AMERICAN GROUND

ALSO BY ROBERT H. FOSSUM AND JOHN K. ROTH

The American Dream 1981

BOOKS BY ROBERT H. FOSSUM

William Styron 1968

Hawthorne's Inviolable Circle 1972

Facing Mirrors (with Sy Kahn) 1980

BOOKS BY JOHN K. ROTH

Freedom and the Moral Life 1969

The Moral Philosophy of William James (ed.) 1969

Problems of the Philosophy of Religion 1971

The Philosophy of Josiah Royce (ed.) 1971

The Moral Equivalent of War and Other Essays (ed.) 1971

The American Religious Experience (with Frederick Sontag) 1972

American Dreams 1976

God and America's Future (with Frederick Sontag) 1977

A Consuming Fire 1979

The Defense of God (ed. with Frederick Sontag) 1985

Ideology and American Experience (ed. with Robert C. Whittemore) 1986

Approaches to Auschwitz (with Richard L. Rubenstein) 1987

The Questions of Philosophy (with Frederick Sontag) 1988

AMERICAN GROUND

VISTAS, VISIONS & REVISIONS

EDITED BY

Robert H. Fossum and *John K. Roth*

PARAGON HOUSE PUBLISHERS
New York

First edition

Published in the United States by

Paragon House Publishers
90 Fifth Avenue
New York, NY 10011

Library of Congress Cataloging-in-Publication Data
American ground.
1. United States—Civilization. 2. American literature.
3. Philosophy, American. I. Fossum, Robert H.
II. Roth, John K.
E169.1.A471987   1987   973   87-20180
ISBN 1-55778-011-0
1-55778-114-1 (pbk.)

For
Our Grandchildren
Alive and Yet to Be

CONTENTS

PART THREE: DREAMS OF SUCCESS
Edward Arlington Robinson   Richard Cory

PART FOUR: IRONY IN AMERICAN LIFE
E. E. Cummings   next to of course god america i

Contents

EPILOGUE: THE SURVEY—FINISHED?

ACKNOWLEDGMENTS

Every attempt has been made to trace the ownership of all copyrighted selections included in this book and to make proper acknowledgment thereof. If error has inadvertently occurred, the editors will make the necessary correction in subsequent editions provided notification is received.

The words "This Land Is Your Land/ This Land Is My Land. . . . This Land Was Made for You and Me," from "This Land Is Your Land," words and music by Woody Guthrie, TRO-© copyright 1956 (renewed 1984), 1958 (renewed 1986) and 1970 by Ludlow Music, Inc., New York, NY.

"The Gift Outright," from *The Poetry of Robert Frost*, edited by Edward Connery Lathem. Copyright © 1942 by Robert Frost. Copyright © 1969 by Holt, Rinehart and Winston. Copyright © 1970 by Lesley Frost Ballantine. Reprinted by permission of Henry Holt and Company, Inc.

"Children of Light," from *Lord Weary's Castle*, copyright © 1946, 1974 by Robert Lowell. Reprinted by permission of Harcourt Brace Jovanovich, Inc.

Selections from *Democracy in America*, by Alexis de Tocqueville, edited by J. P. Mayer and Max Lerner. Translated by George Lawrence: "Concerning the Philosophical Approach of the Americans" and "Concerning the Principal Source of Beliefs Among Democratic Peoples." Copyright © 1966 in the English Translation by Harper and Row Publishers, Inc. Reprinted by permission of Harper and Row Publishers, Inc.

"I Dwell in Possibility" (Poem #657), from *The Complete Poems of Emily Dickinson*, edited by Thomas H. Johnson. Copyright © 1929 by Martha Dickinson Bianchi; copyright © renewed 1957 by Mary L. Hampson. By permission of Little, Brown and Company. Also reprinted by permission of the publishers and the Trustees of Amherst College from *The Poems of Emily Dickinson*, edited by Thomas H. Johnson, Cambridge, MA: The Belknap Press of Harvard University Press, copyright © 1951, 1955, 1979, 1983 by the President and Fellows of Harvard College.

"Provincialism," from Josiah Royce, *Race Questions, Provincialism and Other American Problems*. Reprinted by permission of David Royce.

"The Old Order Changeth," from Woodrow Wilson, *The New Freedom*. Copyright © 1913. Reprinted with the permission of Richard D. Drain, Executor of the Estate of Edith Bolling Wilson.

"Materialism and Idealism in American Life," from George Santayana, *Character and Opinion in the United States*. Reprinted by permission of Mrs. Margot Cory.

"The Body of an American," from John Dos Passos, *1919*. Reprinted by permission of Elizabeth H. Dos Passos.

"Hugh Selwyn Mauberley," in Ezra Pound, *Personae*. Copyright © 1926 by Ezra Pound. Reprinted by permission of New Directions Publishing Corporation.

"Echoes of the Jazz Age," from F. Scott Fitzgerald, *The Crack-Up*. Copyright © 1945 by New Directions Publishing Corporation. Reprinted by permission of New Directions.

"Principles and Ideals of the United States Government," from Herbert Hoover, *The New Day* (Stanford: Stanford University Press, 1928). Reprinted by permissiion of the Herbert Hoover Foundation.

"A Man in the Street," from *The American Jitters* by Edmund Wilson. Copyright © 1932 by Charles Scribner's Sons, copyright © 1958 by Edmund Wilson. Reprinted by permission of Farrar, Straus and Giroux, Inc.

"The United States, Incorporated" and "Toward a New Individualism." Abridged by permission of The Putnam Publishing Group from *Individualism Old and New* by John Dewey. Copyright 1929, 1930 by John Dewey; renewed © 1957, 1958.

Mary Heaton Vorse, "School for Bums," from *The New Republic*, 29 April 1931. Reprinted by permission of *The New Republic*.

"The New Imperative." Reprinted with permission of Macmillan Publishing Company from *The New Imperative* by Walter Lippmann. Copyright © 1935, and renewed 1963, by Walter Lippmann.

"next to of course god america i" is reprinted from *IS 5, Poems by E. E. Cummings*, by permission of Liveright Publishing Corporation. Copyright © 1926 by Horace Liveright. Copyright renewed © 1953 by E. E. Cummings. Copyright © 1985 by E. E. Cummings Trust. Copyright © 1985 by George James Firmage.

"The Forethought," "Of Our Spiritual Strivings," "Of the Passing of the First-Born," "Of the Sorrow Songs," and "Fifty Years After," from *The Souls of Black Folk* by W. E. B. Du Bois. Reprinted by permission of David Graham Du Bois.

Langston Hughes, "Let America Be America Again." From *A New Song* (New York: International Workers Order, 1938). Reprinted by permission of Harold Ober Associates Incorporated. Copyright © 1938 by Langston Hughes. Copyright renewed 1956 by Langston Hughes. Parts of the poem were first published in *Esquire*, July 1936.

PREFACE

NO PEOPLE would have become American without a place of their own. Nor would any place have become American without people who envisioned the vistas of a nation in land that is now the United States. Persons and places conceive each other. If our title evokes that fact, the origins and contents of *American Ground* document it.

We are transplanted Midwesterners whose lives intersect in California, specifically at Claremont McKenna College where we have been colleagues for more than twenty years. For a long time the two of us taught American literature and American philosophy independently, even on opposite ends of our campus. But gradually we discovered that something special could happen if we worked together. In recent years, therefore, we have shared a classroom and team-taught an interdisciplinary course called "Perspectives on the American Dream." It could just as accurately carry the title of this anthology.

Both the course and the book provide selections that exemplify the foundations of characteristic American attitudes, beliefs, ideas, and ideals. In both we try to show that these foundations, like America's land and people, have been composed of richly diverse elements stirred together, sometimes easily and sometimes not, to form a continuously shifting yet fundamentally solid whole. And in both we have included modes of discourse—literary, philosophical, religious, and political—as varied as the elements themselves.

Commitment to diversity created a problem, however: we were unable to find a single book that contained all the readings we wanted to use in our course. *American Ground* does not fully solve that difficulty. For example, although at the end of the book we briefly discuss some novels we have found useful in teaching the course, obviously none of them could be reprinted here. But *American Ground* does contain the shorter pieces which, we have found, successfully provoke discussion of crucial issues and topics. Thereby, we hope, the book will guide those readers who seek a better understanding of the visions and revisions which have helped to shape the character of American life.

Although we have grouped the selections under topic headings, we have also tried to make the order of the groups and the selections within them conform roughly to historical chronology. The most notable exceptions to the principle behind our effort are the poems which, in addition to their intrinsic value, serve as concise thematic preludes to the anthology's major parts. Other exceptions include Nathaniel Hawthorne's

"My Kinsman, Major Molineux," a tale written in the nineteenth century but placed in Part One because its subject is a pre-Revolutionary colonial uprising against British rule, and the passages from W. E. B. Du Bois's *The Souls of Black Folk*, first published in 1903 but placed in Part Four alongside more recent writings about America's racial problems. In general, the fact that a selection appears under one heading does not necessarily mean, of course, that its concerns are limited to a single topic. Like Walt Whitman's *persona* in *Leaves of Grass*, any given reading in this volume may contain multitudes.

Our introductory essays are intended as succinct commentaries on major issues raised in the selections that follow. They do not pretend to provide a detailed picture of American social and political history. Nor do they include more than a few biographical facts about the authors of the selections. The authors' dates appear in the introductions; unless otherwise indicated, the date cited for each selection is the year of its initial publication. At times the original punctuation and spelling in some of the older selections have been modernized for clarity. Information about the sources for the selections is available either in the Acknowledgments or in the occasional notes provided when the selection is part of a larger work or book not otherwise mentioned. To keep the book as spare and lean as possible, however, we have dispensed with most of the usual scholarly apparatus—bibliographies, for instance, and historical footnotes. Comprehensive coverage of such matters is left to those who feel it is essential.

Anthologies can be criticized for what they leave out as well as for what they put in. Ours is no exception. Like other editors, we have been compelled for practical reasons to abridge some of the selections. While we have had to omit much that we would have liked to include, our principle was to emphasize American "classics" and to minimize works of "popular culture." The latter are too likely to be transitory, to lose their significance overnight, whereas the writings published here have for the most part already passed the so-called test of time.

As this book went to press, there was much discussion in the United States about two bestsellers on education. One was *The Closing of the American Mind* by Allan Bloom; the other, by E. D. Hirsch, Jr., was entitled *Cultural Literacy*. Bloom contends that Americans do not inquire enough, while Hirsch argues that Americans do not know enough. Bloom wants American minds to open through questioning, dialogue, and investigation so they can discover what is true. Hirsch thinks Americans pay insufficient attention to teaching and learning about the Western tradition that helps to unify American life.

Hirsch rightly contends that there are some things "every American needs to know." They include those words and documents that "lend coherence to the larger American public culture." Following Horace Kallen, one of the American philosophers who argued for it first, Hirsch specifically affirms that Americans need the vision that a "civil bible" can provide. What such a volume should contain and how its contents might need periodic revision are rightly the subjects of a continuing debate. Nonetheless we hope that the texts found here are worthy of belonging to such a needed canon. Our students, certainly, continue to find that the vistas afforded by such writings open the American mind to concerns as relevant today as they ever were. To all such inheritors of American ground, we offer these collected explorations. In doing so, we express special thanks to Polly Baker, Laura Greeney, William L. Parker, Dianne Pinkowitz, Jonathan Sharp, and Ken Stuart. Their counsel and support made this book possible.

Robert H. Fossum
John K. Roth

Claremont McKenna College
Claremont, California

AMERICAN GROUND

This land is your land, this land is my land,
. . . this land was made for you and me.

Woody Guthrie (1956)

PROLOGUE

THE SURVEY BEGUN

The land was ours before we were the land's.
She was our land more than a hundred years
Before we were her people. She was ours
In Massachusetts, in Virginia,
But we were England's, still colonials,
Possessing what we still were unpossessed by,
Possessed by what we now no more possessed.
Something we were withholding made us weak
Until we found out that it was ourselves
We were withholding from our land of living,
And forthwith found salvation in surrender.
Such as we were we gave ourselves outright
(The deed of gift was many deeds of war)
To the land vaguely realizing westward,
But still unstoried, artless, unenhanced,
Such as she was, such as she would become.

THE GIFT OUTRIGHT
Robert Frost (1936)

NATIONAL BORDERS slice the globe. Typically we take such boundaries for granted, forgetting how recently they have become dominant within our planet's landscape. Although men and women are by nature territorial creatures, human life itself is a newcomer on the cosmic scene. Today people think of themselves as Chinese or German, Russian or American, but there was a time when such distinctions were nonexistent. Millennia passed before those identities and their distinctive political loyalties evolved. Nor have those identities and loyalties stayed the same. Becoming is inescapable and constant.

Dust to dust, ashes to ashes—once born, each of us will perish. In time, most of us disappear without a trace. But what of the life we share by having a country that we call our own? Political rhetoric tries to reassure us that our nation will thrive indefinitely, if not forever. Those promises resonate because much that we hold dear does depend on the national life of which we are a part. On closer inspection, however, such hopes are ill-founded. Nations, too, come and go. Usually they are victims of conflict produced by the very particularity that nations prize.

History, some contend, demonstrates that national pride wastes life. We must concentrate, they say, on transcending national differences. Destructive differences do need to be overcome, especially in our nuclear age, but how? Contingent though they may be, national identities and characteristics are facts of life. Even if we can transcend their destructive features, we must not assume that national loyalties will dissolve of their own accord. If such an outcome were possible, its desirability would be questionable, for cultural diversity nurtured through the world's many national traditions is of great value. Less utopian, and therefore more profoundly idealistic, is a sober view that seeks to build warranted pride in a national identity that not only serves one's own people but also helps to meet the needs all persons share because they are human. Although nationhood and nationality may both be destined for oblivion, the nature and the time of their demise are not ours to know in advance. Making the best of what we have is our lot instead. For millions of persons in the late twentieth century that goal requires coming to terms with the lives they lead on American ground. How Americans cope with their national identity, in turn, affects the fate of the earth.

The nineteenth-century novelist Henry James once observed: "It's a complex fate, being an American." Kris Kristofferson, a contemporary American songwriter, might have had that thought in mind when he described "The Pilgrim—Chapter 33" as "a walking contradiction / Partly truth and partly fiction." And if Robert Frost (1874–1963) had been asked how an American's fate is complicated by the truth and fiction his nation comprises, that great poet might have answered by quoting the lines he recited one January day in 1961. Nearly ninety, Frost favored John F. Kennedy's inaugural with verse. But when he was about to read the poem prepared for that occasion, the Washington wind gusted the lines from his view. From memory, Frost presented "The Gift Outright" instead, reminding Americans, first, that "the land was ours before we were the land's."

American identity is unthinkable without *the land*. Yet the land is a chief ingredient that renders an American fate complex, because how people think about and use American ground puts them at odds. Created by no man or woman, the land was indeed a gift outright. Soon enough, though, it became a "gift" of another kind. The land was there for the taking. Taken it was, too. Long before it was called "American," the territory was home for hundreds of varied tribal cultures that European immigrants came to know indiscriminately as "Indian." The land granted visions of promise—economic, political, religious—but not space enough to satisfy them all. If "this land is your land, this land is my land," *yours* and *mine* have excluded and in many cases shattered the ways of those now called Native Americans. Frost's words add dissonant notes to Woody Guthrie's chorus—"this land was made for you and me"—by remembering that "the deed of gift was many deeds of war."

The land, in a word, meant *possibility* nonetheless. Reality may be frustrating, disappointing, even crushing. But the lure of possibility seems able to transcend all of those. So restless immigrants, their overseas bags and overland trunks packed with hope, entered "the land vaguely realizing westward." Inexorably they occupied the ground, reserving little for the Native American except a trail of tears. Still the land was not theirs, for the immigrants' home was *there*, not *here*. What they found was strange, if not unmapped. The new space was so distant from what they left behind, its future as uncertain as it was unknown. Complicated by the land's problematic development, possibility was a fickle friend. So it is and shall remain.

"Unstoried, artless, unenhanced"—the land was hardly that for the Native Americans who witnessed its European colonization and the aftermath. But for those who, comparatively speaking, were newcomers, and also for the vast majority of us who trace our roots to their arrivals, "the land was ours before we were the land's." The land, moreover, would be less than "our land of living" until the *irony* of being in it was discovered. That irony consisted of intending one thing and unintentionally producing another, which still happens as often as not. The newcomers—"still colonials"—would create and tell stories about the land, enhance it with arts and crafts. While thinking that the United States was "such as she was," Americans old and new would discover that she was becoming—sometimes worse than we knew, sometimes better than we thought.

Only as all Americans, newcomers and natives alike, learn how not to withhold from each other—discovering in the process that American ground has been storied, artful, and enhanced in countless ways unnoticed—will the land be truly made for *you* and *me* and become more fully *ours* as a blessing than as a curse. Yet the complexity of our fate as Americans is that our capacity to give ourselves outright remains in question. As it records a renewing relationship between a father and a son, Robert M. Pirsig's *Zen and the Art of Motorcycle Maintenance* illustrates why that hampered capacity is the case by providing an autobiographical parable about *caring*. In fact, as Chris and his dad bike their way toward each

other, it is clear that their journey within and across American ground
also involves coming to grips with possibility and irony.

Pirsig says his concern is less with "What's new?" and more with
"What's best?" His meditations assay the land and its spirit. Traveling
with spare parts and instruction books on motorcycle repair, he doesn't
want to get stranded or caught unprepared—if he can help it, which is
not always possible. And yet, ironically, "it occurred to me," Pirsig writes,
"there *is* no manual that deals with the *real* business of motorcycle maintenance, the most important aspect of all. Caring about what you are
doing is either considered unimportant or taken for granted." In that
environment, motorcycles are hardware: fueled by gas, not by concern;
sparked by plugs, not by perseverance. Attitudes toward them are in-
consequential. No fiction, of course, could be further from the truth, and
that is Pirsig's point. Turn the motorcycle into yourself, your country,
your world, and the lesson is made the more vital and the more difficult,
partly because in proportion to the problem's growth complexity increases
as your own power diminishes.

Toward the book's end, Chris asks if he can have his own motorcycle
someday. Pirsig tells the boy he can, if he will take care of it. Chris's
questioning continues:

> "What do you have to do?"
> "Lots of things. You've been watching me."
> "Will you show me all of them?"
> "Sure."
> "Is it hard?"
> "Not if you have the right attitudes. It's having the right attitudes that's
> hard."

Chris's father expresses confidence that his son will have the right
attitudes. Indeed, as San Francisco Bay looms ahead, Pirsig concludes:
"Trials never end, of course. Unhappiness and misfortune are bound to
occur as long as people live, but there is a feeling now, that was not here
before, and is not just on the surface of things, but penetrates all the way
through: We've won it. It's going to get better now. You can sort of tell
these things."

Less than five years after Robert Pirsig's still popular narrative appeared, the *San Francisco Chronicle* carried a story about his family: "The
23-year-old son of the author of *Zen and the Art of Motorcycle Maintenance*," its lead paragraph announced, "was stabbed to death Saturday
night two blocks from the Zen Center where he lived, police said yesterday." The article continued by noting that the Pirsig family was scattered. Chris Pirsig had lived at the Zen Center since 1975. His mother
was in Minneapolis. It was uncertain whether his father, who was then

living on a boat off the English coast and writing about Zen and the art of sailing, would be able to attend the funeral.

Being an American is a complex fate because trials do have a way of never ending, even when things seem to be getting better. We Americans prefer to dwell on success stories. We thrive on hopes for the future, too. Hence we are partly truth, but we are also partly fiction insofar as we slight the contradictory character of our nation, which both is and is not what it wants to be and could become. American ground is a scene of epic proportions. It has that quality, however, not only because of optimistic dreams and their accomplishments but also because adversity and failure identify us. Ground together American-style, those realities test our mettle; they reveal our fundamental spirit. Scouting the land, plotting its possibilities, and reckoning with the irony it contains, the pages ahead offer a story to enhance the appreciation that our complex fate is worth having, artful, a gift to share and possess with care.

PART ONE

A NEW COMMONWEALTH

Our fathers wrung their bread from stocks and stones,
And fenced their gardens with the Redman's bones;
Embarking from the Nether Land of Holland,
Pilgrims unhouseled by Geneva's night,
They planted here the Serpent's seeds of light;
And here the pivoting searchlights probe to shock
The riotous glass houses built on rock,
And candles gutter by an empty altar,
And light is where the landless blood of Cain
Is burning, burning the unburied grain.

CHILDREN OF LIGHT
Robert Lowell (1944)

UNDER A MELTING ice cap, the land was here forty thousand years ago, but it was not American ground. Alive with possibility, the terrain became human only as primitive tribes from Asia crossed where the Bering Strait currently flows. As the centuries passed, successive waves of Asiatic immigrants followed those first arrivals and ventured southward from present-day Alaska. The early ancestors of those now identified as Native Americans were among them. Gradually human ways spread widely over what we call North, Central, and South America.

Aztecs in Mexico, Mayas in Central America, Incas in Peru—these civilizations and others produced remarkable empires and traditions long before Christopher Columbus dropped anchor off the Caribbean island of San Salvador on 12 October 1492. There he encountered Arawak tribes. Believing he had reached the Indies—then including India, China, the East Indies, and Japan—Columbus mistakenly called the natives "Indians." The designation stuck, not only for the Arawaks but for all the indigenous peoples who would meet European adventurers bent on exploration and control of a New World.

For more than a century after Columbus's first trans-Atlantic voyage, some one million Native Americans could be found in what is now the United States. Among them were the Iroquois nations in the Northeast, the Nez Percé and many others in the Northwest, the Cherokee and Creek in the Southeast. Pueblo tribes such as the Hopi, Taos, and Zuñi developed their distinctive ways in the Southwest. Somewhat later, the Comanche, Pawnee, and Sioux, utilizing the horse and gun introduced by Spaniards in the seventeenth century, roamed the Great Plains. Over time, all of these tribes and many more were destined to encounter settlers of European stock. If friendly relations prevailed at first, more and more settlers claimed greater amounts of the land. Violence ensued—again and again. By 1890 only 250,000 Native Americans survived. Living very differently from their pre-Columbian forebears, today more than five times that number are citizens of the United States.

How changed is the land, its spirit and people, because the dreams of restless Europeans were enlarged by the discovery of a New World. Depending on a belief in new beginnings, those dreams did not originate in America but often were sustained by a figurative America even before European explorers mapped the coast and probed the interior. His backers entranced by Oriental wealth, Christopher Columbus sought a passage to India. Nonetheless, he imagined that a new kingdom of God, a terrestrial paradise, might be established in the land to which his navigational mistake had led him. In his imaginings, he thus resembled other and later European dreamers who saw their fountain of youth, their New Atlantis, their El Dorado as existing somewhere in that Golden West which turned out to be America. The Atlantic was their frontier, somewhere beyond which lay a place where people could hope to start anew. The hopes, however, were often dashed. Tribal and colonial interests collided. Tensions strained the transplanted European groups as aspirations for personal gain conflicted with visions of communal association. And if those tensions were lacking, the threats of disease and starvation in a supposed land of plenty were never far off. Such gaps between dreams and realities persist. The promised land of the free, now poignantly storied, still shows the scars of its mocking ironies.

PURITANS AND REBELS

Many of the early voyagers were Spanish and French, and their Catholic colonialism marked the land. But the Protestantism of the Puritans was even more influential. The Pilgrims who arrived in 1620 were not the first of that persuasion to immigrate across the sea. Other English-speaking settlements dotted the seaboard before the *Mayflower* spied Cape Cod, a landfall far from her Virginia destination. Still, much of American history is grounded on Plymouth Rock. When the Pilgrims landed there, however, what they found was hardly an earthly paradise. William Bradford (1590–1657), signer of the Mayflower Compact, historian of Plymouth Plantation and its governor for more than thirty years, aptly described their home-to-be as a howling, savage wilderness. Nevertheless, here they could practice their religion. Unimpeded by pressures to tolerate or conform to alien ways, they would restore to Christianity the health which, in the Puritans' opinion, it had lost in the Old World.

By the grace of God, the Puritans claimed, American ground offered the human race a chance to begin anew. As the Mayflower Compact emphasizes, the Pilgrims' efforts to glorify God and to advance the Christian faith enjoined practical political planning, sound economic practice, and shared responsibility for "the general good of the colony." Hence the Compact: a *covenant*, a voluntary agreement, that established a community. But that covenant depended on another. Revealed in Scripture, this prior covenant between God and humankind insisted that the purpose of human life is to glorify God. Willful violation of God's expectations, which divine revelation and human reflection made clear, could not occur with impunity. For those chosen ones who were faithfully obedient, however, God's promise of salvation would never be abrogated.

Puritanism was not a single fixed ideology. It was instead a far-reaching reform movement with diverse and even conflicting tendencies. But if the Pilgrim Separatists who established Plymouth Plantation did not see eye to eye with their less radical and more powerful cousins at Massachusetts Bay, in every Puritan community the sense of covenant expressed in the Mayflower Compact carried substantial weight. As the Puritans' conscience usually understood it, their charge was to "combine ourselves together into a civil body politic" that would serve God by being an example for the rest of the world—a charge that many Americans have taken seriously, if not successfully, ever since.

No one embodied the Puritan conscience better than John Winthrop (1588–1649), who in 1630 led a group of colonists in the *Arbella* across the Atlantic and governed Massachusetts Bay for nearly twenty years. Winthrop's dream was to establish God's New Israel in the New World. Massachusetts Bay, he hoped, would become a true *commonwealth*, a community where civil rectitude, economic prosperity, and religious purity sustained each other. Serving God, this community would provide a fulfilling life for its members. As "a model of Christian charity" it would be a "city upon a hill," influencing human destiny. While still aboard the *Arbella*, Winthrop gathered his followers together and spoke about these possibilities. Stressing "the bond of brotherly affection," he reminded them that they had undertaken a task by "mutual consent." Progress toward their goals entailed "a due form of government both civil and ecclesiastical," the details of such a government, Winthrop believed, having been entrusted to Puritan men by God.

Somewhat later, Winthrop's colleague John Cotton (1584–1652), for many years the most important teacher in the Massachusetts Bay colony, supplemented Puritan idealism with a realistic warning. "Let all the world learn to give mortal men no greater power than they are content they shall use," he admonished, "for use it they will." Rooted in a profound appreciation of the human propensity to sin, that principle stood at the core of Cotton's political philosophy. Without government, individuals will destroy each other. But the remedy must be watched lest it too become deadly. For the same qualities that make government necessary—narrow self-interest, power-grabbing, unchecked desires that produce enslavement—do not disappear in the politically powerful. A proper covenant, therefore, involves a contract between the people and their governors, one that finds the balance between authority and liberty which the public good requires.

Reality fell short of those dreams. One reason was that Winthrop and Cotton could not sustain a consensus rooted in biblical principles. Their plan failed not only because not everyone read God's word exactly alike, but also because many of the early arrivals did not read God's word at all. For only a minority of the colonial settlers dreamed of spiritual renewal, let alone of Christian charity. Hence their understandings of the public good were varied, if they thought of it at all. A covenant is only as real as the shared understanding of its terms; a community exists just to the degree that people hold the same values in common. Puritan ways did not prevail, ironically, partly because they helped to encourage the belief in new beginnings, a conviction that has been widely shared by Americans yet one that keeps them at odds as much as it brings them together. The United States was born, after all, of a bloody revolution.

Despite recurrent attempts to maintain or later to reinstate the Christian vision through Great Awakenings of one sort or another, the Puritans' dream of new beginnings was eventually transmuted into more secular hopes of social, political, economic, psychological, even sexual rebirth. For example, Thomas Paine (1737–1809), political philosopher and revolutionary pamphleteer, illustrates the evolution of religious Protestantism into the political rebelliousness that culminated in the American Revolution. Arriving in Philadelphia from England in 1774, Paine was far less inclined than the Puritans to emphasize God's role in the creation of a new order. His proposition was nothing less than "we have it in our power to begin the world over again." To assume that power and then to act upon it by ridding America of British rule, argued Paine, was not only "Common Sense"; it was virtuous, too, for "the cause of America is in a great measure the cause of all mankind."

Paine's sentiments resound in American history down to the present day. Yet not every American, then or now, would agree that Paine's optimism is warranted. Himself the descendant of New England Puritans, Nathaniel Hawthorne (1804–1864), writing his fiction two generations later, regarded his task as very different from Paine's. No American author has more skillfully dispelled the illusion that there could be a New World totally separable from the Old. Rather, as he showed, persons, places, and peoples always have a past. Indeed, their identity dissolves unless they recognize that they are embedded in history. Hawthorne concurred that the Revolution was necessary and right. But as "My Kinsman, Major Molineux" bears witness, he also urged Americans to remember that their nation grew in soil enriched by British blood. America's rebellious new beginning required a form of parricide. Having fractured the temporal continuity upon which identity, personal or national, is so heavily dependent, Americans would struggle ever after to cope with who they are.

In the main, Hawthorne's point would have been granted by Thomas Jefferson (1743–1826), despite his defense of the sovereignty of the present. For he opened the Declaration of Independence by arguing that the dissolution of longstanding political bonds must not be taken lightly. At the very least, the causes that impelled the separation must be stated publicly. In other ways, however, Jefferson's Declaration carries forward the legacy of turmoil that Hawthorne took to be the price of rupture from the past. That legacy appears in the fact that the Declaration of Independence epitomizes a philosophy not originally American but inspired by a European-based Enlightenment. The heart of this philosophy is a series of fundamental concepts: for example, self-evident truth, unalienable rights, the laws of nature, equality, and happiness. Jefferson banked on a shared understanding of the meaning of those terms. Enough agreement existed that his Declaration still informs American self-understanding; nevertheless, the interpretation of those terms repeatedly divides us. American ground, then, is an arena in which the definitions of governing ideas are debated. The nation's life, fortune, and honor depend on the continuation and quality of that debate.

Naturally, Hawthorne's kind of retrospective caution did not keynote the victory celebrations that followed the British surrender at Yorktown in 1781. More typical were self-congratulations such as those penned by Philip Freneau (1752–1832) in his poem "On the Emigration to America and Peopling the Western Country." Americans, sang Freneau, had left the Old World behind. Its despotic, enslaving chaos would have no privilege in "a happier soil" where virtue and reason thrived, yielding not merely a commonwealth of "heaven-born freedom" but deeds that would prevail over death itself. Freneau's lines were prophetic. Whether they would also prove true would remain in suspense as Americans wrestled with the dilemma of becoming one while being many.

THE ONE AND THE MANY

E Pluribus Unum—Out of Many, One—is the motto of the United States. Following the Revolution, however, serious problems remained about the best ways to create, in Freneau's words, "order from confusion." Politically, opinion clashed over the distribution of power. How much authority should be centralized, how much reserved to the several states; and in either case, what rights would remain to individuals alone? The Constitution drafted at Philadelphia in 1787 represented the culmination of the Founders' thinking on those issues and still enshrines common attitudes toward government. Yet it was no foregone conclusion that eighteenth-century Americans would credit the Constitution's promise "to insure domestic tranquility." A series of arguments by Alexander Hamilton, John Jay, and James Madison (1751–1836)—pseudonymously signed by "Publius" and collectively titled *The Federalist*—were especially influential in winning ratification for the new Constitution. None remains of greater importance than Number 10, which Madison authored.

Within reason's boundaries, the Founders stressed, man could go far to make what he wanted of himself, his surroundings, his institutions, for the God in whom Thomas Jefferson and his comrades trusted was a benevolent Being. Only more insistently than most of those leaders, Madison realistically underscored that "the reason of man remains fallible," that his "self-love" and his "unfriendly passions" may wreck the public good by "the violence of faction," assertions with which Hawthorne was to agree. The causes of factional rivalry, argued Madison, are inseparable from human liberty. A remedy that destroyed them would therefore be worse than the disease itself. A sound government, however, would limit the *effects* of factious spirits while maintaining individual liberty. Through its division of powers, its system of checks and balances, its ability to provide representation for a large and diverse populace, the Constitution was eminently structured to control those effects. Indeed, it would be the best prevention against the formation of the worst threat of all, a majority faction whose pursuit of happiness would tyrannize those outside its ranks. But the optimism within Madison's realistic analysis reasserted itself. For he assumed an affirmative answer to what remains a question where the one and the many are concerned: Will a plurality of factions serve the good of all?

The Constitution that James Madison defended came largely from his own hand. The version approved by the Philadelphia convention on 17 September 1787 prohibited the enactment of *ex post facto* laws, guaranteed trial by jury for criminal offenses, and provided for other basic liberties. Significantly, however, it did not contain what is now referred to as the Bill of Rights, which comprises the first ten amendments to the Constitution, ratified only on 15 December 1791. During the Constitutional convention, relatively little had been said about such a Bill, mainly because the delegates took so seriously the idea that the Constitution spelled out only those powers that belonged explicitly to the federal government. It was clear, at least inferentially, that unless the federal government had a specific mandate to act, it could not do so. Once more, issues concerning the one and the many were not laid to rest for long. Jefferson, for one, argued that too much might be resting on inference, that it would be better to spell out more definitely what the boundaries were between the one central government and its many citizens. But the Jeffersonian solution to the problem actually brings with it more of the same, for once again everything depends on how fundamental concepts— "freedom of speech," for example, or "cruel and unusual punishment"— are interpreted. On American ground, their meaning is not eternally fixed. If the outcome precludes stagnation, it also entrenches a paradox: Americans are kept at odds by the very things on which they agree.

Having led his troops to victory beyond the despair of Valley Forge, George Washington (1732–1799) served the first two terms of the American presidency. His "Farewell Address" is a plea for American unity, revealing now as well as then how elusive unity can be. Urging his contemporaries to esteem "the immense value of your national Union to your collective and individual happiness," he emphasized how the term "American" referred to a single people. They had worked and fought together. With only "slight shades of difference," he added, "you have the same religion, manners, habits and political principles." To enhance the good already achieved, Americans should avoid the "baneful effects" of partisan passions and of entangling affairs with foreign powers. Washington's advice was well conceived, not least because it was occasioned by the very threats he warned against. Whether his recommendations have been followed, however, is another issue. At the bottom of that issue are the facts not only that the course of human events denied America the luxury of isolation but also that Washington underestimated the nation's shades of difference, then and surely later on. Homogeneity has never been a dominant American characteristic. Nor is it likely to be. Unity will always be a rhetorical theme for American presidents—arriving, departing, or in between—because its depth and quality cannot be easily presumed.

Outside observers often understand the United States better than Americans do themselves. A salient example is provided by the French statesman and philosopher Alexis de Tocqueville (1805–1859), whose tour of the country resulted in a classic called *Democracy in America*. Nothing, Tocqueville decided, characterizes Americans so much as their emphasis on *equality*. One effect of that emphasis is that Americans display "a general distaste for accepting any man's word as proof of anything." Instead they rely on "individual effort and judgment" to determine what they believe. Authority and tradition have little status in a land where a premium is placed on figuring out how to do things differently and better. It was no wonder, then, that Americans could not resolve their many differences and adopt one set of shared beliefs. For, ironically, their shared trust in individual judgment made diversity, if not disharmony, inevitable. But Tocqueville also noticed something else: Americans were one as well as many. The point was not only that "without ideas in common . . . there could be no body social." In the American case, the grounding of those ideas was especially intriguing. Tocqueville located it in "public opinion," which he took to be a function of America's stress on democracy, egalitarianism, and self-reliance. Majority sentiment ruled. To Tocqueville, no less than to Washington and Madison before him, that outcome had to be watched, for it could substitute an unthinking, tyrannical conformity for that vitality of being one *and* many which constituted the nation's true health.

In his epic *Leaves of Grass*, the poet Walt Whitman (1819–1892) echoed Tocqueville's concern. Celebrating the multiplicity in American life, Whitman hoped he was a microcosm of the nation when he praised its variety by urging, "I resist any thing better than my own diversity." As he catalogued "the Nation of many nations," Whitman knew that American ground produced countless ways of life and with them a host of questions about how they fitted together. If Americans wanted sound responses to those questions, Whitman argued, they ought not to find them in authority, in tradition, or least of all in that anonymous arbiter, public opinion. Americans could be true to themselves only if they stuck to the characteristic that made them different in the first place: "You must find out for yourself."

Whitman banked on the premise that self-reliance rightly understood would make good the promise of a new commonwealth characterized by the dream of *E Pluribus Unum*. Unfortunately, "finding out for yourself" how far that premise was valid turned into a costly tragedy. For the diversity that America encompassed included the attempt to exist, in

Abraham Lincoln's words, "half *slave* and half *free.*" Sworn to "preserve, protect, and defend the Constitution of the United States," Lincoln (1809–1865) paid the price to keep his word. Only eighty-five years after the Declaration of Independence, a savage Civil War became necessary to keep the Union intact and to certify, as the Thirteenth Amendment did after the war and Lincoln's assassination, that "neither slavery nor involuntary servitude, except as a punishment for crime whereof the party shall have been duly convicted, shall exist within the United States, or any place subject to their jurisdiction."

Today the Civil War battlefields at Chancellorsville, Gettysburg, and Chickamauga are quiet memorials to Confederates and Yankees who fought to the death because they disagreed over the future of the Union and the place of slavery within it. Yet the calm of those places is deceiving, for the violence of faction remains among us. This was understood by the twentieth-century poet Robert Lowell (1917–1977) as he summed up bitterly one strand of American life in the poem that opens this part of our book. The beginnings made by the resolute Europeans who first called the ground American were the birthday of a new world. In many ways they created a better one than had ever before existed. Still, the beginnings were not so new because, as Lowell says, "the Serpent's seeds" were also planted here. Reaping what was sown, the "Children of Light" stained the land with blood, fencing "their gardens with the Redman's bones" in the process. Relatively few Americans can regret without hypocrisy that "our fathers," those Puritans and rebels, embarked "from the Nether Land." Nonetheless, America also retains a wild and savage hue, leaving its sons and daughters to wander in the land, wondering how to make a commonwealth from the one and the many.

PURITANS AND REBELS

The Pilgrim Separatists
The Mayflower Compact
(1620)

IN THE name of God, Amen, We, whose names are underwritten, the loyal subjects of our dread Sovereign Lord King James, by the Grace of God, of Great Britain, France, and Ireland, King, Defender of the Faith, &c. Having undertaken for the glory of God and advancement of the Christian faith, and the honor of our king and country, a voyage to plant the first colony in the northern parts of Virginia; do by these presents, solemnly and mutually, in the presence of God and one another, covenant and combine ourselves together into a civil body politic, for our better ordering and preservation, and furtherance of the ends aforesaid: And by virtue hereof do enact, constitute, and frame, such just and equal laws, ordinances, acts, constitutions, and officers, from time to time, as shall be thought most meet and convenient for the general good of the colony; unto which we promise all due submission and obedience. In witness whereof we have hereunto subscribed our names at Cape Cod the eleventh of November . . . Anno Domini, 1620.

John Carver	John Turner
William Bradford	Francis Eaton
Edward Winslow	James Chilton
William Brewster	John Crakston
Isaac Allerton	John Billington
Myles Standish	Moses Fletcher
John Alden	John Goodman
Samuel Fuller	Degory Priest
Christopher Martin	Thomas Williams
William Mullins	Gilbert Winslow
William White	Edmund Margeson
Richard Warren	Peter Brown

[From the version drafted aboard ship, 11 November 1620.]

John Howland
Stephen Hopkins
Edward Tilley
John Tilley
Francis Cooke
Thomas Rogers
Thomas Tinker
John Rigdale
Edward Fuller

Richard Britterige
George Soule
Richard Clarke
Richard Gardiner
John Allerton
Thomas English
Edward Doty
Edward Leister

John Winthrop
A Model of Christian Charity
(1630)

GOD ALMIGHTY in his most holy and wise providence hath so disposed of the Condition of mankind, as in all times some must be rich some poor, some high and eminent in power and dignity; others mean and in subjection.

THE REASON HEREOF:

1. *First*, to hold conformity with the rest of his works, being delighted to show forth the glory of his wisdom in the variety and difference of the Creatures and the glory of his power, in ordering all these differences for the preservation and good of the whole, and the glory of his greatness that as it is the glory of princes to have many officers, so this great King will have many Stewards counting himself more honoured in dispensing his gifts to man by man, than if he did it by his own immediate hand.

2. *Secondly*, That he might have the more occasion to manifest the work of his Spirit: first, upon the wicked in moderating and restraining them, so that the rich and mighty should not eat up the poor, nor the poor and despised rise up against their superiors and shake off their yoke; secondly, in the regenerate in exercising his graces in them, as in the great ones, their love, mercy, gentleness, temperance, etc., in the poor and inferior sort, their faith patience, obedience, etc.

3. *Thirdly*, That every man might have need of other, and from hence they might be all knit more nearly together in the Bond of brotherly affection: from hence it appears plainly that no man is made more honorable than another or more wealthy, etc., out of any particular and singular respect to himself but for the glory of his Creator and the Common good of the Creature, Man. Therefore God still reserves the property of

[From the version drafted and delivered as a sermon on the voyage to America aboard the *Arbella*.]

these gifts to himself; he there (Ezek. 16:17) calls wealth his gold and his silver, etc. (Prov. 3:9). He claims their service as his due honor the Lord with thy riches, etc. All men being thus (by divine providence) ranked into two sorts, rich and poor; under the first, are comprehended all such as are able to live comfortably by their own means duly improved; and all others are poor according to the former distribution. There are two rules whereby we are to walk one towards another: JUSTICE and MERCY. These are always distinguished in their Act and in their object, yet may they both concur in the same Subject in each respect; as sometimes there may be an occasion of showing mercy to a rich man, in some sudden danger of distress, and also doing of mere Justice to a poor man in regard of some particular contract, etc. There is likewise a double Law by which we are regulated in our conversation one towards another: in both the former respects, the law of nature and the law of grace, or the moral law or the law of the gospel, to omit the rule of Justice as not properly belonging to this purpose otherwise then it may fall into consideration in some particular Cases; by the first of these laws man as he was enabled so withall [is] commanded to love his neighbor as himself, upon this ground stands all the precepts of the moral law, which concerns our dealings with men. To apply this to the works of mercy this law requires two things: first, that every man afford his help to another in every want or distress; secondly, that he perform this out of the same affection, which makes him careful of his own good according to that of our Savior, "Whatsoever ye would that men should do to you" (Matt. 7:12). This was practised by Abraham and Lot in entertaining the Angels and the old man of Gibea.

The Law of Grace or the Gospel hath some difference from the former as in these respects: first, the law of nature was given to man in the estate of innocency; this of the gospel in the estate of regeneracy: secondly, the former propounds one man to another, as the same flesh and Image of God, this as a brother in Christ also, and in the Communion of the same spirit and so teacheth us to put a difference between Christians and others. Do good to all especially to the household of faith; upon this ground the Israelites were to put a difference between the brethren of such as were strangers though not of the Canaanites. Thirdly, the Law of nature could give no rules for dealing with enemies for all are to be considered as friends in the estate of innocency, but the Gospel commands love to an enemy. Proof! "If thine Enemy hunger feed him; Love your Enemies, do good to them that hate you" (Matt. 5:44).

This Law of the Gospel propounds likewise a difference of seasons and occasions. There is a time when a Christian must sell all and give to the poor as they did in the Apostles' times. There is a time also when a Christian (though they give not all yet) must give beyond their ability, as they of Macedonia. Likewise, community of perils calls for extraordinary liberality and so doth Community in some special service for the Church. Lastly, when there is no other means whereby our Christian brother may be relieved in this distress, we must help him beyond our ability, rather than tempt God, in putting him upon help by miraculous or extraordinary means. . . .

It rests now to make some application of this discourse by the present design which gave the occasion of writing of it. Herein are 4 things to be propounded: first, the persons; secondly, the work; thirdly, the end; fourthly, the means.

First, for the persons, we are a Company professing ourselves fellow members of Christ. In which respect only though we were absent from each other many miles, and had our employments as far distant, yet we ought to account ourselves knit together by this bond of love, and live in the exercise of it, if we would have comfort of our being in Christ. . . .

Secondly, for the work we have in hand, it is by a mutual consent through a special overruling providence, and a more than an ordinary approbation of the Churches of Christ to seek out a place of Cohabitation and Consortship under a due form of Government both civil and ecclesiastical. In such cases as this the care of the public must oversway all private respects, by which not only conscience, but mere Civil policy doth bind us; for it is a true rule that particular estates cannot subsist in the ruin of the public.

Thirdly, the end is to improve our lives to do more service to the Lord, the comfort and increase of the body of Christ whereof we are members, that ourselves and posterity may be the better preserved from the Common corruptions of this evil world to serve the Lord and work out our Salvation under the power and purity of his holy Ordinances.

Fourthly, for the means whereby this must be effected, they are twofold: a Conformity with the work and end we aim at; these we see are extraordinary; therefore we must not content ourselves with usual ordinary means. Whatsoever we did or ought to have done when we lived in England, the same must we do and more also where we go. That which the most in their Churches maintain as a truth in profession only, we must bring into familiar and constant practice; as in this duty of love we must love brotherly without dissimulation, we must love one another with a pure heart fervently, we must bear one another's burdens, we must not look only on our own things, but also on the things of our brethren. Neither must we think that the Lord will bear with such failings at our hands as he doth from those among whom we have lived. . . .

Thus stands the cause between God and us. We are entered into Covenant with him for this work, we have taken out a Commission, the Lord hath given us leave to draw our own Articles. We have professed to enterprise these Actions upon these and these ends, we have hereupon besought him of favor and blessing. Now if the Lord shall please to hear us, and bring us in peace to the place we desire, then hath he ratified this Covenant and sealed our Commission, [and] will expect a strict performance of the Articles contained in it; but if we shall neglect the observation of these Articles which are the ends we have propounded, and dissembling with our God, shall fall to embrace this present world and prosecute our carnal intentions, seeking great things for ourselves and our posterity, the Lord will surely break out in wrath against us, be revenged of such a perjured people, and make us know the price of the breach of such a Covenant.

Now the only way to avoid this shipwreck and to provide for our posterity is to follow the Counsel of Micah, to do Justly, to love mercy, to walk humbly with our God. For this end, we must be knit together in this work as one man; we must entertain each other in brotherly Affection; we must be willing to abridge ourselves of our superfluities, for the supply of others' necessities; we must uphold a familiar Commerce together in all meekness, gentleness, patience and liberality; we must delight in each other, make other's Conditions our own, rejoice together, mourn together, labor and suffer together, always having before our eyes our Commission and Community in the work, our Community as members of the same body. So shall we keep the unity of the spirit in the bond of peace. The Lord will be our God and delight to dwell among us as his own people and will command a blessing upon us in all our ways, so that we shall see much more of his wisdom, power, goodness, and truth than formerly we have been acquainted with. We shall find that the God of Israel is among us, when ten of us shall be able to resist a thousand of our enemies, when he shall make us a praise and glory, that men shall say of succeeding plantations: the Lord make it like that of New England. For we must Consider that we shall be as a City upon a Hill, the eyes of all people are upon us. So that if we shall deal falsely with our God in this work we have undertaken and so cause him to withdraw his present help from us, we shall be made a story and a by-word through the world; we shall open the mouths of enemies to speak evil of the ways of God and all professors for God's sake; we shall shame the faces of many of God's worthy servants, and cause their prayers to be turned into Curses upon us till we be consumed out of the good land whither we are going. And to shut up this discourse with that exhortation of Moses, that faithful servant of the Lord, in his last farewell to Israel (Deut. 30). Beloved there is now set before us life and good, death and evil in that we are Commanded this day to love the Lord our God, and to love one another, to walk in his ways and to keep his Commandments and his Ordinance and his laws and the Articles of our Covenant with him, that we may live and be multiplied, and that the Lord our God may bless us in the land whither we go to possess it. But if our hearts shall turn away so that we will not obey, but shall be seduced and worship . . . other gods, our pleasures, and profits, and serve them, it is propounded unto us this day, we shall surely perish out of the good Land whither we pass over this vast Sea to possess it.

> Therefore, let us choose life,
> that we, and our Seed,
> may live; by obeying his
> voice, and cleaving to him,
> for he is our life, and
> our prosperity.

John Cotton
Limitation of Government
(1655)

THIS MAY serve to teach us the danger of allowing to any mortal man an inordinate measure of power to speak great things: to allow to any man uncontrollableness of speech; you see the desperate danger of it.

Let all the world learn to give mortal men no greater power than they are content they shall use—for use it they will. And unless they be better taught of God, they will use it ever and anon: it may be, make it the passage of their proceeding to speak what they will. And they that have liberty to speak great things, you will find it to be true, they will speak great blasphemies. No man would think what desperate deceit and wickedness there is in the hearts of men. And that was the reason why the beast did speak such great things; he might speak and nobody might control him: "What," saith the Lord (in Jer. 3:5), "thou hast spoken and done evil things as thou couldst." If a church or head of a church could have done worse, he would have done it. This is one of the strains of nature: it affects boundless liberty, and to run to the utmost extent. Whatever power he hath received, he hath a corrupt nature that will improve it in one thing or other; if he have liberty, he will think why may he not use it?

Set up the Pope as Lord Paramount over kings and princes, and they shall know that he hath power over them; he will take liberty to depose one and set up another. Give him power to make laws, and he will approve and disapprove as he list: what he approves is canonical, what he disapproves is rejected. Give him that power, and he will so order it at length, he will make such a state of religion, that he that so lives and dies shall never be saved; and all this springs from the vast power that is given to him and from the deep depravation of nature. He will open

[From the version published posthumously in *An Exposition upon the Thirteenth Chapter of the Revelation.*]

his mouth: "His tongue is his own, who is Lord over him" (Psal. 12:3, 4).

It is therefore most wholesome for magistrates and officers in church and commonwealth never to affect more liberty and authority than will do them good, and the people good: for whatever transcendent power is given will certainly overrun those that give it and those that receive it. There is a strain in a man's heart that will sometime or other run out to excess, unless the Lord restrain it; but it is not good to venture it.

It is necessary, therefore, that all power that is on earth be limited, church-power or other. If there be power given to speak great things, then look for great blasphemies, look for a licentious abuse of it. It is counted a matter of danger to the state to limit prerogatives; but it is a further danger not to have them limited: they will be like a tempest if they be not limited. A prince himself cannot tell where he will confine himself, nor can the people tell; but if he have liberty to speak great things, then he will make and unmake, say and unsay, and undertake such things as are neither for his own honor nor for the safety of the state.

It is therefore fit for every man to be studious of the bounds which the Lord hath set: and for the people, in whom fundamentally all power lies, to give as much power as God in His word gives to men. And it is meet that magistrates in the commonwealth, and so officers in churches, should desire to know the utmost bounds of their own power, and it is safe for both. All intrenchment upon the bounds which God hath not given, they are not enlargements, but burdens and snares; they will certainly lead the spirit of a man out of his way, sooner or later.

It is wholesome and safe to be dealt withal as God deals with the vast sea: "Hitherto shalt thou come, but there shalt thou stay thy proud waves." And therefore if they be but banks of simple sand, they will be good enough to check the vast, roaring sea. And so for imperial monarchies: it is safe to know how far their power extends; and then if it be but banks of sand, which is most slippery, it will serve as well as any brazen wall. If you pinch the sea of its liberty, though it be walls of stone or brass, it will beat them down. So it is with magistrates: stint them where God hath not stinted them, and if they were walls of brass, they would beat them down, and it is meet they should; but give them the liberty God allows, and if it be but a wall of sand it will keep them.

As this liquid air in which we breathe, God hath set it for the waters of the clouds to the earth; it is a firmament, it is the clouds, yet it stands firm enough; because it keeps the climate where they are, it shall stand like walls of brass. So let there be due bounds set—and I may apply it to families: it is good for the wife to acknowledge all power and authority to the husband, and for the husband to acknowledge honor to the wife; but still give them that which God hath given them, and no more nor less. Give them the full latitude that God hath given, else you will find you dig pits, and lay snares, and cumber their spirits, if you give them less; there is never peace where full liberty is not given, nor never stable peace where more than full liberty is granted. Let them be duly observed, and give men no more liberty than God doth, nor women, for they will abuse it. The devil will draw them, and God's providence lead them thereunto; therefore give them no more than God gives.

And so for children and servants, or any others you are to deal with: give them the liberty and authority you would have them use, and beyond that stretch not the tether; it will not tend to their good nor yours. And also, from hence gather and go home with this meditation: that certainly here is this distemper in our natures, that we cannot tell how to use liberty, but we shall very readily corrupt ourselves. Oh, the bottomless depth of sandy earth! of a corrupt spirit, that breaks over all bounds, and loves inordinate vastness! That is it we ought to be careful of.

Thomas Paine
Common Sense
(1776)

PERHAPS THE sentiments contained in the following pages are not *yet* sufficiently fashionable to procure them general favor; a long habit of not thinking a thing *wrong* gives it a superficial appearance of being *right*, and raises at first a formidable outcry in defense of custom. But the tumult soon subsides. Time makes more converts than reason.

As a long and violent abuse of power is generally the means of calling the right of it in question (and in matters, too, which might never have been thought of, had not the sufferers been aggravated into the inquiry), and as the King of England has undertaken in his *own right* to support the Parliament in what he calls *theirs*, and as the good people of this country are grievously oppressed by the combination, they have an undoubted privilege to inquire into the pretensions of both and equally to reject the usurpation of either. . . .

The cause of America is in a great measure the cause of all mankind. Many circumstances have and will arise which are not local but universal, and through which the principles of all lovers of mankind are affected and in the event of which their affections are interested. The laying a country desolate with fire and sword, declaring war against the natural rights of all mankind, and extirpating the defenders thereof from the face of the earth is the concern of every man to whom nature has given the power of feeling. . . .

In the following pages I offer nothing more than simple facts, plain arguments, and common sense; and have no other preliminaries to settle with the reader than that he will divest himself of prejudice and prepossession, and suffer his reason and his feelings to determine for themselves; that he will put on, or rather that he will not put off, the true character of a man, and generously enlarge his views beyond the present day.

Volumes have been written on the subject of the struggle between

England and America. Men of all ranks have embarked in the controversy, from different motives and with various designs; but all have been ineffectual, and the period of debate is closed. Arms as the last resource decide the contest; the appeal was the choice of the king, and the continent has accepted the challenge. . . .

The sun never shined on a cause of greater worth. 'Tis not the affair of a city, a county, a province, or a kingdom, but of a continent—of at least one-eighth part of the habitable globe. 'Tis not the concern of a day, a year, or an age; posterity are virtually involved in the contest, and will be more or less affected even to the end of time by the proceedings now. Now is the seedtime of continental union, faith, and honor. The least fracture now will be like a name engraved with the point of a pin on the tender rind of a young oak; the wound would enlarge with the tree, and posterity read it in full-grown characters. . . .

As much has been said of the advantages of reconciliation, which, like an agreeable dream, has passed away and left us as we were, it is but right that we should examine the contrary side of the argument and inquire into some of the many material injuries which these colonies sustain, and always will sustain, by being connected with and dependent on Great Britain. To examine that connection and dependence on the principles of nature and common sense; to see what we have to trust to, if separated, and what we are to expect, if dependent.

I have heard it asserted by some that, as America has flourished under her former connection with Great Britain, the same connection is necessary toward her future happiness and will always have the same effect. Nothing can be more fallacious than this kind of argument. We may as well assert that because a child has thrived upon milk that it is never to have meat, or that the first twenty years of our lives is to become a precedent for the next twenty. But even this is admitting more than is true; for I answer roundly that America would have flourished as much, and probably much more, had no European power had anything to do with her. The commerce by which she has enriched herself are the necessaries of life and will always have a market while eating is the custom of Europe.

But she has protected us, say some. That she has engrossed us is true, and defended the continent at our expense as well as her own is admitted; and she would have defended Turkey from the same motive, viz., for the sake of trade and dominion.

Alas! we have been long led away by ancient prejudices and made large sacrifices to superstition. We have boasted the protection of Great Britain without considering that her motive was *interest*, not *attachment*; and that she did not protect us from *our enemies* on *our account* but from *her enemies* on *her own account*, from those who had no quarrel with us on any *other account* and who will always be our enemies on the *same account*. Let Britain waive her pretensions to the continent or the continent throw off the dependence, and we should be at peace with France and Spain, were they at war with Britain. . . .

But Britain is the parent country, say some. Then the more shame upon her conduct. Even brutes do not devour their young nor savages make war upon their families; wherefore the assertion, if true, turns to her reproach; but it happens not to be true, or only partly so, and the phrase "parent" or "mother country" has been jesuitically adopted by the king and his parasites with a low papistical design of gaining an unfair bias on the credulous weakness of our minds. Europe, and not England, is the parent country of America. This New World has been the asylum for the persecuted lovers of civil and religious liberty from *every part* of Europe. Hither have they fled, not from the tender embraces of the mother, but from the cruelty of the monster; and it is so far true of England that the same tyranny which drove the first emigrants from home pursues their descendants still. . . .

But, admitting that we were all of English descent, what does it amount to? Nothing. Britain, being now an open enemy, extinguishes every other name and title; and to say that reconciliation is our duty is truly farcical. . . .

I challenge the warmest advocate for reconciliation to show a single advantage that this continent can reap by being connected with Great Britain. I repeat the challenge; not a single advantage is derived. Our corn will fetch its price in any market in Europe, and our imported goods must be paid for, buy them where we will.

But the injuries and disadvantages we sustain by that connection are without number, and our duty to mankind at large, as well as to ourselves, instruct us to renounce the alliance; because any submission to or dependence on Great Britain tends directly to involve this continent in European wars and quarrels and sets us at variance with nations who would otherwise seek our friendship and against whom we have neither anger nor complaint. As Europe is our market for trade, we ought to form no partial connection with any part of it. It is the true interest of America to steer clear of European contentions, which she never can do while, by her dependence on Britain, she is made the makeweight in the scale of British politics.

Europe is too thickly planted with kingdoms to be long at peace; and whenever a war breaks out between England and any foreign power, the trade of America goes to ruin *because of her connection with Britain.* The next war may not turn out like the last; and should it not, the advocates for reconciliation now will be wishing for separation then, because neutrality in that case would be a safer convoy than a man-of-war. Everything that is right or natural pleads for separation. The blood of the slain, the weeping voice of nature cries, " '*Tis time to part.*" Even the distance at which the Almighty has placed England and America is a strong and natural proof that the authority of the one over the other was never the design of heaven. The time likewise at which the continent was discovered adds weight to the argument, and the manner in which it was peopled increases the force of it. The Reformation was preceded by the discovery of America—as if the Almighty graciously meant to open a sanctuary to the persecuted in future years, when home should afford neither friendship nor safety.

The authority of Great Britain over this continent is a form of government which sooner or later must have an end. And a serious mind can draw no true pleasure by looking forward, under the painful and positive conviction that what he calls "the present constitution" is merely temporary. As parents, we can have no joy, knowing that this government is not sufficiently lasting to insure anything which we may bequeath to posterity. And by a plain method of argument, as we are running the next generation into debt, we ought to do the work of it; otherwise we use them meanly and pitifully. In order to discover the line of our duty rightly, we should take our children in our hand and fix our station a few years farther into life; that eminence will present a prospect which a few present fears and prejudices conceal from our sight.

Though I would carefully avoid giving unnecessary offense, yet I am inclined to believe that all those who espouse the doctrine of reconciliation may be included within the following descriptions. Interested men, who are not to be trusted, weak men who *cannot* see, prejudiced men who *will not* see, and a certain set of moderate men who think better of the European world than it deserves; and this last class, by an ill-judged deliberation, will be the cause of more calamities to this continent than all the other three. . . .

Men of passive tempers look somewhat lightly over the offenses of Great Britain and, still hoping for the best, are apt to call out, "Come, come, we shall be friends again for all this." But examine the passions and feelings of mankind, bring the doctrine of reconciliation to the touchstone of nature, and then tell me whether you can hereafter love, honor, and faithfully serve the power that has carried fire and sword into your land? If you cannot do all these, then are you only deceiving yourselves, and by your delay bringing ruin upon posterity. Your future connection with Britain, whom you can neither love nor honor, will be forced and unnatural, and being formed only on the plan of present convenience will, in a little time, fall into a relapse more wretched than the first. But if you say you still can pass the violations over, then I ask, has your house been burned? Has your property been destroyed before your face? Are your wife and children destitute of a bed to lie on or bread to live on? Have you lost a parent or a child by their hands, and yourself the ruined and wretched survivor? If you have not, then are you not a judge of those who have. But if you have and can still shake hands with the murderers, then are you unworthy the name of husband, father, friend, or lover; and whatever may be your rank or title in life, you have the heart of a coward and the spirit of a sycophant.

This is not inflaming or exaggerating matters, but trying them by those feelings and affections which nature justifies and without which we should be incapable of discharging the social duties of life or enjoying the felicities of it. I mean not to exhibit horror for the purpose of provoking revenge, but to awaken us from fatal and unmanly slumbers, that we may pursue determinately some fixed object. It is not in the power of Britain or Europe to conquer America, if she do not conquer herself by delay and timidity. . . .

It is repugnant to reason, to the universal order of things, to all examples from former ages, to suppose that this continent can longer remain subject to any external power. The most sanguine in Britain does not think so. The utmost stretch of human wisdom cannot, at this time, compass a plan, short of separation, which can promise the continent even a year's security. Reconciliation is *now* a fallacious dream. Nature has deserted the connection, and art cannot supply her place. For, as Milton wisely expresses, "never can true reconcilement grow where wounds of deadly hate have pierced so deep."

Every quiet method of peace has been ineffectual. Our prayers have been rejected with disdain, and only tended to convince us that nothing flatters vanity or confirms obstinacy in kings more than repeated petitioning—and nothing has contributed more than that very measure to make the kings of Europe absolute. . . . Wherefore, since nothing but blows will do, for God's sake let us come to a final separation, and not leave the next generation to be cutting throats under the violated unmeaning names of parent and child. . . .

As to government matters, it is not in the power of Britain to do this continent justice. The business of it will soon be too weighty and intricate to be managed with any tolerable degree of convenience by a power so distant from us and so very ignorant of us; for if they cannot conquer us, they cannot govern us. To be always running three or four thousand miles with a tale or a petition, waiting four or five months for an answer, which, when obtained, requires five or six more to explain it in, will in a few years be looked upon as folly and childishness. There was a time when it was proper, and there is a proper time for it to cease.

Small islands not capable of protecting themselves are the proper objects for kingdoms to take under their care, but there is something very absurd in supposing a continent to be perpetually governed by an island. In no instance has nature made the satellite larger than its primary planet; and as England and America, with respect to each other, reverse the common order of nature, it is evident they belong to different systems— England to Europe, America to itself.

I am not induced by motives of pride, party, or resentment to espouse the doctrine of separation and independence; I am clearly, positively, and conscientiously persuaded that it is the true interest of this continent to be so; that everything short of *that* is mere patchwork, that it can afford no lasting felicity—that it is leaving the sword to our children, and shrinking back at a time when a little more, a little further, would have rendered this continent the glory of the earth.

As Britain has not manifested the least inclination toward a compromise, we may be assured that no terms can be obtained worthy the acceptance of the continent, or any ways equal to the expense of blood and treasure we have been already put to. . . . As I have always considered the independence of this continent as an event which sooner or later must arrive, so from the late rapid progress of the continent to maturity, the event cannot be far off. Wherefore, on the breaking out of hostilities, it was not worth the while to have disputed a matter which time would have finally redressed, unless we meant to be in earnest; otherwise it is like wasting an estate on a suit at law to regulate the trespasses of a tenant whose lease is just expiring. No man was a warmer wisher for a reconciliation than myself before the fatal nineteenth of April, 1775, but the moment the event of that day was made known I rejected the hardened, sullen-tempered Pharaoh of England forever and disdain the wretch that, with the pretended title of father of his people, can unfeelingly hear of their slaughter and composedly sleep with their blood upon his soul.

But admitting that matters were now made up, what would be the event? I answer, the ruin of the continent. And that for several reasons:

First. The powers of governing still remaining in the hands of the king, he will have a negative over the whole legislation of this continent. And as he has shown himself such an inveterate enemy to liberty and discovered such a thirst for arbitrary power, is he or is he not a proper man to say to these colonies, "You shall make no laws but what I please!"? And is there any inhabitant of America so ignorant as not to know that, according to what is called the "present Constitution," that this continent can make no laws but what the king gives leave to; and is there any man so unwise as not to see that (considering what has happened) he will suffer no law to be made here but such as suits *his* purpose? We may be as effectually enslaved by the want of laws in America as by submitting to laws made for us in England. After matters are made up (as it is called), can there be any doubt but the whole power of the crown will be exerted to keep this continent as low and humble as possible? Instead of going forward we shall go backward, or be perpetually quarrelling, or ridiculously petitioning. We are already greater than the king wishes us to be, and will he not hereafter endeavor to make us less? To bring the matter to one point, is the power who is jealous of our prosperity a proper power to govern us? Whoever says "No" to this question is an independent, for independence means no more than whether we shall make our own laws or whether the king, the greatest enemy this continent has or can have, shall tell us "there shall be no laws but such as I like."

But the king, you will say, has a negative in England; the people there can make no laws without his consent. In point of right and good order, there is something very ridiculous that a youth of twenty-one (which has often happened) shall say to several millions of people older and wiser than himself, "I forbid this or that act of yours to be laws." But in this place I decline this sort of reply, though I will never cease to expose the absurdity of it, and only answer that England being the king's residence, and America not so, makes quite another case. The king's negative *here* is ten times more dangerous and fatal than it can be in England; for *there* he will scarcely refuse his consent to a bill for putting England into as strong a state of defense as possible, and in America he would never suffer such a bill to be passed.

America is only a secondary object in the system of British politics. England consults the good of *this* country no farther than it answers her *own* purpose. Wherefore her own interest leads her to suppress the growth of *ours* in every case which does not promote her advantage or in the least interferes with it. A pretty state we should soon be in under such a secondhand government, considering what has happened! Men do not change from enemies to friends by the alteration of a name. . . .

Secondly. That as even the best terms which we can expect to obtain can amount to no more than a temporary expedient, or a kind of government by guardianship, which can last no longer than till the colonies come of age, so the general face and state of things in the interim will be unsettled and unpromising. Emigrants of property will not choose to come to a country whose form of government hangs but by a thread, and who is every day tottering on the brink of commotion and disturbance; and numbers of the present inhabitants would lay hold of the interval to dispose of their effects and quit the continent.

But the most powerful of all arguments is that nothing but independence, i.e., a continental form of government, can keep the peace of the continent and preserve it inviolate from civil wars. I dread the event of a reconciliation with Britain now, as it is more than probable that it will be followed by a revolt somewhere or other, the consequences of which may be far more fatal than all the malice of Britain.

Thousands are already ruined by British barbarity (thousands more will probably suffer the same fate). Those men have other feelings than us who have nothing suffered. All they now possess is liberty; what they before enjoyed is sacrificed to its service, and having nothing more to lose they disdain submission. Besides, the general temper of the colonies toward a British government will be like that of a youth who is nearly out of his time; they will care very little about her. And a government which cannot preserve the peace is no government at all, and in that case we pay our money for nothing; and pray what is it that Britain can do, whose power will be wholly on paper, should a civil tumult break out the very day after reconciliation? I have heard some men say, many of whom I believe spoke without thinking, that they dreaded an independence, fearing that it would produce civil wars. It is but seldom that our first thoughts are truly correct, and that is the case here; for there are ten times more to dread from a patched-up connection than from independence. I make the sufferer's case my own, and I protest that, were I driven from house and home, my property destroyed, and my circumstances ruined, that as a man, sensible of injuries, I could never relish the doctrine of reconciliation or consider myself bound thereby.

The colonies have manifested such a spirit of good order and obedience to continental government as is sufficient to make every reasonable person easy and happy on that head. No man can assign the least pretense for his fears on any other grounds than such as are truly childish and ridiculous, viz., that one colony will be striving for superiority over another.

Where there are no distinctions, there can be no superiority; perfect equality affords no temptation. The republics of Europe are all (and we may say always) in peace. Holland and Switzerland are without wars, foreign or domestic. Monarchical governments, it is true, are never long at rest; the crown itself is a temptation to enterprising ruffians at home; and that degree of pride and insolence ever attendant on regal authority swells into a rupture with foreign powers in instances where a republican government, by being formed on more natural principles, would negotiate the mistake. . . .

To talk of friendship with those in whom our reason forbids us to have faith and our affections, wounded through a thousand pores, instruct us to detest is madness and folly. Every day wears out the little remains of kindred between us and them; and can there be any reason to hope that, as the relationship expires, the affection will increase, or that we shall agree better when we have ten times more and greater concerns to quarrel over than ever?

Ye that tell us of harmony and reconciliation, can ye restore to us the time that is past? Can ye give to prostitution its former innocence? Neither can ye reconcile Britain and America. The last cord now is broken, the people of England are presenting addresses against us. There are injuries which nature cannot forgive; she would cease to be nature if she did. As well can the lover forgive the ravisher of his mistress as the continent forgive the murders of Britain. The Almighty has implanted in us these unextinguishable feelings for good and wise purposes. They are the guardians of his image in our hearts. They distinguish us from the herd of common animals. The social compact would dissolve and justice be extirpated [from] the earth, or have only a casual existence, were we callous to the touches of affection. The robber and the murderer would often escape unpunished did not the injuries which our tempers sustain provoke us into justice.

O ye that love mankind! Ye that dare oppose not only the tyranny but the tyrant, stand forth! Every spot of the Old World is overrun with oppression. Freedom has been hunted round the globe. Asia and Africa have long expelled her. Europe regards her like a stranger, and England has given her warning to depart. O! receive the fugitive, and prepare in time an asylum for mankind. . . .

I shall conclude these remarks with the following timely and well-intended hints. We ought to reflect that there are three different ways by which an independence may hereafter be effected; and that *one* of those *three* will, one day or other, be the fate of America, viz., by the legal voice of the people in Congress, by a military power, or by a mob. It may not always happen that our soldiers are citizens and the multitude a body of reasonable men; virtue is not hereditary, neither is it perpetual. Should an independence be brought about by the first of those means, we have every opportunity and every encouragement before us to form the noblest, purest constitution on the face of the earth. We have it in our power to begin the world over again. A situation similar to the present has not happened since the days of Noah until now. The birthday of a new world is at hand. . . .

Nathaniel Hawthorne
My Kinsman, Major Molineux
(1832)

AFTER THE kings of Great Britain had assumed the right of appointing the colonial governors, the measures of the latter seldom met with the ready and general approbation, which had been paid to those of their predecessors, under the original charters. The people looked with most jealous scrutiny to the exercise of power, which did not emanate from themselves, and they usually rewarded the rulers with slender gratitude, for the compliances, by which, in softening their instructions from beyond the sea, they had incurred the reprehension of those who gave them. The annals of Massachusetts Bay will inform us, that of six governors, in the space of about forty years from the surrender of the old charter, under James II., two were imprisoned by a popular insurrection; a third, as Hutchinson inclines to believe, was driven from the province by the whizzing of a musket ball; a fourth, in the opinion of the same historian, was hastened to his grave by continual bickerings with the House of Representatives; and the remaining two, as well as their successors, till the Revolution, were favored with few and brief intervals of peaceful sway. The inferior members of the court party, in times of high political excitement, led scarcely a more desirable life. These remarks may serve as preface to the following adventures, which chanced upon a summer night, not far from a hundred years ago. The reader, in order to avoid a long and dry detail of colonial affairs, is requested to dispense with an account of the train of circumstances, that had caused much temporary inflammation of the popular mind.

It was near nine o'clock of a moonlight evening, when a boat crossed the ferry with a single passenger, who had obtained his conveyance, at that unusual hour, by the promise of an extra fare. While he stood on the landing-place, searching in either pocket for the means of fulfilling his agreement, the ferryman lifted a lantern, by the aid of which, and

[Originally published in *The Token* (1832).]

the newly risen moon, he took a very accurate survey of the stranger's figure. He was a youth of barely eighteen years, evidently country-bred, and now, as it should seem, upon his first visit to town. He was clad in a coarse grey coat, well worn, but in excellent repair; his under garments were durably constructed of leather, and sat tight to a pair of serviceable and well-shaped limbs; his stockings of blue yarn, were the incontrovertible handiwork of a mother or a sister; and on his head was a three-cornered hat, which in its better days had perhaps sheltered the graver brow of the lad's father. Under his left arm was a heavy cudgel, formed of an oak sapling, and retaining a part of the hardened root; and his equipment was completed by a wallet, not so abundantly stocked as to incommode the vigorous shoulders on which it hung. Brown, curly hair, well-shaped features, and bright, cheerful eyes, were nature's gifts, and worth all that art could have done for his adornment.

The youth, one of whose names was Robin, finally drew from his pocket the half of a little province-bill of five shillings, which, in the depreciation of that sort of currency, did but satisfy the ferryman's demand, with the surplus of a sexangular piece of parchment valued at three pence. He then walked forward into the town, with as light a step, as if his day's journey had not already exceeded thirty miles, and with as eager an eye, as if he were entering London city, instead of the little metropolis of a New England colony. Before Robin had proceeded far, however, it occurred to him, that he knew not whither to direct his steps; so he paused, and looked up and down the narrow street, scrutinizing the small and mean wooden buildings, that were scattered on either side.

"This low hovel cannot be my kinsman's dwelling," thought he, "nor yonder old house, where the moonlight enters at the broken casement; and truly I see none hereabouts that might be worthy of him. It would have been wise to inquire my way of the ferryman, and doubtless he would have gone with me, and earned a shilling from the Major for his pains. But the next man I meet will do as well."

He resumed his walk, and was glad to perceive that the street now became wider, and the houses more respectable in their appearance. He soon discerned a figure moving on moderately in advance, and hastened his steps to overtake it. As Robin drew nigh, he saw that the passenger was a man in years, with a full periwig of grey hair, a wide-skirted coat of dark cloth, and silk stockings rolled about his knees. He carried a long and polished cane, which he struck down perpendicularly before him, at every step; and at regular intervals he uttered two successive hems, of a peculiarly solemn and sepulchral intonation. Having made these observations, Robin laid hold of the skirt of the old man's coat, just when the light from the open door and windows of a barber's shop, fell upon both their figures.

"Good evening to you, honored Sir," said he, making a low bow, and still retaining his hold of the skirt. "I pray you to tell me whereabouts is the dwelling of my kinsman, Major Molineux?"

The youth's question was uttered very loudly; and one of the barbers, whose razor was descending on a well-soaped chin, and another who was dressing a Ramillies wig, left their occupations, and came to the door. The citizen, in the meantime, turned a long favored countenance upon Robin, and answered him in a tone of excessive anger and annoyance. His two sepulchral hems, however, broke into the very centre of his rebuke, with most singular effect, like a thought of the cold grave obtruding among wrathful passions.

"Let go my garment, fellow! I tell you, I know not the man you speak of. What! I have authority, I have—hem, hem—authority; and if this be the respect you show your betters, your feet shall be brought acquainted with the stocks, by daylight, tomorrow morning!"

Robin released the old man's skirt, and hastened away, pursued by an ill-mannered roar of laughter from the barber's shop. He was at first considerably surprised by the result of his question, but, being a shrewd youth, soon thought himself able to account for the mystery.

"This is some country representative," was his conclusion, "who has never seen the inside of my kinsman's door, and lacks the breeding to answer a stranger civilly. The man is old, or verily—I might be tempted to turn back and smite him on the nose. Ah, Robin, Robin! even the barber's boys laugh at you, for choosing such a guide! You will be wiser in time, friend Robin."

He now became entangled in a succession of crooked and narrow streets, which crossed each other, and meandered at no great distance from the water-side. The smell of tar was obvious to his nostrils, the masts of vessels pierced the moonlight above the tops of the buildings, and the numerous signs, which Robin paused to read, informed him that he was near the centre of business. But the streets were empty, the shops were closed, and lights were visible only in the second stories of a few dwelling-houses. At length, on the corner of a narrow lane, through which he was passing, he beheld the broad countenance of a British hero swinging before the door of an inn, whence proceeded the voices of many guests. The casement of one of the lower windows was thrown back, and a very thin curtain permitted Robin to distinguish a party at supper, round a well-furnished table. The fragrance of the good cheer steamed forth into the outer air, and the youth could not fail to recollect, that the last remnant of his travelling stock of provision had yielded to his morning appetite, and that noon had found, and left him, dinnerless.

"Oh, that a parchment three-penny might give me a right to sit down at yonder table," said Robin, with a sigh. "But the Major will make me welcome to the best of his victuals; so I will even step boldly in, and inquire my way to his dwelling."

He entered the tavern, and was guided by the murmur of voices, and fumes of tobacco, to the public room. It was a long and low apartment, with oaken walls, grown dark in the continual smoke, and a floor, which was thickly sanded, but of no immaculate purity. A number of persons, the larger part of whom appeared to be mariners, or in some way connected with the sea, occupied the wooden benches, or leather-bottomed chairs, conversing on various matters, and occasionally lending their attention to some topic of general interest. Three or four little groups were draining as many bowls of punch, which the great West India trade had long since made a familiar drink in the colony. Others, who had the aspect of men who lived by regular and laborious handicraft, preferred the insulated bliss of an unshared potation, and became more taciturn under its influence. Nearly all, in short, evinced a predilection for the Good Creature in some of its various shapes, for this is a vice, to which, as the Fast-day sermons of a hundred years ago will testify, we have a long hereditary claim. The only guests to whom Robin's sympathies inclined him, were two or three sheepish countrymen, who were using the inn somewhat after the fashion of a Turkish Caravansary; they had gotten themselves into the darkest corner of the room, and, heedless of the Nicotian atmosphere, were supping on the bread of their own ovens, and the bacon cured in their own chimney-smoke. But though Robin felt a sort of brotherhood with these strangers, his eyes were attracted from them, to a person who stood near the door, holding whispered conversation with a group of ill-dressed associates. His features were separately striking almost to grotesqueness, and the whole face left a deep impression in the memory. The forehead bulged out into a double prominence, with a vale between; the nose came boldly forth in an irregular curve, and its bridge was of more than a finger's breadth; the eyebrows were deep and shaggy, and the eyes glowed beneath them like fire in a cave.

While Robin deliberated of whom to inquire respecting his kinsman's dwelling, he was accosted by the innkeeper, a little man in a stained white apron, who had come to pay his professional welcome to the stranger. Being in the second generation from a French Protestant, he seemed to have inherited the courtesy of his parent nation; but no variety of circumstance was ever known to change his voice from the one shrill note in which he now addressed Robin.

"From the country, I presume, Sir?" said he, with a profound bow. "Beg to congratulate you on your arrival, and trust you intend a long stay with us. Fine town here, Sir, beautiful buildings, and much that may interest a stranger. May I hope for the honor of your commands in respect to supper?"

"The man sees a family likeness! the rogue has guessed that I am related to the Major!" thought Robin, who had hitherto experienced little superfluous civility.

All eyes were now turned on the country lad, standing at the door, in his worn three-cornered hat, grey coat, leather breeches, and blue yarn stockings, leaning on an oaken cudgel, and bearing a wallet on his back.

Robin replied to the courteous innkeeper, with such an assumption of consequence, as befitted the Major's relative.

"My honest friend," he said, "I shall make it a point to patronize your house on some occasion, when—" here he could not help lowering his voice—"I may have more than a parchment three-pence in my pocket. My present business," continued he, speaking with lofty confidence, "is merely to inquire the way to the dwelling of my kinsman, Major Molineux."

There was a sudden and general movement in the room, which Robin interpreted as expressing the eagerness of each individual to become his guide. But the innkeeper turned his eyes to a written paper on the wall, which he read, or seemed to read, with occasional recurrences to the young man's figure.

"What have we here?" said he, breaking his speech into little dry fragments. " 'Left the house of the subscriber, bounden servant, Hezekiah Mudge—had on, when he went away, grey coat, leather breeches, master's third best hat. One pound currency reward to whoever shall lodge him in any jail in the province.' Better trudge, boy, better trudge!"

Robin had begun to draw his hand towards the lighter end of the oak cudgel, but a strange hostility in every countenance, induced him to relinquish his purpose of breaking the courteous innkeeper's head. As he turned to leave the room, he encountered a sneering glance from the bold-featured personage whom he had before noticed; and no sooner was he beyond the door, than he heard a general laugh, in which the innkeeper's voice might be distinguished, like the dropping of small stones into a kettle.

"Now is it not strange," thought Robin, with his usual shrewdness, "is it not strange, that the confession of an empty pocket, should outweigh the name of my kinsman, Major Molineux? Oh, if I had one of these grinning rascals in the woods, where I and my oak sapling grew up together, I would teach him that my arm is heavy, though my purse be light!"

On turning the corner of the narrow lane, Robin found himself in a spacious street, with an unbroken line of lofty houses on each side, and a steepled building at the upper end, whence the ringing of a bell announced the hour of nine. The light of the moon, and the lamps from numerous shop windows, discovered people promenading on the pavement, and amongst them, Robin hoped to recognize his hitherto inscrutable relative. The result of his former inquiries made him unwilling to hazard another, in a scene of such publicity, and he determined to walk slowly and silently up the street, thrusting his face close to that of every elderly gentleman, in search of the Major's lineaments. In his progress, Robin encountered many gay and gallant figures. Embroidered garments, of showy colors, enormous periwigs, gold-laced hats, and silver hilted swords, glided past him and dazzled his optics. Travelled youths, imitators of the European fine gentlemen of the period, trod jauntily along, half-dancing to the fashionable tunes which they hummed, and making poor Robin ashamed of his quiet and natural gait. At length, after many pauses to examine the gorgeous display of goods in the shop windows, and after suffering some rebukes for the impertinence of his scrutiny into people's faces, the Major's kinsman found himself near the steepled building, still unsuccessful in his search. As yet, however, he had seen only one side of the thronged street; so Robin crossed, and continued the same sort of inquisition down the opposite pavement, with stronger hopes than the philosopher seeking an honest man, but with no better fortune. He had arrived about midway towards the lower end, from which his course began, when he overheard the approach of someone, who struck down a cane on the flag-stones at every step, uttering, at regular intervals, two sepulchral hems.

"Mercy on us!" quoth Robin, recognizing the sound.

Turning a corner, which chanced to be close at his right hand, he hastened to pursue his researches, in some other part of the town. His patience was now wearing low, and he seemed to feel more fatigue from his rambles since he crossed the ferry, than from his journey of several days on the other side. Hunger also pleaded loudly within him, and Robin began to balance the propriety of demanding, violently and with lifted cudgel, the necessary guidance from the first solitary passenger, whom he should meet. While a resolution to this effect was gaining strength, he entered a street of mean appearance, on either side of which, a row of ill-built houses was straggling towards the harbor. The moonlight fell upon no passenger along the whole extent, but in the third domicile which Robin passed, there was a half-opened door, and his keen glance detected a woman's garment within.

"My luck may be better here," said he to himself.

Accordingly, he approached the door, and beheld it shut closer as he did so; yet an open space remained, sufficing for the fair occupant to observe the stranger, without a corresponding display on her part. All that Robin could discern was a strip of scarlet petticoat, and the occasional sparkle of an eye, as if the moonbeams were trembling on some bright thing.

"Pretty mistress,"—for I may call her so with a good conscience, thought the shrewd youth, since I know nothing to the contrary—"my sweet pretty mistress, will you be kind enough to tell me whereabouts I must seek the dwelling of my kinsman, Major Molineux?"

Robin's voice was plaintive and winning, and the female, seeing nothing to be shunned in the handsome country youth, thrust open the door, and came forth into the moonlight. She was a dainty little figure, with a white neck, round arms, and a slender waist, at the extremity of which her scarlet petticoat jutted out over a hoop, as if she were standing in a balloon. Moreover, her face was oval and pretty, her hair dark beneath the little cap, and her bright eyes possessed a sly freedom, which triumphed over those of Robin.

"Major Molineux dwells here," said this fair woman.

Now her voice was the sweetest Robin had heard that night, the airy counterpart of a stream of melted silver; yet he could not help doubting whether that sweet voice spoke Gospel truth. He looked up and down the mean street, and then surveyed the house before which they stood. It was a small, dark edifice of two stories, the second of which projected over the lower floor; and the front apartment had the aspect of a shop for petty commodities.

"Now truly I am in luck," replied Robin, cunningly, "and so indeed is my kinsman, the Major, in having so pretty a housekeeper. But I prithee trouble him to step to the door; I will deliver him a message from his friends in the country, and then go back to my lodgings at the inn."

"Nay, the Major has been a-bed this hour or more," said the lady of the scarlet petticoat; "and it would be to little purpose to disturb him to-night, seeing his evening draught was of the strongest. But he is a kind-hearted man, and it would be as much as my life's worth, to let a kinsman of his turn away from the door. You are the good old gentleman's very picture, and I could swear that was his rainy-weather hat. Also, he has garments very much resembling those leather—But come in, I pray, for I bid you hearty welcome in his name."

So saying, the fair and hospitable dame took our hero by the hand; and though the touch was light, and the force was gentleness, and though Robin read in her eyes what he did not hear in her words, yet the slender waisted woman, in the scarlet petticoat, proved stronger than the athletic country youth. She had drawn his half-willing footsteps nearly to the threshold, when the opening of a door in the neighborhood, startled the Major's housekeeper, and, leaving the Major's kinsman, she vanished speedily into her own domicile. A heavy yawn preceded the appearance of a man, who, like the Moonshine of Pyramus and Thisbe, carried a lantern, needlessly aiding his sister luminary in the heavens. As he walked sleepily up the street, he turned his broad, dull face on Robin, and displayed a long staff, spiked at the end.

"Home, vagabond, home!" said the watchman, in accents that seemed to fall asleep as soon as they were uttered. "Home, or we'll set you in the stocks by peep of day!"

"This is the second hint of the kind," thought Robin. "I wish they would end my difficulties, by setting me there to-night."

Nevertheless, the youth felt an instinctive antipathy towards the guardian of midnight order, which at first prevented him from asking his usual question. But just when the man was about to vanish behind the corner, Robin resolved not to lose the opportunity, and shouted lustily after him—

"I say, friend! will you guide me to the house of my kinsman, Major Molineux?"

The watchman made no reply, but turned the corner and was gone; yet Robin seemed to hear the sound of drowsy laughter stealing along the solitary street. At that moment, also, a pleasant titter saluted him from the open window above his head; he looked up, and caught the sparkle of a saucy eye; a round arm beckoned to him, and next he heard light footsteps descending the staircase within. But Robin, being of the household of a New England clergyman, was a good youth, as well as a shrewd one; so he resisted temptation, and fled away.

He now roamed desperately, and at random, through the town, almost ready to believe that a spell was on him, like that, by which a wizard of his country, had once kept three pursuers wandering, a whole winter night, within twenty paces of the cottage which they sought. The streets lay before him, strange and desolate, and the lights were extinguished in almost every house. Twice, however, little parties of men, among whom Robin distinguished individuals in outlandish attire, came hurrying along, but though on both occasions they paused to address him, such intercourse did not at all enlighten his perplexity. They did but utter a few words in some language of which Robin knew nothing, and perceiving his inability to answer, bestowed a curse upon him in plain English, and hastened away. Finally, the lad determined to knock at the door of every mansion that might appear worthy to be occupied by his kinsman, trusting that perseverance would overcome the fatality which had hitherto thwarted him. Firm in this resolve, he was passing beneath the walls of a church, which formed the corner of two streets, when, as he turned into the shade of its steeple, he encountered a bulky stranger, muffled in a cloak. The man was proceeding with the speed of earnest business, but Robin planted himself full before him, holding the oak cudgel with both hands across his body, as a bar to further passage.

"Halt, honest man, and answer me a question," said he, very resolutely. "Tell me, this instant, whereabouts is the dwelling of my kinsman, Major Molineux?"

"Keep your tongue between your teeth, fool, and let me pass," said a deep, gruff voice, which Robin partly remembered. "Let me pass, I say, or I'll strike you to the earth!"

"No, no neighbor!" cried Robin, flourishing his cudgel, and then thrusting its larger end close to the man's muffled face. "No, no, I'm not the fool you take me for, nor do you pass, till I have an answer to my question. Whereabouts is the dwelling of my kinsman, Major Molineux?"

The stranger, instead of attempting to force his passage, stept back into the moonlight, unmuffled his own face and stared full into that of Robin.

"Watch here an hour, and Major Molineux will pass by," said he.

Robin gazed with dismay and astonishment, on the unprecedented physiognomy of the speaker. The forehead with its double prominence, the broad-hooked nose, the shaggy eyebrows, and fiery eyes, were those which he had noticed at the inn, but the man's complexion had undergone a singular, or, more properly, a two-fold change. One side of the face blazed of an intense red, while the other was black as midnight, the division line being in the broad bridge of the nose; and a mouth, which seemed to extend from ear to ear, was black or red, in contrast to the color of the cheek. The effect was as if two individual devils, a fiend of fire and a fiend of darkness, had united themselves to form this infernal visage. The stranger grinned in Robin's face, muffled his parti-colored features, and was out of sight in a moment.

"Strange things we travellers see!" ejaculated Robin.

He seated himself, however, upon the steps of the church-door, resolving to wait the appointed time for his kinsman's appearance. A few moments were consumed in philosophical speculations, upon the species of the *genus homo*, who had just left him, but having settled this point shrewdly, rationally, and satisfactorily, he was compelled to look elsewhere for amusement. And first he threw his eyes along the street; it was of more respectable appearance than most of those into which he had wandered, and the moon, "creating, like the imaginative power, a beautiful strangeness in familiar objects," gave something of romance to a scene, that might not have possessed it in the light of day. The irregular, and often quaint architecture of the houses, some of whose roofs were broken into numerous little peaks; while others ascended, steep and narrow, into a single point; and others again were square; the pure milk-white of some of their complexions, the aged darkness of others, and the thousand sparklings, reflected from bright substances in the plastered walls of many; these matters engaged Robin's attention for awhile, and then began to grow wearisome. Next he endeavored to define the forms of distant objects, starting away with almost ghostly indistinctness, just as his eye appeared to grasp them; and finally he took a minute survey of an edifice, which stood on the opposite side of the street, directly in front of the church-door, where he was stationed. It was a large square mansion, distinguished from its neighbors by a balcony, which rested on tall pillars, and by an elaborate Gothic window, communicating therewith.

"Perhaps this is the very house I have been seeking," thought Robin.

Then he strove to speed away the time, by listening to a murmur, which swept continually along the street, yet was scarcely audible, except to an unaccustomed ear like his; it was a low, dull, dreamy sound, compounded of many noises, each of which was at too great a distance to be separately heard. Robin marvelled at this snore of a sleeping town, and marvelled more, whenever its continuity was broken, by now and then a distant shout, apparently loud where it originated. But altogether it was a sleep-inspiring sound, and to shake off its drowsy influence, Robin arose, and climbed a window-frame, that he might view the interior of the church. There the moonbeams came trembling in, and fell down upon the deserted pews, and extended along the quiet aisles. A fainter, yet more awful radiance, was hovering round the pulpit, and one solitary ray had dared to rest upon the opened page of the great Bible. Had Nature, in that deep hour, become a worshipper in the house, which man had builded? Or was that heavenly light the visible sanctity of the place, visible because no earthly and impure feet were within the walls? The scene made Robin's heart shiver with a sensation of loneliness, stronger than he had ever felt in the remotest depths of his native woods; so he turned away, and sat down again before the door. There were graves around the church, and now an uneasy thought obtruded into Robin's breast. What if the object of his search, which had been so often and so strangely thwarted, were all the time mouldering in his shroud? What if his kinsman should glide through yonder gate, and nod and smile to him in passing dimly by?

"Oh, that any breathing thing were here with me!" said Robin.

Recalling his thoughts from this uncomfortable track, he sent them over forest, hill, and stream, and attempted to imagine how that evening of ambiguity and weariness, had been spent by his father's household. He pictured them assembled at the door, beneath the tree, the great old tree, which had been spared for its huge twisted trunk, and venerable shade, when a thousand leafy brethren fell. There, at the going down of the summer sun, it was his father's custom to perform domestic worship, that the neighbors might come and join with him like brothers of the family, and that the wayfaring man might pause to drink at that fountain, and keep his heart pure by freshening the memory of home. Robin distinguished the seat of every individual of the little audience; he saw the good man in the midst, holding the Scriptures in the golden light that shone from the western clouds; he beheld him close the book, and all rise up to pray. He heard the old thanksgivings for daily mercies, the old supplications for their continuance, to which he had so often listened in weariness, but which were now among his dear remembrances. He perceived the slight inequality of his father's voice when he came to speak of the Absent One; he noted how his mother turned her face to the broad and knotted trunk; how his elder brother scorned, because the beard was rough upon his upper lip, to permit his features to be moved; how his younger sister drew down a low hanging branch before her eyes; and how the little one of all, whose sports had hitherto broken the decorum of the scene, understood the prayer for her playmate, and burst into clamorous grief. Then he saw them go in at the door; and when Robin would have entered also, the latch tinkled into its place, and he was excluded from his home.

"Am I here, or there?" cried Robin, starting; for all at once, when his thoughts had become visible and audible in a dream, the long, wide, solitary street shone out before him.

He aroused himself, and endeavored to fix his attention steadily upon the large edifice which he had surveyed before. But still his mind kept vibrating between fancy and reality; by turns, the pillars of the balcony lengthened into the tall, bare stems of pines, dwindled down to human figures, settled again in their true shape and size, and then commenced a new succession of changes. For a single moment, when he deemed himself awake, he could have sworn that a visage, one which he seemed to remember, yet could not absolutely name as his kinsman's, was looking towards him from the Gothic window. A deeper sleep wrestled with, and nearly overcame him, but fled at the sound of footsteps along the opposite pavement. Robin rubbed his eyes, discerned a man passing at the foot of the balcony, and addressed him in a loud, peevish, and lamentable cry.

"Halloo, friend! must I wait here all night for my kinsman, Major Molineux?"

The sleeping echoes awoke, and answered the voice; and the passenger, barely able to discern a figure sitting in the oblique shade of the steeple, traversed the street to obtain a nearer view. He was himself a gentleman in his prime, of open, intelligent, cheerful, and altogether prepossessing countenance. Perceiving a country youth, apparently homeless and without friends, he accosted him in a tone of real kindness, which had become strange to Robin's ears.

"Well, my good lad, why are you sitting here?" inquired he. "Can I be of service to you in any way?"

"I am afraid not, Sir," replied Robin, despondingly; "yet I shall take it kindly, if you'll answer me a single question. I've been searching half the night for one Major Molineux; now, Sir, is there really such a person in these parts, or am I dreaming?"

"Major Molineux! The name is not altogether strange to me," said the gentleman, smiling. "Have you any objection to telling me the nature of your business with him?"

Then Robin briefly related that his father was a clergyman, settled on a small salary, at a long distance back in the country, and that he and Major Molineux were brothers' children. The Major, having inherited riches, and acquired civil and military rank, had visited his cousin in great pomp a year or two before; had manifested much interest in Robin and an elder brother, and, being childless himself, had thrown out hints respecting the future establishment of one of them in life. The elder brother was destined to succeed to the farm, which his father cultivated, in the interval of sacred duties; it was therefore determined that Robin should profit by his kinsman's generous intentions, especially as he had seemed to be rather the favorite, and was thought to possess other necessary endowments.

"For I have the name of being a shrewd youth," observed Robin, in this part of his story.

"I doubt not you deserve it," replied his new friend, good naturedly; "but pray proceed."

"Well, Sir, being nearly eighteen years old, and well grown, as you see," continued Robin, raising himself to his full height, "I thought it high time to begin the world. So my mother and sister put me in handsome trim, and my father gave me half the remnant of his last year's salary, and five days ago I started for this place, to pay the Major a visit. But would you believe it, Sir? I crossed the ferry a little after dusk, and have yet found nobody that would show me the way to his dwelling; only an hour or two since, I was told to wait here, and Major Molineux would pass by."

"Can you describe the man who told you this?" inquired the gentleman.

"Oh, he was a very ill-favored fellow, Sir," replied Robin, "with two great bumps on his forehead, a hook nose, fiery eyes, and, what struck me as the strangest, his face was of two different colors. Do you happen to know such a man, Sir?"

"Not intimately," answered the stranger, "but I chanced to meet him a little time previous to your stopping me. I believe you may trust his word, and that the Major will very shortly pass through this street. In the mean time, as I have a singular curiosity to witness your meeting, I will sit down here upon the steps, and bear you company."

He seated himself accordingly, and soon engaged his companion in animated discourse. It was but of brief continuance, however, for a noise of shouting, which had long been remotely audible, drew so much nearer, that Robin inquired its cause.

"What may be the meaning of this uproar?" asked he. "Truly, if your town be always this noisy, I shall find little sleep, while I am an inhabitant."

"Why, indeed, friend Robin, there do appear to be three or four riotous fellows abroad to-night," replied the gentleman. "You must not expect all the stillness of your native woods, here in our streets. But the watch will shortly be at the heels of these lads, and—"

"Aye, and set them in the stocks by peep of day," interrupted Robin, recollecting his own encounter with the drowsy lantern-bearer. "But, dear Sir, if I may trust my ears, an army of watchmen would never make head against such a multitude of rioters. There were at least a thousand voices went to make up that one shout."

"May not one man have several voices, Robin, as well as two complexions?" said his friend.

"Perhaps a man may; but Heaven forbid that a woman should!" responded the shrewd youth, thinking of the seductive tones of the Major's housekeeper.

The sounds of a trumpet in some neighboring street now became so evident and continual, that Robin's curiosity was strongly excited. In addition to the shouts, he heard frequent bursts from many instruments of discord, and a wild and confused laughter filled up the intervals. Robin rose from the steps, and looked wistfully towards a point, whither several people seemed to be hastening.

"Surely some prodigious merrymaking is going on," exclaimed he. "I have laughed very little since I left home, Sir, and should be sorry to lose an opportunity. Shall we just step round the corner by that darkish house, and take our share of the fun?"

"Sit down again, sit down, good Robin," replied the gentleman, laying his hand on the skirt of the grey coat. "You forget that we must wait here for your kinsman; and there is reason to believe that he will pass by, in the course of a very few moments."

The near approach of the uproar had now disturbed the neighborhood; windows flew open on all sides; and many heads, in the attire of the pillow, and confused by sleep suddenly broken, were protruded to the gaze of whoever had leisure to observe them. Eager voices hailed each other from house to house, all demanding the explanation, which not a soul could give. Half-dressed men hurried towards the unknown commotion, stumbling as they went over the stone steps, that thrust themselves into the narrow foot-walk. The shouts, the laughter, and the tuneless bray, the anti-podes of music, came onward with increasing din, till scattered individuals, and then denser bodies, began to appear round a corner, at the distance of a hundred yards.

"Will you recognize your kinsman, Robin, if he passes in this crowd?" inquired the gentleman.

"Indeed, I can't warrant it, Sir; but I'll take my stand here, and keep a bright look out," answered Robin, descending to the outer edge of the pavement.

A mighty stream of people now emptied into the street, and came rolling slowly towards the church. A single horseman wheeled the corner in the midst of them, and close behind him came a band of fearful wind-instruments, sending forth a fresher discord, now that no intervening buildings kept it from the ear. Then a redder light disturbed the moonbeams, and a dense multitude of torches shone along the street, concealing by their glare whatever object they illuminated. The single horseman, clad in a military dress, and bearing a drawn sword, rode onward as the leader, and, by his fierce and variegated countenance, appeared like war personified; the red of one cheek was an emblem of fire and sword; the blackness of the other betokened the mourning which attends them. In his train, were wild figures in the Indian dress, and many fantastic shapes without a model, giving the whole march a visionary air, as if a dream had broken forth from some feverish brain, and were sweeping visibly through the midnight streets. A mass of people, inactive, except as applauding spectators, hemmed the procession in, and several women ran along the sidewalks, piercing the confusion of heavier sounds, with their shrill voices of mirth or terror.

"The double-faced fellow has his eye upon me," muttered Robin, with an indefinite but uncomfortable idea, that he was himself to bear a part in the pageantry.

The leader turned himself in the saddle, and fixed his glance full upon the country youth, as the steed went slowly by. When Robin had freed his eyes from those fiery ones, the musicians were passing before him, and the torches were close at hand; but the unsteady brightness of the latter formed a veil which he could not penetrate. The rattling of wheels over the stones sometimes found its way to his ear, and confused traces of a human form appeared at intervals, and then melted into the vivid light. A moment more, and the leader thundered a command to halt; the trumpets vomited a horrid breath, and held their peace; the shouts and laughter of the people died away, and there remained only a universal hum, nearly allied to silence. Right before Robin's eyes was an uncovered cart. There the torches blazed the brightest, there the moon shone out like day, and there, in tar-and-feathery dignity, sat his kinsman, Major Molineux!

He was an elderly man, of large and majestic person, and strong, square features, betokening a steady soul; but steady as it was, his enemies had found the means to shake it. His face was pale as death, and far more ghastly; the broad forehead was contracted in his agony, so that his eyebrows formed one grizzled line; his eyes were red and wild, and the foam hung white upon his quivering lip. His whole frame was agitated by a quick, and continual tremor, which his pride strove to quell, even in those circumstances of overwhelming humiliation. But perhaps the bitterest pang of all was when his eyes met those of Robin; for he evidently knew him on the instant, as the youth stood witnessing the foul disgrace of a head that had grown grey in honor. They stared at each other in silence, and Robin's knees shook, and his hair bristled, with a mixture of pity and terror. Soon, however, a bewildering excitement began to seize upon his mind; the preceding adventures of the night, the unexpected appearance of the crowd, the torches, the confused din, and the hush that followed, the spectre of his kinsman reviled by that great multitude, all this, and more than all, a perception of tremendous ridicule in the whole scene, affected him with a sort of mental inebriety. At that moment a voice of sluggish merriment saluted Robin's ears; he turned instinctively, and just behind the corner of the church stood the lantern-bearer, rubbing his eyes, and drowsily enjoying the lad's amazement. Then he heard a peal of laughter like the ringing of silvery bells; a woman twitched his arm, a saucy eye met his, and he saw the lady of the scarlet petticoat. A sharp, dry cachinnation appealed to his memory, and, standing on tiptoe in the crowd, with his white apron over his head, he beheld the courteous little innkeeper. And lastly, there sailed over the heads of the multitude a great, broad laugh, broken in the midst by two sepulchral hems; thus—

"Haw, haw, haw—hem, hem—haw, haw, haw, haw!"

The sound proceeded from the balcony of the opposite edifice, and thither Robin turned his eyes. In front of the Gothic window stood the old citizen, wrapped in a wide gown, his grey periwig exchanged for a nightcap, which was thrust back from his forehead, and his silk stockings hanging down about his legs. He supported himself on his polished cane in a fit of convulsive merriment, which manifested itself on his solemn old features, like a funny inscription on a tomb-stone. Then Robin seemed to hear the voices of the barbers; of the guests of the inn; and of all who had made sport of him that night. The contagion was spreading among the multitude, when, all at once, it seized upon Robin, and he sent forth a shout of laughter that echoed through the street; every man shook his sides, every man emptied his lungs, but Robin's shout was the loudest there. The cloud-spirits peeped from their silvery islands, as the congregated mirth went roaring up the sky! The Man in the Moon heard the far bellow; "Oho," quoth he, "the old Earth is frolicsome to-night!"

When there was a momentary calm in that tempestuous sea of sound, the leader gave the sign, the procession resumed its march. On they went, like fiends that throng in mockery round some dead potentate, mighty no more, but majestic still in his agony. On they went, in counterfeited pomp, in senseless uproar, in frenzied merriment, trampling all on an old man's heart. On swept the tumult, and left a silent street behind.

"Well, Robin, are you dreaming?" inquired the gentleman, laying his hand on the youth's shoulder.

Robin started, and withdrew his arm from the stone post, to which he had instinctively clung, while the living stream rolled by him. His cheek was somewhat pale, and his eye not quite so lively as in the earlier part of the evening.

"Will you be kind enough to show me the way to the ferry?" said he, after a moment's pause.

"You have then adopted a new subject of inquiry?" observed his companion, with a smile.

"Why, yes, Sir," replied Robin, rather dryly. "Thanks to you, and to my other friends, I have at last met my kinsman, and he will scarce desire to see my face again. I begin to grow weary of a town life, Sir. Will you show me the way to the ferry?"

"No, my good friend Robin, not to-night, at least," said the gentleman. "Some few days hence, if you continue to wish it, I will speed you on your journey. Or, if you prefer to remain with us, perhaps, as you are a shrewd youth, you may rise in the world, without the help of your kinsman, Major Molineux."

Thomas Jefferson
The Declaration of Independence
(1776)

WHEN IN the Course of human events, it becomes necessary for one people to dissolve the political bands which have connected them with another, and to assume among the Powers of the earth, the separate and equal station to which the Laws of Nature and of Nature's God entitle them, a decent respect to the opinions of mankind requires that they should declare the causes which impel them to the separation.

We hold these truths to be self-evident, that all men are created equal, that they are endowed by their Creator with certain unalienable Rights, that among these are Life, Liberty and the pursuit of Happiness. That to secure these rights, Governments are instituted among Men, deriving their just powers from the consent of the governed, That whenever any Form of Government becomes destructive of these ends, it is the Right of the People to alter or to abolish it, and to institute new Government, laying its foundation on such principles and organizing its powers in such form, as to them shall seem most likely to effect their Safety and Happiness. Prudence, indeed, will dictate that Governments long established should not be changed for light and transient causes; and accordingly all experience hath shown, that mankind are more disposed to suffer, while evils are sufferable, than to right themselves by abolishing the forms to which they are accustomed. But when a long train of abuses and usurpations, pursuing invariably the same Object evinces a design to reduce them under absolute Despotism, it is their right, it is their duty, to throw off such Government, and to provide new Guards for their future security.—Such has been the patient sufferance of these Colonies; and such is now the necessity which constrains them to alter their former Systems of Government. The history of the present King of Great Britain is a

[From the parchment copy ordered by the Continental Congress on 19 July 1776 and now housed in the National Archives, Washington, D.C.]

history of repeated injuries and usurpations, all having in direct object the establishment of an absolute Tyranny over these States. To prove this, let Facts be submitted to a candid world.

He has refused his Assent to Laws, the most wholesome and necessary for the public good.

He has forbidden his Governors to pass Laws of immediate and pressing importance, unless suspended in their operation till his Assent should be obtained; and when so suspended, he has utterly neglected to attend to them.

He has refused to pass other Laws for the accommodation of large districts of people, unless those people would relinquish the right of Representation in the Legislature, a right inestimable to them and formidable to tyrants only.

He has called together legislative bodies at places unusual, uncomfortable, and distant from the depository of their Public Records, for the sole purpose of fatiguing them into compliance with his measures.

He has dissolved Representative Houses repeatedly, for opposing with manly firmness his invasions on the rights of the people.

He has refused for a long time, after such dissolutions, to cause others to be elected; whereby the Legislative Powers, incapable of Annihilation, have returned to the People at large for their exercise; the State remaining in the mean time exposed to all the dangers of invasion from without, and convulsions within.

He has endeavoured to prevent the population of these States; for that purpose obstructing the Laws of Naturalization of Foreigners; refusing to pass others to encourage their migration hither, and raising the conditions of new Appropriations of Lands.

He has obstructed the Administration of Justice, by refusing his Assent to Laws for establishing Judiciary Powers.

He has made Judges dependent on his Will alone, for the tenure of their offices, and the amount and payment of their salaries.

He has erected a multitude of New Offices, and sent hither swarms of Officers to harass our People, and eat out their substance.

He has kept among us, in times of peace, Standing Armies without the Consent of our legislature.

He has affected to render the Military independent of and superior to the Civil Power.

He has combined with others to subject us to a jurisdiction foreign to our constitution, and unacknowledged by our laws; giving his Assent to their acts of pretended legislation:

For quartering large bodies of armed troops among us:

For protecting them, by a mock Trial, from Punishment for any Murders which they should commit on the Inhabitants of these States:

For cutting off our Trade with all parts of the world:

For imposing taxes on us without our Consent:

For depriving us in many cases, of the benefits of Trial by Jury:

For transporting us beyond Seas to be tried for pretended offences:

For abolishing the free System of English Laws in a neighbouring Province, establishing therein an Arbitrary government, and enlarging its Boundaries so as to render it at once an example and fit instrument for introducing the same absolute rule into these Colonies:

For taking away our Charters, abolishing our most valuable Laws, and altering fundamentally the Forms of our Governments:

For suspending our own Legislature, and declaring themselves invested with Power to legislate for us in all cases whatsoever.

He has abdicated Government here, by declaring us out of his Protection and waging War against us.

He has plundered our seas, ravaged our Coasts, burnt our towns, and destroyed the lives of our people.

He is at this time transporting large armies of foreign mercenaries to compleat the works of death, desolation and tyranny, already begun with circumstances of Cruelty & perfidy scarcely paralleled in the most barbarous ages, and totally unworthy the Head of a civilized nation.

He has constrained our fellow Citizens taken Captive on the high Seas to bear Arms against their Country, to become the executioners of their friends and Brethren, or to fall themselves by their Hands.

He has excited domestic insurrections amongst us, and has endeavoured to bring on the inhabitants of our frontiers, the merciless Indian Savages, whose known rule of warfare, is an undistinguished destruction of all ages, sexes and conditions.

In every stage of these Oppressions We have Petitioned for Redress in the most humble terms: Our repeated Petitions have been answered only by repeated injury. A Prince, whose character is thus marked by every act which may define a Tyrant, is unfit to be the ruler of a free People.

Nor have We been wanting in attention to our British brethren. We have warned them from time to time of attempts by their legislature to extend an unwarrantable jurisdiction over us. We have reminded them of the circumstances of our emigration and settlement here. We have appealed to their native justice and magnanimity, and we have conjured them by the ties of our common kindred to disavow these usurpations, which, would inevitably interrupt our connections and correspondence. They too have been deaf to the voice of justice and of consanguinity. We must, therefore, acquiesce in the necessity, which denounces our Separation, and hold them, as we hold the rest of mankind, Enemies in War, in Peace Friends.

We, therefore, the Representatives of the United States of America, in General Congress, Assembled, appealing to the Supreme Judge of the world for the rectitude of our intentions, do, in the Name, and by Authority of the good People of these Colonies, solemnly publish and declare, That these United Colonies are, and of Right ought to be Free and Independent States; that they are Absolved from all Allegiance to the British Crown, and that all political connection between them and the State of Great Britain, is and ought to be totally dissolved; and that as Free and Independent States, they have full Power to levy War, conclude Peace, contract Alliances, establish Commerce, and to do all other Acts and Things which Independent States may of right do. And for the support of this Declaration, with a firm reliance on the Protection of Divine Providence, we mutually pledge to each other our Lives, our Fortunes and our sacred Honor.

John Hancock.

New Hampshire
Josiah Bartlett,
Wm. Whipple,
Matthew Thornton.

Massachusetts Bay
Saml. Adams,
John Adams,
Robt. Treat Paine,
Elbridge Gerry.

Rhode Island
Step. Hopkins,
William Ellery.

Connecticut
Roger Sherman,
Sam'el Huntington,
Wm. Williams,
Oliver Wolcott.

Georgia
Button Gwinnett,
Lyman Hall,
Geo. Walton.

Maryland
Samuel Chase,
Wm. Paca,
Thos. Stone,
Charles Carroll of
   Carrollton.

Virginia
George Wythe,
Richard Henry Lee,
Th. Jefferson,
Benja. Harrison,
Ths. Nelson, Jr.,
Francis Lightfoot Lee,
Carter Braxton.

New York
Wm. Floyd,
Phil. Livingston,
Frans. Lewis,
Lewis Morris.

North Carolina
Wm. Hooper,
Joseph Hewes,
John Penn.

Pennsylvania
Robt. Morris,
Benjamin Rush,
Benja. Franklin,
John Morton,
Geo. Clymer,
Jas. Smith,
Geo. Taylor,
James Wilson,
Geo. Ross.

Delaware
Caesar Rodney,
Geo. Read,
Tho. M'Kean.

South Carolina
Edward Rutledge,
Thos. Heyward, Junr.,
Thomas Lynch, Junr.,
Arthur Middleton.

New Jersey
Richd. Stockton
Jno. Witherspoon,
Fras. Hopkinson,
John Hart,
Abra. Clark.

Philip Freneau

On the Emigration to America and Peopling the Western Country (1784)

From Europe's proud, despotic shores
Hither the stranger takes his way,
And in our new found world explores
A happier soil, a milder sway,
Where no proud despot holds him down,
No slaves insult him with a crown. . . .

While virtue warms the generous breast,
There heaven-born freedom shall reside,
Nor shall the voice of war molest,
Nor Europe's all-aspiring pride—
There Reason shall new laws devise,
And order from confusion rise. . . .

Far brighter scenes a future age,
The muse predicts, these States will hail,
Whose genius may the world engage,
Whose deeds may over death prevail,
And happier systems bring to view,
Than all the eastern sages knew.

[From the version first published in Bailey's *Pocket Almanac* (1785), stanzas 2, 7, and 10.]

THE ONE AND THE MANY

James Madison
The Federalist, No. 10
(1787)

To the People of the State of New York.

AMONG THE numerous advantages promised by a well constructed Union, none deserves to be more accurately developed than its tendency to break and control the violence of faction. The friend of popular governments never finds himself so much alarmed for their character and fate as when he contemplates their propensity to this dangerous vice. He will not fail therefore to set a due value on any plan which, without violating the principles to which he is attached, provides a proper cure for it. The instability, injustice and confusion introduced into the public councils have in truth been the mortal diseases under which popular governments have every where perished; as they continue to be the favorite and fruitful topics from which the adversaries to liberty derive their most specious declamations. The valuable improvements made by the American Constitutions on the popular models, both ancient and modern, cannot certainly be too much admired; but it would be an unwarrantable partiality to contend that they have as effectually obviated the danger on this side as was wished and expected. Complaints are every where heard from our most considerate and virtuous citizens, equally the friends of public and private faith and of public and personal liberty, that our governments are too unstable; that the public good is disregarded in the conflicts of rival parties; and that measures are too often decided, not according to the rules of justice, and the rights of the minor party, but by the superior force of an interested and over-bearing majority. However anxiously we may wish that these complaints had no foundation, the evidence of known

[From *The Federalist*, which consists of essays first printed in 1787–1788 in the form of letters to the New York *Independent Journal*, *Packet*, and *Daily Advertiser*. They were collected and revised by Alexander Hamilton, in two volumes, in 1788.]

facts will not permit us to deny that they are in some degree true. It will be found indeed, on a candid review of our situation, that some of the distresses under which we labor have been erroneously charged on the operation of our governments; but it will be found, at the same time, that other causes will not alone account for many of our heaviest misfortunes; and particularly, for that prevailing and increasing distrust of public engagements and alarm for private rights, which are echoed from one end of the continent to the other. These must be chiefly, if not wholly, effects of the unsteadiness and injustice with which a factious spirit has tainted our public administrations.

By a faction I understand a number of citizens, whether amounting to a majority or minority of the whole, who are united and actuated by some common impulse of passion, or of interest, adverse to the rights of other citizens, or to the permanent and aggregate interests of the community.

There are two methods of curing the mischiefs of faction: the one, by removing its causes; the other, by controling its effects.

There are again two methods of removing the causes of faction: the one by destroying the liberty which is essential to its existence; the other, by giving to every citizen the same opinions, the same passions, and the same interests.

It could never be more truly said than of the first remedy, that it is worse than the disease. Liberty is to faction, what air is to fire, an aliment without which it instantly expires. But it could not be a less folly to abolish liberty, which is essential to political life, because it nourishes faction than it would be to wish the annihilation of air, which is essential to animal life, because it imparts to fire its destructive agency.

The second expedient is as impracticable as the first would be unwise. As long as the reason of man continues fallible, and he is at liberty to exercise it, different opinions will be formed. As long as the connection subsists between his reason and his self-love, his opinions and his passions will have a reciprocal influence on each other; and the former will be objects to which the latter will attach themselves. The diversity in the faculties of men, from which the rights of property originate, is not less an insuperable obstacle to a uniformity of interests. The protection of these faculties is the first object of Government. From the protection of different and unequal faculties of acquiring property, the possession of different degrees and kinds of property immediately results: and from the influence of these on the sentiments and views of the respective proprietors ensues a division of the society into different interests and parties.

The latent causes of faction are thus sown in the nature of man; and we see them every where brought into different degrees of activity, according to the different circumstances of civil society. A zeal for different opinions concerning religion, concerning Government and many other points, as well of speculation as of practice; an attachment to different leaders ambitiously contending for pre-eminence and power; or to persons of other descriptions whose fortunes have been interesting to the human passions, have in turn divided mankind into parties, inflamed them with mutual animosity, and rendered them much more disposed to vex and oppress each other than to co-operate for their common good. So strong is this propensity of mankind to fall into mutual animosities that where no substantial occasion presents itself the most frivolous and fanciful distinctions have been sufficient to kindle their unfriendly passions and excite their most violent conflicts. But the most common and durable source of factions has been the various and unequal distribution of property. Those who hold and those who are without property, have ever formed distinct interests in society. Those who are creditors and those who are debtors fall under a like discrimination. A landed interest, a manufacturing interest, a mercantile interest, a monied interest, with many lesser interests, grow up of necessity in civilized nations, and divide them into different classes, actuated by different sentiments and views. The regulation of these various and interfering interests forms the principal task of modern Legislation and involves the spirit of party and faction in the necessary and ordinary operations of Government.

No man is allowed to be a judge in his own cause, because his interest would certainly bias his judgment, and, not improbably, corrupt his integrity. With equal, nay with greater reason, a body of men are unfit to be both judges and parties at the same time; yet, what are many of the most important acts of legislation but so many judicial determinations, not indeed concerning the rights of single persons but concerning the rights of large bodies of citizens; and what are the different classes of legislators but advocates and parties to the causes which they determine? Is a law proposed concerning private debts? It is a question to which the creditors are parties on one side and the debtors on the other. Justice ought to hold the balance between them. Yet the parties are and must be themselves the judges; and the most numerous party, or, in other words, the most powerful faction must be expected to prevail. Shall domestic manufactures be encouraged, and in what degree, by restrictions on foreign manufactures? are questions which would be differently decided by the landed and the manufacturing classes, and probably by neither with a sole regard to justice and the public good. The apportionment of taxes on the various descriptions of property is an act which seems to require the most exact impartiality; yet, there is perhaps no legislative act in which greater opportunity and temptation are given to a predominant party to trample on the rules of justice. Every shilling with which they over-burden the inferior number is a shilling saved to their own pockets.

It is in vain to say that enlightened statesmen will be able to adjust these clashing interests and render them all subservient to the public good. Enlightened statesmen will not always be at the helm. Nor, in many cases, can such an adjustment be made at all without taking into view indirect and remote considerations, which will rarely prevail over the immediate interest which one party may find in disregarding the rights of another or the good of the whole.

The inference to which we are brought is that the *causes* of faction cannot be removed, and that relief is only to be sought in the means of controling its *effects*.

If a faction consists of less than a majority, relief is supplied by the republican principle, which enables the majority to defeat its sinister views by regular vote. It may clog the administration, it may convulse the society; but it will be unable to execute and mask its violence under the forms of the Constitution. When a majority is included in a faction, the form of popular government on the other hand enables it to sacrifice to its ruling passion or interest both the public good and the rights of other citizens. To secure the public good and private rights against the danger of such a faction, and at the same time to preserve the spirit and the form of popular government, is then the great object to which our enquiries are directed. Let me add that it is the great desideratum, by which alone this form of government can be rescued from the opprobrium under which it has so long labored and be recommended to the esteem and adoption of mankind.

By what means is this object attainable? Evidently by one of two only. Either the existence of the same passion or interest in a majority at the same time must be prevented; or the majority, having such co-existent passion or interest, must be rendered, by their number and local situation, unable to concert and carry into effect schemes of oppression. If the impulse and the opportunity be suffered to coincide, we well know that neither moral nor religious motives can be relied on as an adequate control. They are not found to be such on the injustice and violence of individuals, and lose their efficacy in proportion to the number combined together; that is, in proportion as their efficacy becomes needful.

From this view of the subject, it may be concluded that a pure Democracy, by which I mean a Society consisting of a small number of citizens who assemble and administer the Government in person, can admit of no cure for the mischiefs of faction. A common passion or interest will, in almost every case, be felt by a majority of the whole; a communication and concert results from the form of Government itself; and there is nothing to check the inducements to sacrifice the weaker party or an obnoxious individual. Hence it is that such Democracies have ever been spectacles of turbulence and contention; have ever been found incompatible with personal security, or the rights of property; and have in general been as short in their lives as they have been violent in their deaths. Theoretic politicians, who have patronized this species of Government, have erroneously supposed that by reducing mankind to a perfect equality in their political rights, they would, at the same time, be perfectly equalized and assimilated in their possessions, their opinions, and their passions.

A Republic, by which I mean a Government in which the scheme of representation takes place, opens a different prospect and promises the cure for which we are seeking. Let us examine the points in which it varies from pure Democracy, and we shall comprehend both the nature of the cure and the efficacy which it must derive from the Union.

The two great points of difference between a Democracy and a Republic are, first, the delegation of the Government, in the latter, to a small number of citizens elected by the rest; secondly, the greater number of citizens and greater sphere of country over which the latter may be extended.

The effect of the first difference is on the one hand to refine and enlarge the public views by passing them through the medium of a chosen body of citizens, whose wisdom may best discern the true interest of their country, and whose patriotism and love of justice will be least likely to sacrifice it to temporary or partial considerations. Under such a regulation, it may well happen that the public voice pronounced by the representatives of the people will be more consonant to the public good than if pronounced by the people themselves convened for the purpose. On the other hand, the effect may be inverted. Men of factious tempers, of local prejudices, or of sinister designs, may by intrigue, by corruption or by other means, first obtain the suffrages, and then betray the interests of the people. The question resulting is whether small or extensive Republics are most favorable to the election of proper guardians of the public weal; and it is clearly decided in favor of the latter by two obvious considerations.

In the first place it is to be remarked that however small the Republic may be, the Representatives must be raised to a certain number in order to guard against the cabals of a few; and that however large it may be, they must be limited to a certain number in order to guard against the confusion of a multitude. Hence the number of Representatives in the two cases, not being in proportion to that of the Constituents, and being proportionally greatest in the small Republic, it follows that if the proportion of fit characters be not less in the large than in the small Republic, the former will present a greater option, and consequently a greater probability of a fit choice.

In the next place, as each Representative will be chosen by a greater number of citizens in the large than in the small Republic, it will be more difficult for unworthy candidates to practise with success the vicious arts by which elections are too often carried; and the suffrages of the people, being more free, will be more likely to centre on men who possess the most attractive merit and the most diffusive and established characters.

It must be confessed that in this, as in most other cases, there is a mean, on both sides of which inconveniencies will be found to lie. By enlarging too much the number of electors, you render the representative too little acquainted with all their local circumstances and lesser interests; as by reducing it too much, you render him unduly attached to these, and too little fit to comprehend and pursue great and national objects. The Federal Constitution forms a happy combination in this respect; the great and aggregate interests being referred to the national, the local and particular to the state legislatures.

The other point of difference is the greater number of citizens and extent of territory which may be brought within the compass of Republican than of Democratic Government; and it is this circumstance principally which renders factious combinations less to be dreaded in the former than in the latter. The smaller the society, the fewer probably will be the distinct parties and interests composing it; the fewer the distinct parties and interests, the more frequently will a majority be found of the same party; and the smaller the number of individuals composing a majority, and the smaller the compass within which they are placed, the more easily will they concert and execute their plans of oppression. Extend the sphere, and you take in a greater variety of parties and interests; you make it less probable that a majority of the whole will have a common motive to invade the rights of other citizens; or if such a common motive exists, it will be more difficult for all who feel it to discover their own strength and to act in unison with each other. Besides other impediments, it may be remarked that, where there is a consciousness of unjust or dishonorable purposes, communication is always checked by distrust in proportion to the number whose concurrence is necessary.

Hence it clearly appears that the same advantage which a Republic has over a Democracy in controling the effects of faction is enjoyed by a large over a small Republic—is enjoyed by the Union over the States composing it. Does this advantage consist in the substitution of Representatives whose enlightened views and virtuous sentiments render them superior to local prejudices and to schemes of injustice? It will not be denied, that the Representation of the Union will be most likely to possess these requisite endowments. Does it consist in the greater security afforded by a greater variety of parties, against the event of any one party being able to outnumber and oppress the rest? In an equal degree does the encreased variety of parties comprised within the Union encrease this security. Does it, in fine, consist in the greater obstacles opposed to the concert and accomplishment of the secret wishes of an unjust and interested majority? Here, again, the extent of the Union gives it the most palpable advantage.

The influence of factious leaders may kindle a flame within their particular States, but will be unable to spread a general conflagration through the other States. A religious sect may degenerate into a political faction in a part of the Confederacy; but the variety of sects dispersed over the entire face of it must secure the national Councils against any danger from that source. A rage for paper money, for an abolition of debts, for an equal division of property, or for any other improper or wicked project, will be less apt to pervade the whole body of the Union than a particular member of it, in the same proportion as such a malady is more likely to taint a particular county or district than an entire State.

In the extent and proper structure of the Union, therefore, we behold a Republican remedy for the diseases most incident to Republican Government. And according to the degree of pleasure and pride we feel in being Republicans ought to be our zeal in cherishing the spirit and supporting the character of Federalists.

PUBLIUS.

The Constitution of the
United States of America
(1787)

WE THE People of the United States, in Order to form a more perfect Union, establish Justice, insure domestic Tranquility, provide for the common defence, promote the general Welfare, and secure the Blessings of Liberty to ourselves and our Posterity, do ordain and establish this CONSTITUTION for the United States of America.

ARTICLE I

Section 1

All legislative Powers herein granted shall be vested in a Congress of the United States, which shall consist of a Senate and House of Representatives.

Section 2

The House of Representatives shall be composed of Members chosen every second Year by the People of the several States, and the Electors in each State shall have the Qualifications requisite for Electors of the most numerous Branch of the State Legislature.

No Person shall be a Representative who shall not have attained to the Age of twenty-five Years, and been seven Years a Citizen of the United States, and who shall not, when elected, be an Inhabitant of that State in which he shall be chosen.

Representatives and direct Taxes[1] shall be apportioned among the several States which may be included within this Union, according to their respective Numbers, which shall be determined by adding to the whole Number of free Persons, including those bound to Service for a Term of Years, and excluding Indians not taxed, three fifths of all other

---

[1] This provision was altered by Amendment XVI.

Persons.[2] The actual Enumeration shall be made within three Years after the first Meeting of the Congress of the United States, and within every subsequent Term of ten Years, in such Manner as they shall by Law direct. The Number of Representatives shall not exceed one for every thirty Thousand, but each State shall have at Least one Representative; and until such enumeration shall be made, the State of New Hampshire shall be entitled to chuse three, Massachusetts eight, Rhode-Island and Providence Plantations one, Connecticut five, New York six, New Jersey four, Pennsylvania eight, Delaware one, Maryland six, Virginia ten, North Carolina five, South Carolina five, and Georgia three.

When vacancies happen in the Representation from any State, the Executive Authority thereof shall issue Writs of Election to fill such Vacancies.

The House of Representatives shall chuse their Speaker and other Officers; and shall have the sole Power of Impeachment.

Section 3
The Senate of the United States shall be composed of two Senators from each State, chosen by the Legislature thereof, for six Years; and each Senator shall have one Vote.

Immediately after they shall be assembled in Consequence of the first Election, they shall be divided as equally as may be into three Classes. The Seats of the Senators of the first Class shall be vacated at the Expiration of the second Year, of the second Class at the Expiration of the fourth Year, and of the third Class at the Expiration of the sixth Year, so that one-third may be chosen every second Year; and if Vacancies happen by Resignation, or otherwise, during the Recess of the Legislature of any State, the Executive thereof may make temporary Appointments until the next Meeting of the Legislature, which shall then fill such Vacancies.

No Person shall be a Senator who shall not have attained to the Age of thirty Years, and been nine Years a Citizen of the United States, and who shall not, when elected, be an Inhabitant of that State for which he shall be chosen.

The Vice President of the United States shall be President of the Senate, but shall have no vote, unless they be equally divided.

The Senate shall chuse their other Officers, and also a President pro tempore, in the absence of the Vice President, or when he shall exercise the Office of President of the United States.

The Senate shall have the sole Power to try all Impeachments. When sitting for that purpose, they shall be on Oath or Affirmation. When the President of the United States is tried, the Chief Justice shall preside:

[2] The "three-fifths" provision was rescinded by Amendment XIV.

And no person shall be convicted without the Concurrence of two thirds of the Members present.

Judgment in Cases of Impeachment shall not extend further than to removel from Office, and disqualification to hold and enjoy any Office of honor, Trust, or Profit under the United States: but the Party convicted shall nevertheless be liable and subject to Indictment, Trial, Judgment, and Punishment, according to Law.

Section 4

The Times, Places and Manner of holding Elections for Senators and Representatives, shall be prescribed in each State by the Legislature thereof; but the Congress may at any time by Law make or alter such Regulations, except as to the Places of Chusing Senators.

The Congress shall assemble at least once in every Year, and such Meeting shall be on the first Monday in December, unless they shall by Law appoint a different Day.

Section 5

Each House shall be the Judge of the Elections, Returns and Qualifications of its own Members, and a Majority of each shall constitute a Quorum to do Business; but a smaller number may adjourn from day to day, and may be authorized to compel the Attendance of absent Members, in such Manner, and under such Penalties, as each House may provide.

Each House may determine the Rules of its Proceedings, punish its Members for disorderly Behaviour, and, with the Concurrence of two thirds, expel a Member.

Each House shall keep a Journal of its Proceedings, and from time to time publish the same, excepting such Parts as may in their Judgment require Secrecy; and the Yeas and Nays of the Members of either House on any question shall, at the Desire of one fifth of those Present, be entered on the Journal.

Neither House, during the Session of Congress, shall, without the Consent of the other, adjourn for more than three days, nor to any other Place than that in which the two Houses shall be sitting.

Section 6

The Senators and Representatives shall receive a Compensation for their Services, to be ascertained by Law, and paid out of the Treasury of the United States. They shall in all Cases, except Treason, Felony, and Breach of the Peace, be privileged from Arrest during their Attendance at the Session of their respective Houses, and in going to and returning from the same; and for any Speech or Debate in either House, they shall not be questioned in any other Place.

No Senator or Representative shall, during the Time for which he was elected, be appointed to any civil Office under the Authority of the United States, which shall have been created, or the Emoluments whereof shall have been increased, during such time; and no Person holding any Office under the United States shall be a Member of either House during his continuance in Office.

Section 7
All Bills for raising Revenue shall originate in the House of Representatives; but the Senate may propose or concur with Amendments as on other bills.

Every Bill which shall have passed the House of Representatives and the Senate, shall, before it become a Law, be presented to the President of the United States; If he approve he shall sign it, but if not he shall return it, with his Objections, to that House in which it shall have originated, who shall enter the Objections at large on their Journal, and proceed to reconsider it. If after such Reconsideration two thirds of that House shall agree to pass the bill, it shall be sent, together with the objections, to the other House, by which it shall likewise be reconsidered, and if approved by two thirds of that House, it shall become a Law. But in all such Cases the Votes of both Houses shall be determined by Yeas and Nays, and the Names of the Persons voting for and against the Bill shall be entered on the Journal of each House respectively. If any Bill shall not be returned by the President within ten Days (Sundays excepted) after it shall have been presented to him, the Same shall be a Law, in like Manner as if he had signed it, unless the Congress by their Adjournment prevent its Return, in which Case it shall not be a Law.

Every Order, Resolution, or Vote to which the Concurrence of the Senate and House of Representatives may be necessary (except on a question of Adjournment) shall be presented to the President of the United States; and before the Same shall take Effect, shall be approved by him, or being disapproved by him, shall be repassed by two thirds of the Senate and House of Representatives, according to the Rules and Limitations prescribed in the Case of a Bill.

Section 8
The Congress shall have Power To lay and collect Taxes, Duties, Imposts and Excises, to pay the Debts and provide for the common Defence and general Welfare of the United States; but all Duties, Imposts and Excises shall be uniform throughout the United States;

To borrow money on the credit of the United States;

To regulate Commerce with foreign Nations, and among the several States, and with the Indian Tribes;

To establish an uniform Rule of Naturalization, and uniform Laws on the subject of bankruptcies throughout the United States;

To coin Money, regulate the Value thereof, and of foreign Coin, and fix the Standard of Weights and Measures;

To provide for the Punishment of counterfeiting the Securities and current Coin of the United States;

To establish Post Offices and post Roads;

To promote the Progress of Science and useful Arts, by securing for limited Times to Authors and Inventors the exclusive Rights to their respective Writings and Discoveries;

To constitute Tribunals inferior to the Supreme Court;

To define and punish Piracies and Felonies committed on the high Seas, and Offenses against the Law of Nations;

To declare War, grant Letters of Marque and Reprisal, and make Rules concerning Captures on Land and Water;

To raise and support Armies, but no Appropriation of Money to that Use shall be for a longer Term than two Years;

To provide and maintain a Navy;

To make Rules for the Government and Regulation of the land and naval forces;

To provide for calling forth the Militia to execute the Laws of the Union, suppress Insurrections and repel Invasions;

To provide for organizing, arming, and disciplining the Militia, and for governing such Part of them as may be employed in the Service of the United States, reserving to the States respectively, the Appointment of the Officers, and the Authority of training the Militia according to the discipline prescribed by Congress;

To exercise exclusive Legislation in all Cases whatsoever, over such District (not exceeding ten Miles square) as may, by Cession of particular States, and the acceptance of Congress, become the Seat of the Government of the United States, and to exercise like Authority over all Places purchased by the consent of the Legislature of the State in which the Same shall be, for the Erection of Forts, Magazines, Arsenals, Dockyards, and other needful Buildings;—And

To make all Laws which shall be necessary and proper for carrying into Execution the foregoing Powers, and all other Powers vested by this Constitution in the Government of the United States, or in any Department or Officer thereof.

Section 9
The Migration or Importation of such Persons as any of the States now existing shall think proper to admit, shall not be prohibited by the Congress prior to the Year one thousand eight hundred and eight, but a tax or duty may be imposed on such Importation, not exceeding ten dollars for each Person.

The privilege of the Writ of Habeas Corpus shall not be suspended, unless when in Cases of Rebellion or Invasion the public Safety may require it.

No bill of Attainder or ex post facto Law shall be passed.

No capitation, or other direct, Tax shall be laid unless in Proportion to the Census or Enumeration herein before directed to be taken.

No Tax or Duty shall be laid on Articles exported from any State.

No Preference shall be given by any Regulation of Commerce or Revenue to the Ports of one State over those of another: nor shall Vessels bound to, or from, one State, be obliged to enter, clear, or pay Duties in another.

No Money shall be drawn from the Treasury, but in Consequence of Appropriations made by Law; and a regular Statement and Account of the Receipts and Expenditures of all public Money shall be published from time to time.

No Title of Nobility shall be granted by the United States: And no Person holding any Office of Profit or Trust under them, shall, without the Consent of the Congress, accept of any present, Emolument, Office, or Title, of any kind whatever, from any King, Prince, or foreign State.

Section 10
No State shall enter into any Treaty, Alliance, or Confederation; grant Letters of Marque and Reprisal; coin Money; emit Bills of Credit; make any Thing but gold and silver Coin a Tender in Payment of Debts; pass any Bill of Attainder, ex post facto Law, or Law impairing the Obligation of Contracts, or grant any Title of Nobility.

No State shall, without the Consent of the Congress, lay any Imposts or Duties on Imports or Exports, except what may be absolutely necessary for executing its inspection Laws: and the net Produce of all Duties and Imposts, laid by any State on Imports or Exports, shall be for the Use of the Treasury of the United States; and all such Laws shall be subject to the Revision and Control of the Congress.

No state shall, without the Consent of Congress, lay any duty of Tonnage, keep Troops, or Ships of War in time of Peace, enter into any Agreement or Compact with another State, or with a foreign Power, or engage in War, unless actually invaded, or in such imminent Danger as will not admit of delay.

ARTICLE II

Section 1
The executive Power shall be vested in a President of the United States of America. He shall hold his Office during the Term of four years, and,

together with the Vice President, chosen for the same Term, be elected, as follows:

Each State shall appoint, in such Manner as the Legislature thereof may direct, a Number of Electors, equal to the whole Number of Senators and Representatives to which the State may be entitled in the Congress: but no Senator or Representative, or Person holding an Office of Trust or Profit under the United States, shall be appointed an Elector.

The Electors shall meet in their respective States, and vote by Ballot for two persons, of whom one at least shall not be an Inhabitant of the same State with themselves. And they shall make a List of all the Persons voted for, and of the Number of Votes for each; which List they shall sign and certify, and transmit sealed to the Seat of the Government of the United States, directed to the President of the Senate. The President of the Senate shall, in the Presence of the Senate and House of Representatives, open all the Certificates, and the Votes shall then be counted. The Person having the greatest Number of Votes shall be the President, if such Number be a Majority of the whole Number of Electors appointed; and if there be more than one who have such Majority, and have an equal Number of Votes, then the House of Representatives shall immediately chuse by Ballot one of them for President; and if no Person have a Majority, then from the five highest on the List the said House shall in the Manner chuse the President. But in chusing the President, the Votes shall be taken by States, the Representation from each State having one Vote; a quorum for this Purpose shall consist of a Member or Members from two-thirds of the States, and a Majority of all the States shall be necessary to a Choice. In every Case, after the Choice of the President, the Person having the greatest Number of Votes of the Electors shall be the Vice President. But if there should remain two or more who have equal votes, the Senate shall chuse from them by Ballot the Vice President.[3]

The Congress may determine the Time of chusing the Electors, and the Day on which they shall give their Votes; which Day shall be the same throughout the United States.

No person except a natural-born Citizen, or a Citizen of the United States, at the time of the Adoption of this Constitution, shall be eligible to the Office of President; neither shall any Person be eligible to that Office who shall not have attained to the Age of thirty-five years, and been fourteen Years a Resident within the United States.

In Case of the Removal of the President from Office, or of his Death, Resignation, or Inability to discharge the Powers and Duties of the said Office, the same shall devolve on the Vice President, and the Congress

[3] This paragraph was revised by Amendment XII.

may by Law provide for the Case of Removal, Death, Resignation, or Inability, both of the President and Vice President, declaring what Officer shall then act as President, and such Officer shall act accordingly, until the disability be removed, or a President shall be elected.

The President shall, at stated Times, receive for his Services a Compensation, which shall neither be increased nor diminished during the Period for which he shall have been elected, and he shall not receive within that Period any other Emolument from the United States, or any of them.

Before he enter on the execution of his Office, he shall take the following Oath or Affirmation:—"I do solemnly swear (or affirm) that I will faithfully execute the Office of President of the United States, and will, to the best of my Ability, preserve, protect, and defend the Constitution of the United States."

Section 2

The President shall be Commander in Chief of the Army and Navy of the United States, and of the Militia of the several States, when called into the actual Service of the United States; he may require the Opinion, in writing, of the principal Officer in each of the executive Departments, upon any subject relating to the Duties of their respective Offices, and he shall have Power to Grant Reprieves and Pardons for Offenses against the United States, except in Cases of Impeachment.

He shall have Power, by and with the Advice and Consent of the Senate, to make Treaties, provided two-thirds of the Senators present concur; and he shall nominate, and by and with the Advice and Consent of the Senate, shall appoint Ambassadors, other public Ministers and Consuls, Judges of the supreme Court, and all other Officers of the United States, whose Appointments are not herein otherwise provided for, and which shall be established by Law: but the Congress may by Law vest the Appointment of such inferior Officers, as they think proper, in the President alone, in the Courts of Law, or in the Heads of Departments.

The President shall have Power to fill up all Vacancies that may happen during the Recess of the Senate, by granting Commissions which shall expire at the End of their next Sesson.

Section 3

He shall from time to time give to the Congress Information of the State of the Union, and recommend to their Consideration such Measures as he shall judge necessary and expedient; he may, on extraordinary occasions, convene both Houses, or either of them, and in Case of Disagreement between them, with respect to the Time of Adjournment, he may adjourn them to such Time as he shall think proper; he shall receive Ambassadors and other public Ministers; he shall take care that the Laws be faithfully executed, and shall Commission all the Officers of the United States.

Section 4
The President, Vice President and all civil Officers of the United States, shall be removed from Office on Impeachment for, and Conviction of, Treason, Bribery, or other High Crimes and Misdemeanors.

ARTICLE III

Section 1
The judicial Power of the United States, shall be vested in one supreme Court, and in such inferior Courts as the Congress may from time to time ordain and establish. The Judges, both of the supreme and inferior Courts, shall hold their Offices during good Behaviour, and shall, at stated Times, receive for their Services, a Compensation, which shall not be diminished during their Continuance in Office.

Section 2
The judicial Power shall extend to all Cases, in Law and Equity, arising under this Constitution, the Laws of the United States, and Treaties made, or which shall be made, under their Authority;—to all Cases affecting ambassadors, other public ministers and consuls;—to all cases of admiralty and maritime Jurisdiction;—to Controversies to which the United States shall be a Party;—to Controversies between two or more States;—between a State and Citizens of another state[4];—between Citizens of different States,—between Citizens of the same State claiming Lands under Grants of different States, and between a State, or the Citizens thereof, and foreign States, Citizens or Subjects.

In all Cases affecting Ambassadors, other public Ministers and Consuls, and those in which a State shall be Party, the supreme Court shall have original Jurisdiction. In all the other Cases before mentioned, the supreme Court shall have appellate Jurisdiction, both as to Law and Fact, with such Exceptions, and under such Regulations as the Congress shall make.

The trial of all Crimes, except in Cases of Impeachment, shall be by Jury; and such Trial shall be held in the State where the said Crimes shall have been committed; but when not committed within any State, the Trial shall be at such Place or Places as the Congress may by Law have directed.

Section 3
Treason against the United States, shall consist only in levying War against them, or in adhering to their Enemies, giving them Aid and Comfort.

[4] This clause was modified by Amendment XI.

No person shall be convicted of Treason unless on the Testimony of two Witnesses to the same overt Act, or on Confession in open Court.

The Congress shall have power to declare the Punishment of Treason, but no Attainder of Treason shall work Corruption of Blood, or Forfeiture except during the Life of the Person attainted.

ARTICLE IV

Section 1
Full Faith and Credit shall be given in each State to the public Acts, Records, and judicial Proceedings of every other State. And the Congress may by general Laws prescribe the Manner in which such Acts, Records and Proceedings shall be proved, and the Effect thereof.

Section 2
The Citizens of each State shall be entitled to all Privileges and Immunities of Citizens in the several States.

A Person charged in any State with Treason, Felony, or other Crime, who shall flee from Justice, and be found in another State, shall on demand of the executive Authority of the State from which he fled, be delivered up, to be removed to the State having Jurisdiction of the crime.

No Person held to Service or Labour in one State, under the Laws thereof, escaping into another, shall, in Consequence of any Law or Regulation therein, be discharged from such Service or Labour, but shall be delivered up on Claim of the Party to whom such Service or Labour may be due.[5]

Section 3
New States may be admitted by the Congress into this Union; but no new State shall be formed or erected within the Jurisdiction of any other State; nor any State be formed by the Junction of two or more States, or parts of States, without the Consent of the Legislatures of the States concerned as well as of the Congress.

The Congress shall have Power to dispose of and make all needful Rules and Regulations respecting the Territory or other Property belonging to the United States; and nothing in this Constitution shall be so construed as to Prejudice any Claims of the United States, or of any particular State.

Section 4
The United States shall guarantee to every State in this Union a Republican Form of Government, and shall protect each of them against In-

[5] This paragraph has been superseded by Amendment XIII.

vasion; and on Application of the Legislature, or of the Executive (when the Legislature cannot be convened) against domestic Violence.

ARTICLE V

The Congress, whenever two-thirds of both Houses shall deem it necessary, shall propose Amendments to this Constitution, or, on the Application of the Legislatures of two-thirds of the several States, shall call a Convention for proposing Amendments, which, in either Case, shall be valid to all Intents and Purposes, as part of this Constitution, when ratified by the Legislatures of three-fourths of the several States, or by Conventions in three-fourths thereof, as the one other Mode of Ratification may be proposed by the Congress; Provided that no Amendment which may be made prior to the Year One thousand eight hundred and eight shall in any Manner affect the first and fourth Clauses in the Ninth Section of the first Article; and that no State, without its Consent, shall be deprived of its equal Suffrage in the Senate.

ARTICLE VI

All Debts contracted and Engagements entered into, before the Adoption of this Constitution, shall be as valid against the United States under this Constitution, as under the Confederation.

This Constitution, and the Laws of the United States which shall be made in Pursuance thereof; and all Treaties made, or which shall be made, under the Authority of the United States, shall be the supreme Law of the Land; and the Judges in every State shall be bound thereby, any Thing in the Constitution or Laws of any State to the Contrary notwithstanding.

The Senators and Representatives before mentioned, and the Members of the several State Legislatures, and all executive and judicial Officers, both of the United States and of the several States, shall be bound by Oath or Affirmation to support this Constitution; but no religious Test shall ever be required as a qualification to any Office or public Trust under the United States.

ARTICLE VII

The Ratification of the Conventions of nine States shall be sufficient for the Establishment of this Constitution between the States so ratifying the same.

Done in Convention by the Unanimous Consent of the States present the Seventeenth Day of September in the Year of our Lord one thousand seven hundred and Eighty seven, and of the Independence of the United States of America the Twelfth. In Witness whereof We have hereunto subscribed our Names.

G.° WASHINGTON—Presid.ᵗ
and deputy from Virginia

New Hampshire
John Langdon
Nicholas Gilman

Massachusetts
Nathaniel Gorham
Rufus King

Connecticut
W.ᵐ Sam. Johnson
Roger Sherman

New York
Alexander Hamilton

New Jersey
Wil: Livingston
David Brearley.
W.ᵐ Paterson.
Iona: Dayton

Pennsylvania
B Franklin
Thomas Mifflin
Robt Morris
Geo. Clymer
Tho.ˢ FitzSimons
Jared Ingersoll
James Wilson
Gouv Morris

Delaware
Geo: Read
Gunning Bedford jun
John Dickinson
Richard Bassett
Jaco: Broom

Maryland
James McHenry
Dan of Sᵗ Tho.ˢ Jenifer
Dan.¹ Carroll

Virginia
John Blair—
James Madison Jr.

North Carolina
W.ᵐ Blount
Rich.ᵈ Dobbs Spraight
Hu Williamson

South Carolina
J. Rutledge
Charles Cotesworth
 Pinckney
Charles Pinckney
Pierce Butler

Georgia
William Few
Abr Baldwin

AMENDMENT I (*I–X adopted 1791*)

Congress shall make no law respecting an establishment of religion, or prohibiting the free exercise thereof; or abridging the freedom of speech, or of the press; or the right of the people peaceably to assemble, and to petition the Government for a redress of grievances.

AMENDMENT II

A well regulated Militia, being necessary to the security of a free State, the right of the people to keep and bear Arms shall not be infringed.

AMENDMENT III

No Soldier shall, in time of peace, be quartered in any house, without the consent of the Owner, nor in time of war, but in a manner to be prescribed by law.

AMENDMENT IV

The right of the people to be secure in their persons, houses, papers, and effects, against unreasonable searches and seizures, shall not be violated, and no Warrants shall issue, but upon probable cause, supported by Oath or affirmation, and particularly describing the place to be searched, and the persons or things to be seized.

AMENDMENT V

No person shall be held to answer for a capital or otherwise infamous crime, unless on a presentment or indictment of a Grand Jury, except in cases arising in the land or naval forces, or in the Militia, when in actual service in time of War or public danger; nor shall any person be subject for the same offence to be twice put in jeopardy of life or limb; nor shall be compelled in any criminal case to be a witness against himself, nor be deprived of life, liberty, or property, without due process of law; nor shall private property be taken for public use, without just compensation.

AMENDMENT VI

In all criminal prosecutions, the accused shall enjoy the right to a speedy and public trial, by an impartial jury of the State and district wherein the crime shall have been committed, which district shall have been previously ascertained by law, and to be informed of the nature and cause of the accusation; to be confronted with the witnesses against him; to have compulsory process for obtaining witnesses in his favour, and to have the Assistance of Counsel for his defence.

AMENDMENT VII

In suits at common law, where the value in controversy shall exceed twenty dollars, the right of trial by jury shall be preserved, and no fact tried by a jury, shall be otherwise reexamined in any Court of the United States, than according to the rules of the common law.

AMENDMENT VIII

Excessive bail shall not be required, nor excessive fines imposed, nor cruel and unusual punishments inflicted.

AMENDMENT IX

The enumeration in the Constitution, of certain rights, shall not be construed to deny or disparage others retained by the people.

AMENDMENT X

The powers not delegated to the United States by the Constitution, nor prohibited by it to the States, are reserved to the States respectively, or to the people.

AMENDMENT XI *(adopted 1798)*

The Judicial power of the United States shall not be construed to extend to any suit in law or equity, commenced or prosecuted against one of the United States by Citizens of another State, or by Citizens or Subjects of any Foreign State.

AMENDMENT XII *(adopted 1804)*

The Electors shall meet in their respective States and vote by ballot for President and Vice-President, one of whom, at least, shall not be an inhabitant of the same State with themselves; they shall name in their ballots the person voted for as President, and in distinct ballots the person voted for as Vice-President, and they shall make distinct lists of all persons voted for as President, and of all persons voted for as Vice-President, and of the number of votes for each, which lists they shall sign and certify, and transmit sealed to the seat of the government of the United States, directed to the President of the Senate;—The President of the Senate shall, in the presence of the Senate and House of Representatives, open all the certificates and the votes shall then be counted;—The person having the greatest number of votes for President, shall be the President, if such number be a majority of the whole number of Electors appointed; and if no person have such majority, then from the persons having the highest numbers not exceeding three on the list of those voted for as President, the House of Representatives shall choose immediately, by ballot, the President. But in choosing the President, the votes shall be taken by states, the representation from each state having one vote; a quorum for this purpose shall consist of a member or members from two-thirds of the states, and a majority of all the states shall be necessary to a choice. And if the House of Representatives shall not choose a President whenever the right of choice shall devolve upon them, before the fourth day of March next following, then the Vice-President shall act as President, as in the case of the death or other constitutional disability of the President.[6]—The person having the greatest number of votes as Vice-President, shall be the Vice-President, if such number be a majority of the whole number of Electors appointed, and if no person have a majority, then from the two highest numbers on the list, the Senate shall choose the Vice-President: a quorum for the purpose shall consist of two-thirds of the whole number of Senators, and a majority of the whole number shall be necessary to a choice. But no person constitutionally ineligible to the office of President shall be eligible to that of Vice-President of the United States.

AMENDMENT XIII *(adopted 1865)*

Section 1
Neither slavery nor involuntary servitude, except as a punishment for crime whereof the party shall have been duly convicted, shall exist within the United States, or any place subject to their jurisdiction.

Section 2
Congress shall have power to enforce this article by appropriate legislation.

AMENDMENT XIV *(adopted 1868)*

Section 1
All persons born or naturalized in the United States, and subject to the jurisdiction thereof, are citizens of the United States and of the State wherein they reside. No State shall abridge the privileges or immunities of citizens of the United States; nor shall any State deprive any person of life, liberty, or property, without due process of law; nor deny to any person within its jurisdiction the equal protection of the laws.

Section 2
Representatives shall be apportioned among the several States according to their respective numbers, counting the whole number of persons in each State, excluding Indians not taxed. But when the right to vote at any election for the choice of electors for President and Vice-President

[6] This sentence has been superseded by Amendment XX, Section 3.

of the United States, Representatives in Congress, the Executive and
Judicial officers of a State, or the members of the Legislature thereof, is
denied to any of the male inhabitants of such State, being twenty-one
years of age,[7] and citizens of the United States, or in any way abridged,
except for participation in rebellion, or other crime, the basis of representation therein shall be reduced in the proportion which the number
of such male citizens shall bear to the whole number of male citizens
twenty-one years of age in such State.

Section 3
No person shall be a Senator or Representative in Congress, or elector
of President and Vice-President, or hold any office, civil or military, under
the United States, or under any State, who, having previously taken an
oath, as a member of Congress, or as an officer of the United States, or
as a member of any State legislature, or as an executive or judicial officer
of any State, to support the Constitution of the United States, shall have
engaged in insurrection or rebellion against the same, or given aid or
comfort to the enemies thereof. But Congress may by a vote of two-thirds
of each House, remove such disability.

Section 4
The validity of the public debt of the United States, authorized by law,
including debts incurred for payment of pensions and bounties for services
in suppressing insurrection or rebellion, shall not be questioned. But
neither the United States nor any State shall assume or pay any debts or
obligation incurred in aid of insurrection or rebellion against the United
States, or any claim for the loss or emancipation of any slave; but all such
debts, obligations, and claims shall be held illegal and void.

Section 5
The Congress shall have the power to enforce, by appropriate legislation,
the provisions of this article.

Amendment XV *(adopted 1870)*

Section 1
The right of citizens of the United States to vote shall not be denied or
abridged by the United States or by any State on account of race, color,
or previous condition of servitude—

Section 2
The Congress shall have power to enforce this article by appropriate
legislation.

---

[7] This clause was modified by Amendment XXVI.

AMENDMENT XVI *(adopted 1913)*

The Congress shall have power to lay and collect taxes on incomes, from whatever source derived, without apportionment among the several States, and without regard to any census or enumeration.

AMENDMENT XVII *(adopted 1913)*

The Senate of the United States shall be composed of two Senators from each State, elected by the people thereof, for six years; and each Senator shall have one vote. The electors in each State shall have the qualifications requisite for electors of the most numerous branch of the State legislatures.

When vacancies happen in the representation of any State in the Senate, the executive authority of such State shall issue writs of election to fill such vacancies: *Provided,* That the legislature of any State may empower the executive thereof to make temporary appointments until the people fill the vacancies by election as the legislature may direct.

This amendment shall not be so construed as to affect the election or term of any Senator chosen before it becomes valid as part of the Constitution.

AMENDMENT XVIII *(adopted 1919)*[8]

Section 1
After one year from the ratification of this article the manufacture, sale, or transportation of intoxicating liquors within, the importation thereof into, or the exportation thereof from the United States and all territory subject to the jurisdiction thereof for beverage purposes is hereby prohibited.

Section 2
The Congress and the several States shall have concurrent power to enforce this article by appropriate legislation.

Section 3
This article shall be inoperative unless it shall have been ratified as an amendment to the Constitution by the legislatures of the several States, as provided in the Constitution, within seven years from the date of the submission hereof to the States by the Congress.

[8] Amendment XVIII was repealed by Amendment XXI.

Amendment XIX *(adopted 1920)*

The right of citizens of the United States to vote shall not be denied or abridged by the United States or by any State on account of sex.

Congress shall have power to enforce this article by appropriate legislation.

Amendment XX *(adopted 1933)*

Section 1
The terms of the President and Vice-President shall end at noon on the 20th day of January, and the terms of Senators and Representatives at noon on the 3d day of January, of the years in which such terms would have ended if this article had not been ratified; and the terms of their successors shall then begin.

Section 2
The Congress shall assemble at least once in every year, and such meeting shall begin at noon on the 3d day of January, unless they shall by law appoint a different day.

Section 3
If, at the time fixed for the beginning of the term of the President, the President elect shall have died, the Vice-President elect shall become President. If a President shall not have been chosen before the time fixed for the beginning of his term, or if the President elect shall have failed to qualify, then the Vice-President elect shall act as President until a President shall have qualified; and the Congress may by law provide for the case wherein neither a President elect nor a Vice-President elect shall have qualified, declaring who shall then act as President, or the manner in which one who is to act shall be selected, and such person shall act accordingly until a President or Vice-President shall have qualified.

Section 4
The Congress may by law provide for the case of the death of any of the persons from whom the House of Representatives may choose a President whenever the right of choice shall have devolved upon them, and for the case of the death of any of the persons from whom the Senate may choose a Vice-President whenever the right of choice shall have devolved upon them.

Section 5
Sections 1 and 2 shall take effect on the 15th day of October following the ratification of this article.

Section 6

This article shall be inoperative unless it shall have been ratified as an amendment to the Constitution by the legislatures of three-fourths of the several States within seven years from the date of its submission.

AMENDMENT XXI *(adopted 1933)*

Section 1

The eighteenth article of amendment to the Constitution of the United States is hereby repealed.

Section 2

The transportation or importation into any State, Territory, or possession of the United States for delivery or use therein of intoxicating liquors, in violation of the laws thereof, is hereby prohibited.

Section 3

This article shall be inoperative unless it shall have been ratified as an amendment to the Constitution by conventions in the several States, as provided in the Constitution, within seven years from the date of the submission hereof to the States by the Congress.

AMENDMENT XXII *(adopted 1951)*

No person shall be elected to the office of the President more than twice, and no person who has held the office of President, or acted as President, for more than two years of a term to which some other person was elected President shall be elected to the office of the President more than once.

But this Article shall not apply to any person holding the office of President when this Article was proposed by the Congress, and shall not prevent any person who may be holding the office of President, or acting as President, during the term within which this Article becomes operative from holding the office of President or acting as President during the remainder of such term.

This article shall be inoperative unless it shall have been ratified as an amendment to the Constitution by the legislatures of three-fourths of the several states within seven years from the date of its submission to the states by the Congress.

AMENDMENT XXIII *(adopted 1961)*

Section 1

The District constituting the seat of Government of the United States shall appoint in such manner as the Congress may direct:

A number of electors of President and Vice-President equal to the whole number of Senators and Representatives in Congress to which the District would be entitled if it were a State, but in no event more than the least populous State; they shall be in addition to those appointed by the States, but they shall be considered, for the purposes of the election of President and Vice-President, to be electors appointed by a State; and they shall meet in the District and perform such duties as provided by the twelfth article of amendment.

Section 2

The Congress shall have power to enforce this article by appropriate legislation.

AMENDMENT XXIV *(adopted 1964)*

Section 1

The right of citizens of the United States to vote in any primary or other election for President or Vice President, for electors for President or Vice President, or for Senator or Representative in Congress, shall not be denied or abridged by the United States or any state by reason of failure to pay any poll tax or other tax.

Section 2

The Congress shall have the power to enforce this article by appropriate legislation.

AMENDMENT XXV *(adopted 1967)*

Section 1

In case of the removal of the President from office or of his death or resignation, the Vice President shall become President.

Section 2

Whenever there is a vacancy in the office of the Vice President, the President shall nominate a Vice President who shall take office upon confirmation by a majority vote of both Houses of Congress.

Section 3

Whenever the President transmits to the President Pro Tempore of the Senate and the Speaker of the House of Representatives his written declaration that he is unable to discharge the powers and duties of his office, and until he transmits to them a written declaration to the contrary, such powers and duties shall be discharged by the Vice President as Acting President.

Section 4

Whenever the Vice President and a majority of either the principal officers of the executive departments or of such other body as Congress may by law provide, transmit to the President Pro Tempore of the Senate and the Speaker of the House of Representatives their written declaration that the President is unable to discharge the powers and duties of his office, the Vice President shall immediately assume the powers and duties of his office as Acting President.

Thereafter, when the President transmits to the President Pro Tempore of the Senate and the Speaker of the House of Representatives his written declaration that no inability exists, he shall resume the powers and duties of his office unless the Vice President and a majority of either the principal officers of the executive departments or of such other body as Congress may by law provide, transmit within four days to the President Pro Tempore of the Senate and the Speaker of the House of Representatives their written declaration that the President is unable to discharge the powers and duties of his office. Thereupon Congress shall decide the issue, assembling within forty-eight hours for that purpose if not in session. If the Congress, within twenty-one days after receipt of the latter written declaration, or, if Congress is not in session, within twenty-one days after Congress is required to assemble, determines by two-thirds vote of both Houses that the President is unable to discharge the powers and duties of his office, the Vice President shall continue to discharge the same as Acting President; otherwise, the President shall resume the powers and duties of his office.

AMENDMENT XXVI *(adopted 1971)*

Section 1

The right of citizens of the United States, who are eighteen years of age or older, to vote shall not be denied or abridged by the United States or by any State on account of age.

Section 2

The Congress shall have power to enforce this article by appropriate legislation.

George Washington
Farewell Address
(1796)

Friends and Fellow-Citizens

THE PERIOD for a new election of a citizen to administer the Executive Government of the United States being not far distant, and the time actually arrived when your thoughts must be employed in designating the person who is to be clothed with that important trust, it appears to me proper, especially as it may conduce to a more distinct expression of the public voice, that I should now apprise you of the resolution I have formed to decline being considered among the number of those out of whom a choice is to be made.

I beg you at the same time to do me the justice to be assured that this resolution has not been taken without a strict regard to all the considerations appertaining to the relation which binds a dutiful citizen to his country; and that in withdrawing the tender of service, which silence in my situation might imply, I am influenced by no diminution of zeal for your future interest, no deficiency of grateful respect for your past kindness, but am supported by a full conviction that the step is compatible with both.

The acceptance of and continuance hitherto in the office to which your suffrages have twice called me have been a uniform sacrifice of inclination to the opinion of duty and to a deference for what appeared to be your desire. I constantly hoped that it would have been much earlier in my power, consistently with motives which I was not at liberty to disregard, to return to that retirement from which I had been reluctantly drawn. The strength of my inclination to do this previous to the last election had even led to the preparation of an address to declare it to you; but mature

[From the version published in *Claypoole's American Daily Advertiser* on 17 September 1796.]

reflection on the then perplexed and critical posture of our affairs with foreign nations and the unanimous advice of persons entitled to my confidence impelled me to abandon the idea. I rejoice that the state of your concerns, external as well as internal, no longer renders the pursuit of inclination incompatible with the sentiment of duty or propriety, and am persuaded, whatever partiality may be retained for my services, that in the present circumstances of our country you will not disapprove my determination to retire.

The impressions with which I first undertook the arduous trust were explained on the proper occasion. In the discharge of this trust I will only say that I have, with good intentions, contributed toward the organization and administration of the Government the best exertions of which a very fallible judgment was capable. Not unconscious in the outset of the inferiority of my qualifications, experience in my own eyes, perhaps still more in the eyes of others, has strengthened the motives to diffidence of myself; and every day the increasing weight of years admonishes me more and more that the shade of retirement is as necessary to me as it will be welcome. Satisfied that if any circumstances have given peculiar value to my services they were temporary, I have the consolation to believe that, while choice and prudence invite me to quit the political scene, patriotism does not forbid it.

In looking forward to the moment which is intended to terminate the career of my political life, my feelings do not permit me to suspend the deep acknowledgment of that debt of gratitude which I owe to my beloved country for the many honors it has conferred upon me; still more for the steadfast confidence with which it has supported me, and for the opportunities I have thence enjoyed of manifesting my inviolable attachment by services faithful and persevering, though in usefulness unequal to my zeal. If benefits have resulted to our country from these services, let it always be remembered to your praise and as an instructive example in our annals that under circumstances in which the passions, agitated in every direction, were liable to mislead; amidst appearances sometimes dubious; vicissitudes of fortune often discouraging; in situations in which not unfrequently want of success has countenanced the spirit of criticism, the constancy of your support was the essential prop of the efforts and a guaranty of the plans by which they were effected. Profoundly penetrated with this idea, I shall carry it with me to my grave as a strong incitement to unceasing vows that Heaven may continue to you the choicest tokens of its beneficence; that your union and brotherly affection may be perpetual; that the free Constitution which is the work of your hands may be sacredly maintained; that its administration in every department may be stamped with wisdom and virtue; that, in fine, the happiness of the people of these States, under the auspices of liberty, may be made com-

plete by so careful a preservation and so prudent a use of this blessing
as will acquire to them the glory of recommending it to the applause, the
affection, and adoption of every nation which is yet a stranger to it.

Here, perhaps, I ought to stop. But a solicitude for your welfare which
can not end but with my life, and the apprehension of danger natural to
that solicitude, urge me on an occasion like the present to offer to your
solemn contemplation and to recommend to your frequent review some
sentiments which are the result of much reflection, of no inconsiderable
observation, and which appear to me all important to the permanency of
your felicity as a people. These will be offered to you with the more
freedom as you can only see in them the disinterested warnings of a
parting friend, who can possibly have no personal motive to bias his
counsel. Nor can I forget as an encouragement to it your indulgent reception of my sentiments on a former and not dissimilar occasion.

Interwoven as is the love of liberty with every ligament of your hearts,
no recommendation of mine is necessary to fortify or confirm the attachment.

The unity of government which constitutes you one people is also now
dear to you. It is justly so, for it is a main pillar in the edifice of your real
independence, the support of your tranquillity at home, your peace abroad,
of your safety, of your prosperity, of that very liberty which you so highly
prize. But as it is easy to foresee that from different causes and from
different quarters much pains will be taken, many artifices employed, to
weaken in your minds the conviction of this truth, as this is the point in
your political fortress against which the batteries of internal and external
enemies will be most constantly and actively (though often covertly and
insidiously) directed, it is of definite moment that you should properly
estimate the immense value of your national union to your collective and
individual happiness; that you should cherish a cordial, habitual, and
immovable attachment to it; accustoming yourselves to think and speak
of it as of the palladium of your political safety and prosperity; watching
for its preservation with jealous anxiety; discountenancing whatever may
suggest even a suspicion that it can in any event be abandoned, and
indignantly frowning upon the first dawning of every attempt to alienate
any portion of our country from the rest or to enfeeble the sacred ties
which now link together the various parts.

For this you have every inducement of sympathy and interest. Citizens
by birth or choice of a common country, that country has a right to
concentrate your affections. The name of American, which belongs to you
in your national capacity, must always exalt the just pride of patriotism
more than any appellation derived from local discriminations. With slight
shades of difference, you have the same religion, manners, habits, and
political principles. You have in a common cause fought and triumphed

together. The independence and liberty you possess are the work of joint councils and joint efforts, of common dangers, sufferings, and successes.

But these considerations, however powerfully they address themselves to your sensibility, are greatly outweighed by those which apply more immediately to your interest. Here every portion of our country finds the most commanding motives for carefully guarding and preserving the union of the whole.

The *North*, in an unrestrained intercourse with the *South*, protected by the equal laws of a common government, finds in the products of the latter great additional resources of maritime and commerical enterprise and precious materials of manufacturing industry. The *South*, in the same intercourse, benefiting by the same agency of the *North*, sees its agriculture grow and its commerce expand. Turning partly into its own channels the seamen of the *North*, it finds its particular navigation invigorated; and while it contributes in different ways to nourish and increase the general mass of the national navigation, it looks forward to the protection of a maritime strength to which itself is unequally adapted. The *East*, in a like intercourse with the *West*, already finds, and in the progressive improvement of interior communications by land and water will more and more find, a valuable vent for the commodities which it brings from abroad or manufactures at home. The *West* derives from the *East* supplies requisite to its growth and comfort, and what is perhaps of still greater consequence, it must of necessity owe the *secure* enjoyment of indispensable *outlets* for its own productions to the weight, influence, and the future maritime strength of the Atlantic side of the Union, directed by an indissoluble community of interest as *one nation*. Any other tenure by which the *West* can hold this essential advantage, whether derived from its own separate strength or from an apostate and unnatural connection with any foreign power, must be intrinsically precarious.

While, then, every part of our country thus feels an immediate and particular interest in union, all the parts combined can not fail to find in the united mass of means and efforts greater strength, greater resource, proportionably greater security from external danger, a less frequent interruption of their peace by foreign nations, and what is of inestimable value, they must derive from union an exemption from those broils and wars between themselves which so frequently afflict neighboring countries not tied together by the same governments, which their own rivalships alone would be sufficient to produce, but which opposite foreign alliances, attachments, and intrigues would stimulate and imbitter. Hence, likewise, they will avoid the necessity of those overgrown military establishments which, under any form of government, are inauspicious to liberty, and which are to be regarded as particularly hostile to republican liberty. In this sense it is that your union ought to be considered as a main prop of your liberty, and that the love of the one ought to endear to you the preservation of the other.

These considerations speak a persuasive language to every reflecting and virtuous mind, and exhibit the continuance of the union as a primary object of patriotic desire. Is there a doubt whether a common government can embrace so large a sphere? Let experience solve it. To listen to mere speculation in such a case were criminal. We are authorized to hope that a proper organization of the whole, with the auxiliary agency of governments for the respective subdivisions, will afford a happy issue to the experiment. It is well worth a fair and full experiment. With such powerful and obvious motives to union affecting all parts of our country, while experience shall not have demonstrated its impracticability, there will always be reason to distrust the patriotism of those who in any quarter may endeavor to weaken its bands.

In contemplating the causes which may disturb our union it occurs as matter of serious concern that any ground should have been furnished for characterizing parties by *geographical* discriminations—*Northern* and *Southern*, *Atlantic* and *Western*—whence designing men may endeavor to excite a belief that there is a real difference of local interests and views. One of the expedients of party to acquire influence within particular districts is to misrepresent the opinions and aims of other districts. You can not shield yourselves too much against the jealousies and heart-burnings which spring from these misrepresentations; they tend to render alien to each other those who ought to be bound together by fraternal affection. The inhabitants of our Western country have lately had a useful lesson on this head. They have seen in the negotiation by the Executive and in the unanimous ratification by the Senate of the treaty with Spain, and in the universal satisfaction at that event throughout the United States, a decisive proof how unfounded were the suspicions propagated among them of a policy in the General Government and in the Atlantic States unfriendly to their interests in regard to the Mississippi. They have been witnesses to the formation of two treaties—that with Great Britain and that with Spain—which secure to them everything they could desire in respect to our foreign relations toward confirming their prosperity. Will it not be their wisdom to rely for the preservation of these advantages on the union by which they were procured? Will they not henceforth be deaf to those advisers, if such there are, who would sever them from their brethren and connect them with aliens?

To the efficacy and permanency of your union a government for the whole is indispensable. No alliances, however strict, between the parts can be an adequate substitute. They must inevitably experience the infractions and interruptions which all alliances in all times have experienced. Sensible of this momentous truth, you have improved upon your first essay by the adoption of a Constitution of Government better calculated than your former for an intimate union and for the efficacious management of your common concerns. This Government, the offspring of your own choice, uninfluenced and unawed, adopted upon full investigation and mature deliberation, completely free in its principles, in the distribution of its powers, uniting security with energy, and containing within itself a provision for its own amendment, has a just claim to your confidence and your support. Respect for its authority, compliance with its laws, acquiescence in its measures, are duties enjoined by the fundamental maxims of true liberty. The basis of our political systems is the right of the people to make and to alter their constitutions of government. But the constitution which at any time exists till changed by an explicit and authentic act of the whole people is sacredly obligatory upon all. The very idea of the power and the right of the people to establish government presupposes the duty of every individual to obey the established government.

All obstructions to the execution of the laws, all combinations and associations, under whatever plausible character, with the real design to direct, control, counteract, or awe the regular deliberation and action of the constituted authorities, are destructive of this fundamental principle and of fatal tendency. They serve to organize faction; to give it an artificial and extraordinary force; to put in the place of the delegated will of the nation the will of a party, often a small but artful and enterprising minority of the community, and, according to the alternate triumphs of different parties, to make the public administration the mirror of the ill-concerted and incongruous projects of faction rather than the organ of consistent and wholesome plans, digested by common counsels and modified by mutual interests.

However combinations or associations of the above description may now and then answer popular ends, they are likely in the course of time and things to become potent engines by which cunning, ambitious, and unprincipled men will be enabled to subvert the power of the people, and to usurp for themselves the reins of government, destroying afterwards the very engines which have lifted them to unjust dominion.

Toward the preservation of your Government and the permanency of your present happy state, it is requisite not only that you steadily discountenance irregular oppositions to its acknowledged authority, but also that you resist with care the spirit of innovation upon its principles, however specious the pretexts. One method of assault may be to effect in the forms of the Constitution alterations which will impair the energy of the system, and thus to undermine what can not be directly overthrown. In all the changes to which you may be invited remember that time and habit are at least as necessary to fix the true character of governments as of other human institutions; that experience is the surest standard by which to test the real tendency of the existing constitution of a country; that facility in changes upon the credit of mere hypothesis and opinion exposes to perpetual change, from the endless variety of hypothesis and opinion; and remember especially that for the efficient management of your common interests in a country so extensive as ours a government of as much vigor as is consistent with the perfect security of liberty is indispensable. Liberty itself will find in such a government, with powers properly distributed and adjusted, its surest guardian. It is, indeed, little else than a name where the government is too feeble to withstand the enterprises of faction, to confine each member of the society within the limits prescribed by the laws, and to maintain all in the secure and tranquil enjoyment of the rights of person and property.

I have already intimated to you the danger of parties in the State, with particular reference to the founding of them on geographical discriminations. Let me now take a more comprehensive view, and warn you in the most solemn manner against the baneful effects of the spirit of party generally.

This spirit, unfortunately, is inseparable from our nature, having its root in the strongest passions of the human mind. It exists under different shapes in all governments, more or less stifled, controlled, or repressed; but in those of the popular form it is seen in its greatest rankness and is truly their worst enemy.

The alternate domination of one faction over another, sharpened by the spirit of revenge natural to party dissension, which in different ages and countries has perpetrated the most horrid enormities, is itself a frightful despotism. But this leads at length to a more formal and permanent despotism. The disorders and miseries which result gradually incline the minds of men to seek security and repose in the absolute power of an individual, and sooner or later the chief of some prevailing faction, more able or more fortunate than his competitors, turns this disposition to the purposes of his own elevation on the ruins of public liberty.

Without looking forward to an extremity of this kind (which nevertheless ought not to be entirely out of sight), the common and continual mischiefs of the spirit of party are sufficient to make it the interest and duty of a wise people to discourage and restrain it.

It serves always to distract the public councils and enfeeble the public administration. It agitates the community with ill-founded jealousies and false alarms; kindles the animosity of one part against another; foments occasionally riot and insurrection. It opens the door to foreign influence and corruption, which find a facilitated access to the government itself through the channels of party passion. Thus the policy and the will of one country are subjected to the policy and will of another.

There is an opinion that parties in free countries are useful checks upon the administration of the government, and serve to keep alive the spirit of liberty. This within certain limits is probably true; and in governments of a monarchical cast patriotism may look with indulgence, if not with favor, upon the spirit of party. But in those of the popular character, in governments purely elective, it is a spirit not to be encouraged. From their natural tendency it is certain there will always be enough of that spirit for every salutary purpose; and there being constant danger of excess, the effort ought to be by force of public opinion to mitigate and assuage it. A fire not to be quenched, it demands a uniform vigilance to prevent its bursting into a flame, lest, instead of warming, it should consume.

It is important, likewise, that the habits of thinking in a free country should inspire caution in those intrusted with its administration to confine themselves within their respective constitutional spheres, avoiding in the exercise of the powers of one department to encroach upon another. The spirit of encroachment tends to consolidate the powers of all the departments in one, and thus to create, whatever the form of government, a real despotism. A just estimate of that love of power and proneness to abuse it which predominates in the human heart is sufficient to satisfy us of the truth of this position. The necessity of reciprocal checks in the exercise of political power, by dividing and distributing it into different depositories, and constituting each the guardian of the public weal against invasions by the others, has been evinced by experiments ancient and modern, some of them in our country and under our own eyes. To preserve them must be as necessary as to institute them. If in the opinion of the people the distribution or modification of the constitutional powers be in any particular wrong, let it be corrected by an amendment in the way which the Constitution designates. But let there be no change by usurpation; for though this in one instance may be the instrument of good, it is the customary weapon by which free governments are destroyed. The precedent must always greatly overbalance in permanent evil any partial or transient benefit which the use can at any time yield.

Of all the dispositions and habits which lead to political prosperity, religion and morality are indispensable supports. In vain would that man claim the tribute of patriotism who should labor to subvert these great pillars of human happiness—these firmest props of the duties of men and citizens. The mere politician, equally with the pious man, ought to respect and to cherish them. A volume could not trace all their connections with private and public felicity. Let it simply be asked, Where is the security for property, for reputation, for life, if the sense of religious obligation *desert* the oaths which are the instruments of investigation in courts of justice? And let us with caution indulge the supposition that morality can be maintained without religion. Whatever may be conceded to the influence of refined education on minds of peculiar structure, reason and experience both forbid us to expect that national morality can prevail in exclusion of religious principle.

It is substantially true that virtue or morality is a necessary spring of popular government. The rule indeed extends with more or less force to every species of free government. Who that is a sincere friend to it can look with indifference upon attempts to shake the foundation of the fabric? Promote, then, as an object of primary importance, institutions for the general diffusion of knowledge. In proportion as the structure of a government gives force to public opinion, it is essential that public opinion should be enlightened.

As a very important source of strength and security, cherish public credit. One method of preserving it is to use it as sparingly as possible, avoiding occasions of expense by cultivating peace, but remembering also that timely disbursements to prepare for danger frequently prevent much greater disbursements to repel it; avoiding likewise the accumulation of debt, not only by shunning occasions of expense, but by vigorous exertions in time of peace to discharge the debts which unavoidable wars have occasioned, not ungenerously throwing upon posterity the burthen which we ourselves ought to bear. The execution of these maxims belongs to your representatives; but it is necessary that public opinion should cooperate. To facilitate to them the performance of their duty it is essential that you should practically bear in mind that toward the payment of debts there must be revenue; that to have revenue there must be taxes; that no taxes can be devised which are not more or less inconvenient and unpleasant; that the intrinsic embarrassment inseparable from the selection of the proper objects (which is always a choice of difficulties), ought to be a decisive motive for a candid construction of the conduct of the Government in making it, and for a spirit of acquiescence in the measures for obtaining revenue which the public exigencies may at any time dictate.

Observe good faith and justice toward all nations. Cultivate peace and harmony with all. Religion and morality enjoin this conduct. And can it be that good policy does not equally enjoin it? It will be worthy of a free, enlightened, and at no distant period a great nation to give to mankind the magnanimous and too novel example of a people always guided by an exalted justice and benevolence. Who can doubt that in the course of time and things the fruits of such a plan would richly repay any temporary advantages which might be lost by a steady adherence to it? Can it be that Providence has not connected the permanent felicity of a nation with its virtue? The experiment, at least, is recommended by every sentiment which ennobles human nature. Alas! is it rendered impossible by its vices?

In the execution of such a plan nothing is more essential than that

permanent, inveterate antipathies against particular nations and passionate attachments for others should be excluded, and that in place of them
just and amicable feelings toward all should be cultivated. The nation
which indulges toward another an habitual hatred or an habitual fondness
is in some degree a slave. It is a slave to its animosity or to its affection,
either of which is sufficient to lead it astray from its duty and its interest.
Antipathy in one nation against another disposes each more readily to
offer insult and injury, to lay hold of slight causes of umbrage, and to be
haughty and intractable when accidental or trifling occasions of dispute
occur.

Hence frequent collisions, obstinate, envenomed, and bloody contests.
The nation prompted by ill will and resentment sometimes impels to war
the government contrary to the best calculations of policy. The government sometimes participates in the national propensity, and adopts through
passion what reason would reject. At other times it makes the animosity
of the nation subservient to projects of hostility, instigated by pride,
ambition, and other sinister and pernicious motives. The peace often,
sometimes perhaps the liberty, of nations has been the victim.

So, likewise, a passionate attachment of one nation for another produces
a variety of evils. Sympathy for the favorite nation, facilitating the illusion
of an imaginary common interest in cases where no real common interest
exists, and infusing into one the enmities of the other, betrays the former
into a participation in the quarrels and wars of the latter without adequate
inducement or justification. It leads also to concessions to the favorite
nation of privileges denied to others, which is apt doubly to injure the
nation making the concession by unnecessarily parting with what ought
to have been retained, and by exciting jealousy, ill-will, and a disposition
to retaliate in the parties from whom equal privileges are withheld; and
it gives to ambitious, corrupted, or deluded citizens (who devote themselves to the favorite nation) facility to betray or sacrifice the interests of
their own country without odium, sometimes even with popularity, gild-
ing with the appearances of a virtuous sense of obligation, a commendable
deference for public opinion, or a laudable zeal for public good the base
or foolish compliances of ambition, corruption, or infatuation.

As avenues to foreign influence in innumerable ways, such attachments
are particularly alarming to the truly enlightened and independent patriot.
How many opportunities do they afford to tamper with domestic factions,
to practice the arts of seduction, to mislead public opinion, to influence
or awe the public councils! Such an attachment of a small or weak toward
a great and powerful nation dooms the former to be the satellite of the
latter. Against the insidious wiles of foreign influence (I conjure you to
believe me, fellow-citizens) the jealousy of a free people ought to be
constantly awake, since history and experience prove that foreign influ-

ence is one of the most baneful foes of republican government. But that jealousy, to be useful, must be impartial, else it becomes the instrument of the very influence to be avoided, instead of a defense against it. Excessive partiality for one foreign nation and excessive dislike of another cause those whom they actuate to see danger only on one side, and serve to veil and even second the arts of influence on the other. Real patriots who may resist the intrigues of the favorite are liable to become suspected and odious, while its tools and dupes usurp the applause and confidence of the people to surrender their interests.

The great rule of conduct for us in regard to foreign nations is, in extending our commercial relations to have with them as little *political* connection as possible. So far as we have already formed engagements let them be fulfilled with perfect good faith. Here let us stop.

Europe has a set of primary interests which to us have none or a very remote relation. Hence she must be engaged in frequent controversies, the causes of which are essentially foreign to our concerns. Hence, therefore, it must be unwise in us to implicate ourselves by artificial ties in the ordinary vicissitudes of her politics or the ordinary combinations and collisions of her friendships or enmities.

Our detached and distant situation invites and enables us to pursue a different course. If we remain one people, under an efficient government, the period is not far off when we may defy material injury from external annoyance; when we may take such an attitude as will cause the neutrality we may at any time resolve upon to be scrupulously respected; when belligerent nations, under the impossibility of making acquisitions upon us, will not lightly hazard the giving us provocation; when we may choose peace or war, as our interest, guided by justice, shall counsel.

Why forgo the advantages of so peculiar a situation? Why quit our own to stand upon foreign ground? Why, by interweaving our destiny with that of any part of Europe, entangle our peace and prosperity in the toils of European ambition, rivalship, interest, humor, or caprice?

It is our true policy to steer clear of permanent alliances with any portion of the foreign world, so far, I mean, as we are now at liberty to do it; for let me not be understood as capable of patronizing infidelity to existing engagements. I hold the maxim no less applicable to public than to private affairs that honesty is always the best policy. I repeat, therefore, let those engagements be observed in their genuine sense. But in my opinion it is unnecessary and would be unwise to extend them.

Taking care always to keep ourselves by suitable establishments on a respectable defensive posture, we may safely trust to temporary alliances for extraordinary emergencies.

Harmony, liberal intercourse with all nations are recommended by policy, humanity, and interest. But even our commercial policy should hold an equal and impartial hand, neither seeking nor granting exclusive favors or preferences; consulting the natural course of things; diffusing and diversifying by gentle means the streams of commerce, but forcing nothing; establishing with powers so disposed, in order to give trade a stable course, to define the rights of our merchants, and to enable the Government to support them, conventional rules of intercourse, the best that present circumstances and mutual opinion will permit, but temporary and liable to be from time to time abandoned or varied as experience and circumstance shall dictate; constantly keeping in view that it is folly in one nation to look for disinterested favors from another; that it must pay with a portion of its independence for whatever it may accept under that character; that by such acceptance it may place itself in the condition of having given equivalents for nominal favors, and yet of being reproached with ingratitude for not giving more. There can be no greater error than to expect or calculate upon real favors from nation to nation. It is an illusion which experience must cure, which a just pride ought to discard.

In offering to you, my countrymen, these counsels of an old and affectionate friend I dare not hope they will make the strong and lasting impression I could wish—that they will control the usual current of the passions or prevent our nation from running the course which has hitherto marked the destiny of nations. But if I may even flatter myself that they may be productive of some partial benefit, some occasional good—that they may now and then recur to moderate the fury of party spirit, to warn against the mischiefs of foreign intrigue, to guard against the impostures of pretended patriotism—this hope will be a full recompense for the solicitude for your welfare by which they have been dictated.

How far in the discharge of my official duties I have been guided by the principles which have been delineated the public records and other evidences of my conduct must witness to you and to the world. To myself, the assurance of my own conscience is that I have at least believed myself to be guided by them.

In relation to the still subsisting war in Europe my proclamation of the 22d of April, 1793, is the index to my plan. Sanctioned by your approving voice and by that of your representatives in both Houses of Congress, the spirit of that measure has continually governed me, uninfluenced by any attempts to deter or divert me from it.

After deliberate examination, with the aid of the best lights I could obtain, I was well satisfied that our country, under all the circumstances of the case, had a right to take, and was bound in duty and interest to take, a neutral position. Having taken it, I determined as far as should depend upon me to maintain it with moderation, perseverance, and firmness.

The considerations which respect the right to hold this conduct it is not necessary on this occasion to detail. I will only observe that, according to my understanding of the matter, that right, so far from being denied by any of the belligerent powers, has been virtually admitted by all.

The duty of holding a neutral conduct may be inferred, without anything more, from the obligation which justice and humanity impose on every nation, in cases in which it is free to act, to maintain inviolate the relations of peace and amity toward other nations.

The inducements of interest for observing that conduct will best be referred to your own reflections and experience. With me a predominant motive has been to endeavor to gain time to our country to settle and mature its yet recent institutions, and to progress without interruption to that degree of strength and consistency which is necessary to give it, humanly speaking, the command of its own fortunes.

Though in reviewing the incidents of my Administration I am unconscious of intentional error, I am nevertheless too sensible of my defects not to think it probable that I may have committed many errors. Whatever they may be, I fervently beseech the Almighty to avert or mitigate the evils to which they may tend. I shall also carry with me the hope that my country will never cease to view them with indulgence, and that, after forty-five years of my life dedicated to its service with an upright zeal, the faults of incompetent abilities will be consigned to oblivion, as myself must soon be to the mansions of rest.

Relying on its kindness in this as in other things, and actuated by that fervent love toward it which is so natural to a man who views in it the native soil of himself and his progenitors for several generations, I anticipate with pleasing expectation that retreat in which I promise myself to realize without alloy the sweet enjoyment of partaking in the midst of my fellow-citizens the benign influence of good laws under a free government—the ever-favorite object of my heart, and the happy reward, as I trust, of our mutual cares, labors, and dangers.

Alexis de Tocqueville
Democracy in America
(1840)

CONCERNING THE PHILOSOPHICAL
APPROACH OF THE AMERICANS

LESS ATTENTION, I suppose, is paid to philosophy in the United States than in any other country of the civilized world. The Americans have no school of philosophy peculiar to themselves, and they pay very little attention to the rival European schools. Indeed they hardly know their names. Nevertheless, it is noticeable that the people of the United States almost all have a uniform method and rules for the conduct of intellectual inquiries. So, though they have not taken the trouble to define the rules, they have a philosophical method shared by all.

To escape from imposed systems, the yoke of habit, family maxims, class prejudices, and to a certain extent national prejudices as well; to treat tradition as valuable for information only and to accept existing facts as no more than a useful sketch to show how things could be done differently and better; to seek by themselves and in themselves for the only reason for things, looking to results without getting entangled in the means toward them and looking through forms to the basis of things—such are the principal characteristics of what I would call the American philosophical method.

To carry the argument further and to select the chief among these various features, and the one which includes almost all the others within itself, I should say that in most mental operations each American relies on individual effort and judgment.

So, of all countries in the world, America is the one in which the precepts of Descartes are least studied and best followed. No one should be surprised at that.

The Americans never read Descartes's works because their state of

[From *Democracy in America*, Volume II (1840). Volume I had been published in 1835.]

society distracts them from speculative inquiries, and they follow his precepts because this same state of society naturally leads them to adopt them.

The continuous activity which prevails in a democratic society leads to the relaxation or the breaking of the links between generations. It is easy for a man to lose track of his ancestors' conceptions or not to bother about them.

Men living in such a society cannot base their beliefs on the opinions of the class to which they belong, for, one may almost say, there are no more classes, and such as do still exist are composed of such changing elements that they can never, as a body, exercise real power over their members.

When it comes to the influence of one man's mind over another's, that is necessarily very restricted in a country where the citizens have all become more or less similar, see each other at very close quarters, and since they do not recognize any signs of incontestable greatness or superiority in any of their fellows, are continually brought back to their own judgment as the most apparent and accessible test of truth. So it is not only confidence in any particular man which is destroyed. There is a general distaste for accepting any man's word as proof of anything.

So each man is narrowly shut up in himself, and from that basis makes the pretension to judge the world.

This American way of relying on themselves alone to control their judgment leads to other mental habits.

Seeing that they are successful in resolving unaided all the little difficulties they encounter in practical affairs, they are easily led to the conclusion that everything in the world can be explained and that nothing passes beyond the limits of intelligence.

Thus they are ready to deny anything which they cannot understand. Hence they have little faith in anything extraordinary and an almost invincible distaste for the supernatural.

Being accustomed to rely on the witness of their own eyes, they like to see the object before them very clearly. They therefore free it, as far as they can, from its wrappings and move anything in the way and anything that hides their view of it, so as to get the closest view they can in broad daylight. This turn of mind soon leads them to a scorn of forms, which they take as useless, hampering veils put between them and truth.

So the Americans have needed no books to teach them philosophic method, having found it in themselves. Much the same can be said of what has happened in Europe.

This same method has only become established and popular in Europe as conditions of life have become more equal and men more like one another.

Let us turn our attention for a moment to the chronological development.

The sixteenth-century reformers subjected some of the dogmas of the ancient faith to individual reason, but they still refused to allow all the others to be discussed by it. In the seventeenth century Bacon, in natural science, and Descartes, in philosophy strictly so called, abolished accepted formulas, destroyed the dominion of tradition, and upset the authority of masters.

The eighteenth-century philosopher turned this same principle into a general rule and undertook to submit the object of all his beliefs to each man's individual examination.

It is surely clear that Luther, Descartes, and Voltaire all used the same method, and they differed only in the greater or lesser extent to which they held it should be applied.

How did it happen that the reformers were shut in so narrowly within the circle of religious ideas? Why did Descartes, not wanting to use his method except for certain subjects, declare that one should judge philosophical questions for oneself, but not political ones? Why did men in the eighteenth century suddenly draw general conclusions from this same method, which Descartes and his forerunners had either not noticed or refused to observe? Finally, why was it at that time that this method suddenly came out of the schools, worked its way into society, and became the common coin of thought; moreover, when the French had spread its popularity, why was it openly adopted or secretly followed by all the peoples of Europe?

It was possible for this philosophic method to come into the world in the sixteenth century and to be defined and generalized in the seventeenth, but it could not be commonly accepted in either of those centuries. The political laws, the state of society, and habits of thought, all deriving from first causes of their own, were opposed to it.

It was discovered at a time when men were beginning to grow more equal and more like each other. It could not be generally followed except in centuries when conditions had become more or less similar and people like each other.

It follows that the eighteenth-century philosophic method is not just French, but democratic, and that explains its easy admission throughout Europe, which has been so greatly changed partly by its means. The reason the French turned the world upside down is not simply that they changed their ancient beliefs and modified their ancient morality. The reason is that they were the first to generalize and call attention to a philosophic method by which all ancient things could be attacked and the way opened for everything new.

If I am asked why nowadays that method is more often and more strictly applied by the French than by the Americans, though liberty is as complete and of longer date among the latter, I reply that that is partly due to two circumstances that must first be understood.

It was religion that gave birth to the English colonies in America. One must never forget that. In the United States religion is mingled with all the national customs and all those feelings which the word fatherland evokes. For that reason it has peculiar power.

There is another circumstance equally potent in its influence. In America religion has, if one may put it so, defined its own limits. There the structure of religious life has remained entirely distinct from the political organization. It has therefore been easy to change ancient laws without shaking the foundations of ancient beliefs.

In this way Christianity has kept a strong hold over the minds of Americans, and—this is the point I wish to emphasize—its power is not just that of a philosophy which has been examined and accepted, but that of a religion believed in without discussion.

In the United States there are an infinite variety of ceaselessly changing Christian sects. But Christianity itself is an established and irresistible fact which no one seeks to attack or to defend.

Since the Americans have accepted the main dogmas of the Christian religion without examination, they are bound to receive in like manner a great number of moral truths derived therefrom and attached thereto. This puts strict limits on the field of action left open to individual analysis and keeps out of this field many of the most important subjects about which men can have opinions.

The other circumstance which I referred to is this:

The state of society and the Constitution in America are democratic, but there has been no democratic revolution. They were pretty well as they now are when they first arrived in the land. That is a very important point.

Every revolution must shake ancient beliefs, sap authority, and cloud shared ideas. So any revolution, to a greater or lesser extent, throws men back on themselves and opens to each man's view an almost limitless empty space.

When standards of equality have resulted from a long struggle between the different classes of which the old society was composed, envy, hatred, and distrust of his neighbor, together with pride and exaggerated confidence in himself, invade the human heart and for some time hold dominion there. That fact, without reference to equality, works powerfully to divide men and to ensure that they be mistrustful of one another's judgment and look for enlightenment only in themselves.

Consequently each man undertakes to be sufficient to himself and glories in the fact that his beliefs about everything are peculiar to himself.

No longer do ideas, but interests only, form the links between men, and it would seem that human opinions were no more than a sort of mental dust open to the wind on every side and unable to come together and take shape.

Thus the independence of mind which equality supposes to exist is never so great and never shows itself so excessive as at the moment when equality begins to be established and during the pangs of its birth. One must make a careful distinction between that type of intellectual liberty which can result from equality and the anarchy brought in by revolution. Each of these two elements must be considered separately if we are not to conceive exaggerated hopes and fears for the future.

I think that the men who live in the new societies will often make use of individual judgment, but I am far from believing that they will often abuse it.

The reason for this, which I reserve for the next chapter, is something of more general application to democratic countries, something which must in the long run hold the independence of individual thought within fixed, indeed sometimes narrow, bounds.

CONCERNING THE PRINCIPAL SOURCE OF BELIEFS AMONG DEMOCRATIC PEOPLES

Dogmatic beliefs are more or less numerous at different periods. They come into existence in various ways and can change both form and substance. But it can never happen that there are no dogmatic beliefs, that is to say, opinions which men take on trust without discussion. If each man undertook to make up his mind about everything himself and to pursue truth only along roads that he himself had cleared, it is unlikely that any large number of people would ever succeed in agreeing on any common belief.

However, it is easy to see that no society could prosper without such beliefs, or rather that there are no societies which manage in that way. For without ideas in common, no common action would be possible, and without common action, men might exist, but there could be no body social. So for society to exist and, even more, for society to prosper, it is essential that all the minds of the citizens should always be rallied and held together by some leading ideas; and that could never happen unless each of them sometimes came to draw his opinions from the same source and was ready to accept some beliefs ready made.

Moreover, considering each man by himself, dogmatic beliefs seem no less indispensable for living alone than for acting in common with his fellows.

If man had to prove for himself all the truths of which he makes use every day, he would never come to an end of it. He would wear himself out proving preliminary points and make no progress. Since life is too short for such a course and human faculties are too limited, man has to accept as certain a whole heap of facts and opinions which he has neither leisure nor power to examine and verify for himself, things which cleverer men than he have discovered and which the crowd accepts. On that foundation he then builds the house of his own thoughts. He does not act so from any conscious choice, for the inflexible laws of his existence compel him to behave like that.

No philosopher in the world, however great, can help believing a million things on trust from others or assuming the truth of many things besides those he has proved.

Such behavior is desirable as well as necessary. Anyone who undertook to go into everything himself could give but little time or attention to each question. He would keep his mental faculties in a state of perpetual excitement, which would prevent his going deeply into any truth or being firmly convinced of anything at all. His intelligence would be independent but weak. So a choice must be made among all the things about which men have opinions, and some beliefs must be accepted without discussion so that it is possible to go deeply into a few selected ones for examination.

It is true that any man accepting any opinion on trust from another puts his mind in bondage. But it is a salutary bondage, which allows him to make good use of freedom.

So somewhere and somehow authority is always bound to play a part in intellectual and moral life. The part may vary, but some part there must be. The independence of the individual may be greater or less but can never be unlimited. Therefore we need not inquire about the existence of intellectual authority in democratic ages, but only where it resides and what its limits are.

The last chapter showed how standards of equality give men a sort of instinctive incredulity about the supernatural and a very high and often thoroughly exaggerated conception of human reason.

Thus men who live in times of equality find it hard to place the intellectual authority to which they submit, beyond and outside humanity. Generally speaking, they look into themselves or into their fellows for the sources of truth. That is enough to prove that no new religion could become established in such periods and that any attempts to bring one into existence would be not only impious but also ridiculous and unreasonable. One can anticipate that democratic peoples will not easily believe in divine missions, that they will be quick to laugh at new prophets, and that they will wish to find the chief arbiter of their beliefs within, and not beyond, the limits of their kind.

When standards are unequal and men unalike, there are some very enlightened and learned individuals whose intelligence gives them great power, while the multitude is very ignorant and blinkered. As a result men living under an aristocracy are naturally inclined to be guided in their views by a more thoughtful man or class, and they have little inclination to suppose the masses infallible.

In times of equality the opposite happens.

The nearer men are to a common level of uniformity, the less are they inclined to believe blindly in any man or any class. But they are readier to trust the mass, and public opinion becomes more and more mistress of the world.

Not only is public opinion the only guide left to aid private judgment, but its power is infinitely greater in democracies than elsewhere. In times of equality men, being so like each other, have no confidence in others, but this same likeness leads them to place almost unlimited confidence in the judgment of the public. For they think it not unreasonable that, all having the same means of knowledge, truth will be found on the side of the majority.

The citizen of a democracy comparing himself with the others feels proud of his equality with each. But when he compares himself with all his fellows and measures himself against this vast entity, he is overwhelmed by a sense of his insignificance and weakness.

The same equality which makes him independent of each separate citizen leaves him isolated and defenseless in the face of the majority.

So in democracies public opinion has a strange power of which aristocratic nations can form no conception. It uses no persuasion to forward its beliefs, but by some mighty pressure of the mind of all upon the intelligence of each it imposes its ideas and makes them penetrate men's very souls.

The majority in the United States takes over the business of supplying the individual with a quantity of ready-made opinions and so relieves him of the necessity of forming his own. So there are many theories of philosophy, morality, and politics which everyone adopts unexamined on the faith of public opinion. And if one looks very closely into the matter, one finds that religion is strong less as a revealed doctrine than as part of common opinion.

I know that American political laws give the majority the sovereign right to rule society, and that considerably increases the dominion it has anyhow over men's minds. For nothing comes more natural to man than to recognize the superior wisdom of his oppressor.

So this political omnipotence simply augments the power which public opinion would have had without it over each citizen, but it is not the foundation thereof. One must look to equality itself for the source of that influence, and not to the more or less popular institutions which egalitarian men have created for themselves. One may suppose that the intellectual dominion of the greatest number would be less absolute among a democratic people subject to a king than in a pure democracy. But it will always be very nearly absolute in times of equality, and no matter what political laws men devise for themselves, it is safe to foresee that trust in common opinion will become a sort of religion, with the majority as its prophet.

Thus intellectual authority will be different, but it will not be less. Far from believing that it is likely to disappear, I anticipate that it may easily become too great and that possibly it will confine the activity of private judgment within limits too narrow for the dignity and happiness of mankind. I see clearly two tendencies in equality; one turns each man's attention to new thoughts, while the other would induce him freely to give up thinking at all. I can see how, abetted by certain laws, democracy might extinguish that freedom of the mind which a democratic social condition favors. Thus it might happen that, having broken down all the bonds which classes or men formerly imposed on it, the human spirit might bind itself in tight fetters to the general will of the greatest number.

If democratic peoples substituted the absolute power of a majority for all the various powers that used excessively to impede or hold back the upsurge of individual thought, the evil itself would only have changed its form. Men would by no means have found the way to live in independence; they would only have succeeded in the difficult task of giving slavery a new face. There is matter for deep reflection there. I cannot say this too often for all those who see freedom of the mind as something sacred and who hate not only despots but also despotism. For myself, if I feel the hand of power heavy on my brow, I am little concerned to know who it is that oppresses me; I am no better inclined to pass my head under the yoke because a million men hold it for me.

Walt Whitman
Song of Myself
(1855)

I am of old and young, of the foolish as much as the wise,
Regardless of others, ever regardful of others,
Maternal as well as paternal, a child as well as a man,
Stuff'd with the stuff that is coarse and stuff'd with the stuff that is fine,
One of the Nation of many nations, the smallest the same and the largest
    the same,
A Southerner soon as a Northerner, a planter nonchalant and hospitable
    down by the Oconee I live,
A Yankee bound my own way ready for trade, my joints the limberest
    joints on earth and the sternest joints on earth,
A Kentuckian walking the vale of the Elkhorn in my deer-skin leggings,
    a Louisianian or Georgian,
A boatman over lakes or bays or along coasts, a Hoosier, a Badger, Buck-
    eye;
At home on Kanadian snow-shoes or up in the bush, or with fishermen
    off Newfoundland,
At home in the fleet of ice-boats, sailing with the rest and tacking,
At home on the hills of Vermont or in the woods of Maine, or the Texan
    ranch,
Comrade of Californians, comrade of Free North-Westerners, (loving
    their big proportions,)
Comrade of raftsmen and coalmen, comrade of all who shake hands and
    welcome to drink and meat,
A learner with the simplest, a teacher of the thoughtfullest,

[From *Leaves of Grass*. Reprinted here are stanzas 16 and 46 of "Song of Myself" as that poem appears in the version of *Leaves of Grass* that is variously called the ninth, the 1891–1892, or the deathbed edition. Whitman preferred this version of the original, which was published in Brooklyn in 1855.]

A novice beginning yet experient of myriads of seasons,
Of every hue and caste am I, of every rank and religion,
A farmer, mechanic, artist, gentleman, sailor, quaker,
Prisoner, fancy-man, rowdy, lawyer, physician, priest.

I resist any thing better than my own diversity,
Breathe the air but leave plenty after me,
And am not stuck up, and am in my place.

(The moth and the fish-eggs are in their place,
The bright suns I see and the dark suns I cannot see are in their place,
The palpable is in its place and the impalpable is in its place.)

.   .   .   .   .

I know I have the best of time and space, and was never measured and
        never will be measured.

I tramp a perpetual journey, (come listen all!)
My signs are a rain-proof coat, good shoes, and a staff cut from the woods,
No friend of mine takes his ease in my chair,
I have no chair, no church, no philosophy,
I lead no man to a dinner-table, library, exchange,
But each man and each woman of you I lead upon a knoll,
My left hand hooking you round the waist,
My right hand pointing to landscapes of continents and the public road.

Not I, not any one else can travel that road for you,
You must travel it for yourself.

It is not far, it is within reach,
Perhaps you have been on it since you were born and did not know,
Perhaps it is everywhere on water and on land.

Shoulder your duds dear son, and I will mine, and let us hasten forth,
Wonderful cities and free nations we shall fetch as we go.

If you tire, give me both burdens, and rest the chuff of your hand on my
        hip,
And in due time you shall repay the same service to me,
For after we start we never lie by again.

This day before dawn I ascended a hill and look'd at the crowded heaven,
And I said to my spirit *When we become the enfolders of those orbs, and
        the pleasure and knowledge of every thing in them, shall we be
        fill'd and satisfied then?*
And my spirit said *No, we but level that lift to pass and continue beyond.*

You are also asking me questions and I hear you,
I answer that I cannot answer, you must find out for yourself.

Sit a while dear son,
Here are biscuits to eat and here is milk to drink,
But as soon as you sleep and renew yourself in sweet clothes, I kiss you
    with a good-by kiss and open the gate for your egress hence.

Long enough have you dream'd contemptible dreams,
Now I wash the gum from your eyes,
You must habit yourself to the dazzle of the light and of every moment
    of your life.

Long have you timidly waded holding a plank by the shore,
Now I will you to be a bold swimmer,
To jump off in the midst of the sea, rise again, nod to me, shout, and
    laughingly dash with your hair.

Abraham Lincoln
The Gettysburg Address
(1863)

FOURSCORE AND seven years ago our fathers brought forth, on this continent, a new nation, conceived in Liberty, and dedicated to the proposition that all men are created equal.

Now we are engaged in a great civil war, testing whether that nation, or any nation so conceived, and so dedicated, can long endure. We are met on a great battlefield of that war. We have come to dedicate a portion of that field, as a final resting-place for those who here gave their lives, that that nation might live. It is altogether fitting and proper that we should do this.

But, in a larger sense, we can not dedicate—we can not consecrate—we can not hallow—this ground. The brave men, living and dead, who struggled here, have consecrated it far above our poor power to add or detract. The world will little note, nor long remember what we say here, but it can never forget what they did here. It is for us the living, rather, to be dedicated here to the unfinished work which they who fought here have thus far so nobly advanced. It is rather for us to be here dedicated to the great task remaining before us—that from these honored dead we take increased devotion to that cause for which they here gave the last full measure of devotion—that we here highly resolve that these dead shall not have died in vain—that this nation, under God, shall have a new birth of freedom—and that government of the people, by the people, for the people, shall not perish from the earth.

[From the version delivered at Gettysburg, Pennsylvania, on 19 November 1863.]

Abraham Lincoln
The Second Inaugural Address
(1865)

Fellow Countrymen:

AT THIS second appearing to take the oath of the presidential office, there is less occasion for an extended address than there was at the first. Then a statement, somewhat in detail, of a course to be pursued, seemed fitting and proper. Now, at the expiration of four years, during which public declarations have been constantly called forth on every point and phase of the great contest which still absorbs the attention, and engrosses the energies of the nation, little that is new could be presented. The progress of our arms, upon which all else chiefly depends, is as well known to the public as to myself; and it is, I trust, reasonably satisfactory and encouraging to all. With high hope for the future, no prediction in regard to it is ventured.

On the occasion corresponding to this four years ago, all thoughts were anxiously directed to an impending civil-war. All dreaded it—all sought to avert it. While the inaugural address was being delivered from this place, devoted altogether to *saving* the Union without war, insurgent agents were in the city seeking to *destroy* it without war—seeking to dissolve the Union, and divide effects, by negotiation. Both parties deprecated war; but one of them would *make* war rather than let the nation survive; and the other would *accept* war rather than let it perish. And the war came.

One eighth of the whole population were colored slaves, not distributed generally over the Union, but localized in the Southern part of it. These slaves constituted a peculiar and powerful interest. All knew that this interest was, somehow, the cause of the war. To strengthen, perpetuate, and extend this interest was the object for which the insurgents would

[From the version delivered in Washington, D.C., on 4 March 1865.]

rend the Union, even by war; while the government claimed no right to do more than to restrict the territorial enlargement of it. Neither party expected for the war, the magnitude, or the duration, which it has already attained. Neither anticipated that the *cause* of the conflict might cease with, or even before, the conflict itself should cease. Each looked for an easier triumph, and a result less fundamental and astounding. Both read the same Bible, and pray to the same God; and each invokes His aid against the other. It may seem strange that any men should dare to ask a just God's assistance in wringing their bread from the sweat of other men's faces; but let us judge not that we be not judged. The prayers of both could not be answered; that of neither has been answered fully. The Almighty has His own purposes. "Woe unto the world because of offences! for it must needs be that offences come; but woe to that man by whom the offence cometh!" If we shall suppose that American Slavery is one of those offences which, in the providence of God, must needs come, but which, having continued through His appointed time, He now wills to remove, and that He gives to both North and South, this terrible war, as the woe due to those by whom the offence came, shall we discern therein any departure from those divine attributes which the believers in a Living God always ascribe to Him? Fondly do we hope—fervently do we pray—that this mighty scourge of war may speedily pass away. Yet, if God wills that it continue, until all the wealth piled by the bond-man's two hundred and fifty years of unrequited toil shall be sunk, and until every drop of blood drawn with the lash, shall be paid by another drawn with the sword, as was said three thousand years ago, so still it must be said "the judgments of the Lord, are true and righteous altogether."

With malice toward none; with charity for all; with firmness in the right, as God gives us to see the right, let us strive on to finish the work we are in; to bind up the nation's wounds; to care for him who shall have borne the battle, and for his widow, and his orphan—to do all which may achieve and cherish a just, and a lasting peace, among ourselves, and with all nations.

PART TWO

PLURALISTIC FRONTIERS

I dwell in Possibility—
A fairer House than Prose—
More numerous of Windows—
Superior—for Doors—

Of Chambers, as the Cedars—
Impregnable of Eye—
And for an Everlasting Roof
The Gambrels of the Sky.

Of Visitors—the fairest—
For Occupation—This—
The spreading wide my narrow Hands
To gather Paradise—

I DWELL IN POSSIBILITY
Emily Dickinson (1862)

IN 1893, at the World's Columbian Exposition in Chicago, a young American professor read a paper to a conference of fellow historians. The scholar was Frederick Jackson Turner (1861–1932), and the paper, "The Significance of the Frontier in American History," eventually became one of the most influential interpretations of American ground ever attempted. Put simply, Turner's argument was that the conditions of frontier life were the most significant facts of the nation's history to that point. Noting America's succession of westward-moving frontiers, Turner claimed that each one afforded settlers contact with untouched nature, a "perennial rebirth," an "escape from the bondage of the past . . . and scorn of older society," and above all, the opportunity which, he declared, has become another name for America. Moreover, frontier existence fostered the individualism, self-reliance and self-determination, democracy, faith in man, and courage to adapt to change that Turner believed characterized Americans in general.

That the course of American history has been marked by a series of frontiers is of course indisputable. At first, it was the Eastern seaboard, that "waste and howling wilderness" (as the poet Michael Wigglesworth described it in 1662) confronted by the Puritans and other early settlers; later, it was successively the Alleghenies, the Mississippi, the Missouri, the Great Plains, the Rockies, and finally the shores of the Pacific Ocean. Turner has been criticized, however, for exaggerating the influence of the frontier on American ideals and on the American character. He has also been accused of confusing actual frontier existence with the romantic myths that have grown up around it. Whether such criticism is justified or not, to dismiss Turner's thesis altogether is to dismiss the powerful effects that the *idea* of the frontier, and of the West in general, has had on the American imagination. It is, moreover, to take too lightly the effects of the romantic myths themselves. Those effects have been profound. They help to account for the concept of Manifest Destiny, with all the implications of that concept. They help to explain why, to so many Americans past and present, the West with its temporal as well as spatial connotations has stood for a condition in which an idealized past can merge with an idealized future to make anything seem possible. And they surely account for the fact that the most indigenous American heroes are Western frontiersmen: historical personages such as Daniel Boone, Davy Crockett, Wyatt Earp, even Andrew Jackson and Abraham Lincoln; fictional creations such as James Fenimore Cooper's Leatherstocking and his many avatars, including the strong, stoical, individualistic figures portrayed on film by the likes of Gary Cooper, Henry Fonda, John Wayne, and Clint Eastwood.

This is not to say that the effects of the myth have always been salutary. Myths may constitute "a fairer house than Prose" but not necessarily a sounder one. The myth of the West may have misled Americans into believing that the future is absolutely open and unaffected by the past, or that simple physical movement from one place to another will inevitably improve the quality of one's life, or that the nation's space and natural resources are inexhaustible. For good or for ill, however, the myth of the West is the ground from which innumerable American dreams have sprung and continue to spring.

THE DREAM OF THE WEST

From the time of the first American colonists, if not before, the land to the West was a symbol of the unknown, of the unexplored, and of future possibilities. Still, the very fact that it was regarded as a *tabula rasa* on which, supposedly, anything could be written made it fearsome as well as alluring. True, it was a potential Garden of the World; but it was also a place fraught with possible (and, as it turned out, real) terrors and hardships. It was a place where many believed a new Adam might arise; but it was also a place where men and women might revert to a primal savagery, not escaping from the bondage of the past at all but plunging back into a barbarism from which civilization had presumably rescued them. It was a place that promised individuals a tempting freedom from social restraints; but it was also a place that threatened them with the agonies of isolation, with cultural deprivation, and with a loss of the comfort and security of historical tradition.

Turner himself exemplifies some of this ambivalence. Although he recognizes that frontier life was merely a step toward the development of a higher civilization, the subtly elegiac tone of his essay suggests that a part of him laments its passage. Turner's ambivalence is not unique. It is discernible in the works of earlier American writers who sang the praises of untouched nature yet identified America's glorious destiny with the settling of the West.

Several such tensions are evident in J. Hector St. John de Crèvecoeur's *Letters from an American Farmer*. Born in France, Crèvecoeur (1735–1813) had immigrated to Canada and subsequently to New York where he took up farming and, probably in the decade preceding the Revolution (which he opposed), wrote most of his *Letters*. They were first published under his pseudonym J. Hector St. John. In some respects, Crèvecoeur's account smacks of a pastoral idyl. Describing agrarian life on a relatively early frontier along the Eastern seaboard, he speaks sentimentally about the morally uplifting effects of the farmer's direct contact with the land. Like Turner after him, Crèvecoeur asserts that frontier life encourages democracy, and he stresses the opportunity, intellectual as well as economic, which the simple fact of *space* affords Americans. Moreover, in industrious immigrants, farming on this continent produces a "sort of resurrection," he states, for they are "inspired with those new thoughts which constitute an American." Dwelling in possibility, the American is in fact a "new man," free of the ancient principles, prejudices, and social inequalities of the European.

Yet in this sunny romantic picture some darker hues appear. A "mild government" makes America the "most perfect society now existing in the world"; still, Crèvecoeur is appalled by the horrors of slavery he witnesses in Carolina. He is especially disturbed by the sight of a black man in a cage because the slave has been put there not by uncivilized persons but by men "in a more improved situation." Evidently their "improvement" consists mainly of an outlook which tells them that the "laws of self-preservation" render "such executions necessary." As for nature, it can be beneficent, and life in nature is on the whole preferable to life in a complex society that fosters such rationalized brutality as slavery; but nature can also be capriciously cruel. And while Crèvecoeur believes that contact with nature tends to soothe the breast of the farmer, it has the opposite effect on those pioneers who venture into the wilderness. Exhibiting the "most hideous parts of our society," the hunter, for example, takes on the characteristics of his prey. Crèvecoeur's man of the wild is a far cry from Natty Bumppo, Cooper's "saint with a gun." He is instead, like Cooper's despised half-breeds, a combination of the most odious vices of Europeans and Indians alike, a personification of Turner's "meeting point between savagery and civilization" in the worst sense. Indeed, to Crèvecoeur humans in general are hardly "that class of beings which we vainly think ourselves to be." Because human nature is "poisoned" in its "most essential parts," it must be as carefully cultivated and controlled as the land itself. Even America's "new man" cannot be allowed complete freedom of expression. It is clear that in the long run Crèvecoeur's experience did not foster in him the "faith in man" that Turner attributes to frontier existence.

Nathaniel Hawthorne never lived on the frontier. Yet he shared some of Crèvecoeur's ambivalence and skepticism, and he was more keenly aware of the ironies of American life and American aspirations. Always careful in his writings to acknowledge humanity's capacity for goodness and its need for faith in moral progress, he was a child of the Puritans and thus acutely conscious of the "magnetic chain" of evil and fractious passions linking all the sons and daughters of Adam. Nor did Hawthorne believe that any land was truly virginal. Eden had fallen long ago, and humanity with it; hence, no escape from the bondage of the past was possible. As his "My Kinsman, Major Molineux" has illustrated, severing all ties with the past was to Hawthorne not even desirable, morally or otherwise.

These convictions are all expressed in "Earth's Holocaust." Set on "one of the broadest prairies of the West," Hawthorne's sketch depicts the efforts of a group of radical reformers to burn all vestiges of the past. Here, on a blank expanse of seemingly boundless possibilities, they dream that an earthly paradise can be created. Hawthorne implies at once that their hope is illusory. Whether the scene is "in time past or time to come" is, he says, "of little or no moment," because dreams of a totally new beginning on the frontier are as doomed to failure, now or in the future, as they have always been. For, ironically, the incendiaries act not as the rational enlightened New Adams they seek to be but rather as a passionate, unruly mob. Considering everything old to be *ipso facto* bad, they savagely set fire to good and bad alike. For a while, Hawthorne's narrator defends them. Mildly disturbed when great literary and philosophical works are thrown into the fire, he nevertheless argues that "nature [is] better than a book," and that "if we read it aright, it will be to us a volume of eternal truth." But when even the Bible is consigned to the flames as but "a fable of the world's infancy," he begins to see that the "Titan of innovation . . . at first shaking down only the old and rotten shapes of things, had . . . laid his terrible hand upon the main pillars which supported the whole edifice of our moral and spiritual state." Furthermore, he is reminded by a "dark-complexioned personage" that the reformers have neglected to destroy the prime source of evil, namely, the human heart. Hawthorne would seem to agree that the heart is indeed the only truly "boundless sphere wherein existed the original wrong of which the crime and misery of this outward world were merely types." He would also seem to agree that until that "foul cavern" is purified the world will be the old world yet—even in the American West. It is worth noting, however, that the dark stranger is described as a satanic figure and, as such, a purveyor of only half-truths. Hawthorne suggests that the whole truth lies elsewhere, on a frontier, so to speak, between a blind optimism and a despairing pessimism.

When one considers the violence and lawlessness, the exploitation and extermination of the Indians to which Chiefs Meninock (c. 1840–c. 1930) and Washakie (c. 1804–1900) allude in selections that follow, the spoliation and pollution of nature, the ruthless land speculation that sacrificed human rights to property rights on the frontier, then one may be tempted to adopt the darker sides of Crèvecoeur's and Hawthorne's views. At the very least, if the West was indeed another name for possibility and opportunity, then the possibilities realized and opportunities exercised were a mixed moral matter.

PHILOSOPHICAL FRONTIERS

In his 1966 introduction to Alexis de Tocqueville's *Democracy in America*, Max Lerner says that during the 1830s America had a "triple frontier": geographical, industrial-commercial, and democratic, the latter personified by Andrew Jackson, the nation's first Western president. To these, Lerner might have added a fourth: the philosophical frontier called Transcendentalism, which opened not in the West but in the East.

Under the leadership of lecturer, essayist, and former minister Ralph Waldo Emerson (1803–1882), a diverse group of New England thinkers and writers—including Theodore Parker, Margaret Fuller, and Henry David Thoreau—set off a second American Revolution of sorts. Theirs was not a violent revolution, nor even one that sought power for partisan purposes. It did have political implications, however, for the Transcendentalists urged their fellow Americans to consider anew what it means to be alive.

Three targets drew the Transcendentalists' fire. First, they broke from the vestiges of Puritan theology that still influenced American religion. That tradition, being too much dependent on acceptance of specific doctrine, so the Trancendentalists claimed, further sapped genuine spirituality by proclaiming an excessively pessimistic view of human nature. According to the Transcendentalists, this "mumps and measles of the soul," as Emerson called it, made creation a tragedy by portraying depraved human sinners in the hands of a God whose righteous anger slackened only enough to elect a few for salvation.

Although the Transcendentalists were thus hopeful about God and humankind alike, they certainly did not find that the United States was living up to its potential. Hence a second target of their rebellion urged Americans to desist from imitating European styles and to develop our own distinctive art, literature, and philosophy. The third, the crux of the Transcendentalists' revolution, was even closer to home. Americans, these intellectual pioneers feared, were in danger of losing their individuality and their souls as well. Being like everybody else—that was the threat in the former case. Making the accumulation of money and property one's top priority—such was the danger in the latter.

When the Transcendentalists criticized Americans for being half asleep, for being too comfortable and too lethargic to take advantage of the frontier within, these thinkers were motivated by a cluster of shared convictions, which Emerson might have summed up as follows:

(1) The most genuine human life is characterized by moral sensitivity and spiritual awareness. Intuition—the combined power of reason, feeling, and imagination—can lead one beyond the appearances of sense experience to discovery of the fundamental unity, beauty, and goodness of all existence.

(2) The Puritans had a point in considering nature a symbol of spiritual reality, but they erred insofar as they saw any part of it as the "devil's territory." All of nature reflects a divine moral idea. Its apparently disparate parts actually form an essential harmony corresponding to the organic unity of a person, for both consist of matter infused with spirit. Nature, then, provides a kind of language which, read correctly, can teach people what they are and how to live. And since America at its best is, like nature, both Many and One, the nation is potentially a social manifestation of the divine plan. The problem, however, is that America, intent on developing its productive power, concentrates its energies on

matter as matter rather than on the spiritual meanings that matter signifies. The result leads to mistaking a mediocre conformity for a unity in which each individual is vital and essential.

(3) Realization of one's relations with others should be coupled with a self-reliance rooted in the development of one's personal, moral, and spiritual qualities. The true claims of the individual can be reconciled with those that are proper to society as a whole if we recognize the existence of a fundamental spiritual force—Emerson called it the Oversoul—from which all things arise and which permeates everything and everyone. Through such a reconciliation the spirit of democracy is nourished.

Contrary to what Emerson may have wished, Transcendentalism, like the dream of the West, was not an entirely original American creation. He and his companions blended strands of European philosophy and Oriental religion and adapted them in various ways to American conditions. Nor was Transcendentalism a systematic body of thought. Its very emphasis on individualism inevitably led to differences of outlook and opinion among members of the group. Furthermore, their view of reality as a process of Becoming easily accommodated changes in attitude, even logical contradictions, as was probably to be expected in a rapidly changing nation. Emerson himself, for example, was not always as optimistic as his public utterances suggest. In a sense, the Transcendentalists' philosophical frontier was as fluid as the country's geographical frontiers.

For all their praise of nature and notwithstanding Emerson's preference for an agrarian society because it puts man in touch with the true "work of the world" and his exhortation to Americans to establish "an original relationship" to the physical universe, the Transcendentalists had little interest in the literal frontier. It was the symbolic West that enticed them: the West as a symbol of humanity's unexplored interior spaces, of its infinite spiritual possibilities, of its ability to attain rebirth by throwing off the authority and excrescences of history while recognizing that its archetypal elements are eternally present. The expansion of the nation was important to the Transcendentalists only insofar as it corresponded to the expansion of the self.

Emerson's "Nature" (1836) was the first great Transcendentalist document, the most thoroughgoing expression of his view of the physical world and man's relationship to it. His "The American Scholar" was in turn a classic declaration of America's cultural independence from the "courtly muses of Europe" and, more generally, from the authority of the past. And his "Self-Reliance" became the quintessential statement of America's faith in that individualism which, according to Turner, was nurtured by the frontier. In that famous essay, Emerson urges his countrymen to trust the "aboriginal Self on which a universal reliance may be grounded," to cultivate the "unaffected . . . innocence of the child" which, he believed, the American society of his day was conspiring to destroy. Emerson thus seems to suggest that his ideal American is a kind of noble savage. Not so. While he agreed with his friend Thoreau that, as Emerson put it in his essay on "Politics," the "less government we have the better," there is nothing anarchic or savage about Emerson's ideal individual. The "aboriginal self" to which he refers is instead the buried "genius" within everyone. It is the "divine idea which each of us represents," the image of the Oversoul whose "primary wisdom," lying in the "deep forests of the heart" beneath a socially conditioned consciousness, is the best weapon against an emasculating conformity to the "smooth mediocrity and squalid contentment of the times." Only by trusting that wisdom can Americans bring about a "new day" and realize an Absolute West, a truly moral and spiritual democracy.

Thoreau (1817–1862), Emerson's most famous disciple, was at one and the same time more outspoken about social issues—slavery, for example, and labor conditions in the textile mills of Lowell, Massachusetts—and more the radical nonconformist than his mentor. He also lived in closer contact to the land and wrote more concretely about the natural world. For all his naturalistic pursuits and descriptions, however, they were not in themselves his principal concerns. Keenly conscious of the "doubleness of all things," he too, like Emerson, was primarily concerned with nature as a symbol of certain "higher laws." To focus on the physical as physical, nothing more, would be to give oneself over entirely to one's "animal nature" and to subordinate one's spiritual faculties. It would correspond to a "life without principle." Thus Thoreau's frontier is, like Emerson's, an interior region, the West he contemplated a country of the soul. True, in his early essay "Walking" he speaks of the West in standard nineteenth-century terms as representing progress, fertility, and the future; its physical spaciousness, he indicates, may actually produce an intellectual expansion. Yet even in this essay his westward walking principally symbolizes his exploration of the "wildness" within himself, and one suspects that his advice to young men to go west is, unlike Horace Greeley's, more than slightly disingenuous.

Thoreau's comments in "Life without Principle" more accurately represent his attitudes. Declaring that the "ways by which you may get money almost without exception lead downward," and lamenting the incessant activity of his money-minded neighbors, Thoreau also believes that physical movement in itself—westward or otherwise—can be a distraction from that spiritual voyaging, that plunge into the profound depths of soul, which is the important business of life. Hence he derides the rush for gold in California. Since the only truly precious metal is the gold within, one need go no farther than the Concord woods to mine it. Once found, it shines like the "ever-glorious morning," one of Thoreau's favorite metaphors for the rediscovery of that primal innocence which to him as to Emerson is the basis of moral principle. How to live and what to live for—the answers to those questions were the objects of his famous sojourn at Walden Pond, emblem of his pioneering venture on his personal frontier and of his questing in general.

Born at the height of the Transcendentalist movement and son of a father sympathetic to some aspects of it, William James (1842–1910), leading exponent of the American philosophy known as Pragmatism, would nevertheless seem to have little in common with Emerson and Thoreau. In contrast to them, James argued for what he called "the pluralistic side," stressing the flux and variety of experience in "a world imperfectly unified still, and perhaps always to remain so." Like the Transcendentalists, he did believe that reality is in process—but to such an extent that truth itself, far from being eternal, is in the making as propositions are acted upon and tested in concrete situations. Human freedom, James affirmed, determines what the world will be. His accent on an open, evolving universe, on the world as possibility and opportunity, on the virtues of the "strenuous mood"—all of these are compatible enough with Transcendental optimism. But Emerson's sometimes fuzzy mysticism and the symbolic mode inherent to Transcendentalist writing are lacking in James. He is surely more tolerant and less ironic than Thoreau. Indeed, James's "On a Certain Blindness in Human Beings" sounds like a criticism of Thoreau's contempt for people who are apparently concerned only with making a living. One has no right, James says, to pass hasty judgment on the labor of others, for that labor may have significance to them beyond what we perceive. It may reward them with a sense of duty fulfilled or of a victory in the face of obstacles. It all depends on the "eagerness" of their pursuit. Thoreau asserts that most men and women are blind to themselves; James says they are more likely to be blind to the motives of others. The blindness that separates one consciousness from another constitutes a frontier that should be crossed.

In other ways, however, James resembles Emerson and Thoreau more than might be expected. A psychologist as well as philosopher, student of the "varieties of religious experience," James too is vitally concerned with what he calls the "ejective world," the "vast world of inner life beyond us, so different from that of outer seeming," a sense of which can come upon us from nature and from other people alike. Despite his tolerance, James too deplores Americans' obsession with "practical interest." He even goes so far as to suggest, Thoreau-like, that a person may have to be a "loafer" to gain insight into the truly significant and thus be able to "change the usual standards of human value." And, recalling both Emerson and Thoreau, James asserts the sovereignty of the present: "This world never did anywhere or at any time contain more of essential divinity, or of eternal meaning," than it does here and now. In short, James's West also is an interior space, discovered by descending to a "more profound and primitive level."

New England intellectual, Harvard professor, cultured member of a cultured family, James could still speak of desirable conditions in terms usually associated with the more physically adventurous pioneers. Too many of his educated peers, he declares, have "got far, far away from Nature." He is uneasy about the Chautauqua Lake community because it is too well-ordered, secure, civilized. He longs instead "for something primordial and savage." Human existence needs "intensity and danger"; it needs struggle; it should provoke such frontier virtues as "pluck and will" and "dogged endurance." For the real world is a "wilderness" of "heights and depths," of "precipices . . . and steep ideals," of the "awful and infinite." He might be describing the American West.

Josiah Royce (1855–1916), James's friend and Harvard colleague, was born in California. Yet his "Provincialism" is an implicit criticism of the typical American attitude that if we do not like where we are, we can always light out for some new territory. Royce's essay is a plea on behalf of stability, community loyalty, a history that dignifies the present. Acknowledging that "economic conditions rather than deliberate choice" frequently dictate movement from one place to another, Royce urges that new opportunities be opened within local communities themselves. For while independence of spirit requires people to believe that they can pursue an "ideal to a new realm," commitment to a community is also necessary.

Royce's argument—which has a decidedly contemporary ring to it—springs from his fear that America is sacrificing individuals to the collective. Recalling the Hawthorne of "My Kinsman, Major Molineux" in noting that one great problem of popular government is finding ways to avoid mob rule in which individual will and initiative are lost, Royce proposes in effect that the "realm of the province" is a social unit analogous to the individual. Only its will can effectively battle the "overwhelming forces of consolidation," the centralization of industry, education, and communication. His argument would have appealed to Thoreau and Emerson. Admittedly less mystical than Emerson but more monistic than James, Royce at one point echoes the sage of Concord describing the Oversoul. "All the unique individuals of the truly spiritual order," contends Royce, "stand in relation to the same universal light, to the same divine whole in relation to which they win their individuality."

By the time Royce wrote "Provincialism," the frontier had closed. Still, ideas and language associated with it resound in Royce's essay. They continue to resound today, especially—sometimes with unintended irony, sometimes with shrewd calculation—in political speeches. They are a part of the national rhetoric. They are embedded in American ground.

THE DREAM OF THE WEST

J. Hector St. John de Crèvecoeur
Letters from an American Farmer
(1782)

WHAT IS AN AMERICAN

I WISH I could be acquainted with the feelings and thoughts which must agitate the heart and present themselves to the mind of an enlightened Englishman, when he first lands on this continent. He must greatly rejoice that he lived at a time to see this fair country discovered and settled; he must necessarily feel a share of national pride, when he views the chain of settlements which embellishes these extended shores. When he says to himself, this is the work of my countrymen, who, when convulsed by factions, afflicted by a variety of miseries and wants, restless and impatient, took refuge here. They brought along with them their national genius, to which they principally owe what liberty they enjoy, and what substance they possess. Here he sees the industry of his native country displayed in a new manner, and traces in their works the embrios of all the arts, sciences, and ingenuity which flourish in Europe. Here he beholds fair cities, substantial villages, extensive fields, an immense country filled with decent houses, good roads, orchards, meadows, and bridges, where an hundred years ago all was wild, woody and uncultivated! What a train of pleasing ideas this fair spectacle must suggest; it is a prospect which must inspire a good citizen with the most heartfelt pleasure. The difficulty consists in the manner of viewing so extensive a scene. He is arrived on a new continent; a modern society offers itself to his contemplation, different from what he had hitherto seen. It is not composed, as in Europe, of great lords who possess every thing, and of a herd of people who have nothing. Here are no aristocratical families, no courts, no kings, no bishops, no ecclesiastical dominion, no invisible power giving to a few a very visible one; no great manufacturers employing thousands, no great refinements of luxury. The rich and the poor are not so far removed from each other as they are in Europe. Some few towns excepted, we are all

[From *Letters from an American Farmer*, which was first published at London in 1782. Letters III and IX are reprinted here.]

tillers of the earth, from Nova Scotia to West Florida. We are a people
of cultivators, scattered over an immense territory, communicating with
each other by means of good roads and navigable rivers, united by the
silken bands of mild government, all respecting the laws, without dreading
their power, because they are equitable. We are all animated with the
spirit of an industry which is unfettered and unrestrained, because each
person works for himself. If he travels through our rural districts he views
not the hostile castle, and the haughty mansion, contrasted with the clay-
built hut and miserable cabbin, where cattle and men help to keep each
other warm, and dwell in meanness, smoke, and indigence. A pleasing
uniformity of decent competence appears throughout our habitations. The
meanest of our log-houses is a dry and comfortable habitation. Lawyer
or merchant are the fairest titles our towns afford; that of a farmer is the
only appellation of the rural inhabitants of our country. It must take some
time ere he can reconcile himself to our dictionary, which is but short in
words of dignity and names of honour. There, on a Sunday, he sees a
congregation of respectable farmers and their wives, all clad in neat
homespun, well mounted, or riding in their own humble waggons. There
is not among them an esquire, saving the unlettered magistrate. There
he sees a parson as simple as his flock, a farmer who does not riot on the
labour of others. We have no princes, for whom we toil, starve, and bleed:
we are the most perfect society now existing in the world. Here man is
free as he ought to be; nor is this pleasing equality so transitory as many
others are. Many ages will not see the shores of our great lakes replenished
with inland nations, nor the unknown bounds of North America entirely
peopled. Who can tell how far it extends? Who can tell the millions of
men whom it will feed and contain? For no European foot has as yet
travelled half the extent of this mighty continent!

The next wish of this traveller will be to know whence came all these
people? They are a mixture of English, Scotch, Irish, French, Dutch,
Germans, and Swedes. From this promiscuous breed, that race now called
Americans have arisen. The eastern provinces must indeed be excepted,
as being the unmixed descendents of Englishmen. I have heard many
wish that they had been more intermixed also: for my part, I am no
wisher, and think it much better as it has happened. They exhibit a most
conspicuous figure in this great and variegated picture; they too enter for
a great share in the pleasing perspective displayed in these thirteen provinces. I know it is fashionable to reflect on them, but I respect them for
what they have done; for the accuracy and wisdom with which they have
settled their territory; for the decency of their manners; for their early
love of letters; their ancient college, the first in this hemisphere; for their
industry; which to me who am but a farmer, is the criterion of everything.
There never was a people, situated as they are, who with so ungrateful

a soil have done more in so short a time. Do you think that the monarchical ingredients which are more prevalent in other governments have purged them from all foul stains? Their histories assert the contrary.

In this great American asylum, the poor of Europe have by some means met together, and in consequence of various causes; to what purpose should they ask one another what countrymen they are? Alas, two thirds of them had no country. Can a wretch who wanders about, who works and starves, whose life is a continual scene of sore affliction or pinching penury; can that man call England or any other kingdom his country? A country that had no bread for him, whose fields procured him no harvest, who met with nothing but the frowns of the rich, the severity of the laws, with jails and punishments; who owned not a single foot of the extensive surface of this planet? No! urged by a variety of motives, here they came. Every thing has tended to regenerate them; new laws, a new mode of living, a new social system; here they are become men: in Europe they were as so many useless plants, wanting vegitative mould, and refreshing showers; they withered, and were mowed down by want, hunger, and war; but now by the power of transplantation, like all other plants they have taken root and flourished! Formerly they were not numbered in any civil lists of their country, except in those of the poor; here they rank as citizens. By what invisible power has this surprising metamorphosis been performed? By that of the laws and that of their industry. The laws, the indulgent laws, protect them as they arrive, stamping on them the symbol of adoption; they receive ample rewards for their labours; these accumulated rewards procure them lands; those lands confer on them the title of freemen, and to that title every benefit is affixed which men can possibly require. This is the great operation daily performed by our laws. From whence proceed these laws? From our government. Whence the government? It is derived from the original genius and strong desire of the people ratified and confirmed by the crown. . . .

What then is the American, this new man? He is either an European, or the descendant of an European, hence that strange mixture of blood, which you will find in no other country. I could point out to you a family whose grandfather was an Englishman, whose wife was Dutch, whose son married a French woman, and whose present four sons have now four wives of different nations. *He* is an American, who leaving behind him all his ancient prejudices and manners, receives new ones from the new mode of life he has embraced, the new government he obeys, and the new rank he holds. He becomes an American by being received in the broad lap of our great *Alma Mater*. Here individuals of all nations are melted into a new race of men, whose labours and posterity will one day cause great changes in the world. Americans are the western pilgrims, who are carrying along with them that great mass of arts, sciences, vigour, and industry which began long since in the east; they will finish the great circle. The Americans were once scattered all over Europe; here they are incorporated into one of the finest systems of population which has ever appeared, and which will hereafter become distinct by the power of the different climates they inhabit. The American ought therefore to love this country much better than that wherein either he or his fore-fathers were born. Here the rewards of his industry follow with equal steps the progress of his labour; his labour is founded on the basis of nature, *self-interest*; can it want a stronger allurement? Wives and children, who before in vain demanded of him a morsel of bread, now, fat and frolicsome, gladly help their father to clear those fields whence exuberant crops are to arise to feed and to clothe them all; without any part being claimed, either by a despotic prince, a rich abbot, or a mighty lord. Here religion demands but little of him; a small voluntary salary to the minister, and gratitude to God; can he refuse these? The American is a new man, who acts upon new principles; he must therefore entertain new ideas, and form new opinions. From involuntary idleness, servile dependence, penury, and useless labour, he has passed to toils of a very different nature, rewarded by ample subsistence. —This is an American.

British America is divided into many provinces, forming a large association, scattered along a coast 1500 miles extent and about 200 wide. This society I would fain examine, at least such as it appears in the middle provinces; if it does not afford that variety of tinges and gradations which may be observed in Europe, we have colours peculiar to ourselves. For instance, it is natural to conceive that those who live near the sea, must be very different from those who live in the woods; the intermediate space will afford a separate and distinct class.

Men are like plants; the goodness and flavour of the fruit proceeds from the peculiar soil and exposition in which they grow. We are nothing but what we derive from the air we breathe, the climate we inhabit, the government we obey, the system of religion we profess, and the nature of our employment. Here you will find but few crimes; these have acquired as yet no root among us. I wish I were able to trace all my ideas; if my ignorance prevents me from describing them properly, I hope I shall be able to delineate a few of the outlines, which are all I propose.

Those who live near the sea, feed more on fish than on flesh, and often encounter that boisterous element. This renders them more bold and enterprising; this leads them to neglect the confined occupations of the land. They see and converse with a variety of people; their intercourse with mankind becomes extensive. The sea inspires them with a love of traffic, a desire of transporting produce from one place to another; and leads them to a variety of resources which supply the place of labour. Those who inhabit the middle settlements, by far the most numerous, must be very different; the simple cultivation of the earth purifies them, but the indulgences of the government, the soft remonstrances of religion, the rank of independent freeholders, must necessarily inspire them with sentiments, very little known in Europe among people of the same class. What do I say? Europe has no such class of men; the early knowledge they acquire, the early bargains they make, give them a great degree of sagacity. As freemen they will be litigious; pride and obstinacy are often the cause of law suits; the nature of our laws and governments may be another. As citizens it is easy to imagine, that they will carefully read the newspapers, enter into every political disquisition, freely blame or censure governors and others. As farmers they will be careful and anxious to get as much as they can, because what they get is their own. As northern men they will love the cheerful cup. As Christians, religion curbs them not in their opinions; the general indulgence leaves every one to think for themselves in spiritual matters; the laws inspect our actions, our thoughts are left to God. Industry, good living, selfishness, litigiousness, country politics, the pride of freemen, religious indifference, are their characteristics. If you recede still farther from the sea, you will come into more modern settlements; they exhibit the same strong lineaments, in a ruder appearance. Religion seems to have still less influence, and their manners are less improved.

Now we arrive near the great woods, near the last inhabited districts; there men seem to be placed still farther beyond the reach of government, which in some measure leaves them to themselves. How can it pervade every corner; as they were driven there by misfortunes, necessity of beginnings, desire of acquiring large tracks of land, idleness, frequent want of economy, ancient debts; the re-union of such people does not afford a very pleasing spectacle. When discord, want of unity and friendship; when either drunkenness or idleness prevail in such remote districts; contention, inactivity, and wretchedness must ensue. There are not the same remedies to these evils as in a long established community. The few magistrates they have, are in general little better than the rest; they are often in a perfect state of war; that of man against man, sometimes decided by blows, sometimes by means of the law; that of man against every wild inhabitant of these venerable woods, of which they are come to dispossess them. There men appear to be no better than carnivorous animals of a superior rank, living on the flesh of wild animals when they can catch them, and when they are not able, they subsist on grain. He who would wish to see America in its proper light, and have a true idea of its feeble beginnings and barbarous rudiments, must visit our extended line of frontiers where the last settlers dwell, and where he may see the first labours of settlement, the mode of clearing the earth, in all their different appearances; where men are wholly left dependent on their native tempers, and on the spur of uncertain industry, which often fails when not sanctified by the efficacy of a few moral rules. There, remote from the power of example, and check of shame, many families exhibit the most hideous parts of our society. They are a kind of forlorn hope, preceding by ten or twelve years the most respectable army of veterans which come after them. In that space, prosperity will polish some, vice and the law will drive off the rest, who uniting again with others like themselves will recede still farther; making room for more industrious people, who will finish their improvements, convert the loghouse into a convenient habitation, and rejoicing that the first heavy labours are finished, will change in a few years that hitherto barbarous country into a fine fertile, well regulated district. Such is our progress, such is the march of the Europeans toward the interior parts of this continent. In all societies there are off-casts; this impure part serves as our precursors or pioneers; my father himself was one of that class, but he came upon honest principles, and was therefore one of the few who held fast; by good conduct and temperance, he transmitted to me his fair inheritance, when not above one in fourteen of his contemporaries had the same good fortune.

Forty years ago this smiling country was thus inhabited; it is now purged, a general decency of manners prevails thoughout, and such has been the fate of our best countries.

Exclusive of those general characteristics, each province has its own, founded on the government, climate, mode of husbandry, customs, and peculiarity of circumstances. Europeans submit insensibly to these great powers, and become, in the course of a few generations, not only Americans in general, but either Pennsylvanians, Virginians, or provincials under some other name. Whoever traverses the continent must easily observe those strong differences, which will grow more evident in time. The inhabitants of Canada, Massachusetts, the middle provinces, the southern ones will be as different as their climates; their only points of unity will be those of religion and language. . . .

DESCRIPTION OF CHARLES-TOWN; THOUGHTS ON SLAVERY; ON PHYSICAL EVIL; A MELANCHOLY SCENE.

Charles-town is, in the north, what Lima is in the south; both are Capitals of the richest provinces of their respective hemispheres: you may therefore conjecture, that both cities must exhibit the appearances necessarily resulting from riches. Peru abounding in gold, Lima is filled with inhabitants who enjoy all those gradations of pleasure, refinement, and luxury, which proceed from wealth. Carolina produces commodities, more valuable perhaps than gold, because they are gained by greater industry; it exhibits also on our northern stage, a display of riches and luxury, inferior indeed to the former, but far superior to what are to be seen in our northern towns. Its situation is admirable, being built at the confluence of two large rivers, which receive in their course a great number of inferior streams; all navigable in the spring, for flat boats. Here the produce of this extensive territory concentres; here therefore is the seat of the most valuable exportation; their wharfs, their docks, their magazines, are extremely convenient to facilitate this great commercial business. The inhabitants are the gayest in America; it is called the centre of our beau monde, and it is always filled with the richest planters of the province, who resort hither in quest of health and pleasure. . . .

The three principal classes of inhabitants are, lawyers, planters, and merchants; this is the province which has afforded to the first the richest spoils, for nothing can exceed their wealth, their power, and their influence. They have reached the *ne plus ultra* of worldly felicity; no plantation is secured, no title is good, no will is valid, but what they dictate, regulate, and approve. The whole mass of provincial property is become tributary to this society; which, far above priests and bishops, disdain to be satisfied with the poor Mosaical portion of the tenth. I appeal to the many inhabitants, who, while contending perhaps for their right to a few hundred acres, have lost by the mazes of the law their whole patrimony. These men are more properly law givers than interpreters of the law; and have united here, as well as in most other provinces, the skill and dexterity of the scribe with the power and ambition of the prince: who can tell where this may lead in a future day? The nature of our laws, and the spirit of freedom, which often tends to make us litigious, must necessarily throw the greatest part of the property of the colonies into the hands of these gentlemen. In another century, the law will possess in the north, what now the church possesses in Peru and Mexico.

While all is joy, festivity, and happiness in Charles-Town, would you imagine that scenes of misery overspread in the country? Their ears by habit are become deaf, their hearts are hardened; they neither see, hear, nor feel for the woes of their poor slaves, from whose painful labours all their wealth proceeds. Here the horrors of slavery, the hardship of incessant toils, are unseen; and no one thinks with compassion of those showers of sweat and of tears which from the bodies of Africans, daily drop, and moisten the ground they till. The cracks of the whip urging these miserable beings to excessive labour, are far too distant from the gay Capital to be heard. The chosen race eat, drink, and live happy, while the unfortunate one grubs up the ground, raises indigo, or husks the rice; exposed to a sun full as scorching as their native one; without the support of good food, without the cordials of any chearing liquor. This great contrast has often afforded me subjects of the most afflicting meditation. On the one side, behold a people enjoying all that life affords most bewitching and pleasurable, without labour, without fatigue, hardly sub-jected to the trouble of wishing. With gold, dug from Peruvian mountains, they order vessels to the coasts of Guinea; by virtue of that gold, wars, murders, and devastations are committed in some harmless, peaceable African neighbourhood, where dwelt innocent people, who even knew not but that all men were black. The daughter torn from her weeping mother, the child from the wretched parents, the wife from the loving husband; whole families swept away and brought through storms and tempests to this rich metropolis! There, arranged like horses at a fair, they are branded like cattle, and then driven to toil, to starve, and to languish for a few years on the different plantations of these citizens. And for whom must they work? For persons they know not, and who have no other power over them than that of violence; no other right than what this accursed metal has given them! Strange order of things! Oh, Nature, where art thou?—Are not these blacks thy children as well as we? On the other side, nothing is to be seen but the most diffusive misery and wretchedness, unrelieved even in thought or wish! Day after day they drudge on without any prospect of ever reaping for themselves; they are obliged to devote their lives, their limbs, their will, and every vital ex-ertion to swell the wealth of masters; who look not upon them with half the kindness and affection with which they consider their dogs and horses. Kindness and affection are not the portion of those who till the earth, who carry the burdens, who convert the logs into useful boards. This reward, simple and natural as one would conceive it, would border on humanity; and planters must have none of it! . . .

. . . We certainly are not that class of beings which we vainly think ourselves to be; man an animal of prey, seems to have rapine and the love of bloodshed implanted in his heart; nay, to hold it the most hon-ourable occupation in society: we never speak of a hero of mathematics, a hero of knowledge of humanity; no, this illustrious appellation is re-served for the most successful butchers of the world. If Nature has given us a fruitful soil to inhabit, she has refused us such inclinations and propensities as would afford us the full enjoyment of it. Extensive as the surface of this planet is, not one half of it is yet cultivated, not half replenished; she created man, and placed him either in the woods or plains, and provided him with passions which must for ever oppose his happiness; every thing is submitted to the power of the strongest; men, like the elements, are always at war; the weakest yield to the most potent; force, subtilty, and malice, always triumph over unguarded honesty, and simplicity. Benignity, moderation, and justice, are virtues adapted only to the humble paths of life: we love to talk of virtue and to admire its beauty, while in the shade of solitude, and retirement; but when we step forth into active life, if it happen to be in competition with any passion or desire, do we observe it to prevail? Hence so many religious impostors have triumphed over the credulity of mankind, and have rendered their frauds the creeds of succeeding generations, during the course of many ages; until worne away by time, they have been replaced by new ones. Hence the most unjust war, if supported by the greatest force, always succeeds; hence the most just ones, when supported only by their justice, as often fail. Such is the ascendancy of power; the supreme arbiter of all the revolutions which we observe in this planet: so irresistible is power, that it often thwarts the tendency of the most forcible causes, and prevents their subsequent salutary effects, though ordained for the good of man by the Governor of the universe. Such is the perverseness of human nature; who can describe it in all its latitude?

In the moments of our philanthropy we often talk of an indulgent nature, a kind parent, who for the benefit of mankind has taken singular pains to vary the genera of plants, fruits, grain, and the different productions of the earth; and has spread peculiar blessings in each climate. This is undoubtedly an object of contemplation which calls forth our warmest gratitude; for so singularly benevolent have those parental intentions been, that where barrenness of soil or severity of climate prevail, there she has implanted in the heart of man, sentiments which overbalance every misery, and supply the place of every want. She has given to the inhabitants of these regions, an attachment to their savage rocks and wild shores, unknown to those who inhabit the fertile fields of the temperate zone. Yet if we attentively view this globe, will it not appear rather a place of punishment, than of delight? And what misfortune! that those punishments should fall on the innocent, and its few delights be enjoyed by the most unworthy. Famine, diseases, elementary convulsions, human feuds, dissensions, &c. are the produce of every climate; each climate produces besides, vices, and miseries peculiar to its latitude. View the frigid sterility of the north, whose famished inhabitants hardly acquainted with the sun, live and fare worse than the bears they hunt: and to which they are superior only in the faculty of speaking. View the arctic and antarctic regions, those huge voids, where nothing lives; regions of eternal snow: where winter in all his horrors has established his throne, and arrested every creative power of nature. Will you call the miserable stragglers in these countries by the name of men? Now contrast this frigid power of the north and south with that of the sun; examine the parched lands of the torrid zone, replete with sulphureous exhalations; view those countries of Asia subject to pestilential infections which lay nature waste; view this globe often convulsed both from within and without; pouring forth from several mouths, rivers of boiling matter, which are imperceptibly leaving immense subterranean graves, wherein millions will one day perish! Look at the poisonous soil of the equator, at those putrid slimy tracks, teeming with horrid monsters, the enemies of the human race; look next at the sandy continent, scorched perhaps by the fatal approach of some ancient comet, now the abode of desolation. Examine the rains,the convulsive storms of those climates, where masses of sulphur, bitumen, and electrical fire, combining their dreadful powers, are incessantly hovering and bursting over a globe threatened with dissolution. On this little shell, how very few are the spots where man can live and flourish? even under those mild climates which seem to breathe peace and happiness, the poison of slavery, the fury of despotism, and the rage of superstition, are all combined against man! There only the few live and rule, whilst the many starve and utter ineffectual complaints: there, human nature appears more debased, perhaps than in the less favoured climates. The fertile plains of Asia, the rich low lands of Egypt and of Diarbeck, the fruitful fields bordering on the Tigris and the Euphrates, the extensive country of the East-Indies in all its separate districts; all these must to the geographical eye, seem as if intended for terrestrial paradises: but though surrounded with the spontaneous riches of nature though her kindest favours seem to be shed on those beautiful regions with the most profuse hand; yet there in general we find the most wretched people in the world. Almost every where, liberty so natural to mankind, is refused, or rather enjoyed but by their tyrants; the word slave, is the appellation of every rank, who adore as a divinity, a being worse than themselves; subject to every caprice, and to every lawless rage which unrestrained power can give. Tears are shed, perpetual groans are heard, where only the accents of peace, alacrity, and gratitude should resound. There the very delirium of tyranny tramples on the best gifts of nature, and sports with the fate, the happiness, the lives of millions: there the extreme fertility of the ground always indicates the extreme misery of the inhabitants!

Every where one part of the human species are taught the art of shedding the blood of the other; of setting fire to their dwellings; of levelling the works of their industry: half of the existence of nations regularly employed in destroying other nations. What little political felicity is to be met with here and there, has cost oceans of blood to purchase; as if good was never to be the portion of unhappy man. Republics, kingdoms, monarchies, founded either on fraud or successful violence, increase by pursuing the steps of the same policy, until they are destroyed in their turn, either by the influence of their own crimes, or by more successful but equally criminal enemies.

If from this general review of human nature, we descend to the examination of what is called civilized society; there the combination of every natural and artifical want, makes us pay very dear for what little share of political felicity we enjoy. It is a strange heterogeneous assem-

blage of vices and virtues, and of a variety of other principles, for ever
at war, for ever jarring, for ever producing some dangerous, some dis-
tressing extreme. Where do you conceive then that nature intended we
should be happy? Would you prefer the state of men in the woods, to
that of men in a more improved situation? Evil preponderates in both;
in the first they often eat each other for want of food, and in the other
they often starve each other for want of room. For my part, I think the
vices and miseries to be found in the latter, exceed those of the former;
in which real evil is more scarce, more supportable, and less enormous.
Yet we wish to see the earth peopled; to accomplish the happiness of
kingdoms, which is said to consist in numbers. Gracious God! to what
end is the introduction of so many beings into a mode of existence in
which they must grope amidst as many errors, commit as many crimes,
and meet with as many diseases, wants, and sufferings!

The following scene will I hope account for these melancholy reflections, and apologize for the gloomy thoughts with which I have filled this
letter: my mind is, and always has been, oppressed since I became a
witness to it. I was not long since invited to dine with a planter who lived
three miles from ———, where he then resided. In order to avoid the
heat of the sun, I resolved to go on foot, sheltered in a small path, leading
through a pleasant wood. I was leisurely travelling along, attentively
examining some peculiar plants which I had collected, when all at once
I felt the air strongly agitated; though the day was perfectly calm and
sultry. I immediately cast my eyes toward the cleared ground, from which
I was but at a small distance, in order to see whether it was not occasioned
by a sudden shower; when at that instant a sound resembling a deep
rough voice, uttered, as I thought, a few inarticulate monosyllables. Alarmed
and surprized, I precipitately looked all round, when I perceived at about
six rods distance something resembling a cage, suspended to the limbs
of a tree; all the branches of which appeared covered with large birds of
prey, fluttering about, and anxiously endeavouring to perch on the cage.
Actuated by an involuntary motion of my hands, more than by any design
of my mind, I fired at them; they all flew to a short distance, with a most
hideous noise: when, horrid to think and painful to repeat, I perceived
a negro, suspended in the cage, and left there to expire! I shudder when
I recollect that the birds had already picked out his eyes, his cheek bones
were bare; his arms had been attacked in several places, and his body
seemed covered with a multitude of wounds. From the edges of the hollow
sockets and from the lacerations with which he was disfigured, the blood
slowly dropped, and tinged the ground beneath. No sooner were the
birds flown, than swarms of insects covered the whole body of this unfortunate wretch, eager to feed on his mangled flesh and to drink his blood.
I found myself suddenly arrested by the power of affright and terror; my

nerves were convulsed; I trembled, I stood motionless, involuntarily contemplating the fate of this negro, in all its dismal latitude. The living
spectre, though deprived of his eyes, could still distinctly hear, and in
his uncouth dialect begged me to give him some water to allay his thirst.
Humanity herself would have recoiled back with horror; she would have
balanced whether to lessen such reliefless distress, or mercifully with one
blow to end this dreadful scene of agonizing torture! Had I had a ball in
my gun, I certainly should have despatched him; but finding myself unable
to perform so kind an office, I sought, though trembling, to relieve him
as well as I could. A shell ready fixed to a pole, which had been used by
some negroes, presented itself to me; filled it with water, and with trembling hands I guided it to the quivering lips of the wretched sufferer.
Urged by the irresistible power of thirst, he endeavoured to meet it, as
he instinctively guessed its approach by the noise it made in passing
through the bars of the cage. "Tankè, you whitè man, tankè you, putè
somè poison and givè me." How long have you been hanging there? I
asked him. "Two days, and me no die; the birds, the birds; aaah me!"
Oppressed with the reflections which this shocking spectacle afforded
me, I mustered strength enough to walk away, and soon reached the
house at which I intended to dine. There I heard that the reason for this
slave being thus punished, was on account of his having killed the overseer
of the plantation. They told me that the laws of self-preservation rendered
such executions necessary; and supported the doctrine of slavery with the
arguments generally made use of to justify the practice; with the repetition
of which I shall not trouble you at present.

Nathaniel Hawthorne
Earth's Holocaust
(1844)

ONCE UPON a time—but whether in time past or time to come, is a matter of little or no moment—this wide world had become so overburthened with an accumulation of worn-out trumpery, that the inhabitants determined to rid themselves of it by a general bonfire. The site fixed upon, at the representation of the Insurance Companies, and as being as central a spot as any other on the globe, was one of the broadest prairies of the West, where no human habitation would be endangered by the flames, and where a vast assemblage of spectators might commodiously admire the show. Having a taste for sights of this kind, and imagining, likewise, that the illumination of the bonfire might reveal some profundity of moral truth, heretofore hidden in mist or darkness, I made it convenient to journey thither and be present. At my arrival, although the heap of condemned rubbish was as yet comparatively small, the torch had already been applied. Amid that boundless plain, in the dusk of evening, like a far-off star alone in the firmament, there was merely visible one tremulous gleam, whence none could have anticipated so fierce a blaze as was destined to ensue. With every moment, however, there came foot-travellers, women holding up their aprons, men on horseback, wheelbarrows, lumbering baggage-wagons, and other vehicles great and small, and from far and near, laden with articles that were judged fit for nothing but to be burnt.

"What materials have been used to kindle the flames?" inquired I of a bystander; for I was desirous of knowing the whole process of the affair, from beginning to end.

The person whom I addressed was a grave man, fifty years old or thereabout, who had evidently come thither as a looker-on; he struck me immediately as having weighed for himself the true value of life and its

[Originally published in *Graham's Magazine* (May 1844).]

circumstances, and therefore as feeling little personal interest in whatever judgment the world might form of them. Before answering my question, he looked me in the face, by the kindling light of the fire.

"Oh, some very dry combustibles," replied he, "and extremely suitable to the purpose—no other, in fact, than yesterday's newspapers, last month's magazines, and last year's withered leaves. Here, now, comes some antiquated trash, that will take fire like a handfull of shavings."

As he spoke, some rough-looking men advanced to the verge of the bonfire, and threw in, as it appeared, all the rubbish of the Herald's Office; the blazonry of coat-armor; the crests and devices of illustrious families; pedigrees that extended back, like lines of light, into the mist of the dark ages; together with stars, garters, and embroidered collars; each of which, as paltry a bauble as it might appear to the uninstructed eye, had once possessed vast significance, and was still, in truth, reckoned among the most precious of moral or material facts, by the worshippers of the gorgeous past. Mingled with this confused heap, which was tossed into the flames by armsfull at once, were innumerable badges of knighthood; comprising those of all the European sovereignties, and Napoleon's decoration of the Legion of Honor, the ribands of which were entangled with those of the ancient order of St. Louis. There, too, were the medals of our own society of Cincinnati, by means of which, as history tells us, an order of hereditary knights came near being constituted out of the king-quellers of the Revolution. And, besides, there were the patents of nobility of German counts and barons, Spanish grandees, and English peers, from the worm-eaten instrument signed by William the Conqueror, down to the bran-new parchment of the latest lord, who has received his honors from the fair hand of Victoria.

At sight of the dense volumes of smoke, mingled with vivid jets of flame, that gushed and eddied forth from this immense pile of earthly distinctions, the multitude of plebeian spectators set up a joyous shout, and clapt their hands with an emphasis that made the welkin echo. That was their moment of triumph, achieved after long ages, over creatures of the same clay and same spiritual infirmities, who had dared to assume the privileges due only to Heaven's better workmanship. But now there rushed towards the blazing heap a gray-haired man, of stately presence, wearing a coat from the breast of which some star, or other badge of rank, seemed to have been forcibly wrenched away. He had not the tokens of intellectual power in his face; but still there was the demeanor—the habitual, and almost native dignity—of one who had been born to the idea of his own social superiority, and had never felt it questioned, till that moment.

"People," cried he, gazing at the ruin of what was dearest in his eyes, with grief and wonder, but, nevertheless, with a degree of stateliness—

"people, what have you done! This fire is consuming all that marked your advance from barbarism, or that could have prevented your relapse thither. We—the men of the privileged orders—were those who kept alive, from age to age, the old chivalrous spirit; the gentle and generous thought; the higher, the purer, the more refined and delicate life! With the nobles, too, you cast off the poet, the painter, the sculptor—all the beautiful arts;—for we were their patrons, and created the atmosphere in which they flourish. In abolishing the majestic distinctions of rank, society loses not only its grace, but its steadfastness—"

More he would doubtless have spoken; but here there arose an outcry, sportive, contemptuous, and indignant, that altogether drowned the appeal of the fallen nobleman; insomuch that, casting one look of despair at his own half-burnt pedigree, he shrunk back into the crowd, glad to shelter himself under his new-found insignificance.

"Let him thank his stars that we have not flung him into the same fire!" shouted a rude figure, spurning the embers with his foot. "And, henceforth, let no man dare to show a piece of musty parchment, as his warrant for lording it over his fellows! If he have strength of arm, well and good; it is one species of superiority. If he have wit, wisdom, courage, force of character, let these attributes do for him what they may. But, from this day forward, no mortal must hope for place and consideration, by reckoning up the mouldy bones of his ancestors! That nonsense is done away."

"And in good time," remarked the grave observer by my side—in a low voice however—"if no worse nonsense come in its place. But at all events, this species of nonsense has fairly lived out its life."

There was little space to muse or moralize over the embers of this time-honored rubbish; for, before it was half burnt out, there came another multitude from beyond the sea, bearing the purple robes of royalty, and the crowns, globes, and sceptres of emperors and kings. All these had been condemned as useless baubles; playthings, at best, fit only for the infancy of the world, or rods to govern and chastise it in its nonage; but with which universal manhood, at its full-grown stature, could no longer brook to be insulted. Into such contempt had these regal insignia now fallen, that the gilded crown and tinselled robes of the player-king, from Drury Lane Theatre, had been thrown in among the rest, doubtless as a mockery of his brother-monarchs, on the great stage of the world. It was a strange sight, to discern the crown-jewels of England, glowing and flashing in the midst of the fire. Some of them had been delivered down from the times of the Saxon princes; others were purchased with vast revenues, or, perchance, ravished from the dead brows of the native potentates of Hindostan; and the whole now blazed with a dazzling lustre, as if a star had fallen in that spot, and been shattered into fragments. The

splendor of the ruined monarchy had no reflection, save in those inestimable precious-stones. But, enough on this subject! It were but tedious
to describe how the Emperor of Austria's mantle was converted to tinder,
and how the posts and pillars of the French throne became a heap of
coals, which it was impossible to distinguish from those of any other wood.
Let me add, however, that I noticed one of the exiled Poles, stirring up
the bonfire with the Czar of Russia's sceptre, which he afterwards flung
into the flames.

"The smell of singed garments is quite intolerable here," observed my
new acquaintance, as the breeze enveloped us in the smoke of a royal
wardrobe. "Let us get to windward, and see what they are doing on the
other side of the bonfire."

We accordingly passed round, and were just in time to witness the
arrival of a vast procession of Washingtonians—as the votaries of temperance call themselves now-a-days—accompanied by thousands of the
Irish disciples of Father Mathew, with that great apostle at their head.
They brought a rich contribution to the bonfire; being nothing less than
all the hogsheads and barrels of liquor in the world, which they rolled
before them across the prairie.

"Now, my children," cried Father Mathew, when they reached the
verge of the fire—"one shove more, and the work is done! And now let
us stand off, and see Satan deal with his own liquor!"

Accordingly, having placed their wooden vessels within reach of the
flames, the procession stood off at a safe distance, and soon beheld them
burst into a blaze that reached the clouds, and threatened to set the sky
itself on fire. And well it might. For here was the whole world's stock of
spirituous liquors, which, instead of kindling a frenzied light in the eyes
of individual topers as of yore, soared upward with a bewildering gleam
that startled all mankind. It was the aggregate of that fierce fire, which
would otherwise have scorched the hearts of millions. Meantime, numberless bottles of precious wine were flung into the blaze; which lapped
up the contents as if it loved them, and grew, like other drunkards, the
merrier and fiercer for what it quaffed. Never again will the insatiable
thirst of the fire-fiend be so pampered! Here were the treasures of famous
bon-vivants—liquors that had been tossed on ocean, and mellowed in the
sun, and hoarded long in the recesses of the earth—the pale, the gold,
the ruddy juice of whatever vineyards were most delicate—the entire
vintage of Tokay—all mingling in one stream with the vile fluids of the
common pot-house, and contributing to heighten the self-same blaze.
And while it rose in a gigantic spire, that seemed to wave against the
arch of the firmament, and combine itself with the light of stars, the
multitude gave a shout, as if the broad earth were exulting in its deliv-
erance from the curse of ages.

But the joy was not universal. Many deemed that human life would be gloomier than ever, when that brief illumination should sink down. While the reformers were at work, I had overheard muttered expostulations from several respectable gentlemen with red noses, and wearing gouty shoes; and a ragged worthy, whose face looked like a hearth where the fire is burnt out, now expressed his discontent more openly and boldly.

"What is this world good for," said the Last Toper, "now that we can never be jolly any more? What is to comfort the poor man in sorrow and perplexity?—how is he to keep his heart warm against the cold winds of this cheerless earth?—and what do you propose to give him, in exchange for the solace that you take away? How are old friends to sit together by the fireside, without a cheerful glass between them? A plague upon your reformation! It is a sad world, a cold world, a selfish world, a low world, not worth an honest fellow's living in, now that good-fellowship is gone forever!"

This harangue excited great mirth among the bystanders. But, preposterous as was the sentiment, I could not help commiserating the forlorn condition of the Last Toper, whose boon-companions had dwindled away from his side, leaving the poor fellow without a soul to countenance him in sipping his liquor, nor, indeed, any liquor to sip. Not that this was quite the true state of the case; for I had observed him, at a critical moment, filch a bottle of fourth-proof brandy that fell beside the bonfire, and hide it in his pocket.

The spirituous and fermented liquors being thus disposed of, the zeal of the reformers next induced them to replenish the fire with all the boxes of tea and bags of coffee in the world. And now came the planters of Virginia, bringing their crops of tobacco. These, being cast upon the heap of inutility, aggregated it to the size of a mountain, and incensed the atmosphere with such potent fragrance, that methought we should never draw pure breath again. The present sacrifice seemed to startle the lovers of the weed, more than any that they had hitherto witnessed.

"Well;—they've put my pipe out," said an old gentleman, flinging it into the flames in a pet. "What is this world coming to? Everything rich and racy—all the spice of life—is to be condemned as useless. Now that they have kindled the bonfire, if these nonsensical reformers would fling themselves into it, all would be well enough!"

"Be patient," responded a staunch conservative;—"it will come to that in the end. They will first fling us in, and finally themselves."

From the general and systematic measures of reform, I now turned to consider the individual contributions to this memorable bonfire. In many instances, these were of a very amusing character. One poor fellow threw in his empty purse, and another, a bundle of counterfeit or insolvable bank-notes. Fashionable ladies threw in their last season's bonnets, to-

gether with heaps of ribbon, yellow lace, and much other half-worn mil-
liner's ware; all of which proved even more evanescent in the fire, than
it had been in the fashion. A multitude of lovers, of both sexes—discarded
maids or bachelors, and couples, mutually weary of one another—tossed
in bundles of perfumed letters and enamored sonnets. A hack-politician,
being deprived of bread by the loss of office, threw in his teeth, which
happened to be false ones. The Rev. Sydney Smith—having voyaged
across the Atlantic for that sole purpose—came up to the bonfire, with a
bitter grin, and threw in certain repudiated bonds, fortified though they
were with the broad seal of a sovereign state. A little boy of five years
old, in the premature manliness of the present epoch, threw in his playthings; a college-graduate, his diploma; an apothecary, ruined by the
spread of homœopathy, his whole stock of drugs and medicines; a physician, his library; a parson, his old sermons; and a fine gentleman of the
old school, his code of manners, which he had formerly written down for
the benefit of the next generation. A widow, resolving on a second marriage, slyly threw in her dead husband's miniature. A young man, jilted
by his mistress, would willingly have flung his own desperate heart into
the flames, but could find no means to wrench it out of his bosom. An
American author, whose works were neglected by the public, threw his
pen and paper into the bonfire, and betook himself to some less discouraging occupation. It somewhat startled me to overhear a number of
ladies, highly respectable in appearance, proposing to fling their gowns
and petticoats into the flames, and assume the garb, together with the
manners, duties, offices, and responsibilities, of the opposite sex.

What favor was accorded to this scheme, I am unable to say; my
attention being suddenly drawn to a poor, deceived, and half-delirious
girl, who, exclaiming that she was the most worthless thing alive or dead,
attempted to cast herself into the fire, amid all that wrecked and broken
trumpery of the world. A good man, however, ran to her rescue.

"Patience, my poor girl!" said he, as he drew her back from the fierce
embrace of the destroying angel. "Be patient, and abide Heaven's will.
So long as you possess a living soul, all may be restored to its first freshness. These things of matter, and creations of human fantasy, are fit for
nothing but to be burnt, where once they have had their day. But your
day is Eternity!"

"Yes," said the wretched girl, whose frenzy seemed now to have sunk
down into deep despondence;—"yes; and the sunshine is blotted out of
it!"

It was now rumored among the spectators, that all the weapons and
munitions of war were to be thrown into the bonfire; with the exception
of the world's stock of gunpowder, which, as the safest mode of disposing
of it, had already been drowned in the sea. This intelligence seemed to

awaken great diversity of opinion. The hopeful philanthropist esteemed it a token that the millennium was already come; while persons of another stamp, in whose view mankind was a breed of bull-dogs, prophesied that all the old stoutness, fervor, nobleness, generosity, and magnanimity of the race, would disappear; these qualities, as they affirmed, requiring blood for their nourishment. They comforted themselves, however, in the belief that the proposed abolition of war was impracticable, for any length of time together.

Be that as it might, numberless great guns, whose thunder had long been the voice of battle—the artillery of the Armada, the battering-trains of Marlborough, and the adverse cannon of Napoleon and Wellington— were trundled into the midst of the fire. By the continual addition of dry combustibles, it had now waxed so intense, that neither brass nor iron could withstand it. It was wonderful to behold, how those terrible instruments of slaughter melted away like playthings of wax. Then the armies of the earth wheeled around the mighty furnace, with their military music playing triumphant marches, and flung in their muskets and swords. The standard-bearers, likewise, cast one look upward at their banners, all tattered with shot-holes, and inscribed with the names of victorious fields; and giving them a last flourish on the breeze, they lowered them into the flame, which snatched them upward in its rush towards the clouds. This ceremony being over, the world was left without a single weapon in its hands, except, possibly, a few old King's arms and rusty swords, and other trophies of the Revolution, in some of our state-armories. And now the drums were beaten and the trumpets brayed all together, as a prelude to the proclamation of universal and eternal peace, and the announcement that glory was no longer to be won by blood; but that it would henceforth be the contention of the human race, to work out the greatest mutual good; and that beneficence, in the future annals of the earth, would claim the praise of valor. The blessed tidings were accordingly promulgated, and caused infinite rejoicings among those who had stood aghast at the horror and absurdity of war.

But I saw a grim smile pass over the scarred visage of a stately old commander—by his war-worn figure and rich military dress, he might have been one of Napoleon's famous marshals—who, with the rest of the world's soldiery, had just flung away the sword, that had been familiar to his right hand for half-a-century.

"Aye, aye!" grumbled he. "Let them proclaim what they please; but, in the end, we shall find that all this foolery has only made more work for the armorers and cannon-founderies."

"Why, Sir," exclaimed I, in astonishment, "do you imagine that the human race will ever so far return on the steps of its past madness, as to weld another sword, or cast another cannon?"

"There will be no need," observed, with a sneer, one who neither felt benevolence, nor had faith in it. "When Cain wished to slay his brother, he was at no loss for a weapon."

"We shall see," replied the veteran commander.—"If I am mistaken, so much the better; but, in my opinion—without pretending to philosophize about the matter—the necessity of war lies far deeper than these honest gentlemen suppose. What! Is there a field for all the petty disputes of individuals, and shall there be no great law-court for the settlement of national difficulties? The battle-field is the only court where such suits can be tried!"

"You forget, General," rejoined I, "that, in this advanced stage of civilization, Reason and Philanthropy combined will constitute just such a tribunal as is requisite."

"Ah, I had forgotten that, indeed!" said the old warrior, as he limped away.

The fire was now to be replenished with materials that had hitherto been considered of even greater importance to the well-being of society, than the warlike munitions which we had already seen consumed. A body of reformers had travelled all over the earth, in quest of the machinery by which the different nations were accustomed to inflict the punishment of death. A shudder passed through the multitude, as these ghastly emblems were dragged forward. Even the flames seemed at first to shrink away, displaying the shape and murderous contrivance of each in a full blaze of light, which, of itself, was sufficient to convince mankind of the long and deadly error of human law. Those old implements of cruelty—those horrible monsters of mechanism—those inventions which it seemed to demand something worse than man's natural heart to contrive, and which had lurked in the dusky nooks of ancient prisons, the subject of terror-stricken legends—were now brought forth to view. Headsmen's axes, with the rust of noble and royal blood upon them, and a vast collection of halters that had choked the breath of plebeian victims, were thrown in together. A shout greeted the arrival of the guillotine, which was thrust forward on the same wheels that had borne it from one to another of the blood-stained streets of Paris. But the loudest roar of applause went up, telling the distant sky of the triumph of the earth's redemption, when the gallows made its appearance. An ill-looking fellow, however, rushed forward, and putting himself in the path of the reformers, bellowed hoarsely, and fought with brute fury to stay their progress.

It was little matter of surprise, perhaps, that the executioner should thus do his best to vindicate and uphold the machinery by which he himself had his livelihood, and worthier individuals their death. But it deserved special note, that men of a far different sphere—even of that consecrated class in whose guardianship the world is apt to trust its benevolence—were found to take the hangman's view of the question.

"Stay, my brethren!" cried one of them. "You are misled by a false philanthropy!—you know not what you do. The gallows is a heaven-oriented instrument! Bear it back, then, reverently, and set it up in its old place; else the world will fall to speedy ruin and desolation!"

"Onward, onward!" shouted a leader in the reform. "Into the flames with the accursed instrument of man's bloody policy! How can human law inculcate benevolence and love, while it persists in setting up the gallows as its chief symbol? One heave more, good friends; and the world will be redeemed from its greatest error!"

A thousand hands, that, nevertheless, loathed the touch, now lent their assistance, and thrust the ominous burthen far, far, into the centre of the raging furnace. There its fatal and abhorred image was beheld, first black, then a red coal, then ashes.

"That was well done!" exclaimed I.

"Yes; it was well done," replied—but with less enthusiasm than I expected—the thoughtful observer who was still at my side; "well done, if the world be good enough for the measure. Death, however, is an idea that cannot easily be dispensed with, in any condition between the primal innocence and that other purity and perfection, which, perchance, we are destined to attain, after travelling round the full circle. But, at all events, it is well that the experiment should now be tried."

"Too cold!—too cold!" impatiently exclaimed the young and ardent leader in this triumph. "Let the heart have its voice here, as well as the intellect. And as for ripeness—and as for progress—let mankind always do the highest, kindest, noblest thing, that, at any given period, it has attained to the perception of; and surely that thing cannot be wrong, nor wrongly timed!"

I know not whether it were the excitement of the scene, or whether the good people around the bonfire were really growing more enlightened, every instant; but they now proceeded to measures, in the full length of which I was hardly prepared to keep them company. For instance, some threw their marriage-certificates into the flames, and declared themselves candidates for a higher, holier, and more comprehensive union than that which had subsisted from the birth of time, under the form of the connubial tie. Others hastened to the vaults of banks, and to the coffers of the rich—all of which were open to the first-comer, on this fated occasion—and brought entire bales of paper-money to enliven the blaze, and tons of coin to be melted down by its intensity. Henceforth, they said, universal benevolence, uncoined and exhaustless, was to be the golden currency of the world. At this intelligence, the bankers, and speculators in the stocks, grew pale; and a pick-pocket, who had reaped a rich harvest among the crowd, fell down in a deadly fainting-fit. A few men of business burnt their day-books and ledgers, the notes and obligations of their creditors, and all other evidences of debts due to themselves; while perhaps a somewhat larger number satisfied their zeal for reform with the sacrifice of any uncomfortable recollection of their own indebtment. There was then a cry, that the period was arrived, when the title-deeds of landed property should be given to the flames, and the whole soil of the earth revert to the public, from whom it had been wrongfully abstracted, and most unequally distributed among individuals. Another party demanded, that all written constitutions, set forms of government, legislative acts, statute-books, and everything else on which human invention had endeavored to stamp its arbitrary laws, should at once be destroyed, leaving the consummated world as free as the man first created.

Whether any ultimate action was taken with regard to these propositions, is beyond my knowledge; for, just then, some matters were in progress that concerned my sympathies more nearly.

"See!—see!—what heaps of books and pamphlets," cried a fellow, who did not seem to be a lover of literature. "Now we shall have a glorious blaze!"

"That's just the thing," said a modern philosopher. "Now we shall get rid of the weight of dead men's thought, which has hitherto pressed so heavily on the living intellect, that it has been incompetent to any effectual self-exertion. Well done, my lads! Into the fire with them! Now you are enlightening the world, indeed!"

"But what is to become of the Trade?" cried a frantic bookseller.

"Oh, by all means, let them accompany their merchandise," coolly observed an author. "It will be a noble funeral-pile!"

The truth was, that the human race had now reached a stage of progress, so far beyond what the wisest and wittiest men of former ages had ever dreamed of, that it would have been a manifest absurdity to allow the earth to be any longer encumbered with their poor achievements in the literary line. Accordingly, a thorough and searching investigation had swept the booksellers' shops, hawkers' stands, public and private libraries, and even the little book-shelf by the country fireside, and had brought the world's entire mass of printed paper, bound or in sheets, to swell the already mountain-bulk of our illustrious bonfire. Thick, heavy folios, containing the labors of lexicographers, commentators, and encyclopediasts, were flung in, and, falling among the embers with a leaden thump, smouldered away to ashes, like rotten wood. The small, richly-gilt, French tomes, of the last age, with the hundred volumes of Voltaire among them, went off in a brilliant shower of sparkles, and little jets of flame; while the current literature of the same nation burnt red and blue, and threw an infernal light over the visages of the spectators, converting them all to the aspect of parti-colored fiends. A collection of German stories emitted a scent of brimstone. The English standard authors made excellent fuel, generally exhibiting the properties of sound oak logs. Milton's works, in particular, sent up a powerful blaze, gradually reddening into a coal, which promised to endure longer than almost any other material of the pile. From Shakspeare there gushed a flame of such marvellous splendor, that men shaded their eyes as against the sun's meridian glory; nor, even when the works of his own elucidators were flung upon him, did he cease to flash forth a dazzling radiance, from beneath the ponderous heap. It is my belief, that he is still blazing as fervidly as ever.

"Could a poet but light a lamp at that glorious flame," remarked I, "he might then consume the midnight oil to some good purpose."

"That is the very thing which modern poets have been too apt to do— or, at least, to attempt," answered a critic. "The chief benefit to be expected from this conflagration of past literature, undoubtedly is, that writers will henceforth be compelled to light their lamps at the sun or stars."

"If they can reach so high," said I. "But that task requires a giant, who may afterwards distribute the light among inferior men. It is not every one that can steal the fire from Heaven, like Prometheus; but when once he had done the deed, a thousand hearths were kindled by it."

It amazed me much to observe, how indefinite was the proportion between the physical mass of any given author, and the property of brilliant and long-continued combustion. For instance, there was not a quarto volume of the last century—nor, indeed, of the present—that could compete, in that particular, with a child's little gilt-covered book, containing Mother Goose's Melodies. The Life and Death of Tom Thumb outlasted the biography of Marlborough. An epic—indeed, a dozen of them—was converted to white ashes, before the single sheet of an old ballad was half-consumed. In more than one case, too, when volumes of applauded verse proved incapable of anything better than a stifling smoke, an unregarded ditty of some nameless bard—perchance, in the corner of a newspaper—soared up among the stars, with a flame as brilliant as their own. Speaking of the properties of flame, methought Shelley's poetry emitted a purer light than almost any other productions of his day; contrasting beautifully with the fitful and lurid gleams, and gushes of black vapor, that flashed and eddied from the volumes of Lord Byron. As for Tom Moore, some of his songs diffused an odor like a burning pastille.

I felt particular interest in watching the combustion of American authors, and scrupulously noted, by my watch, the precise number of moments that changed most of them from shabbily-printed books to indistinguishable ashes. It would be invidious, however, if not perilous, to betray these awful secrets; so that I shall content myself with observing, that it was not invariably the writer most frequent in the public mouth, that made the most splendid appearance in the bonfire. I especially remember, that a great deal of excellent inflammability was exhibited in a thin volume of poems by Ellery Channing; although, to speak the truth, there were certain portions that hissed and spluttered in a very disagreeable fashion. A curious phenomenon occurred, in reference to several writers, native as well as foreign. Their books, though of highly respectable figure, instead of bursting into a blaze, or even smouldering out their substance in smoke, suddenly melted away, in a manner that proved them to be ice.

If it be no lack of modesty to mention my own works, it must here be confessed, that I looked for them with fatherly interest, but in vain. Too probably, they were changed to vapor by the first action of the heat; at best, I can only hope, that, in their quiet way, they contributed a glimmering spark or two to the splendor of the evening.

"Alas, and woe is me!" thus bemoaned himself a heavy-looking gentleman in green spectacles. "The world is utterly ruined, and there is nothing to live for any longer! The business of my life is snatched from me. Not a volume to be had for love or money!"

"This," remarked the sedate observer beside me, "is a book-worm—one of those men who are born to gnaw dead thoughts. His clothes, you see, are covered with the dust of libraries. He has no inward fountain of ideas; and, in good earnest, now that the old stock is abolished, I do not see what is to become of the poor fellow. Have you no word of comfort for him?"

"My dear Sir," said I to the desperate book-worm, "is not Nature better than a book?—is not the human heart deeper than any system of philosophy?—is not life replete with more instruction than past observers have found it possible to write down in maxims? Be of good cheer! The great book of Time is still spread wide open before us; and, if we read it aright, it will be to us a volume of eternal Truth."

"Oh, my books, my books, my precious, printed books!" reiterated the forlorn book-worm. "My only reality was a bound volume; and now they will not leave me even a shadowy pamphlet!"

In fact, the last remnant of the literature of all the ages was now descending upon the blazing heap, in the shape of a cloud of pamphlets from the press of the New World. These, likewise, were consumed in the twinkling of an eye, leaving the earth, for the first time since the days of Cadmus, free from the plague of letters—an enviable field for the authors of the next generation!

"Well—and does anything remain to be done?" inquired I, somewhat anxiously. "Unless we set fire to the earth itself, and then leap boldly off into infinite space, I know not that we can carry reform to any further point."

"You are vastly mistaken, my good friend," said the observer. "Believe me, the fire will not be allowed to settle down, without the addition of fuel that will startle many persons, who have lent a willing hand thus far."

Nevertheless, there appeared to be a relaxation of effort, for a little time, during which, probably, the leaders of the movement were considering what should be done next. In the interval, a philosopher threw his theory into the flames; a sacrifice, which, by those who knew how to estimate it, was pronounced the most remarkable that had yet been made. The combustion, however, was by no means brilliant. Some indefatigable people, scorning to take a moment's ease, now employed themselves in collecting all the withered leaves and fallen boughs of the forest, and thereby recruited the bonfire to a greater height than ever. But this was mere by-play.

"Here comes the fresh fuel that I spoke of," said my companion.

To my astonishment, the persons who now advanced into the vacant space, around the mountain of fire, bore surplices and other priestly garments, mitres, crosiers, and a confusion of popish and protestant emblems, with which it seemed their purpose to consummate this great Act of Faith. Crosses, from the spires of old cathedrals, were cast upon the heap, with as little remorse as if the reverence of centuries, passing in long array beneath the lofty towers, had not looked up to them as the holiest of symbols. The font, in which infants were consecrated to God; the sacramental vessels, whence Piety had received the hallowed draught; were given to the same destruction. Perhaps it most nearly touched my heart, to see, among these devoted relics, fragments of the humble communion-tables and undecorated pulpits, which I recognized as having been torn from the meeting-houses of New-England. Those simple edifices might have been permitted to retain all of sacred embellishment that their Puritan founders had bestowed, even though the mighty structure of St. Peter's had sent its spoils to the fire of this terrible sacrifice. Yet I felt that these were but the externals of religion, and might most safely be relinquished by spirits that best knew their deep significance.

"All is well," said I, cheerfully. "The wood-paths shall be the aisles of our cathedral—the firmament itself shall be its ceiling! What needs an earthly roof between the Deity and his worshipper? Our faith can well afford to lose all the drapery that even the holiest men have thrown around it, and be only the more sublime in its simplicity."

"True," said my companion. "But will they pause here?"

The doubt, implied in his question, was well-founded. In the general destruction of books, already described, a holy volume—that stood apart from the catalogue of human literature, and yet, in one sense, was at its head—had been spared. But the Titan of innovation—angel or fiend, double in his nature, and capable of deeds befitting both characters—at first shaking down only the old and rotten shapes of things, had now, as it appeared, laid his terrible hand upon the main pillars, which supported the whole edifice of our moral and spiritual state. The inhabitants of the earth had grown too enlightened to define their faith within a form of words, or to limit the spiritual by any analogy to our material existence. Truths, which the Heavens trembled at, were now but a fable of the world's infancy. Therefore, as the final sacrifice of human eror, what else remained, to be thrown upon the embers of that awful pile, except the Book, which, though a celestial revelation to past ages, was but a voice from a lower sphere, as regarded the present race of man? It was done! Upon the blazing heap of falsehood and worn-out truth—things that the earth had never needed, or had ceased to need, or had grown childishly weary of—fell the ponderous church-Bible, the great old volume, that had lain so long on the cushions of the pulpit, and whence the pastor's solemn voice had given holy utterances, on so many a Sabbath-day. There, likewise, fell the family-Bible, which the long-buried patriarch had read to his children—in prosperity or sorrow, by the fireside, and in the summer-shade of trees—and had bequeathed downward, as the heirloom of generations. There fell the bosom-Bible, the little volume that had been the soul's friend of some sorely tried Child of Dust, who thence took courage, whether his trial were for life or death, steadfastly confronting both, in the strong assurance of Immortality.

All these were flung into the fierce and riotous blaze; and then a mighty wind came roaring across the plain, with a desolate howl, as if it were the angry lamentation of the Earth for the loss of Heaven's sunshine; and it shook the gigantic pyramid of flame, and scattered the cinders of half-consumed abominations around upon the spectators.

"This is terrible!" said I, feeling that my cheek grew pale, and seeing a like change in the visages about me.

"Be of good courage yet," answered the man with whom I had so often spoken. He continued to gaze steadily at the spectacle, with a singular calmness, as if it concerned him merely as an observer.—"Be of good courage—nor yet exult too much; for there is far less both of good and evil, in the effect of this bonfire, than the world might be willing to believe."

"How can that be?" exclaimed I, impatiently.—"Has it not consumed everything? Has it not swallowed up, or melted down, every human or divine appendage of our mortal state, that had substance enough to be acted on by fire? Will there be anything left us, tomorrow morning, better or worse than a heap of embers and ashes?"

"Assuredly there will," said my grave friend. "Come hither tomorrow morning—or whenever the combustible portion of the pile shall be quite burnt out—and you will find among the ashes everything really valuable that you have seen cast into the flames. Trust me; the world of tomorrow will again enrich itself with the gold and diamonds, which have been cast off by the world of to-day. Not a truth is destroyed—nor buried so deep among the ashes, but it will be raked up at last."

This was a strange assurance. Yet I felt inclined to credit it; the more especially as I beheld, among the wallowing flames, a copy of the Holy Scriptures, the pages of which, instead of being blackened into tinder, only assumed a more dazzling whiteness, as the finger-marks of human imperfection were purified away. Certain marginal notes and commentaries, it is true, yielded to the intensity of the fiery test, but without detriment to the smallest syllable that had flamed from the pen of inspiration.

"Yes;—there is the proof of what you say," answered I, turning to the observer. "But, if only what is evil can feel the action of the fire, then, surely, the conflagration has been of inestimable utility. Yet, if I understand aright, you intimate a doubt whether the world's expectation of benefit will be realized by it."

"Listen to the talk of these worthies," said he, pointing to a group in front of the blazing pile.—"Possibly, they may teach you something useful, without intending it."

The persons, whom he indicated, consisted of that brutal and most earthy figure, who had stood forth so furiously in defence of the gallows—the hangman, in short—together with the Last Thief and the Last Murderer; all three of whom were clustered about the Last Toper. The latter was liberally passing the brandy-bottle, which he had rescued from the general destruction of wines and spirits. This little convivial party seemed at the lowest pitch of despondency; as considering that the purified world must needs be utterly unlike the sphere that they had hitherto known, and therefore but a strange and desolate abode for gentlemen of their kidney.

"The best counsel for all of us, is," remarked the hangman, "that—as soon as we have finished the last drop of liquor—I help you, my three friends, to a comfortable end upon the nearest tree, and then hang myself on the same bough. This is no world for us, any longer."

"Poh, poh, my good fellows!" said a dark-complexioned personage, who now joined the group—his complexion was indeed fearfully dark; and his eyes glowed with a redder light than that of the bonfire—"Be not so cast down, my dear friends; you shall see good days yet. There is one thing that these wiseacres have forgotten to throw into the fire, and without which all the rest of the conflagration is just nothing at all—yes; though they had burnt the earth itself to a cinder!"

"And what may that be?" eagerly demanded the Last Murderer.

"What, but the human heart itself!" said the dark-visaged stranger, with a portentous grin. "And, unless they hit upon some method of purifying that foul cavern, forth from it will re-issue all the shapes of wrong and misery—the same old shapes, or worse ones—which they have taken such a vast deal of trouble to consume to ashes. I have stood by, this live-long night, and laughed in my sleeve at the whole business. Oh, take my word for it, it will be the old world yet!"

This brief conversation supplied me with a theme for lengthened thought. How sad a truth—if true it were—that Man's age-long endeavor for perfection had served only to render him the mockery of the Evil Principle, from the fatal circumstance of an error at the very root of the matter! The Heart—the Heart—there was the little, yet boundless sphere, wherein existed the original wrong, of which the crime and misery of this outward world were merely types. Purify that inner sphere; and the many shapes of evil that haunt the outward, and which now seem almost our only realities, will turn to shadowy phantoms, and vanish of their own accord. But, if we go no deeper than the Intellect, and strive, with merely that feeble instrument, to discern and rectify what is wrong, our whole accomplishment will be a dream; so unsubstantial, that it matters little whether the bonfire, which I have so faithfully described, were what we choose to call a real event, and a flame that would scorch the finger—or only a phosphoric radiance, and a parable of my own brain!

Meninock
An Indian Voice
(1915)

GOD CREATED this Indian country and it was like He spread out a big blanket. He put the Indians on it. They were created here in this country, truly and honestly, and that was the time this river started to run. Then God created fish in this river and put deer in these mountains and made laws through which has come the increase of fish and game. Then the Creator gave us Indians life; we awakened and as soon as we saw the game and fish we knew that they were made for us. For the women God made roots and berries to gather, and the Indians grew and multiplied as a people. When we were created we were given our ground to live on, and from that time these were our rights. This is all true. We had the fish before the missionaries came, before the white man came. We were put here by the Creator and these were our rights as far as my memory to my great-grandfather. This was the food on which we lived. My mother gathered berries; my father fished and killed the game. These words are mine and they are true. It matters not how long I live, I cannot change these thoughts. My strength is from the fish; my blood is from the fish, from the roots and the berries. The fish and the game are the essence of my life. I was not brought from a foreign country and did not come here. I was put here by the Creator. We had no cattle, no hogs, no grain, only berries and roots and game and fish. We never thought we would be troubled about these things, and I tell my people, and I believe it, it is not wrong for us to get this food. Whenever the seasons open I raise my heart in thanks to the Creator for his bounty that this food has come. . . .

[This text consists of testimony by Meninock, a Yakima chief, responding in court to charges brought in 1915 that he had broken a Washington state law on salmon fishing. The Yakimas argued that the law violated an 1855 treaty guaranteeing them fishing rights in perpetuity. Meninock was found guilty.]

Washakie
An Indian Voice
(1878)

THE WHITE man, who possesses this whole vast country from sea to sea, who roams over it at pleasure and lives where he likes, cannot know the cramp we feel in this little spot, with the undying remembrance of the fact, which you know as well as we, that every foot of what you proudly call America, not very long ago belonged to the Red Man. The Great Spirit gave it to us, there was room enough for all his tribes; all were happy in their freedom.

The white man had, in ways we know not of, learned some things we had not learned: among them how to make superior tools and terrible weapons, better for war then bows and arrows, and there seemed no end to the hordes of men that followed them from other lands beyond the sea.

And so, at last, our fathers were steadily driven out, or killed. We, their sons, but sorry remnants of tribes once mighty, are cornered in little spots of the earth, all ours by right—cornered like guilty prisoners, and watched by men with guns who are more than anxious to kill us off.

[This text is from a speech by Washakie, a Shoshone chief, given at a council called by the governor of Wyoming in 1878.]

Frederick Jackson Turner
The Significance of the Frontier
in American History
(1893)

IN A recent bulletin of the Superintendent of the Census for 1890 appear these significant words: "Up to and including 1880 the country had a frontier of settlement, but at present the unsettled area has been so broken into by isolated bodies of settlement that there can hardly be said to be a frontier line. In the discussion of its extent, its westward movement, etc., it can not, therefore, any longer have a place in the census reports." This brief official statement marks the closing of a great historic movement. Up to our own day American history has been in a large degree the history of the colonization of the Great West. The existence of an area of free land, its continuous recession, and the advance of American settlement westward, explain American development.

Behind institutions, behind constitutional forms and modifications, lie the vital forces that call these organs into life and shape them to meet changing conditions. The peculiarity of American institutions is the fact that they have been compelled to adapt themselves to the changes of an expanding people—to the changes involved in crossing a continent, in winning a wilderness, and in developing at each area of this progress out of the primitive economic and political conditions of the frontier into the complexity of city life. Said Calhoun in 1817, "We are great, and rapidly— I was about to say fearfully—growing!" So saying, he touched the distinguishing feature of American life. All peoples show development; the germ theory of politics has been sufficiently emphasized. In the case of most nations, however, the development has occurred in a limited area;

[From *The Report of the American Historical Association* (1893). Reprinted in Turner's *The Frontier in American History* (1920).]

and if the nation has expanded, it has met other growing peoples whom it has conquered. But in the case of the United States we have a different phenomenon. Limiting our attention to the Atlantic coast, we have the familiar phenomenon of the evolution of institutions in a limited area, such as the rise of representative government; the differentiation of simple colonial governments into complex organs; the progress from primitive industrial society, without division of labor, up to manufacturing civilization. But we have in addition to this a recurrence of the process of evolution in each western area reached in the process of expansion. Thus American development has exhibited not merely advance along a single line, but a return to primitive conditions on a continually advancing frontier line, and a new development for that area. American social development has been continually beginning over again on the frontier. This perennial rebirth, this fluidity of American life, this expansion westward with its new opportunities, its continuous touch with the simplicity of primitive society, furnish the forces dominating American character. The true point of view in the history of this nation is not the Atlantic coast, it is the Great West. Even the slavery struggle . . . occupies its important place in American history because of its relation to westward expansion.

In this advance, the frontier is the outer edge of the wave—the meeting point between savagery and civilization. Much has been written about the frontier from the point of view of border warfare and the chase, but as a field for the serious study of the economist and the historian it has been neglected.

The American frontier is sharply distinguished from the European frontier—a fortified boundary line running through dense populations. The most significant thing about the American frontier is that it lies at the hither edge of free land. In the census reports it is treated as the margin of that settlement which has a density of two or more to the square mile. The term is an elastic one, and for our purposes does not need sharp definition. We shall consider the whole frontier belt, including the Indian country and the outer margin of the "settled area" of the census reports. This paper will make no attempt to treat the subject exhaustively; its aim is simply to call attention to the frontier as a fertile field for investigation, and to suggest some of the problems which arise in connection with it.

In the settlement of America we have to observe how European life entered the continent, and how America modified and developed that life and reacted on Europe. Our early history is the study of European germs developing in an American environment. Too exclusive attention has been paid by institutional students to the Germanic origins, too little to the American factors. The frontier is the line of most rapid and effective Americanization. The wilderness masters the colonist. It finds him a European in dress, industries, tools, modes of travel, and thought. It takes him from the railroad car and puts him in a birch canoe. It strips off the garments of civilization and arrays him in the hunting shirt and the moccasin. It puts him in the log cabin of the Cherokee and Iroquois and runs an Indian palisade around him. Before long he has gone to planting Indian corn and plowing with a sharp stick; he shouts the war cry and takes the scalp in orthodox Indian fashion. In short, at the frontier the environment is at first too strong for the man. He must accept the conditions which it furnishes, or perish, and so he fits himself into the Indian clearings and follows the Indian trails. Little by little he transforms the wilderness, but the outcome is not the old Europe, not simply the development of Germanic germs, any more than the first phenomenon was a case of reversion to the Germanic mark. The fact is that here is a new product that is American. At first, the frontier was the Atlantic coast. It was the frontier of Europe in a very real sense. Moving westward, the frontier became more and more American. As successive terminal moraines result from successive glaciations, so each frontier leaves its traces behind it, and when it becomes a settled area the region still partakes of the frontier characteristics. Thus the advance of the frontier has meant a steady movement away from the influence of Europe, a steady growth of independence on American lines. And to study this advance, the men who grew up under these conditions, and the political, economic, and social results of it, is to study the really American part of our history. . . .

In these successive frontiers we find natural boundary lines which have served to mark and to affect the characteristics of the frontiers, namely: the "fall line;" the Alleghany Mountains; the Mississippi; the Missouri where its direction approximates north and south; the line of the arid lands, approximately the ninety-ninth meridian; and the Rocky Mountains. The fall line marked the frontier of the seventeenth century; the Alleghanies that of the eighteenth; the Mississippi that of the first quarter of the nineteenth; the Missouri that of the middle of this century (omitting the California movement); and the belt of the Rocky Mountains and the arid tract, the present frontier. Each was won by a series of Indian wars.

At the Atlantic frontier one can study the germs of processes repeated at each successive frontier. We have the complex European life sharply precipitated by the wilderness into the simplicity of primitive conditions. The first frontier had to meet its Indian question, its question of the disposition of the public domain, of the means of intercourse with older settlements, of the extension of political organization, of religious and educational activity. And the settlement of these and similar questions for one frontier served as a guide for the next. The American student needs not to go to the "prim little townships of Sleswick" for illustrations of the law of continuity and development. For example, he may study

the origin of our land policies in the colonial land policy; he may see how
the system grew by adapting the statutes to the customs of the successive
frontiers. He may see how the mining experience in the lead regions of
Wisconsin, Illinois, and Iowa was applied to the mining laws of the Sierras,
and how our Indian policy has been a series of experimentations on
successive frontiers. Each tier of new States has found in the older ones
material for its constitutions. Each frontier has made similar contributions
to American character. . . .

But with all these similarities there are essential differences, due to
the place element and the time element. . . . It would be a work worth
the historian's labors to mark these various frontiers and in detail compare
one with another. Not only would there result a more adequate conception
of American development and characteristics, but invaluable additions
would be made to the history of society.

Loria, the Italian economist, has urged the study of colonial life as an
aid in understanding the stages of European development, affirming that
colonial settlement is for economic science what the mountain is for ge-
ology, bringing to light primitive stratifications. "America," he says, "has
the key to the historical enigma which Europe has sought for centuries
in vain, and the land which has no history reveals luminously the course
of universal history." There is much truth in this. The United States lies
like a huge page in the history of society. Line by line as we read this
continental page from West to East we find the record of social evolution.
It begins with the Indian and the hunter; it goes on to tell of the disin-
tegration of savagery by the entrance of the trader, the path-finder of
civilization; we read the annals of the pastoral stage in ranch life; the
exploitation of the soil by the raising of unrotated crops of corn and wheat
in sparsely settled farming communities; the intensive culture of the
denser farm settlement; and finally the manufacturing organization with
city and factory system. . . . Particularly in eastern States this page is a
palimpsest. What is now a manufacturing State was in an earlier decade
an area of intensive farming. Earlier yet it had been a wheat area, and
still earlier the "range" had attracted the cattle-herder. Thus Wisconsin,
now developing manufacture, is a State with varied agricultural interests.
But earlier it was given over to almost exclusive grain-raising, like North
Dakota at the present time.

Each of these areas has had an influence in our economic and political
history; the evolution of each into a higher stage has worked political
transformations. But what constitutional historian has made any adequate
attempt to interpret political facts by the light of these social areas and
changes?

The Atlantic frontier was compounded of fisherman, fur-trader, miner,
cattle-raiser, and farmer. Excepting the fisherman, each type of industry

was on the march toward the West, impelled by an irresistible attraction. Each passed in successive waves across the continent. Stand at Cumberland Gap and watch the procession of civilization, marching single file— the buffalo following the trail to the salt springs, the Indian, the fur-trader and hunter, the cattle-raiser, the pioneer farmer—and the frontier has passed by. Stand at South Pass in the Rockies a century later and see the same procession with wider intervals between. The unequal rate of advance compels us to distinguish the frontier into the trader's frontier, the rancher's frontier, or the miner's frontier, and the farmer's frontier. When the mines and the cow pens were still near the fall line the traders' pack trains were tinkling across the Alleghanies, and the French on the Great Lakes were fortifying their posts, alarmed by the British trader's birch canoe. When the trappers scaled the Rockies, the farmer was still near the mouth of the Missouri. . . .

From the time the mountains rose between the pioneer and the seaboard, a new order of Americanism arose. The West and the East began to get out of touch of each other. The settlements from the sea to the mountains kept connection with the rear and had a certain solidarity. But the over-mountain men grew more and more independent. The East took a narrow view of American advance, and nearly lost these men. Kentucky and Tennessee history bears abundant witness to the truth of this statement. The East began to try to hedge and limit westward expansion. Though Webster could declare that there were no Alleghanies in his politics, yet in politics in general they were a very solid factor.

The exploitation of the beasts took hunter and trader to the west, the exploitation of the grasses took the rancher west, and the exploitation of the virgin soil of the river valleys and prairies attracted the farmer. Good soils have been the most continuous attraction to the farmer's frontier. The land hunger of the Virginians drew them down the rivers into Carolina, in early colonial days; the search for soils took the Massachusetts men to Pennsylvania and to New York. As the eastern lands were taken up migration flowed across them to the west. . . .

Omitting those of the pioneer farmers who move from the love of adventure, the advance of the more steady farmer is easy to understand. Obviously the immigrant was attracted by the cheap lands of the frontier, and even the native farmer felt their influence strongly. Year by year the farmers who lived on soil whose returns were diminished by unrotated crops were offered the virgin soil of the frontier at nominal prices. Their growing families demanded more lands, and these were dear. The competition of the unexhausted, cheap, and easily tilled prairie lands compelled the farmer either to go west and continue the exhaustion of the soil on a new frontier, or to adopt intensive culture. Thus the census of 1890 shows, in the Northwest, many counties in which there is an absolute or a relative decrease of population. These States have been sending farmers to advance the frontier on the plains, and have themselves begun to turn to intensive farming and to manufacture. A decade before this, Ohio had shown the same transition stage. Thus the demand for land and the love of wilderness freedom drew the frontier ever onward.

Having now roughly outlined the various kinds of frontiers, and their modes of advance, chiefly from the point of view of the frontier itself, we may next inquire what were the influences on the East and on the Old World. . . .

First, we note that the frontier promoted the formation of a composite nationality for the American people. The coast was preponderantly English, but the later tides of continental immigration flowed across to the free lands. This was the case from the early colonial days. The Scotch-Irish and the Palatine Germans, or "Pennsylvania Dutch," furnished the dominant element in the stock of the colonial frontier. With these peoples were also the freed indented servants, or redemptioners, who at the expiration of their time of service passed to the frontier. . . . Very generally these redemptioners were of non-English stock. In the crucible of the frontier the immigrants were Americanized, liberated, and fused into a mixed race, English in neither nationality nor characteristics. The process has gone on from the early days to our own. Burke and other writers in the middle of the eighteenth century believed that Pennsylvania was "threatened with the danger of being wholly foreign in language, manners, and perhaps even inclinations." The German and Scotch-Irish elements in the frontier of the South were only less great. In the middle of the present century the German element in Wisconsin was already so considerable that leading publicists looked to the creation of a German state out of the commonwealth by concentrating their colonization. Such examples teach us to beware of misinterpreting the fact that there is a common English speech in America into a belief that the stock is also English.

In another way the advance of the frontier decreased our dependence on England. The coast, particularly of the South, lacked diversified industries, and was dependent on England for the bulk of its supplies. In the South there was even a dependence on the Northern colonies for articles of food. . . . Before long the frontier created a demand for merchants. As it retreated from the coast it became less and less possible for England to bring her supplies directly to the consumer's wharfs, and carry away staple crops, and staple crops began to give way to diversified agriculture for a time. The effect of this phase of the frontier action upon the northern section is perceived when we realize how the advance of the frontier aroused seaboard cities like Boston, New York, and Baltimore, to engage in rivalry for what Washington called "the extensive and valuable trade of a rising empire."

The legislation which most developed the powers of the national government, and played the largest part in its activity, was conditioned on the frontier. Writers have discussed the subjects of tariff, land, and internal improvement, as subsidiary to the slavery question. . . .

This is a wrong perspective. The pioneer needed the goods of the coast, and so the grand series of internal improvement and railroad legislation began, with potent nationalizing effects. Over internal improvements occurred great debates, in which grave constitutional questions were discussed. Sectional groupings appear in the votes, profoundly significant for the historian. Loose construction increased as the nation marched westward. But the West was not content with bringing the farm to the factory. Under the lead of Clay—"Harry of the West"—protective tariffs were passed, with the cry of bringing the factory to the farm. The disposition of the public lands was a third important subject of national legislation influenced by the frontier. . . .

It is safe to say that the legislation with regard to land, tariff, and internal improvements—the American system of the nationalizing Whig party—was conditioned on frontier ideas and needs. But it was not merely in legislative action that the frontier worked against the sectionalism of the coast. The economic and social characteristics of the frontier worked against sectionalism. The men of the frontier had closer resemblances to the Middle region than to either of the other sections. Pennsylvania had been the seed-plot of frontier emigration, and, although she passed on her settlers along the Great Valley into the west of Virginia and the Carolinas, yet the industrial society of these Southern frontiersmen was always more like that of the Middle region than like that of the tide-water portion of the South, which later came to spread its industrial type throughout the South.

The Middle region, entered by New York harbor, was an open door to all Europe. The tide-water part of the South represented typical Englishmen, modified by a warm climate and servile labor, and living in baronial fashion on great plantations; New England stood for a special English movement—Puritanism. The Middle region was less English than the other sections. It had a wide mixture of nationalities, a varied society, the mixed town and county system of local government, a varied economic life, many religious sects. In short, it was a region mediating between New England and the South, and the East and the West. It represented that composite nationality which the contemporary United States exhibits, that juxtaposition of non-English groups, occupying a valley or a little settlement, and presenting reflections of the map of Europe in their variety. It was democratic and nonsectional, if not national; "easy, tolerant, and contented;" rooted strongly in material prosperity. It was typical of the modern United States. It was least sectional, not only because it lay between North and South, but also because with no barriers to shut out its frontiers from its settled region, and with a system of connecting waterways, the Middle region mediated between East and West as well as between North and South. Thus it became the typically American region. Even the New Englander, who was shut out from the frontier by the Middle region, tarrying in New York or Pennsylvania on his westward march, lost the acuteness of his sectionalism on the way. . . .

It was this nationalizing tendency of the West that transformed the democracy of Jefferson into the national republicanism of Monroe and the democracy of Andrew Jackson. The West of the War of 1812, the West of Clay, and Benton and Harrison, and Andrew Jackson, shut off by the Middle States and the mountains from the coast sections, had a solidarity of its own with national tendencies. On the tide of the Father of Waters, North and South met and mingled into a nation. Interstate migration went steadily on—a process of cross-fertilization of ideas and institutions. The fierce struggle of the sections over slavery on the western frontier does not diminish the truth of this statement; it proves the truth of it. Slavery was a sectional trait that would not down, but in the West it could not remain sectional. It was the greatest of frontiersmen who declared: "I believe this Government can not endure permanently half slave and half free. It will become all of one thing or all of the other." Nothing works for nationalism like intercourse within the nation. Mobility of population is death to localism, and the western frontier worked irresistibly in unsettling population. The effect reached back from the frontier and affected profoundly the Atlantic coast and even the Old World.

But the most important effect of the frontier has been in the promotion of democracy here and in Europe. As has been indicated, the frontier is productive of individualism. Complex society is precipitated by the wilderness into a kind of primitive organization based on the family. The tendency is anti-social. It produces antipathy to control, and particularly to any direct control. The tax-gatherer is viewed as a representative of oppression. . . . Frontier conditions prevalent in the colonies are important factors in the explanation of the American Revolution, where individual liberty was sometimes confused with absence of all effective government. The same conditions aid in explaining the difficulty of instituting a strong government in the period of the confederacy. The frontier individualism has from the beginning promoted democracy.

The frontier States that came into the Union in the first quarter of a century of its existence came in with democratic suffrage provisions, and had reactive effects of the highest importance upon the older States whose peoples were being attracted there. An extension of the franchise became essential. It was *western* New York that forced an extension of suffrage in the constitutional convention of that State in 1821; and it was *western* Virginia that compelled the tide-water region to put a more liberal suffrage provision in the constitution framed in 1830, and to give to the frontier region a more nearly proportionate representation with the tide-water aristocracy. The rise of democracy as an effective force in the nation came in with western preponderance under Jackson and William Henry Harrison, and it meant the triumph of the frontier—with all of its good and with all of its evil elements.

So long as free land exists, the opportunity for a competency exists, and economic power secures political power. But the democracy born of free land, strong in selfishness and individualism, intolerant of administrative experience and education, and pressing individual liberty beyond its proper bounds, has its dangers as well as its benefits. Individualism in America has allowed a laxity in regard to governmental affairs which has rendered possible the spoils system and all the manifest evils that follow from the lack of a highly developed civic spirit. In this connection may be noted also the influence of frontier conditions in permitting lax business honor, inflated paper currency and wild-cat banking. The colonial and revolutionary frontier was the region whence emanated many of the worst forms of an evil currency. The West in the War of 1812 repeated the phenomenon on the frontier of that day, while the speculation and wild-cat banking of the period of the crisis of 1837 occurred on the new frontier belt of the next tier of States. Thus each one of the periods of lax financial integrity coincides with periods when a new set of frontier communities had arisen, and coincides in area with these successive frontiers, for the most part. . . . A primitive society can hardly be expected to show the intelligent appreciation of the complexity of business interests in a developed society. . . . But the attempts to limit the boundaries, to restrict land sales and settlement, and to deprive the West of its share of political power were all in vain. Steadily the frontier of settlement advanced and carried with it individualism, democracy, and nationalism, and powerfully affected the East and the Old World.

The most effective efforts of the East to regulate the frontier came through its educational and religious activity, exerted by interstate migration and by organized societies. Speaking in 1835, Dr. Lyman Beecher . . . pointed out that the population of the West "is assembled from all the States of the Union and from all the nations of Europe, and is rushing in like the waters of the flood, demanding for its moral preservation the immediate and universal action of those institutions which discipline the mind and arm the conscience and the heart. And so various are the opinions and habits, and so recent and imperfect is the acquaintance, and so sparse are the settlements of the West, that no homogeneous public sentiment can be formed to legislate immediately into being the requisite institutions. And yet they are all needed immediately in their utmost perfection and power. A nation is being 'born in a day.' . . . But what

will become of the West if her prosperity rushes up to such a majesty of
power, while those great institutions linger which are necessary to form
the mind and the conscience and the heart of that vast world. It must
not be permitted. . . . Let no man at the East quiet himself and dream
of liberty, whatever may become of the West. . . . Her destiny is our
destiny."

With the appeal to the conscience of New England, he adds appeals
to her fears lest other religious sects anticipate her own. The New England
preacher and school-teacher left their mark on the West. The dread of
Western emancipation from New England's political and economic control was paralleled by her fears lest the West cut loose from her religion.
. . . As seaboard cities like Philadelphia, New York, and Baltimore strove
for the mastery of Western trade, so the various denominations strove
for the possession of the West. Thus an intellectual stream from New
England sources fertilized the West. Other sections sent their missionaries; but the real struggle was between sects. The contest for power and
the expansive tendency furnished to the various sects by the existence
of a moving frontier must have had important results on the character
of religious organization in the United States. The multiplication of
rival churches in the little frontier towns had deep and lasting social effects. . . .

From the conditions of frontier life came intellectual traits of profound
importance. The works of travelers along each frontier from colonial days
onward describe certain common traits, and these traits have, while softening down, still persisted as survivals in the place of their origin, even
when a higher social organization succeeded. The result is that to the
frontier the American intellect owes its striking characteristics. That
coarseness and strength combined with acuteness and inquisitiveness;
that practical, inventive turn of mind, quick to find expedients; that masterful grasp of material things, lacking in the artistic but powerful to effect
great ends; that restless, nervous energy; that dominant individualism,
working for good and for evil, and withal that buoyancy and exuberance
which comes with freedom—these are traits of the frontier, or traits called
out elsewhere because of the existence of the frontier. Since the days
when the fleet of Columbus sailed into the waters of the New World,
America has been another name for opportunity, and the people of the
United States have taken their tone from the incessant expansion which
has not only been open but has even been forced upon them. He would
be a rash prophet who should assert that the expansive character of American life has now entirely ceased. Movement has been its dominant fact,
and unless this training has no effect upon a people, the American energy
will continually demand a wider field for its exercise. But never again
will such gifts of free land offer themselves. For a moment, at the frontier,

the bonds of custom are broken and unrestraint is triumphant. There is no *tabula rasa*. The stubborn American environment is there with its imperious summons to accept its conditions; the inherited ways of doing things are also there; and yet, in spite of environment, and in spite of custom, each frontier did indeed furnish a new field of opportunity, a gate of escape from the bondage of the past; and freshness, and confidence, and scorn of older society, impatience of its restraints and its ideas, and indifference to its lessons, have accompanied the frontier. What the Mediterranean Sea was to the Greeks, breaking the bond of custom, offering new experiences, calling out new institutions and activities, that, and more, the ever retreating frontier has been to the United States directly, and to the nations of Europe more remotely. And now, four centuries from the discovery of America, at the end of a hundred years of life under the Constitution, the frontier has gone, and with its going has closed the first period of American history.

PHILOSOPHICAL FRONTIERS

Ralph Waldo Emerson
Self-Reliance
(1841)

I READ the other day some verses written by an eminent painter which were original and not conventional. The soul always hears an admonition in such lines, let the subject be what it may. The sentiment they instil is of more value than any thought they may contain. To believe your own thought, to believe that what is true for you in your private heart is true for all men—that is genius. Speak your latent conviction, and it shall be the universal sense; for the inmost in due time becomes the outmost, and our first thought is rendered back to us by the trumpets of the Last Judgment. Familiar as the voice of the mind is to each, the highest merit we ascribe to Moses, Plato and Milton is that they set at naught books and traditions, and spoke not what men, but what *they* thought. A man should learn to detect and watch that gleam of light which flashes across his mind from within, more than the lustre of the firmament of bards and sages. Yet he dismisses without notice his thought, because it is his. In every work of genius we recognize our own rejected thoughts; they come back to us with a certain alienated majesty. . . .

Trust thyself: every heart vibrates to that iron string. Accept the place the divine providence has found for you, the society of your contemporaries, the connection of events. Great men have always done so, and confided themselves childlike to the genius of their age, betraying their perception that the absolutely trustworthy was seated at their heart, working through their hands, predominating in all their being. And we are now men, and must accept in the highest mind the same transcendent destiny; and not minors and invalids in a protected corner, not cowards fleeing before a revolution, but guides, redeemers and benefactors, obeying the Almighty effort and advancing on Chaos and the Dark. . . .

[From *Essays: First Series.*]

Society everywhere is in conspiracy against the manhood of every one of its members. Society is a joint-stock company, in which the members agree, for the better securing of his bread to each shareholder, to surrender the liberty and culture of the eater. The virtue in most request is conformity. Self-reliance is its aversion. It loves not realities and creators but names and customs.

Whoso would be a man, must be a nonconformist. He who would gather immortal palms must not be hindered by the name of goodness, but must explore if it be goodness. Nothing is at last sacred but the integrity of your own mind. Absolve you to yourself, and you shall have the suffrage of the world. I remember an answer which when quite young I was prompted to make to a valued adviser who was wont to importune me with the dear old doctrines of the church. On my saying, "What have I to do with the sacredness of traditions, if I live wholly from within?" my friend suggested—"But these impulses may be from below, not from above." I replied, "They do not seem to me to be such; but if I am the Devil's child, I will live then from the Devil." No law can be sacred to me but that of my nature. Good and bad are but names very readily transferable to that or this; the only right is what is after my constitution; the only wrong what is against it. A man is to carry himself in the presence of all opposition as if every thing were titular and ephemeral but he. I am ashamed to think how easily we capitulate to badges and names, to large societies and dead institutions. . . .

What I must do is all that concerns me, not what the people think. This rule, equally arduous in actual and in intellectual life, may serve for the whole distinction between greatness and meanness. It is the harder because you will always find those who think they know what is your duty better than you know it. It is easy in the world to live after the world's opinion; it is easy in solitude to live after your own; but the great man is he who in the midst of the crowd keeps with perfect sweetness the independence of solitude.

The objection to conforming to usages that have become dead to you is that it scatters your force. It loses your time and blurs the impression of your character. If you maintain a dead church, contribute to a dead Bible-society, vote with a great party either for the government or against it, spread your table like base housekeepers—under all these screens I have difficulty to detect the precise man you are: and of course so much force is withdrawn from your proper life. But do your work, and I shall know you. Do your work, and you shall reinforce yourself. A man must consider what a blindman's-buff is this game of conformity. If I know your sect I anticipate your argument. I hear a preacher announce for his text and topic the expediency of one of the institutions of his church. Do I not know beforehand that not possibly can he say a new and spontaneous word? Do I not know that with all this ostentation of examining the grounds of the institution he will do no such thing? Do I not know that he is pledged to himself not to look but at one side, the permitted side, not as a man, but as a parish minister? He is a retained attorney, and these airs of the bench are the emptiest affectation. Well, most men have bound their eyes with one or another handkerchief, and attached themselves to some one of these communities of opinion. This conformity makes them not false in a few particulars, authors of a few lies, but false in all particulars. . . .

The other terror that scares us from self-trust is our consistency; a reverence for our past act or word because the eyes of others have no other data for computing our orbit than our past acts, and we are loth to disappoint them.

But why should you keep your head over your shoulder? Why drag about this corpse of your memory, lest you contradict somewhat you have stated in this or that public place? Suppose you should contradict yourself; what then? It seems to be a rule of wisdom never to rely on your memory alone, scarcely even in acts of pure memory, but to bring the past for judgment into the thousand-eyed present, and live ever in a new day. In your metaphysics you have denied personality to the Deity, yet when the devout motions of the soul come, yield to them heart and life, though they should clothe God with shape and color. Leave your theory, as Joseph his coat in the hand of the harlot, and flee.

A foolish consistency is the hobgoblin of little minds, adored by little statesmen and philosophers and divines. With consistency a great soul has simply nothing to do. He may as well concern himself with his shadow on the wall. Speak what you think now in hard words and to-morrow speak what to-morrow thinks in hard words again, though it contradict every thing you said to-day.—'Ah, so you shall be sure to be misunderstood.'—Is it so bad then to be misunderstood? Pythagoras was misunderstood, and Socrates, and Jesus, and Luther, and Copernicus, and Galileo, and Newton, and every pure and wise spirit that ever took flesh. To be great is to be misunderstood. . . .

The magnetism which all original action exerts is explained when we inquire the reason of self-trust. Who is the Trustee? What is the aboriginal Self, on which a universal reliance may be grounded? What is the nature and power of that science-baffling star, without parallax, without calculable elements, which shoots a ray of beauty even into trivial and impure actions, if the least mark of independence appear? The inquiry leads us to that source, at once the essence of genius, of virtue, and of life, which we call Spontaneity or Instinct. We denote this primary wisdom as Intuition, whilst all later teachings are tuitions. In that deep force, the last fact behind which analysis cannot go, all things find their common origin. . . . Here is the fountain of action and of thought. Here are the lungs of that inspiration which giveth man wisdom and which cannot be denied without impiety and atheism. We lie in the lap of immense intelligence, which makes us receivers of its truth and organs of its activity. When we discern justice, when we discern truth, we do nothing of ourselves, but allow a passage to its beams. If we ask whence this comes, if we seek to pry into the soul that causes, all philosophy is at fault. Its presence or its absence is all we can affirm. . . .

The relations of the soul to the divine spirit are so pure that it is profane to seek to interpose helps. It must be that when God speaketh he should communicate, not one thing, but all things; should fill the world with his voice; should scatter forth light, nature, time, souls, from the centre of the present thought; and new date and new create the whole. Whenever a mind is simple and receives a divine wisdom old things pass away— means, teachers, texts, temples fall; it lives now, and absorbs past and future into the present hour. All things are made sacred by relation to it—one as much as another. All things are dissolved to their centre by their cause, and in the universal miracle petty and particular miracles disappear. If therefore a man claims to know and speak of God and carries you backward to the phraseology of some old mouldered nation in another country, in another world, believe him not. Is the acorn better than the oak which is its fullness and completion? Is the parent better than the child into whom he has cast his ripened being? Whence then this worship of the past? The centuries are conspirators against the sanity and authority of the soul. Time and space are but physiological colors which the eye makes, but the soul is light: where it is, is day; where it was, is night; and history is an impertinence and an injury if it be any thing more than a cheerful apologue or parable of my being and becoming . . . .

This should be plain enough. Yet see what strong intellects dare not yet hear God himself unless he speak the phraseology of I know not what David, or Jeremiah, or Paul. We shall not always set so great a price on a few texts, on a few lives. . . . When we have new perception, we shall gladly disburden the memory of its hoarded treasures as old rubbish. When a man lives with God, his voice shall be as sweet as the murmur of the brook and the rustle of the corn.

And now at last the highest truth on this subject remains unsaid; probably cannot be said; for all that we say is the far-off remembering of the intuition. That thought by what I can now nearest approach to say it, is this. When good is near you, when you have life in yourself, it is not by any known or accustomed way; you shall not discern the footprints of any other; you shall not see the face of man; you shall not hear any name; the way, the thought, the good, shall be wholly strange and new. It shall exclude example and experience. . . .

Henry David Thoreau
Life without Principle
(1863)

AT A lyceum, not long since, I felt that the lecturer had chosen a theme too foreign to himself, and so failed to interest me as much as he might have done. He described things not in or near to his heart, but toward his extremities and superficies. There was, in this sense, no truly central or centralizing thought in the lecture. I would have had him deal with his privatest experience, as the poet does. The greatest compliment that was ever paid me was when one asked me what *I thought*, and attended to my answer. I am surprised, as well as delighted, when this happens, it is such a rare use he would make of me, as if he were acquainted with the tool. Commonly, if men want anything of me, it is only to know how many acres I make of their land,—since I am a surveyor—or, at most, what trivial news I have burdened myself with. They never will go to law for my meat; they prefer the shell. A man once came a considerable distance to ask me to lecture on Slavery; but on conversing with him, I found that he and his clique expected seven eighths of the lecture to be theirs, and only one eighth mine; so I declined. I take it for granted, when I am invited to lecture anywhere,—for I have had a little experience in that business,—that there is a desire to hear what *I think* on some subject, though I may be the greatest fool in the country,—and not that I should say pleasant things merely, or such as the audience will assent to; and I resolve, accordingly, that I will give them a strong dose of myself. They have sent for me, and engaged to pay for me, and I am determined that they shall have me, though I bore them beyond all precedent.

So now I would say something similar to you, my readers. Since *you* are my readers, and I have not been much of a traveler, I will not talk about people a thousand miles off, but come as near home as I can. As the time is short, I will leave out all the flattery, and retain all the criticism.

[Published posthumously in the *Atlantic Monthly* (October 1863).]

Let us consider the way in which we spend our lives.

This world is a place of business. What an infinite bustle! I am awaked almost every night by the panting of the locomotive. It interrupts my dreams. There is no sabbath. It would be glorious to see mankind at leisure for once. It is nothing but work, work, work. I cannot easily buy a blank-book to write thoughts in; they are commonly ruled for dollars and cents. An Irishman, seeing me making a minute in the fields, took it for granted that I was calculating my wages. If a man was tossed out of a window when an infant, and so made a cripple for life, or scared out of his wits by the Indians, it is regretted chiefly because he was thus incapacitated for—business! I think that there is nothing, not even crime, more opposed to poetry, to philosophy, ay, to life itself, than this incessant business.

There is a coarse and boisterous money-making fellow in the outskirts of our town, who is going to build a bank-wall under the hill along the edge of his meadow. The powers have put this into his head to keep him out of mischief, and he wishes me to spend three weeks digging there with him. The result will be that he will perhaps get some more money to hoard, and leave for his heirs to spend foolishly. If I do this, most will commend me as an industrious and hard-working man; but if I choose to devote myself to certain labors which yield more real profit, though but little money, they may be inclined to look on me as an idler. Nevertheless, as I do not need the police of meaningless labor to regulate me, and do not see anything praiseworthy in this fellow's undertaking any more than in many an enterprise of our own or foreign governments, however amusing it may be to him or them, I prefer to finish my education at a different school.

If a man walk in the woods for love of them half of each day, he is in danger of being regarded as a loafer; but if he spends his whole day as a speculator, shearing off those woods and making earth bald before her time, he is esteemed an industrious and enterprising citizen. As if a town had no interest in its forests but to cut them down! . . .

The ways by which you may get money almost without exception lead downward. To have done anything by which you earned money *merely* is to have been truly idle or worse. If the laborer gets no more than the wages which his employer pays him, he is cheated, he cheats himself. If you would get money as a writer or lecturer, you must be popular, which is to go down perpendicularly. Those services which the community will most readily pay for, it is most disagreeable to render. You are paid for being something less than a man. The State does not commonly reward a genius any more wisely. . . .

The aim of the laborer should be, not to get his living, to get "a good job," but to perform well a certain work; and, even in a pecuniary sense, it would be economy for a town to pay its laborers so well that they would not feel that they were working for low ends, as for a livelihood merely, but for scientific, or even moral ends. Do not hire a man who does your work for money, but him who does it for love of it.

It is remarkable that there are few men so well employed, so much to their minds, but that a little money or fame would commonly buy them off from their present pursuit. I see advertisements for *active* young men, as if activity were the whole of a young man's capital. Yet I have been surprised when one has with confidence proposed to me, a grown man, to embark in some enterprise of his, as if I had absolutely nothing to do, my life having been a complete failure hitherto. What a doubtful compliment this to pay me! As if he had met me halfway across the ocean beating up against the wind, but bound nowhere, and proposed to me to go along with him! If I did, what do you think the underwriters would say? No, no! I am not without employment at this stage of the voyage. To tell the truth, I saw an advertisement for able-bodied seamen, when I was a boy, sauntering in my native port, and as soon as I came of age I embarked.

The community has no bribe that will tempt a wise man. You may raise money enough to tunnel a mountain, but you cannot raise money enough to hire a man who is minding *his own* business. An efficient and valuable man does what he can, whether the community pay him for it or not. . . .

Perhaps I am more than usually jealous with respect to my freedom. I feel that my connection with and obligation to society are still very slight and transient. Those slight labors which afford me a livelihood, and by which it is allowed that I am to some extent serviceable to my contemporaries, are as yet commonly a pleasure to me, and I am not often reminded that they are a necessity. So far I am successful. But I foresee that if my wants should be much increased, the labor required to supply them would become a drudgery. If I should sell both my forenoons and afternoons to society, as most appear to do, I am sure that for me there would be nothing left worth living for. I trust that I shall never thus sell my birthright for a mess of pottage. I wish to suggest that a man may be very industrious, and yet not spend his time well. There is no more fatal blunderer than he who consumes the greater part of his life getting his living. All great enterprises are self-supporting. The poet, for instance, must sustain his body by his poetry, as a steam planing-mill feeds its boilers with the shavings it makes. You must get your living by loving. But as it is said of the merchants that ninety-seven in a hundred fail, so the life of men generally, tried by this standard, is a failure, and bankruptcy may be surely prophesied. . . .

It is remarkable that there is little or nothing to be remembered written on the subject of getting a living; how to make getting a living not merely honest and honorable, but altogether inviting and glorious; for if *getting a living* is not so, then living is not. One would think, from looking at literature, that this question had never disturbed a solitary individual's musings. Is it that men are too much disgusted with their experience to speak of it? The lesson of value which money teaches, which the Author of the Universe has taken so much pains to teach us, we are inclined to skip altogether. As for the means of living, it is wonderful how indifferent men of all classes are about it, even reformers, so called,—whether they inherit, or earn, or steal it. I think that Society has done nothing for us in this respect, or at least has undone what she has done. Cold and hunger seem more friendly to my nature than those methods which men have adopted and advise to ward them off.

The title *wise* is, for the most part, falsely applied. How can one be a wise man, if he does not know any better how to live than other men?— if he is only more cunning and intellectually subtle? Does Wisdom work in a treadmill? or does she teach how to succeed *by her example*? Is there any such thing as wisdom not applied to life? Is she merely the miller who grinds the finest logic? It is pertinent to ask if Plato got his *living* in a better way or more successfully than his contemporaries,—or did he succumb to the difficulties of life like other men? Did he seem to prevail over some of them merely by indifference, or by assuming grand airs? or find it easier to live, because his aunt remembered him in her will? The ways in which most men get their living, that is, live, are mere make-shifts, and a shirking of the real business of life,—chiefly because they do not know, but partly because they do not mean, any better.

The rush to California, for instance, and the attitude, not merely of merchants, but of philosophers and prophets, so called, in relation to it, reflect the greatest disgrace on mankind. That so many are ready to live by luck, and so get the means of commanding the labor of others less lucky, without contributing any value to society! And that is called enterprise! I know of no more startling development of the immorality of trade, and all the common modes of getting a living. The philosophy and poetry and religion of such a mankind are not worth the dust of a puff-ball. The hog that gets his living by rooting, stirring up the soil so, would be ashamed of such company. If I could command the wealth of all the worlds by lifting my finger, I would not pay *such* a price for it. Even Mahomet knew that God did not make this world in jest. It makes God to be a moneyed gentleman who scatters a handful of pennies in order to see mankind scramble for them. The world's raffle! A subsistence in the domains of Nature a thing to be raffled for! What a comment, what a satire, on our institutions! The conclusion will be, that mankind will hang itself upon a tree. And have all the precepts in all the Bibles taught men only this? and is the last and most admirable invention of the human race only an improved muck-rake? Is this the ground on which Orientals and Occidentals meet? Did God direct us so to get our living, digging where we never planted,—and He would, perchance, reward us with lumps of gold?

God gave the righteous man a certificate entitling him to food and raiment, but the unrighteous man found a facsimile of the same in God's coffers, and appropriated it, and obtained food and raiment like the former. It is one of the most extensive systems of counterfeiting that the world has seen. I did not know that mankind were suffering for want of gold. I have seen a little of it. I know that it is very malleable, but not so malleable as wit. A grain of gold will gild a great surface, but not so much as a grain of wisdom.

The gold-digger in the ravines of the mountains is as much a gambler as his fellow in the saloons of San Francisco. What difference does it make whether you shake dirt or shake dice? If you win, society is the loser. The gold-digger is the enemy of the honest laborer, whatever checks and compensations there may be. It is not enough to tell me that you worked hard to get your gold. So does the Devil work hard. The way of transgressors may be hard in many respects. The humblest observer who goes to the mines sees and says that gold-digging is of the character of a lottery; the gold thus obtained is not the same thing with the wages of honest toil. But, practically, he forgets what he has seen, for he has seen only the fact, not the principle, and goes into trade there, that is, buys a ticket in what commonly proves another lottery, where the fact is not so obvious.

After reading Howitt's account of the Australian gold-diggings one evening, . . . I was thinking, accidentally, of my own unsatisfactory life, doing as others do; and with that vision of the diggings still before me, I asked myself why *I* might not be washing some gold daily, though it were only the finest particles,—why *I* might not sink a shaft down to the gold within me, and work that mine. *There* is a Ballarat, a Bendigo for you,— what though it were a sulky-gully? At any rate, I might pursue some path, however solitary and narrow and crooked, in which I could walk with love and reverence. Wherever a man separates from the multitude, and goes his own way in this mood, there indeed is a fork in the road, though ordinary travelers may see only a gap in the paling. His solitary path across lots will turn out the *higher way* of the two.

Men rush to California and Australia as if the true gold were to be found in that direction; but that is to go to the very opposite extreme to where it lies. They go prospecting farther and farther away from the true lead, and are most unfortunate when they think themselves most successful. Is not our *native* soil auriferous? Does not a stream from the golden mountains flow through our native valley? and has not this for more than geologic ages been bringing down the shining particles and forming the nuggets for us? Yet, strange to tell, if a digger steal away, prospecting for this true gold, into the unexplored solitudes around us, there is no danger that any will dog his steps, and endeavor to supplant him. He may claim and undermine the whole valley even, both the cultivated and the uncultivated portions, his whole life long in peace, for no one will ever dispute his claim. . . .

It is remarkable that among all the preachers there are so few moral teachers. The prophets are employed in excusing the ways of men. Most reverend seniors, the *illuminati* of the age, tell me, with a gracious, reminiscent smile, betwixt an aspiration and a shudder, not to be too tender about these things,—to lump all that, that is, make a lump of gold of it. The highest advice I have heard on these subjects was groveling. The burden of it was,—It is not worth your while to undertake to reform the world in this particular. Do not ask how your bread is buttered; it will make you sick, if you do,—and the like. A man had better starve at once than lose his innocence in the process of getting his bread. If within the sophisticated man there is not an unsophisticated one, then he is but one of the Devil's angels. As we grow old, we live more coarsely, we relax a little in our disciplines, and, to some extent, cease to obey our finest instincts. But we should be fastidious to the extreme of sanity, disregarding the gibes of those who are more unfortunate than ourselves. . . .

I hardly know an *intellectual* man, even, who is so broad and truly liberal that you can think aloud in his society. Most with whom you endeavor to talk soon come to a stand against some institution in which they appear to hold stock,—that is, some particular, not universal, way of viewing things. They will continually thrust their own low roof, with its narrow skylight, between you and the sky, when it is the unobstructed heavens you would view. Get out of the way with your cobwebs, wash your windows, I say! In some lyceums they tell me that they have voted to exclude the subject of religion. But how do I know what their religion is, and when I am near to or far from it? I have walked into such an arena and done my best to make a clean breast of what religion I have experienced, and the audience never suspected what I was about. The lecture was as harmless as moonshine to them. Whereas, if I had read to them the biography of the greatest scamps in history, they might have thought that I had written the lives of the deacons of their church. Ordinarily, the inquiry is, Where did you come from? or, Where are you going? That was a more pertinent question which I overheard one of my auditors put to another once,—"What does he lecture for?" It made me quake in my shoes.

To speak impartially, the best men that I know are not serene, a world in themselves. For the most part, they dwell in forms, and flatter and study effect only more finely than the rest. We select granite for the underpinning of our houses and barns; we build fences of stone; but we do not ourselves rest on an underpinning of granitic truth, the lowest primitive rock. Our sills are rotten. What stuff is the man made of who is not coexistent in our thought with the purest and subtilest truth? I often accuse my finest acquaintances of an immense frivolity; for, while there are manners and compliments we do not meet, we do not teach one another the lessons of honesty and sincerity that the brutes do, or of steadiness and solidity that the rocks do. The fault is commonly mutual, however; for we do not habitually demand any more of each other. . . .

Just so hollow and ineffectual, for the most part, is our ordinary conversation. Surface meets surface. When our life ceases to be inward and private, conversation degenerates into mere gossip. We rarely meet a man who can tell us any news which he has not read in a newspaper, or been told by his neighbor; and, for the most part, the only difference between us and our fellow is that he has seen the newspaper, or been out to tea, and we have not. In proportion as our inward life fails, we go more constantly and desperately to the post-office. You may depend on it, that the poor fellow who walks away with the greatest number of letters proud of his extensive correspondence has not heard from himself this long while.

I do not know but it is too much to read one newspaper a week. I have tried it recently, and for so long it seems to me that I have not dwelt in my native region. The sun, the clouds, the snow, the trees say not so much to me. You cannot serve two masters. It requires more than a day's devotion to know and to possess the wealth of a day.

We may well be ashamed to tell what things we have read or heard in our day. I do not know why my news should be so trivial,—considering what one's dreams and expectations are, why the developments should be so paltry. The news we hear, for the most part, is not news to our genius. It is the stalest repetition. . . .

All summer, and far into the autumn, perchance, you unconsciously went by the newspapers and the news, and now you find it was because the morning and the evening were full of news to you. Your walks were full of incidents. You attended, not to the affairs of Europe, but to your own affairs in Massachusetts fields. If you chance to live and move and have your being in that thin stratum in which the events that make the news transpire,—thinner than the paper on which it is printed,—then these things will fill the world for you; but if you soar above or dive below that plane, you cannot remember nor be reminded of them. Really to see the sun rise or go down every day, so to relate ourselves to a universal fact, would preserve us sane forever. . . . I find it so difficult to dispose of the few facts which to me are significant, that I hesitate to burden my attention with those which are insignificant, which only a divine mind could illustrate. Such is, for the most part, the news in newspapers and conversation. It is important to preserve the mind's chastity in this respect. . . .

By all kinds of traps and signboards, threatening the extreme penalty of the divine law, exclude such trespassers from the only ground which can be sacred to you. It is so hard to forget what it is worse than useless to remember! If I am to be a thoroughfare, I prefer that it be to the mountain-brooks, the Parnassian streams, and not the town-sewers. There is inspiration, that gossip which comes to the ear of the attentive mind from the courts of heaven. There is the profane and stale revelation of the bar-room and the police court. The same ear is fitted to receive both communications. Only the character of the hearer determines to which it shall be open, and to which closed. I believe that the mind can be permanently profaned by the habit of attending to trivial things, so that all our thoughts shall be tinged with triviality. Our very intellect shall be macadamized, as it were,—its foundation broken into fragments for the wheels of travel to roll over; and if you would know what will make the most durable pavement, surpassing rolled stones, spruce blocks, and asphaltum, you have only to look into some of our minds which have been subjected to this treatment so long.

If we have thus desecrated ourselves,—as who has not?—the remedy will be wariness and devotion to reconsecrate ourselves, and make once more a fane of the mind. We should treat our minds, that is, ourselves, as innocent and ingenuous children, whose guardians we are, and be careful what objects and what subjects we thrust on their attention. Read not the Times. Read the Eternities. Conventionalities are at length as bad as impurities. Even the facts of science may dust the mind by their dryness, unless they are in a sense effaced each morning, or rather rendered fertile by the dews of fresh and living truth. Knowledge does not come to us by details, but in flashes of light from heaven. Yes, every thought that passes through the mind helps to wear and tear it, and to deepen the ruts, which, as in the streets of Pompeii, evince how much it has been used. How many things there are concerning which we might well deliberate whether we had better know them,—had better let their peddling-carts be driven, even at the slowest trot or walk, over that bridge of glorious span by which we trust to pass at last from the farthest brink of time to the nearest shore of eternity! Have we no culture, no refinement,—but skill only to live coarsely and serve the Devil?—to acquire a little worldly wealth, or fame, or liberty, and make a false show with it, as if we were all husk and shell, with no tender and living kernel to us?

Shall our institutions be like those chestnut-burs which contain abortive nuts, perfect only to prick the fingers?

America is said to be the arena on which the battle of freedom is to be fought; but surely it cannot be freedom in a merely political sense that is meant. Even if we grant that the American has freed himself from a political tryant, he is still the slave of an economical and moral tyrant. Now that the republic—the *res-publica*—has been settled, it is time to look after *res-privata*,—the private state, to see, as the Roman senate charged its consuls, *"ne quid res-*PRIVATA *detrimenti caperet,"* that the *private* state receive no detriment.

Do we call this the land of the free? What is it to be free from King George and continue the slaves of King Prejudice? What is it to be born free and not to live free? What is the value of any political freedom, but as a means to moral freedom? Is it a freedom to be slaves, or a freedom to be free, of which we boast? We are a nation of politicians, concerned about the outmost defenses only of freedom. It is our children's children who may perchance be really free. We tax ourselves unjustly. There is a part of us which is not represented. It is taxation without representation. We quarter troops, we quarter fools and cattle of all sorts upon ourselves. We quarter our gross bodies on our poor souls, till the former eat up all the latter's substance.

With respect to a true culture and manhood, we are essentially provincial still, not metropolitan,—mere Jonathans. We are provincial, because we do not find at home our standards; because we do not worship truth, but the reflection of truth; because we are warped and narrowed by an exclusive devotion to trade and commerce and manufactures and agriculture and the like, which are but means, and not the end. . . .

Government and legislation: these I thought were respectable professions. We have heard of heaven-born Numas, Lycurguses, and Solons, in the history of the world, whose *names* at least may stand for ideal legislators; but think of legislating to *regulate* the breeding of slaves, or the exportation of tobacco! What have divine legislators to do with the exportation or the importation of tobacco? what humane ones with the breeding of slaves? Suppose you were to submit the question to any son of God,—and has He no children in the nineteenth century? is it a family which is extinct?—in what condition would you get it again? What shall a State like Virginia say for itself at the last day, in which these have been the principal, the staple productions? What ground is there for patriotism in such a State? I derive my facts from statistical tables which the States themselves have published.

A commerce that whitens every sea in quest of nuts and raisins, and makes slaves of its sailors for this purpose! I saw, the other day, a vessel which had been wrecked, and many lives lost, and her cargo of rags, juniper-berries, and bitter almonds were strewn along the shore. It seemed hardly worth the while to tempt the dangers of the sea between Leghorn and New York for the sake of a cargo of juniper-berries and bitter almonds. America sending to the Old World for her bitters! Is not the sea-brine, is not shipwreck, bitter enough to make the cup of life go down here? Yet such, to a great extent, is our boasted commerce; and there are those who style themselves statesmen and philosophers who are so blind as to think that progress and civilization depend on precisely this kind of interchange and activity,—the activity of flies about a molasses-hogshead. Very well, observes one, if men were oysters. And very well, answer I, if men were mosquitoes. . . . When we want culture more than potatoes, and illumination more than sugar-plums, then the great resources of a world are taxed and drawn out, and the result, or staple production, is, not slaves, nor operatives, but men,—those rare fruits called heroes, saints, poets, philosophers, and redeemers. . . .

What is called politics is comparatively something so superficial and inhuman, that practically I have never fairly recognized that it concerns me at all. The newspapers, I perceive, devote some of their columns specially to politics or government without charge; and this, one would say, is all that saves it; but as I love literature and to some extent the truth also, I never read those columns at any rate. I do not wish to blunt my sense of right so much. I have not got to answer for having read a single President's Message. A strange age of the world this, when empires, kingdoms, and republics come a-begging to a private man's door, and utter their complaints at his elbow! I cannot take up a newspaper but I find that some wretched government or other, hard pushed, and on its last legs, is interceding with me, the reader, to vote for it. . . . The poor President, what with preserving his popularity and doing his duty, is completely bewildered. The newspapers are the ruling power. Any other government is reduced to a few marines at Fort Independence. . . .

Those things which now most engage the attention of men, as politics and the daily routine, are, it is true, vital functions of human society, but should be unconsciously performed, like the corresponding functions of the physical body. They are *infra*-human, a kind of vegetation. I sometimes awake to a half-consciousness of them going on about me, as a man may become conscious of some of the processes of digestion in a morbid state, and so have the dyspepsia, as it is called. It is as if a thinker submitted himself to be rasped by the great gizzard of creation. Politics is, as it were, the gizzard of society, full of grit and gravel, and the two political parties are its two opposite halves,—sometimes split into quarters, it may be, which grind on each other. Not only individuals, but states, have thus a confirmed dyspepsia, which expresses itself, you can imagine by what sort of eloquence. Thus our life is not altogether a forgetting, but also, alas! to a great extent, a remembering, of that which we should never have been conscious of, certainly not in our waking hours. Why should we not meet, not always as dyspeptics, to tell our bad dreams, but sometimes as *eu*peptics, to congratulate each other on the ever-glorious morning? I do not make an exorbitant demand, surely.

William James
On a Certain Blindness
in Human Beings
(1899)

OUR JUDGMENTS concerning the worth of things, big or little, depend on the *feelings* the things arouse in us. Where we judge a thing to be precious in consequence of the *idea* we frame of it, this is only because the idea is itself associated already with a feeling. If we were radically feelingless, and if ideas were the only things our mind could entertain, we should lose all our likes and dislikes at a stroke, and be unable to point to any one situation or experience in life more valuable or significant than any other.

Now the blindness in human beings, of which this discourse will treat, is the blindness with which we all are afflicted in regard to the feelings of creatures and people different from ourselves.

We are practical beings, each of us with limited functions and duties to perform. Each is bound to feel intensely the importance of his own duties and the significance of the situations that call these forth. But this feeling is in each of us a vital secret, for sympathy with which we vainly look to others. The others are too much absorbed in their own vital secrets to take an interest in ours. Hence the stupidity and injustice of our opinions, so far as they deal with the significance of alien lives. Hence the falsity of our judgments, so far as they presume to decide in an absolute way on the value of other persons' conditions or ideals.

Take our dogs and ourselves, connected as we are by a tie more intimate than most ties in this world; and yet, outside of that tie of friendly fondness, how insensible, each of us, to all that makes life significant for the other!—we to the rapture of bones under hedges, or smells of trees and

[From *Talks to Teachers on Psychology: And to Students on Some of Life's Ideals* (1899).]

lamp-posts, they to the delights of literature and art. As you sit reading the most moving romance you ever fell upon, what sort of a judge is your fox-terrier of your behavior? With all his good will toward you, the nature of your conduct is absolutely excluded from his comprehension. To sit there like a senseless statue, when you might be taking him to walk and throwing sticks for him to catch! What queer disease is this that comes over you every day, of holding things and staring at them like that for hours together, paralyzed of motion and vacant of all conscious life? The African savages came nearer the truth; but they, too, missed it, when they gathered wonderingly round one of our American travellers who, in the interior, had just come into possession of a stray copy of the New York *Commercial Advertiser*, and was devouring it column by column. When he got through, they offered him a high price for the mysterious object; and, being asked for what they wanted it, they said: "For an eye medicine,"—that being the only reason they could conceive of for the protracted bath which he had given his eyes upon its surface.

The spectator's judgment is sure to miss the root of the matter, and to possess no truth. The subject judged knows a part of the world of reality which the judging spectator fails to see, knows more while the spectator knows less; and, wherever there is conflict of opinion and difference of vision, we are bound to believe that the truer side is the side that feels the more, and not the side that feels the less.

Let me take a personal example of the kind that befalls each one of us daily:—

Some years ago, while journeying in the mountains of North Carolina, I passed by a large number of "coves," as they call them there, or heads of small valleys between the hills, which had been newly cleared and planted. The impression on my mind was one of unmitigated squalor. The settler had in every case cut down the more manageable trees, and left their charred stumps standing. The larger trees he had girdled and killed, in order that their foliage should not cast a shade. He had then built a log cabin, plastering its chinks with clay, and had set up a tall zigzag rail fence around the scene of his havoc, to keep the pigs and cattle out. Finally, he had irregularly planted the intervals between the stumps and trees with Indian corn, which grew among the chips; and there he dwelt with his wife and babes—an axe, a gun, a few utensils, and some pigs and chickens feeding in the woods, being the sum total of his possessions.

The forest had been destroyed; and what had "improved" it out of existence was hideous, a sort of ulcer, without a single element of artificial grace to make up for the loss of Nature's beauty. Ugly, indeed, seemed the life of the squatter, scudding, as the sailors say, under bare poles, beginning again away back where our first ancestors started, and by hardly a single item the better off for all the achievements of the intervening generations.

Talk about going back to nature! I said to myself, oppressed by the dreariness, as I drove by. Talk of a country life for one's old age and for one's children! Never thus, with nothing but the bare ground and one's bare hands to fight the battle! Never, without the best spoils of culture woven in! The beauties and commodities gained by the centuries are sacred. They are our heritage and birthright. No modern person ought to be willing to live a day in such a state of rudimentariness and denudation.

Then I said to the mountaineer who was driving me, "What sort of people are they who have to make these new clearings?" "All of us," he replied. "Why, we ain't happy here, unless we are getting one of these coves under cultivation." I instantly felt that I had been losing the whole inward significance of the situation. Because to me the clearings spoke of naught but denudation, I thought that to those whose sturdy arms and obedient axes had made them they could tell no other story. But, when *they* looked on the hideous stumps, what they thought of was personal victory. The chips, the girdled trees, and the vile split rails spoke of honest sweat, persistent toil and final reward. The cabin was a warrant of safety for self and wife and babes. In short, the clearing, which to me was a mere ugly picture on the retina, was to them a symbol redolent with moral memories and sang a very pæan of duty, struggle, and success.

I had been as blind to the peculiar ideality of their conditions as they certainly would also have been to the ideality of mine, had they had a peep at my strange indoor academic ways of life at Cambridge. . . .

And now what is the result of all these considerations . . . It is negative in one sense, but positive in another. It absolutely forbids us to be forward in pronouncing on the meaninglessness of forms of existence other than our own; and it commands us to tolerate, respect, and indulge those whom we see harmlessly interested and happy in their own ways, however unintelligible these may be to us. Hands off: neither the whole of truth nor the whole of good is revealed to any single observer, although each observer gains a partial superiority of insight from the peculiar position in which he stands. Even prisons and sick-rooms have their special revelations. It is enough to ask of each of us that he should be faithful to his own opportunities and make the most of his own blessings, without presuming to regulate the rest of the vast field.

William James
What Makes a Life Significant
(1899)

IN MY previous talk, "On a Certain Blindness," I tried to make you feel how soaked and shot-through life is with values and meanings which we fail to realize because of our external and insensible point of view. The meanings are there for the others, but they are not there for us. There lies more than a mere interest of curious speculation in understanding this. It has the most tremendous practical importance. I wish that I could convince you of it as I feel it myself. It is the basis of all our tolerance, social, religious, and political. The forgetting of it lies at the root of every stupid and sanguinary mistake that rulers over subject-peoples make. The first thing to learn in intercourse with others is noninterference with their own peculiar ways of being happy, provided those ways do not assume to interfere by violence with ours. No one has insight into all the ideals. No one should presume to judge them off-hand. The pretension to dogmatize about them in each other is the root of most human injustices and cruelties, and the trait in human character most likely to make the angels weep.

Every Jack sees in his own particular Jill charms and perfections to the enchantment of which we stolid onlookers are stone-cold. And which has the superior view of the absolute truth, he or we? Which has the more vital insight into the nature of Jill's existence, as a fact? Is he in excess, being in this matter a maniac? or are we in defect, being victims of a pathological anæsthesia as regards Jill's magical importance? Surely the latter; surely to Jack are the profounder truths revealed; surely poor Jill's palpitating little life-throbs *are* among the wonders of creation, *are* worthy of this sympathetic interest; and it is to our shame that the rest of us cannot feel like Jack. For Jack realizes Jill concretely, and we do not. He struggles toward a union with her inner life, divining her feelings, antic-

[From *Talks to Teachers on Psychology: And to Students on Some of Life's Ideals* (1899).]

ipating her desires, understanding her limits as manfully as he can, and yet inadequately, too; for he is also afflicted with some blindness, even here. Whilst we, dead clods that we are, do not even seek after these things, but are contented that that portion of eternal fact named Jill should be for us as if it were not. Jill, who knows her inner life, knows that Jack's way of taking it—so importantly—is the true and serious way; and she responds to the truth in him by taking him truly and seriously, too. May the ancient blindness never wrap its clouds about either of them again! Where would any of *us* be, were there no one willing to know us as we really are or ready to repay us for *our* insight by making recognizant return? We ought, all of us, to realize each other in this intense, pathetic, and important way.

If you say that this is absurd, and that we cannot be in love with everyone at once, I merely point out to you that, as a matter of fact, certain persons do exist with an enormous capacity for friendship and for taking delight in other people's lives; and that such persons know more of truth than if their hearts were not so big. The vice of ordinary Jack and Jill affection is not its intensity, but its exclusions and its jealousies. Leave those out, and you see that the ideal I am holding up before you, however impracticable to-day, yet contains nothing intrinsically absurd.

We have unquestionably a great cloud-bank of ancestral blindness weighing down upon us, only transiently riven here and there by fitful revelations of the truth. It is vain to hope for this state of things to alter much. Our inner secrets must remain for the most part impenetrable by others, for beings as essentially practical as we are are necessarily short of sight. But, if we cannot gain much positive insight into one another, cannot we at least use our sense of our own blindness to make us more cautious in going over the dark places? Cannot we escape some of those hideous ancestral intolerances and cruelties, and positive reversals of the truth?

For the remainder of this hour I invite you to seek with me some principle to make our tolerance less chaotic. And, as I began my previous lecture by a personal reminiscence, I am going to ask your indulgence for a similar bit of egotism now.

A few summers ago I spent a happy week at the famous Assembly Grounds on the borders of Chautauqua Lake. The moment one treads that sacred enclosure, one feels one's self in an atmosphere of success. Sobriety and industry, intelligence and goodness, orderliness and ideality, prosperity and cheerfulness, pervade the air. It is a serious and studious picnic on a gigantic scale. Here you have a town of many thousands of inhabitants, beautifully laid out in the forest and drained, and equipped with means for satisfying all the necessary lower and most of the superfluous higher wants of man. You have a first-class college in full blast.

You have magnificent music—a chorus of seven hundred voices, with possibly the most perfect open-air auditorium in the world. You have every sort of athletic exercise from sailing, rowing, swimming, bicycling, to the ball-field and the more artificial doings which the gymnasium affords. You have kindergartens and model secondary schools. You have general religious services and special club-houses for the several sects. You have perpetually running soda-water fountains, and daily popular lectures by distinguished men. You have the best of company, and yet no effort. You have no zymotic diseases, no poverty, no drunkenness, no crime, no police. You have culture, you have kindness, you have cheapness, you have equality, you have the best fruits of what mankind has fought and bled and striven for under the name of civilization for centuries. You have, in short, a foretaste of what human society might be, were it all in the light, with no suffering and no dark corners.

I went in curiosity for a day. I stayed for a week, held spell-bound by the charm and ease of everything, by the middle-class paradise, without a sin, without a victim, without a blot, without a tear.

And yet what was my own astonishment, on emerging into the dark and wicked world again, to catch myself quite unexpectedly and involuntarily saying: "Ouf! what a relief! Now for something primordial and savage, even though it were as bad as an Armenian massacre, to set the balance straight again. This order is too tame, this culture too second-rate, this goodness too uninspiring. This human drama without a villain or a pang; this community so refined that ice-cream soda-water is the utmost offering it can make to the brute animal in man; this city simmering in the tepid lakeside sun; this atrocious harmlessness of all things,—I cannot abide with them. Let me take my chances again in the big outside worldly wilderness with all its sins and sufferings. There are the heights and depths, the precipices and the steep ideals, the gleams of the awful and the infinite; and there is more hope and help a thousand times than in this dead level and quintessence of every mediocrity."

Such was the sudden right-about-face performed for me by my lawless fancy! There had been spread before me the realization—on a small, sample scale of course—of all the ideals for which our civilization has been striving: security, intelligence, humanity, and order; and here was the instinctive hostile reaction, not of the natural man, but of a so-called cultivated man upon such a Utopia. There seemed thus to be a self-contradiction and paradox somewhere, which I, as a professor drawing a full salary, was in duty bound to unravel and explain, if I could.

So I meditated. And, first of all, I asked myself what the thing was that was so lacking in this Sabbatical city, and the lack of which kept one forever falling short of the higher sort of contentment. And I soon recognized that it was the element that gives to the wicked outer world all its moral style, expressiveness and picturesqueness,—the element of precipitousness, so to call it, of strength and strenuousness, intensity and danger. What excites and interests the looker-on at life, what the romances and the statues celebrate and the grim civic monuments remind us of, is the everlasting battle of the powers of light with those of darkness; with heroism, reduced to its bare chance, yet ever and anon snatching victory from the jaws of death. But in this unspeakable Chautauqua there was no potentiality of death in sight anywhere, and no point of the compass visible from which danger might possibly appear. The ideal was so completely victorious already that no sign of any previous battle remained, the place just resting on its oars. But what our human emotions seem to require is the sight of the struggle going on. The moment the fruits are being merely eaten, things become ignoble. Sweat and effort, human nature strained to its uttermost and on the rack, yet getting through alive, and then turning its back on its success to pursue another more rare and arduous still—this is the sort of thing the presence of which inspires us, and the reality of which it seems to be the function of all the higher forms of literature and fine art to bring home to us and suggest. At Chautauqua there were no racks, even in the place's historical museum; and no sweat, except possibly the gentle moisture on the brow of some lecturer, or on the sides of some player in the ball-field.

Such absence of human nature *in extremis* anywhere seemed, then, a sufficient explanation for Chautauqua's flatness and lack of zest. . . .

With these thoughts in my mind, I was speeding with the train toward Buffalo, when, near that city, the sight of a workman doing something on the dizzy edge of a sky-scaling iron construction brought me to my senses very suddenly. And now I perceived, by a flash of insight, that I had been steeping myself in pure ancestral blindness, and looking at life with the eyes of a remote spectator. Wishing for heroism and the spectacle of human nature on the rack, I had never noticed the great fields of heroism lying round about me, I had failed to see it present and alive. I could only think of it as dead and embalmed, labelled and costumed, as it is in the pages of romance. And yet there it was before me in the daily lives of the laboring classes. Not in clanging fights and desperate marches only is heroism to be looked for, but on every railway bridge and fire-proof building that is going up to-day. On freight-trains, on the decks of vessels, in cattleyards and mines, on lumber-rafts, among the firemen and the policemen, the demand for courage is incessant; and the supply never fails. There, every day of the year somewhere, is human nature *in extremis* for you. And wherever a scythe, an axe, a pick, or a shovel is wielded, you have it sweating and aching and with its powers of patient endurance racked to the utmost under the length of hours of the strain.

As I awoke to all this unidealized heroic life around me, the scales seemed to fall from my eyes; and a wave of sympathy greater than anything I had ever before felt with the common life of common men began to fill my soul. It began to seem as if virtue with horny hands and dirty skin were the only virtue genuine and vital enough to take account of. Every other virtue poses; none is absolutely unconscious and simple, and unexpectant of decoration or recognition, like this. . . .

You see, my friends, how the plot now thickens; and how strangely the complexities of this wonderful human nature of ours begin to develop under our hands. We have seen the blindness and deadness to each other which are our natural inheritance; and, in spite of them, we have been led to acknowledge an inner meaning which passeth show, and which may be present in the lives of others where we least descry it. And now we are led to say that such inner meaning can be *complete* and *valid for us also*, only when the inner joy, courage, and endurance are joined with an ideal.

But what, exactly, do we mean by an ideal? Can we give no definite account of such a word?

To a certain extent we can. An ideal, for instance, must be something intellectually conceived, something of which we are not unconscious, if we have it; and it must carry with it that sort of outlook, uplift, and brightness that go with all intellectual facts. Secondly, there must be *novelty* in an ideal,—novelty at least for him whom the ideal grasps. Sodden routine is incompatible with ideality, although what is sodden routine for one person may be ideal novelty for another. This shows that there is nothing absolutely ideal: ideals are relative to the lives that entertain them. To keep out of the gutter is for us here no part of consciouness at all, yet for many of our brethren it is the most legitimately engrossing of ideals.

Now, taken nakedly, abstractly, and immediately, you see that mere ideals are the cheapest things in life. Everybody has them in some shape or other, personal or general, sound or mistaken, low or high; and the most worthless sentimentalists and dreamers, drunkards, shirks and verse-makers, who never show a grain of effort, courage, or endurance, possibly have them on the most copious scale. Education, enlarging as it does our horizon and perspective, is a means of multiplying our ideals, of bringing new ones into view. And your college professor, with a starched shirt and spectacles, would, if a stock of ideals were all alone by itelf enough to render a life significant, be the most absolutely and deeply significant of men. . . .

But such consequences as this, you instinctively feel, are erroneous. The more ideals a man has, the more contemptible, on the whole, do you continue to deem him, if the matter ends there for him, and if none of the laboring man's virtues are called into action on his part,—no courage shown, no privations undergone, no dirt or scars contracted in the attempt to get them realized. It is quite obvious that something more than the mere possession of ideals is required to make a life significant in any sense that claims the spectator's admiration. Inner joy, to be sure, it may *have*, with its ideals; but that is its own private sentimental matter. To extort from us, outsiders as we are, with our own ideals to look after, the tribute of our grudging recognition, it must back its ideal visions with what the laborers have, the sterner stuff of manly virtue; it must multiply their sentimental surface by the dimension of the active will, if we are to have *depth*, if we are to have anything cubical and solid in the way of character.

The significance of a human life for communicable and publicly recognizable purposes is thus the offspring of a marriage of two different parents, either of whom alone is barren. The ideals taken by themselves give no reality, the virtues by themselves no novelty. And let the orientalists and pessimists say what they will, the thing of deepest—or, at any rate, of comparatively—deepest—significance in life does seem to be its character of *progress*, or that strange union of reality with ideal novelty which it continues from one moment to another to present. . . .

But, with all this beating and tacking on my part, I fear you take me to be reaching a confused result. I seem to be just taking things up and dropping them again. First I took up Chautauqua, and dropped that; then . . . the heroism of common toil; . . . finally, I took up ideals, and seem now almost dropping those. But please observe in what sense it is that I drop them. It is when they pretend *singly* to redeem life from insignificance. Culture and refinement all alone are not enough to do so. Ideal aspirations are not enough, when uncombined with pluck and will. But neither are pluck and will, dogged endurance and insensibility to danger enough, when taken all alone. There must be some sort of fusion, some chemical combination among these principles, for a life objectively and thoroughly significant to result.

Of course, this is a somewhat vague conclusion. But in a question of significance, of worth, like this, conclusions can never be precise. The answer of appreciation, of sentiment, is always a more or a less, a balance struck by sympathy, insight, and good will. But it is an answer, all the same, a real conclusion. And, in the course of getting it, it seems to me that our eyes have been opened to many important things. Some of you are, perhaps, more livingly aware than you were an hour ago of the depths of worth that lie around you, hid in alien lives. And, when you ask how much sympathy you ought to bestow, although the amount is, truly enough, a matter of ideal on your own part, yet in this notion of the combination of ideals with active virtues you have a rough standard for shaping your decision. In any case, your imagination is extended. You divine in the world about you matter for a little more humility on your own part, and tolerance, reverence, and love for others; and you gain a certain inner joyfulness at the increased importance of our common life. Such joyfulness is a religious inspiration and an element of spiritual health, and worth more than large amounts of that sort of technical and accurate information which we professors are supposed to be able to impart. To show the sort of thing I mean by these words, I will just make one brief practical illustration, and then close.

We are suffering to-day in America from what is called the labor-question; and, when you go out into the world, you will each and all of you be caught up in its perplexities. I use the brief term labor-question to cover all sorts of anarchistic discontents and socialistic projects, and the conservative resistances which they provoke. So far as this conflict is unhealthy and regrettable,—and I think it is so only to a limited extent,— the unhealthiness consists solely in the fact that one-half of our fellow-countrymen remain entirely blind to the internal significance of the lives of the other half. They miss the joys and sorrows, they fail to feel the moral virtue, and they do not guess the presence of the intellectual ideals. They are at cross-purposes all along the line, regarding each other as they might regard a set of dangerously gesticulating automata, or, if they seek to get at the inner motivation, making the most horrible mistakes. Often all that the poor man can think of in the rich man is a cowardly greediness for safety, luxury, and effeminacy, and a boundless affectation. What he is, is not a human being, but a pocket-book, a bank-account. And a similar greediness, turned by disappointment into envy, is all that many rich men can see in the state of mind of the dissatisfied poor. And, if the rich man begins to do the sentimental act over the poor man, what senseless blunders does he make, pitying him for just those very duties and those very immunities which, rightly taken, are the condition of his most abiding and characteristic joys! Each, in short, ignores the fact that happiness and unhappiness and significance are a vital mystery; each pins them absolutely on some ridiculous feature of the external situation; and everybody remains outside of everybody else's sight.

Society has, with all this, undoubtedly got to pass toward some newer and better equilibrium, and the distribution of wealth has doubtless slowly got to change: such changes have always happened, and will happen to the end of time. But if, after all that I have said, any of you expect that they will make any *genuine vital difference* on a large scale, to the lives of our descendants, you will have missed the significance of my entire lecture. The solid meaning of life is always the same eternal thing,—the marriage, namely, of some unhabitual ideal, however special, with some fidelity, courage, and endurance; with some man's or woman's pains.— And, whatever or wherever life may be, there will always be the chance for that marriage to take place. . . .

In this solid and tridimensional sense, so to call it, those philosophers are right who contend that the world is a standing thing, with no progress, no real history. The changing conditions of history touch only the surface of the show. The altered equilibriums and redistributions only diversify our opportunities and open chances to us for new ideals. But, with each new ideal that comes into life, the chance for a life based on some old ideal will vanish; and he would needs be a presumptuous calculator who should with confidence say that the total sum of significances is positively and absolutely greater at any one epoch than at any other of the world.

I am speaking broadly, I know, and omitting to consider certain qualifications in which I myself believe. But one can only make one point in one lecture, and I shall be well content if I have brought my point home to you this evening in even a slight degree. *There are compensations*: and no outward changes of condition in life can keep the nightingale of its eternal meaning from singing in all sorts of different men's hearts. That is the main fact to remember. If we could not only admit it with our lips, but really and truly believe it, how our convulsive insistencies, how our antipathies and dreads of each other, would soften down! If the poor and the rich could look at each other in this way, *sub specie æternatis*, how gentle would grow their disputes! what tolerance and good humor, what willingness to live and let live, would come into the world!

Josiah Royce
Provincialism
(1908)

THE WORD "provincialism," which I have used as my title, has been chosen because it is the best single word that I have been able to find to suggest the group of social tendencies to which I want to call your especial attention. I intend to use this word in a somewhat elastic sense, which I may at once indicate. . . . For me, then, a province shall mean any one part of a national domain, which is, geographically and socially, sufficiently unified to have a true consciousness of its own unity, to feel a pride in its own ideals and customs, and to possess a sense of its distinction from other parts of the country. And by the term "provincialism" I shall mean, first, the tendency of such a province to possess its own customs and ideals; secondly, the totality of these customs and ideals themselves; and thirdly, the love and pride which leads the inhabitants of a province to cherish as their own these traditions, beliefs, and aspirations. . . . My thesis is that, in the present state of the world's civilization, and of the life of our own country, the time has come to emphasize, with a new meaning and intensity, the positive value, the absolute necessity for our welfare, of a wholesome provincialism, as a saving power to which the world in the near future will need more and more to appeal.

The time was (and not very long since), when, in our own country, we had to contend against very grave evils due to false forms of provincialism. What has been called sectionalism long threatened our national unity. Our Civil War was fought to overcome the ills due to such influences. There was, therefore, a time when the virtue of true patriotism had to be founded upon a vigorous condemnation of certain powerful forms of provincialism. And our national education at that time depended both upon our learning common federal ideals, and upon our looking to foreign lands for the spiritual guidance of older civilizations. Furthermore, not only have these things been so in the past, but similar needs will, of course, be felt in the future. We shall always be required to take counsel of the other nations in company with whom we are at work upon the tasks of civilization. Nor have we outgrown our spiritual dependence upon older forms of civilization. In fact we shall never outgrow a certain inevitable degree of such dependence. Our national unity, moreover, will always require of us a devotion that will transcend in some directions the limits of all our provincial ideas. A common sympathy between the different sections of our country will, in future, need a constantly fresh cultivation. Against the evil forms of sectionalism we shall always have to contend. All this I well know, and these things I need not in your presence emphasize. But what I am to emphasize is this: The present state of civilization, both in the world at large, and with us, in America, is such as to define a new social mission which the province alone, but not the nation, is able to fulfil. False sectionalism, which disunites, will indeed always remain as great an evil as ever it was. But the modern world has reached a point where it needs, more than ever before, the vigorous development of a highly organized provincial life. Such a life, if wisely guided, will not mean disloyalty to the nation; and it need not mean narrowness of spirit, nor yet the further development of jealousies between various communities. What it will mean, or at least may mean,— this, so far as I have time, I wish to set forth in the following discussion. My main intention is to define the right form and the true office of provincialism,—to portray what, if you please, we may well call the Higher Provincialism,—to portray it, and then to defend it, to extol it, and to counsel you to further just such provincialism.

Since this is my purpose, let me at once say that I address myself, in the most explicit terms, to men and women who, as I hope and presuppose, are and wish to be, in the wholesome sense, provincial. Every one, as I maintain, ought, ideally speaking, to be provincial,—and that no matter how cultivated, or humanitarian, or universal in purpose or in experience he may be or may become. If in our own country, where often so many people are still comparative strangers to the communities in which they have come to live, there are some of us who, like myself, have changed our provinces during our adult years, and who have so been unable to become and to remain in the sense of European countries provincial; and if, moreover, the life of our American provinces everywhere has still too brief a tradition,—all that is our misfortune, and not our advantage. As our country grows in social organization, there will be, in absolute measure, more and not less provincialism amongst our people. To be sure, as I hope, there will also be, in absolute measure, more and not less patriotism, closer and not looser national ties, less and not more mutual sectional misunderstanding. But the two tendencies, the tendency toward national unity and that toward local independence of spirit, must henceforth grow together. They cannot prosper apart. The national unity must not kill out, nor yet hinder, the provincial self-consciousness. The loyalty to the Republic must not lessen the love and the local pride of the individual community. The man of the future must love his province more than he does to-day. His provincial customs and ideals must be more and not less highly developed, more and not less self-conscious, well-established, and earnest. And therefore, I say, I appeal to you as to a company of people who are, and who mean to be, provincial as well as patriotic,—servants and lovers of your own community and of its ways, as well as citizens of the world. . . .

With this programme in mind, let me first tell you what seem to me to be in our modern world, and, in particular, in our American world, the principal evils which are to be corrected by a further development of a true provincial spirit, and which cannot be corrected without such a development.

The first of these evils I have already mentioned. It is a defect incidental, partly to the newness of our own country, but partly also to those world-wide conditions of modern life which make travel, and even a change of home, both attractive and easy to dwellers in the most various parts of the globe. In nearly every one of our American communities, at least in the northern and in the western regions of our country, there is a rather large proportion of people who either have not grown up where they were born, or who have changed their dwelling-place in adult years. I can speak all the more freely regarding this class of our communities, because, in my own community, I myself, as a native of California, now resident in New England, belong to such a class. Such classes, even in modern New England, are too large. The stranger, the sojourner, the newcomer, is an inevitable factor in the life of most American communities. To make him welcome is one of the most gracious of the tasks in which our people have become expert. To give him his fair chance is the rule of our national life. But it is not on the whole well when the affairs of a community remain too largely under the influence of those who mainly feel either the wanderer's or the new resident's interest in the region where they are now dwelling. To offset the social tendencies due to such frequent changes of dwelling-place we need the further development and the intensification of the community spirit. The sooner the new resident learns to share this spirit, the better for him and for his community. A sound instinct, therefore, guides even our newer communities, in the more fortunate cases, to a rapid development of such a local sentiment as makes the stranger feel that he must in due measure conform if he would be permanently welcome, and must accept the local spirit if he is to enjoy the advantages of his community. As a Californian I have been interested to see both the evidences and the nature of this rapid evolution of the genuine provincial spirit in my own state. How swiftly, in that country, the Californians of the early days seized upon every suggestion that could give a sense of the unique importance of their new provincial life. The associations that soon clustered about the tales of the life of Spanish missionaries and Mexican colonists in the years before 1846,— these our American Californians cherished from the outset. This, to us often half-legendary past, gave us a history of our own. The wondrous events of the early mining life,—how earnestly the pioneers later loved to rehearse that story; and how proud every young Californian soon became of the fact that his father had had his part therein. Even the Californian's well-known and largely justified glorification of his climate was, in his own mind, part of the same expression of his tendency to idealize whatever tended to make his community, and all its affairs, seem unique, beloved, and deeply founded upon some significant natural basis. Such a foundation was, indeed, actually there; nature had, indeed, richly blessed his land; but the real interest that made one emphasize and idealize all these things, often so boastfully, was the interest of the loyal citizen in finding his community an object of pride. Now you, who know well your own local history, will be able to observe the growth amongst you of this tendency to idealize your past, to glorify the bounties that nature has showered upon you, all in such wise as to give the present life of your community more dignity, more honor, more value in the eyes of yourselves and of strangers. In fact, that we all do thus glorify our various provinces, we well know; and with what feelings we accompany the process, we can all observe for ourselves. But it is well to remember that the special office, the principal use, the social justification, of such mental tendencies in ourselves lies in the aid that they give us in becoming loyal to our community, and in assimilating to our own social order the strangers that are within our gates. . . . So learn to view your new community that every stranger who enters it shall at once feel the dignity of its past, and the unique privilege that is offered to him when he is permitted to belong to its company of citizens. . . .

[A] second modern evil arises from, and constitutes, one aspect of the levelling tendency of recent civilization. That such a levelling tendency exists, most of us recognize. That it is the office of the province to contend against some of the attendant evils of this tendency, we less often observe. By the levelling tendency in question I mean that aspect of modern civilization which is most obviously suggested by the fact that, because of the ease of communication amongst distant places, because of the spread of popular education, and because of the consolidation and of the centralization of industries and of social authorities, we tend all over the nation, and, in some degree, even throughout the civilized world, to read the same daily news, to share the same general ideas, to submit to the same overmastering social forces, to live in the same external fashions, to discourage individuality, and to approach a dead level of harassed mediocrity. One of the most marked of all social tendencies is in any age that toward the mutual assimilation of men in so far as they are in social relations with one another. One of the strongest human predispositions is that toward imitation. But our modern conditions have greatly favored the increase of the numbers of people who read the same books and newspapers, who repeat the same phrases, who follow the same social fashions, and who thus, in general, imitate one another in constantly more and more ways. The result is a tendency to crush the individual. Furthermore there are modern economic and industrial developments, too well known to all of you to need any detailed mention here, which lead toward similar results. The independence of the small trader or manufacturer becomes lost in the great commercial or industrial combination. The vast corporation succeeds and displaces the individual. Ingenuity and initiative become subordinated to the discipline of an impersonal social order. And each man, becoming, like his fellow, the servant of masters too powerful for him to resist, and too complex in their undertakings for him to understand, is, in so far, disposed unobtrusively to conform to the ways of his innumerable fellow-servants, and to lose all sense of his unique moral destiny as an individual.

I speak here merely of tendencies. As you know, they are nowhere unopposed tendencies. Nor do I for an instant pretend to call even these levelling tendencies wholly, or principally, evil. But for the moment I call attention to what are obviously questionable, and in some degree are plainly evil, aspects of these modern tendencies. Imitation is a good thing. All civilization depends upon it. But there may be a limit to the number of people who ought to imitate precisely the same body of ideas and customs. For imitation is not man's whole business. There ought to be some room left for variety. Modern conditions have often increased too much what one might call the purely mechanical carrying-power of certain ruling social influences. There are certain metropolitan newspapers, for instance, which have far too many readers for the good of the social order in which they circulate. These newspapers need not always be very mischievous ones. But when read by too vast multitudes, they tend to produce a certain monotonously uniform triviality of mind in a large proportion of our city and suburban population. It would be better if the same readers were divided into smaller sections, which read different newspapers, even if these papers were of no higher level. For then there would at least be a greater variety in the sorts of triviality which from day to day occupied their minds. And variety is the beginning of individual independence of insight and of conviction. As for the masses of people who are under the domination of the great corporations that employ them, I am here not in the least dwelling upon their economic difficulties. I am pointing out that the lack of initiative in their lives tends to make their spiritual range narrower. They are too little disposed to create their own world. Now every man who gets into a vital relation to God's truth becomes, in his own way, a creator. And if you deprive a man of all incentive to create, you in so far tend to cut him off from God's truth. Or, in more common language, independence of spirit flourishes only when a man at least believes that he has a chance to change his fortunes if he persistently wills to do so. But the servant of some modern forms of impersonal social organization tends to lose this belief that he has a chance. Hence he tends to lose independence of spirit.

Well, this is the second of the evils of the modern world which, as I have said, provincialism may tend to counteract. Local spirit, local pride, provincial independence, influence the individual man precisely because they appeal to his imitative tendencies. But thereby they act so as to render him more or less immune in presence of the more trivial of the influences that, coming from without his community, would otherwise be likely to reduce him to the dead level of the customs of the whole nation. A country district may seem to a stranger unduly crude in its ways; but it does not become wiser in case, under the influence of city newspapers and of summer boarders, it begins to follow city fashions merely for the sake of imitating. Other things being equal, it is better in proportion as it remains self-possessed,—proud of its own traditions, not unwilling indeed to learn, but also quite ready to teach the stranger its own wisdom. And in similar fashion provincial pride helps the individual man to keep his self-respect even when the vast forces that work toward industrial consolidation, and toward the effacement of individual initiative, are besetting his life at every turn. For a man is in large measure what his social consciousness makes him. Give him the local community that he loves and cherishes, that he is proud to honor and to serve,— make his ideal of that community lofty,—give him faith in the dignity of his province,—and you have given him a power to counteract the levelling tendencies of modern civilization.

The third of the evils with which a wise provincialism must contend is closely connected with the second. I have spoken of the constant tendency of modern life to the mutual assimilation of various parts of the social order. Now this assimilation may occur slowly and steadily, as in great measure it normally does; or, on the other hand, it may take more sudden and striking forms, at moments when the popular mind is excited, when great emotions affect the social order. At such times of emotional disturbance, society is subject to tendencies which have recently received a good deal of psychological study. They are the tendencies to constitute what has often been called the spirit of the crowd or of the mob. . . .

I use the term "mob-spirit" as an abbreviation for a very large range of phenomena, phenomena which may indeed be classed with all the rest of the imitative phenomena as belonging to one genus. But the mob-phenomena are distinguished from the other imitative phenomena by certain characteristic emotional tendencies which belong to excited crowds of people, and which do not belong to the more strictly normal social activities. Man, as an imitative animal, naturally tends, as we have seen, to do whatever his companions do, so long as he is not somehow aroused to independence and to individuality. Accordingly, he easily shares the beliefs and temperaments of those who are near enough to him to influence him. But now suppose a condition of things such as may readily occur in any large group of people who have somehow come to feel strong sympathy with one another, and who are for any reason in a relatively passive and impressible state of mind. In such a company of people let any idea which has a strong emotional coloring come to be suggested, by the words of the leader, by the singing of a song, by the beginning of any social activity that does not involve clear thinking, that does not call upon a man to assert his own independence. Such an idea forthwith tends to take possession in an extraordinarily strong degree of every member of the social group in question. As a consequence, the individual may come to be, as it were, hypnotized by his social group. He may reach a stage where he not merely lacks a disposition to individual initiative, but becomes for the time simply unable to assert himself, to think his own thoughts, or even to remember his ordinary habits and principles of conduct. His judgment for the time becomes one with that of the mass. He may not himself observe this fact. Like the hypnotized subject, the member of the excited mob may feel as if he were very independently expressing himself. He may say: "This idea is my own idea," when as a fact the ruling idea is suggested by the leaders of the mob, or even by the accident of the momentary situation. The individual may be led to acts of which he says: "These things are my duty, my sacred privilege, my right," when as a fact the acts in question are forced upon him by the suggestions of the social mass of which at the instant he is merely a helpless member. As the hypnotized subject, again, thinks his will free when an observer can see that he is obliged to follow the suggestions of the hypnotizer, so the member of the mob may feel all the sense of pure initiative, although as a fact he is in bondage to the will of another, to the motives of the moment.

All such phenomena are due to very deep-seated and common human tendencies. It is no individual reproach to any one of us that, under certain conditions, he would lose his individuality and become the temporary prey of the mob-spirit. Moreover, by the word "mob" itself, or by the equivalent word "crowd," I here mean no term that reflects upon the personal characters or upon the private intelligence of the individuals who chance to compose any given mob. In former ages when the defenders of aristocratic or of monarchical institutions used to speak with contempt of the mob, and oppose to the mob the enlightened portion of the community, the wise who ought to rule, or the people whom birth and social position secured against the defects of the mob, the term was used without a true understanding of the reason why crowds of people are upon occasion disposed to do things that are less intelligent than the acts of normal and thoughtful people would be. For the modern student of the psychology of crowds, a crowd or a mob means not in any wise a company of wicked, of debased, or even of ignorant persons. The term means merely a company of people who, by reason of their sympathies, have for the time being resigned their individual judgment. A mob might be a mob of saints or of cutthroats, of peasants or of men of science. If it were a mob it would lack due social wisdom whatever its membership might be. For the members of the mob are sympathizing rather than criticising. . . . Opposed to the mob in which the good sense of individuals is lost in blur of emotion, and in a helpless suggestibility,—opposed to the mob, I say, is the small company of thoughtful individuals who are taking counsel together. Now our modern life, with its vast unions of people, with its high development of popular sentiments, with its passive and sympathetic love for knowing and feeling whatever other men know and feel, is subject to the disorders of larger crowds, of more dangerous mobs, than have ever before been brought into sympathetic union. One great problem of our time, then, is how to carry on popular government without being at the mercy of the mob-spirit. It is easy to give this mob-spirit noble names. Often you hear of it as "grand popular enthusiasm." Often it is highly praised as a loyal party spirit or as patriotism. But psychologically it is the mob-spirit whenever it is the spirit of a large company of people who are no longer either taking calm counsel together in small groups, or obeying an already established law or custom, but who are merely sympathizing with one another, listening to the words of leaders, and believing the large print headings of their newspapers. Every such company of people is, in so far, a mob. Though they spoke with the tongues of men and of angels, you could not then trust them. Wisdom is not in them nor in their mood. However highly trained they may be as individuals, their mental processes, as a mob, are degraded. Their suffrages, as a mob, ought not to count. Their deeds come of evil. The next mob may undo their work. Accident may render their enthusiasm relatively harmless. But, as a mere crowd, they cannot be wise. They cannot be safe rulers. Who, then, are the men who wisely think and rightly guide? They are, I repeat, the men who take counsel together in small groups, who respect one another's individuality, who meanwhile criticise one another constantly, and earnestly, and who suspect whatever the crowd teaches. In such men there need be no lack of wise sympathy, but there is much besides sympathy. There is individuality, and there is a willingness to doubt both one another and themselves. To such men, and to such groups, popular government ought to be intrusted.

Now these principles are responsible for the explanation of the well-known contrast between those social phenomena which illustrate the wisdom of the enlightened social order, and the phenomena which, on the contrary, often seem such as to make us despair for the moment of the permanent success of popular government. In the rightly constituted social group where every member feels his own responsibility for his part of the social enterprise which is in hand, the result of the interaction of individuals is that the social group may show itself wiser than any of its individuals. In the mere crowd, on the other hand, the social group may be, and generally is, more stupid than any of its individual members. Compare a really successful town meeting in a comparatively small community with the accidental and sometimes dangerous social phenomena of a street mob or of a great political convention. In the one case every individual may gain wisdom from his contact with the social group. In the other case every man concerned, if ever he comes again to himself, may feel ashamed of the absurdity of which the whole company was guilty. Social phenomena of the type that may result from the higher social group, the group in which individuality is respected, even while social loyalty is demanded,—these phenomena may lead to permanent social results which as tradition gives them a fixed character may gradually lead to the formation of permanent institutions, in which a wisdom much higher than that of any individual man may get embodied. . . . There are social groups that are not subject to the mob-spirit. And now if you ask how such social groups are nowadays to be fostered, to be trained, to be kept alive for the service of the nation, I answer that the place for fostering such groups is the province, for such groups flourish under conditions that arouse local pride, the loyalty to one's own community, the willingness to remember one's own ways and ideals, even at the moment when the nation is carried away by some levelling emotion. The lesson would then be: Keep the province awake, that the nation may be saved from the disastrous hypnotic slumber so characteristic of excited masses of mankind. . . . Freedom, I should say, dwells now in the small social group, and has its securest home in the provincial life. The nation by itself, apart from the influence of the province, is in danger of becoming an incomprehensible monster, in whose presence the individual loses his right, his self-consciousness, and his dignity. The province must save the individual.

But, you may ask, in what way do I conceive that the wise provincialism of which I speak ought to undertake and carry on its task? How is it to meet the evils of which I have been speaking? In what way is its influence to be exerted against them? And how can the province cultivate its self-consciousness without tending to fall back again into the ancient narrowness from which small communities were so long struggling to escape? How can we keep broad humanity and yet cultivate provincialism? How can we be loyally patriotic, and yet preserve our consciousness of the peculiar and unique dignity of our own community? In what form are our wholesome provincial activities to be carried on?

I answer, of course, in general terms, that the problem of the wholesome provincial consciousness is closely allied to the problem of any individual form of activity. An individual tends to become narrow when he is what we call self-centred. But, on the other hand, philanthropy that is not founded upon a personal loyalty of the individual to his own family and to his own personal duties is notoriously a worthless abstraction. We love the world better when we cherish our own friends the more faithfully. We do not grow in grace by forgetting individual duties in behalf of remote social enterprises. Precisely so, the province will not serve the nation best by forgetting itself, but by loyally emphasizing its own duty to the nation and therefore its right to attain and to cultivate its own unique wisdom. Now all this is indeed obvious enough, but this is precisely what in our days of vast social consolidation we are some of us tending to forget.

Now as to the more concrete means whereby the wholesome provincialism is to be cultivated and encouraged, let me appeal directly to the loyal member of any provincial community, be it the community of a small town, or of a great city, or of a country district. Let me point out what kind of work is needed in order to cultivate that wise provincialism which, as you see, I wish to have grow not in opposition to the interests of the nation, but for the very sake of saving the nation from the modern evil tendencies of which I have spoken.

First, then, I should say a wholesome provincialism is founded upon the thought that while local pride is indeed a praiseworthy accompaniment of every form of social activity, our province, like our own individuality, ought to be to all of us rather an ideal than a mere boast. And here, as I think, is a matter which is too often forgotten. Everything valuable is, in our present human life, known to us as an ideal before it becomes an attainment, and in view of our human imperfections, remains to the end of our short lives much more a hope and an inspiration than it becomes a present achievement. Just because the true issues of human life are brought to a finish not in time but in eternity, it is necessary that in our temporal existence what is most worthy should appear to us as an ideal, as an Ought, rather than as something that is already in our hands. The old saying about the bird in the hand being worth two in the bush does not rightly apply to the ideal goods of a moral agent working under human limitations. For him the very value of life includes the fact that its goal as something infinite can never at any one instant be attained. In this fact the moral agent glories, for it means that he has something to do. Hence the ideal in the bush, so to speak, is always worth infinitely more to him than the food or the plaything of time that happens to be just now in his hands. The difference between vanity and self-respect depends largely upon this emphasizing of ideals in the case of the higher forms of self-consciousness, as opposed to the emphasis upon transient temporal attainments in the case of the lower forms. Now what holds true of individual self-consciousness ought to hold true of the self-consciousness of the community. Boasting is often indeed harmless and may prove a stimulus to good work. It is therefore to be indulged as a tribute to our human weakness. But the better aspect of our provincial consciousness is always its longing for the improvement of the community.

And now, in the second place, a wise provincialism remembers that it is one thing to seek to make ideal values in some unique sense our own, and it is quite another thing to believe that if they are our own, other people cannot possess such ideal values in their own equally unique fashion. A realm of genuinely spiritual individuality is one where each individual has his own unique significance, so that none could take another's place. But for just that very reason all the unique individuals of the truly spiritual order stand in relation to the same universal light, to the same divine whole in relation to which they win their individuality. Hence all the individuals of the true spiritual order have ideal goods in common, as the very means whereby they can win each his individual place with reference to the possession and the employment of these common goods. Well, it is with provinces as with individuals. The way to win independence is by learning freely from abroad, but by then insisting upon our own interpretation of the common good. . . .

And therefore, thirdly, I say in developing your provincial spirit, be quite willing to encourage your young men to have relations with other communities. But on the other hand, encourage them also to make use of what they thus acquire for the furtherance of the life of their own community. Let them win aid from abroad, but let them also have, so far as possible, an opportunity to use this which they acquire in the service of their home. Of course economic conditions rather than deliberate choice commonly determine how far the youth of a province are able to remain for their lifetime in a place where they grow up. But so far as a provincial spirit is concerned, it is well to avoid each of two extremes in the treatment of the young men of the community,—extremes that I have too often seen exemplified. The one extreme consists in maintaining that if young men mean to be loyal to their own province, to their own state, to their own home, they ought to show their loyalty by an unwillingness to seek guidance from foreign literature, from foreign lands, in the patronizing of foreign or distant institutions, or in the acceptance of the customs and ideas of other communities than their own. Against this extreme let the Japanese be our typical instance. They have wandered far. They have studied abroad. They have assimilated the lore of other communities. And they have only gained in local consciousness, in independence of spirit, by the ordeal. The other extreme is the one expressed in that tendency to wander and to encourage wandering, which has led so many of our communities to drive away the best and most active of their young men. We want more of the determination to find, if possible, a place for our youth in their own communities.

Finally, let the province more and more seek its own adornment. Here I speak of a matter that in all our American communities has been until recently far too much neglected. Local pride ought above all to centre, so far as its material objects are concerned, about the determination to give the surroundings of the community nobility, dignity, beauty. We Americans spend far too much of our early strength and time in our newer communities upon injuring our landscapes, and far too little upon endeavoring to beautify our towns and cities. We have begun to change all that, and while I have no right to speak as an æsthetic judge concerning the growth of the love of the beautiful in our country, I can strongly insist that no community can think any creation of genuine beauty and dignity in its public buildings or in the surroundings of its towns and cities too good a thing for its own deserts. For we deserve what in such realms we can learn how to create or to enjoy, or to make sacrifices for. And no provincialism will become dangerously narrow so long as it is constantly accompanied by a willingness to sacrifice much in order to put in the form of great institutions, of noble architecture, and of beautiful surroundings an expression of the worth that the community attaches to its own ideals.

PART THREE

DREAMS OF SUCCESS

Whenever Richard Cory went down town,
We people on the pavement looked at him:
He was a gentleman from sole to crown,
Clean favored, and imperially slim.

And he was always quietly arrayed,
And he was always human when he talked;
But still he fluttered pulses when he said,
"Good-morning," and he glittered when he walked.

And he was rich—yes, richer than a king—
And admirably schooled in every grace:
In fine, we thought that he was everything
To make us wish that we were in his place.

So on we worked, and waited for the light,
And went without the meat, and cursed the bread;
And Richard Cory, one calm summer night,
Went home and put a bullet through his head.

RICHARD CORY
Edwin Arlington Robinson (1897)

T HE DREAM of success is one of the oldest and most enduring of American dreams. And in America, success has always been defined, at least in part, by material prosperity. Granted, to the Puritans success meant establishing a Christian commonwealth of God's chosen people bound together by brotherly affection and a mutual dedication to spiritual

[From *The Children of the Night* (Boston: Richard G. Badger and Company, 1897).]

salvation. Material well-being was nevertheless important to them, if only as a sign that God approved of their endeavors. Similarly, to Thomas Jefferson and his compatriots success meant forming a "more perfect union," free of the social and political ills of Europe, in which men might exercise their "unalienable rights" to "life, liberty, and the pursuit of happiness." Yet no one has ever doubted that the latter included the pursuit of material goods. Indeed, in *The Federalist*, James Madison implies that the most unalienable right of all is the right to private property. Surely, too, the impetus behind the westward movement was not merely a desire to escape what Crèvecoeur called the "ancient prejudices and manners" of the Old World. Perhaps more than anything else, free land and, eventually, the discovery of gold in California induced Americans to venture farther and farther west.

As early as the 1840s, however, some eloquent voices lamented that the moral and spiritual grounds of the American dream were being submerged under a rising tide of materialism. Emerson, for example, in his "Ode: Inscribed to W. H. Channing" (1846), cried that "Things are in the saddle / And ride mankind." Thoreau deplored his neighbors' concern with "business" rather than with the principles by which their lives could be made spiritually and morally richer. In fact, one of the reasons for Thoreau's vehement opposition to slavery was that slaves were treated not as human beings but as pieces of property. Nor did he consider Northern industrialists morally superior to Southern slaveholders. For purposes of economic gain, the former were exploiting an entire class of white laborers.

The industrialization that disturbed Thoreau exploded after the Civil War. The agrarian life that both Crèvecoeur and Jefferson felt would best insure a democratic order seemed doomed. Steel manufacture, the railroads, the meat-packing and oil industries all grew apace on American ground. And with the growth of industry and big business came urbanization, the cities filling with young men who fled the farm and with European immigrants drawn by stories of the gold-paved streets of the New World. A serpent had apparently entered the American Garden in the form of the Machine.

Such developments led to the formation of a new American wealthy class and to a modified, if not entirely new, measure of success. The Rockefellers, the Carnegies, the Morgans built enormous fortunes by shrewdly manipulating natural resources, the market, and the cheap labor of immigrants who, as a class, were largely dependent on industrial employment for their survival. To some Americans, these "captains of industry" were titans, updated versions of the strong, self-reliant American hero, a superior breed exemplifying in human affairs the concept of "survival of the fittest." To others, they were no better than pirates, "robber barons," ruthless men who would sacrifice everything and everyone to their lust for wealth and power, who controlled not only the economy but those politicians willing to overlook, in the name of a *laissez faire* policy, the entrepreneurs' wrongdoings.

Even more disturbing to some observers, Americans in general seemed increasingly ready to accept a strictly monetary concept of success. All well and good if, like Horatio Alger's heroes, riches could be achieved without sacrificing ethical principles. But even if principles had to be shaded slightly, wealth was still the goal most worth striving for. William James thought this attitude so insidiously pervasive that in a famous letter to H. G. Wells in 1906 he complained that his countrymen worshiped "the bitch-goddess SUCCESS." Other nations, James said, already thought the emblem of the United States should be a hog. To be "richer than a king," as Edwin Arlington Robinson (1869–1935) described Richard Cory, seemed Americans' only aim, James's "strenuous mood" to be exercised only in pursuit of money. Mark Twain sometimes shared James's view. In 1873 he co-authored with Charles Dudley Warner a satirical novel that not only depicted the corruption, gross opportunism, and vulgarity of the times but also gave the era a name. The novel was entitled *The Gilded Age*.

GILDED DREAMS

In many ways, the most forceful criticism of the gilded age came from an unexpected source: Walt Whitman. True, Whitman's high hopes for America had been shaken by the Civil War; yet the dominant tone of the first four editions of his long epic poem *Leaves of Grass* had been optimistic, celebrating American democracy, its high place on the evolutionary ladder, its spiritual as well as its physical energy. The celebration of American ideals is still present in *Democratic Vistas*. So is much of Whitman's typical optimism. The keynote of the essay, however, is that America's "justification and success" have not yet been realized; they depend "almost entirely on the future," for so far, ironically, the nation had "morally and artistically originated nothing." Indeed, Whitman states that America suffers from a disease characterized by deceit, hypocrisy, corruption, falsehood, and vulgarity. "Never was there, perhaps, more hollowness of heart than at present, and here in the United States. . . . The underlying principles of the States are not honestly believed in." Rather than a universal culture, art, and literature reflecting the true American idea, the nation is in thrall to business, whose "sole object is, by any means, pecuniary gain." In fact, Whitman asserts, the "depravity of the business classes of our country is not less than has been supposed but infinitely greater." The same is true of government. To the concept of self-reliance, Whitman still says yes; to opportunistic self-seeking, he says no, for the latter is not his definition of the road to success.

Although the tone of Thorstein Veblen's *The Theory of the Leisure Class* is less impassioned than that of *Democratic Vistas*, its mode more analytical, its attack on the business mentality and the caste system is even more devastating. Veblen (1857–1929)—economist, iconoclastic social theorist, university professor—does not restrict his analysis of the leisure class to its American version, but his picture clearly reflects the late nineteenth-century American scene. As he describes it, the leisure class flaunts its high position by a "conspicuous consumption" and display of symbols of wealth. Its relation "to the economic process is a pecuniary relation—a relation of acquisition, not of production; of exploitation, not of serviceability." Out of instinct and self-interest, the leisure class is also inherently conservative, opposing any changes in institutions, policies, or habits of thought which threaten to undermine its power. It is actually regressive, since the economic relations it defends are holdovers from the "predatory stage" of social development. And by resisting change, it impedes the evolution of an entire society. As to those classes that would gain the most from innovation, their creative energies are exhausted in simply making a living, while their habits of thought, their ideas of what is good and right, the symbols of success they esteem are inculcated in them by the very class that exploits their labor. Veblen's theory was bitterly attacked not only by members of the leisure class itself but also by his fellow academicians. Nonetheless, it influenced American economic thought and contributed to a rising sympathy with social control.

The policy of *laissez faire* which Veblen implicitly criticized had, it could be and was argued, served the country well at one time and was not easily dismissed as obsolete. Furthermore, any kind of governmental control, even if designed to "promote the general Welfare," was bound to be viewed suspiciously by a people who prized individual freedom as highly as Americans always have. Even those who would have benefited most from governmental regulation of the economy were loath to accept the need for it, perhaps for the reasons Veblen mentions. If an Andrew Carnegie could rise from his humble beginnings to become a steel magnate and millionaire, thereby realizing the prevailing dream of success, so could anyone else. Or so the thinking went.

Yale professor of political and social science William Graham Sumner (1840–1910) was among the defenders of the *laissez faire* philosophy. In *What Social Classes Owe to Each Other*, Sumner's answer to the question raised by his title is simple and forthright: they owe each other nothing. Believing that "God and nature have ordained the chances and conditions of life on earth once and for all," Sumner distinguishes between "ills which belong to the struggle for existence" and ills "due to the faults of human institutions." Only the latter, according to Sumner, should be the concern of "associated effort." And since the United States already has a set of institutions that adjust rights when one person's actions impinge on the freedom of another's, the best thing to do is not tamper with those institutions. All that society needs is to be let alone. Although within a "natural social order" there are bound to be unjust inequalities, some of these will be remedied by "natural adjustments," others by voluntary concessions. The cost of trying to remedy them by other means, however, is too high: the price is loss of freedom. "A society based on contract," Sumner insists, "is a society of free and independent men. . . . It follows . . . that one man, in a free state, cannot claim help from, and cannot be charged to give help to, another." What the Puritans called "brotherly affections" are thus socially irrelevant, for Sumner believes that "In a state based on contract *sentiment* is out of place." What, then, is success? According to Sumner, it is "making the best of one's self individually," which is "not a separate thing from the duty of filling one's place in society." The condition for both social and personal success is unrestricted freedom.

Personification in his own right of the rags-to-riches dream, Andrew Carnegie (1835–1919) was also one of the most articulate exponents of Social Darwinism. Declaring in "Wealth" that "upon the sacredness of property civilization itself depends" and that the "problem of our age is the proper administration of wealth," Carnegie agrees with Sumner that "nature's laws" should not be tampered with. Foremost among these is the law of competition which, though "sometimes hard for the individual," is in the long run "best for the race, because it insures the survival of the fittest in every department." Implicitly, the fittest individuals are those capable of amassing the most wealth, and progress for the race consists largely if not entirely of improved material conditions. In short, Carnegie assumes that success is wealth. Unlike Sumner, however, Carnegie believes that the wealthy are morally obligated to help the less successful who are willing to help themselves. No advocate of "indiscriminate charity," as well as somewhat of a puritan, Carnegie urges the wealthy to live unostentatiously and philanthropically administer their surplus wealth in the form of parks, libraries, and other institutions designed to "improve the general condition of the people." Thus the "true Gospel" according to Andrew attempts to reconcile an unfettered individualism with a social conscience, material success with moral, intellectual, and aesthetic values.

Ironically the great industrialists were not in fact as much averse to governmental interference in the economy as they professed to be. They supported it when, as in the case of high tariffs, it worked to their advantage. By the turn of the century, it was becoming increasingly apparent to more and more Americans that the ever-widening gap between rich and poor was not going to be bridged by philanthropy, nor social justice be achieved by the kind of economic and political order that the Sumners and Carnegies advocated. It was time, many felt, for the government to intercede on behalf of the have-nots as well as the haves, not only because of the social problems involved but also because the principles of justice that America supposedly stood for were being violated. Americans generally were no less enamored of materialistic success than before, but they were less convinced that the prevailing economic system provided everyone with a fair and equal opportunity to succeed. Hence, as the nineteenth century came to an end, the Progressive movement in its various forms was born. Helped along by popular muckraking writers such as Upton Sinclair and Lincoln Steffens, Progressive leaders Robert La Follette, Theodore Roosevelt, and others sought to control the trusts, to reduce the power of corrupt political machines, and to effect legislation that would more directly involve people in choosing who would govern them.

Like Theodore Roosevelt before him, Woodrow Wilson (1856–1924) was a powerful Progressive spokesman for regulation of the trusts and monopolies. Academic historian turned statesman, Wilson shared Veblen's perception that institutions must change to accommodate changing conditions. And the old order had changed. The very opportunities for success that Carnegie had insisted were indispensable to the progress of the race were being denied, Wilson felt, by the very system Carnegie and Sumner had defended, in that a handful of powerful men and corporations were doing all they could to violate the "law of competition." Writing in *The New Freedom*, Wilson disagrees with Sumner that "sentiment" has no place in the social contract. Instead, he deplores the fact that the current economic system is "heartless" and that the country's laws do not "prevent the strong from crushing the weak." Wilson was not so much convinced as Roosevelt that big government was the answer; nevertheless, he calls for legislation that will "look after the men who are on the make rather than the men who are already made." It was a call typical of the Progressive movement.

George Santayana (1863–1952) was neither a politician nor an economist. A poet and author of one novel (*The Last Puritan*) as well as a philosopher, the European-born Santayana grew up in Boston and taught philosophy for several years at Harvard. From 1914 until his death in 1952, however, he lived abroad. His *Character and Opinion in the United States* is therefore the work of a cosmopolitan. Still, his portrait of the typical American corresponds closely to the descriptions limned by earlier, more provincial writers. Santayana notes, for example, the American's scorn for the past, his self-confidence, his restless mobility, his belief in the "categorical excellence of work, growth, enterprise, reform, and prosperity." Above all, Santayana observes, the American's definition of success is singularly based on quantity rather than on quality. Reminding one of Thoreau, Santayana says: "To be poor in order to be simple, to produce less in order that the product may be more choice and beautiful . . . is an ideal not articulate in the American mind." The American is not unimaginative, but his imagination centers on the practical: "He is an idealist working on matter." Convinced that God and nature are on his side, he envisions the perfectibility of material existence on American ground. Perhaps, Santayana suggests, the American holds this view because he has "never yet had to face the trials of Job."

DISENCHANTMENT AND DEPRESSION

Writing in 1920, Santayana may have been correct. Traumatic as the Civil War had been, the Union had been saved; and America's participation in World War I had been brief and victorious. Yet the very idealism that Santayana found to be characteristically American was shaken by World War I and its aftermath. In one sense, entry into that war violated the advice offered by George Washington in his Farewell Address and the policy stated in the Monroe Doctrine: that we should guard against foreign entanglements if we were to protect our political purity as well as our geographical hegemony. In another sense, however, our involvement was an extension of an idea stated initially by John Winthrop and reasserted by Thomas Paine: that America was destined to be a model to the rest of the world. For whatever material self-interest prompted Congress to declare war on Germany, the professed moral reason was that America had a mission to "make the world safe for democracy," an almost religious imperative to defend righteousness wherever it was threatened. Wilson's commitment to the League of Nations was the postwar equivalent of that mission. The repudiation of the League, America's attempted reversion to isolationism, was in turn partly the result of a widespread feeling that the mission was not worth the cost. The war had not saved civilization. Europe was beyond salvation; from now on, America should take care of itself and remain free of the Old World's contaminating influences.

Moreover, a number of people came to doubt that the United States had fought for moral reasons in the first place. Who, after all, had profited from the war? Was it the common citizen or was it the big industrialists, the munitions makers, the House of Morgan as John Dos Passos (1896–1970) capitalized it? It was certainly not those who had actually experienced the horrors of a technological warfare, a warfare that called into question the very doctrine of benign scientific progress. Dos Passos, the distinguished writer who had driven an ambulance on the Western front and was a liberal activist during the twenties and thirties, expresses the disenchantment of his generation in "The Body of an American." Ironically juxtaposing the death of the Unknown Soldier with American bigotry, with the impersonalism of the military, with jingoistic and sentimental platitudes, Dos Passos implies that the cause for which the young man died was an illusion, the nation's self-righteousness a mockery. In the passages from "Hugh Selwyn Mauberley," the poet Ezra Pound (1885–1972) responds similarly. An expatriate since 1908 and later a supporter of Mussolini, Pound too derides the empty rhetoric of the politicians, the irony of dying for a "botched civilization," and the deceit, infamy, and greed exposed by the war. Dos Passos and Pound, like the hero of Ernest Hemingway's *A Farewell to Arms*, had seen "nothing sacred" about a war that was supposed to end all wars.

Nor was postwar America likely to lighten the hearts of liberal reformers, for the decade of the twenties was in general politically conservative. The Progressive movement did not die out altogether, of course; there were still calls for social reform, and organized labor began to take an active political role. But, tired of causes and evidently suspicious of any idea that smacked remotely of such "foreign ideologies" as socialism or communism, the voters sent to the White House three conservative Republicans—Warren G. Harding, Calvin Coolidge, and Herbert Hoover. Despite corruption in the Harding administration, the victory of the monopolies over the trust busters, and the exclusion of factory workers and farmers from the benefits of the postwar economic boom, it was not merely a conservative but a confident decade. To the middle class, at least, the nation seemed about to realize its dream of success: unlimited prosperity for virtually everyone.

The conservatism did not, curiously enough, extend to morals and manners. The twenties also included what F. Scott Fitzgerald (1896–1940) called the "greatest, gaudiest spree in history." Starting with the younger generation but soon extending to its elders, a revolt against nineteenth-century sexual taboos, frugality, and self-restraint took place. In such novels as *The Great Gatsby* and *Tender Is the Night*, Fitzgerald dramatized the reckless gaiety, hedonism, worship of money, and moral irresponsibility of the era. "Echoes of the Jazz Age" treats these characteristics with an ambivalence typical of Fitzgerald. Admitting to some nostalgia for the "utter confidence" of the age ("Even when you were broke you didn't worry about money, because it was in such profusion around you"), and regretting that he and his generation "will never feel quite so intensely about our surroundings anymore," Fitzgerald also recognizes that during the decade America seemed to have abandoned its dedication to work and moral decency and social justice in favor of the frivolous, the superficial, and the self-indulgent. In Santayana's terms, Fitzgerald's Americans were no longer idealists working on matter; they were simply vulgar materialists.

The gaudy spree ended, as all sprees must, one dark day in 1929 when the financial structure of the United States collapsed beneath a tangled heap of stock-market ticker tape. In a 1928 campaign speech, published in *The New Day*, Herbert Hoover (1874–1964) had extolled the prosperity that a "rugged individualism" and free competition had brought to the nation. His message turned out to be sadly ironic. Acknowledging, as Wilson had done, that changing conditions made a policy of complete *laissez faire* obsolete, that the government must protect the people against domination by any group, business or political, Hoover's speech warns principally against the danger of governmental interference. Government should be an "umpire," not a "player in the economic game." Even after the 1929 crash, when he finally agreed to extend aid to faltering industries, he disapproved of directly helping the unemployed. It is not surprising that when the makeshift dwellings of the dispossessed began to multiply around the nation they were popularly called "Hoovervilles." It is equally unsurprising that Hoover lost the 1932 presidential election to the liberal, reform-minded Franklin Delano Roosevelt.

The problem of the thirties was indeed, as Carnegie had said of an earlier age, the "proper administration of wealth"; but the solutions proposed then by Sumner and Carnegie and now by Hoover, the Liberty League, Al Smith, and others were no longer defensible. Not in a country, still blessed with plentiful natural resources, where banks and businesses were failing, where the lines of the homeless and unemployed grew steadily longer, where cities were turning into what Mary Heaton Vorse (1874–1966) called "A School for Bums," and where wages for migrant farm workers fell below the subsistence level. As both Vorse and Edmund Wilson (1895–1972) describe conditions during the Great Depression— some of them, unfortunately, persist even now—skilled craftsmen, commercial and professional, the educated as well as the uneducated shared in the "massed misery." Wilson's "man in the street" is depicted as "able-bodied and self-dependent," but he "looks dazed." A once-confident American, he cannot understand what has happened to his formerly secure world. Prosperity may be "just around the corner," as he was repeatedly told, but that corner seems to recede ever farther down the long street. What had happened to the American dream of success? To the land of opportunity where people willing to work could prosper according to their ability and industry?

In *Individualism Old and New*, the pragmatist philosopher John Dewey (1859–1952), noting the "troubled and tangled economic scene," argues that one reason for the bewilderment is that while the nation "has steadily moved from an earlier pioneer individualism to a condition of dominant corporateness," too many Americans believe that the old concept is still viable. Dewey does not propose to forgo individualism altogether. But he declares that since not even government regulation can restore the earlier condition, Americans must recognize that corporateness is an accomplished fact, that they must redefine individualism, and that they must learn to use the new science and technology for the "liberation and enrichment of human life" rather than for the pecuniary advantage of the few. Echoing Veblen, Dewey insists that ways of thinking, desires, and purposes must change as the social order changes, despite opposition from those who fear that innovative thought will deprive them of their economic power. What is needed is a "new psychological and moral type" of individual, one "integrated within itself and with a liberated function in the society wherein it exists." In short, Dewey believes that qualitative culture must catch up with quantitative material culture.

Walter Lippmann (1889–1974), the influential newspaper columnist and social philosopher, also remarks on the confusion of the times. He too observes that, ironically, the nation's industrial and financial leaders who defend but do not themselves practice a *laissez faire* doctrine are thereby able to control the economy for their own benefit. Admitting that he would rather have "economic liberty than centralized direction and control," Lippmann concedes that such liberty must now be deliberately maintained by governmental authority. The "new imperative" is to strike a balance between liberty and authority. To insist that the ironic paradoxes of poverty and economic stagnation in a naturally bountiful and technologically advanced nation can be resolved without a coherent governmental policy is to undermine American traditions and tempt the young to turn to communism or fascism.

Franklin Delano Roosevelt's actions upon assuming the presidency in 1932 were attempts to do what Lippmann was still advocating in 1935. Convinced that the sorry state of the economy demanded more government intervention than ever before, Roosevelt immediately declared a bank holiday to protect savings, created federal agencies to relieve unemployment, lent government money to businesses large and small, enforced the antitrust laws, initiated old-age and unemployment insurance. Some of his New Deal measures were declared unconstitutional by the Supreme Court, others were rejected by Congress, and not every citizen regarded Roosevelt as a savior. On the whole, however, public sympathy was so overwhelmingly in his favor that he was reelected by a landslide vote in 1936, for an unprecedented third term in 1940, and still again in 1944 while America was at war.

Despite Roosevelt's efforts, it took the industrial boom consequent upon the United States entering into World War II to put a final end to the Great Depression. And although numerous aspects of the national life, economic and otherwise, were markedly changed during the thirties, certain characteristic American attitudes remained the same. However disenchanting the decade may have been, most Americans clung to their belief that the country was still the last, best hope of the world, that it offered more freedom and opportunity than any other nation, and that tomorrow would be better than today. No economic problems, no contradictions between the country's stated ideals and social reality, not even the prospects of a Second World War could change that.

GILDED DREAMS

Walt Whitman
Democratic Vistas
(1871)

. . . AMERICA, FILLING the present with greatest deeds and problems, cheerfully accepting the past, including feudalism (as, indeed, the present is but the legitimate birth of the past, including feudalism), counts, as I reckon, for her justification and success, (for who, as yet, dare claim success?) almost entirely on the future. Nor is that hope unwarranted. To-day, ahead, though dimly yet, we see, in vistas, a copious, sane, gigantic offspring. For our New World I consider far less important for what it has done, or what it is, than for results to come. Sole among nationalities, these States have assumed the task to put in forms of lasting power and practicality, on areas of amplitude rivaling the operations of the physical kosmos, the moral political speculations of ages, long, long deferr'd, the democratic republican principle, and the theory of development and perfection by voluntary standards and self-reliance. Who else, indeed, except the United States, in history, so far, have accepted in unwitting faith, and, as we now see, stand, act upon, and go security for, these things?

But preluding no longer, let me strike the key-note of the following strain. First premising that, though the passages of it have been written at widely different times, (it is, in fact, a collection of memoranda, perhaps for future designers, comprehenders,) and though it may be open to the charge of one part contradicting another—for there are opposite sides to the great question of democracy, as to every great question—I feel the parts harmoniously blended in my own realization and convictions, and present them to be read only in such oneness, each page and each claim and assertion modified and temper'd by the others. Bear in mind, too, that they are not the result of studying up in political economy, but of the ordinary sense, observing, wandering among men, these States, these stirring years of war and peace. I will not gloss over the appalling dangers of universal suffrage in the United States. In fact, it is to admit and face these dangers I am writing. To him or her within whose thought rages the battle, advancing, retreating, between democracy's convictions, aspirations, and the people's crudeness, vice, caprices, I mainly write this essay. I shall use the words America and democracy as convertible terms. Not an ordinary one is the issue. The United States are destined either to surmount the gorgeous history of feudalism, or else prove the most tremendous failure of time. Not the least doubtful am I on any prospects of their material success. . . .

Admitting all this, with the priceless value of our political institutions, general suffrage, (and fully acknowledging the latest, widest opening of the doors,) I say that, far deeper than these, what finally and only is to make of our western world a nationality superior to any hither known, and out-topping the past, must be vigorous, yet unsuspected Literatures, perfect personalities, and sociologies, original, transcendental, and expressing (what, in highest sense, are not yet express'd at all,) democracy and the modern. With these, and out of these, I promulgate new races of Teachers, and of perfect Women, indispensable to endow the birth-stock of a New World. For feudalism, caste, the ecclesiastic traditions, though palpably retreating from political institutions, still hold essentially, by their spirit, even in this country, entire possession of more important fields, indeed the very subsoil, of education, and of social standards and literature.

I say that democracy can never prove itself beyond cavil, until it founds and luxuriantly grows its own forms of art, poems, schools, theology, displacing all that exists, or that has been produced anywhere in the past, under opposite influences. . . . Our fundamental want to-day in the United States, with closest, amplest reference to present conditions, and to the future, is of a class, and the clear idea of a class, of native authors, literatuses, far different, far higher in grade than any yet known, sacerdotal, modern, fit to cope with our occasions, lands, permeating the whole mass of American mentality, taste, belief, breathing into it a new breath of life, giving it decision, affecting politics far more than the popular superficial suffrage, with results inside and underneath the elections of Presidents or Congresses—radiating, begetting appropriate teachers, schools, manners, and, as its grandest result, accomplishing, (what neither the schools nor the churches and their clergy have hitherto accomplish'd, and without which this nation will no more stand, permanently, soundly, than a house will stand without a substratum,) a religious and moral character beneath the political and productive and intellectual bases of the States. . . .

I say we had best look our times and lands searchingly in the face, like a physician diagnosing some deep disease. Never was there, perhaps, more hollowness at heart than at present, and here in the United States.

Genuine belief seems to have left us. The underlying principles of the States are not honestly believ'd in, (for all this hectic glow, and these melodramatic screamings,) nor is humanity itself believ'd in. What penetrating eye does not everywhere see through the mask? The spectacle is appalling. We live in an atmosphere of hypocrisy throughout. The men believe not in the women, nor the women in the men. A scornful superciliousness rules in literature. The aim of all the *littérateurs* is to find something to make fun of. A lot of churches, sects, &c., the most dismal phantasms I know, usurp the name of religion. Conversation is a mass of badinage. From deceit in the spirit, the mother of all false deeds, the offspring is already incalculable. . . . The depravity of the business classes of our country is not less than has been supposed, but infinitely greater. The official services of America, national, state, and municipal, in all their branches and departments, except the judiciary, are saturated in corruption, bribery, falsehood, maladministration; and the judiciary is tainted. The great cities reek with respectable as much as non-respectable robbery and scoundrelism. In fashionable life, flippancy, tepid amours, weak infidelism, small aims, or no aims at all, only to kill time. In business, (this all-devouring modern word, business,) the one sole object is, by any means, pecuniary gain. The magician's serpent in the fable ate up all the other serpents; and moneymaking is our magician's serpent, remaining today sole master of the field. The best class we show, is but a mob of fashionably dress'd speculators and vulgarians. True, indeed, behind this fantastic farce, enacted on the visible stage of society, solid things and stupendous labors are to be discover'd, existing crudely and going on in the background, to advance and tell themselves in time. Yet the truths are none the less terrible. I say that our New World democracy, however great a success in uplifting the masses out of their sloughs, in materialistic development, products, and in a certain highly-deceptive superficial popular intellectuality, is, so far, an almost complete failure in its social aspects, and in really grand religious, moral, literary, and esthetic results. . . .

Then still the thought returns, (like the thread-passage in overtures,) giving the key and echo to these pages. When I pass to and fro, different latitudes, different seasons, beholding the crowds of the great cities, New York, Boston, Philadelphia, Cincinnati, Chicago, St. Louis, San Francisco, New Orleans, Baltimore—when I mix with these interminable swarms of alert, turbulent, good-natured, independent citizens, mechanics, clerks, young persons—at the idea of this mass of men, so fresh and free, so loving and so proud, a singular awe falls upon me. I feel, with dejection and amazement, that among our geniuses and talented writers or speakers, few or none have yet really spoken to this people, created a single image-making work for them, or absorb'd the central spirit and the idiosyncrasies which are theirs—and which, thus, in highest ranges, so far remain entirely uncelebrated, unexpress'd.

Dominion strong is the body's; dominion stronger is the mind's. What has fill'd, and fills to-day our intellect, our fancy, furnishing the standards therein, is yet foreign. The great poems, Shakspere included, are poisonous to the idea of the pride and dignity of the common people, the life-blood of democracy. The models of our literature, as we get it from other lands, ultra-marine, have had their birth in courts, bask'd and grown in castle sunshine; all smells of princes' favors. Of workers of a certain sort, we have, indeed, plenty, contributing after their kind; many elegant, many learn'd, all complacent. But touch'd by the national test, or tried by the standards of democratic personality, they wither to ashes. I say I have not seen a single writer, artist, lecturer, or what not, that has confronted the voiceless but ever erect and active, pervading, underlying will and typic aspiration of the land, in a spirit kindred to itself. Do you call those genteel little creatures American poets? Do you term that perpetual, pistareen, paste-pot work, American art, American drama, taste, verse? I think I hear, echoed as from some mountaintop afar in the west, the scornful laugh of the Genius of these States. . . .

America has yet morally and artistically originated nothing. She seems singularly unaware that the models of persons, books, manners, &c., appropriate for former conditions and for European lands, are but exiles and exotics here. No current of her life, as shown on the surfaces of what is authoritatively called her society, accepts or runs into social or esthetic democracy; but all the currents set squarely against it. Never, in the Old World, was thoroughly upholster'd exterior appearance and show, mental and other, built entirely on the idea of caste, and on the sufficiency of mere outside acquisition—never were glibness, verbal intellect, more the test, the emulation—more loftily elevated as head and sample—than they are on the surface of our republican States this day. The writers of a time hint the mottoes of its gods. The word of the modern, say these voices, is the word Culture.

We find ourselves abruptly in close quarters with the enemy. This word Culture, or what it has come to represent, involves, by contrast, our whole theme, and has been, indeed, the spur, urging us to engagement. Certain questions arise. As now taught, accepted and carried out, are not the processes of culture rapidly creating a class of supercilious infidels, who believe in nothing? Shall a man lose himself in countless masses of adjustments, and be so shaped with reference to this, that, and the other, that the simply good and healthy and brave parts of him are reduced and clipped away, like the bordering of box in a garden? You can cultivate corn and roses and orchards—but who shall cultivate the mountain peaks, the ocean, and the tumbling gorgeousness of the clouds?

Lastly—is the readily-given reply that culture only seeks to help, systematize, and put in attitude, the elements of fertility and power, a conclusive reply?

I do not so much object to the name, or word, but I should certainly insist, for the purposes of these States, on a radical change of category, in the distribution of precedence. I should demand a programme of culture, drawn out, not for a single class alone, or for the parlors or lecture-rooms, but with an eye to practical life, the west, the working-men, the facts of farms and jack-planes and engineers, and of the broad range of the women also of the middle and working strata, and with reference to the perfect equality of women, and of a grand and powerful motherhood. I should demand of this programme or theory a scope generous enough to include the widest human area. It must have for its spinal meaning the formation of a typical personality of character, eligible to the uses of the high average of men—and *not* restricted by conditions ineligible to the masses. The best culture will always be that of the manly and courageous instincts, and loving perceptions, and of self-respect—aiming to form, over this continent, an idiocrasy of universalism, which, true child of America, will bring joy to its mother, returning to her in her own spirit, recruiting myriads of offspring, able, natural, perceptive, tolerant, devout believers in her, America, and with some definite instinct why and for what she has arisen, most vast, most formidable of historic births, and is, now and here, with wonderful step, journeying through Time. . . .

William Graham Sumner
What Social Classes
Owe to Each Other
(1883)

ON A NEW PHILOSOPHY: THAT POVERTY IS
THE BEST POLICY

IT IS commonly asserted that there are in the United States no classes, and any allusion to classes is resented. On the other hand, we constantly read and hear discussions of social topics in which the existence of social classes is assumed as a simple fact. "The poor," "the weak," "the laborers," are expressions which are used as if they had exact and well-understood definition. Discussions are made to bear upon the assumed rights, wrongs, and misfortunes of certain social classes; and all public speaking and writing consists, in a large measure, of the discussion of general plans for meeting the wishes of classes of people who have not been able to satisfy their own desires. These classes are sometimes discontented, and sometimes not. Sometimes they do not know that anything is amiss with them until the "friends of humanity" come to them with offers of aid. Sometimes they are discontented and envious. They do not take their achievements as a fair measure of their rights. They do not blame themselves or their parents for their lot, as compared with that of other people. Sometimes they claim that they have a right to everything of which they feel the need for their happiness on earth. To make such a claim against God or Nature would, of course, be only to say that we claim a right to live on earth if we can. But God and Nature have ordained the chances and conditions of life on earth once for all. The case cannot be reopened. We cannot get a revision of the laws of human life. We are absolutely shut up to the need and duty, if we would learn how to live happily, of

[From *What Social Classes Owe to Each Other* (New York: Harper & Brothers, 1883).]

investigating the laws of Nature, and deducing the rules of right living in the world as it is. These are very wearisome and commonplace tasks. They consist in labor and self-denial repeated over and over again in learning and doing. When the people whose claims we are considering are told to apply themselves to these tasks they become irritated and feel almost insulted. They formulate their claims as rights against society—that is, against some other men. In their view they have a right, not only to *pursue* happiness, but to *get* it; and if they fail to get it, they think they have a claim to the aid of other men—that is, to the labor and self-denial of other men—to get it for them. They find orators and poets who tell them that they have grievances, so long as they have unsatisfied desires.

Now, if there are groups of people who have a claim to other people's labor and self-denial, and if there are other people whose labor and self-denial are liable to be claimed by the first groups, then there certainly are "classes," and classes of the oldest and most vicious type. For a man who can command another man's labor and self-denial for the support of his own existence is a privileged person of the highest species conceivable on earth. Princes and paupers meet on this plane, and no other men are on it at all. On the other hand, a man whose labor and self-denial may be diverted from his maintenance to that of some other man is not a free man, and approaches more or less toward the position of a slave. Therefore we shall find that, in all the notions which we are to discuss, this elementary contradiction, that there are classes and that there are not classes, will produce repeated confusion and absurdity. We shall find that, in our efforts to eliminate the old vices of class government, we are impeded and defeated by new products of the worst class theory. We shall find that all the schemes for producing equality and obliterating the organization of society produce a new differentiation based on the worst possible distinction—the right to claim and the duty to give one man's effort for another man's satisfaction. We shall find that every effort to realize equality necessitates a sacrifice of liberty. . . .

Certain ills belong to the hardships of human life. They are natural. They are part of the struggle with Nature for existence. We cannot blame our fellow-men for our share of these. My neighbor and I are both struggling to free ourselves from these ills. The fact that my neighbor has succeeded in this struggle better than I constitutes no grievance for me. Certain other ills are due to the malice of men, and to the imperfections or errors of civil institutions. These ills are an object of agitation, and a subject of discussion. The former class of ills is to be met only by manly effort and energy; the latter may be corrected by associated effort. The former class of ills is constantly grouped and generalized, and made the object of social schemes. We shall see, as we go on, what that means.

The second class of ills may fall on certain social classes, and reform will take the form of interference by other classes in favor of that one. The last fact is, no doubt, the reason why people have been led, not noticing distinctions, to believe that the same method was applicable to the other class of ills. The distinction here made between the ills which belong to the struggle for existence and those which are due to the faults of human institutions is of prime importance. . . .

There is no possible definition of "a poor man." A pauper is a person who cannot earn his living; whose producing powers have fallen positively below his necessary consumption; who cannot, therefore, pay his way. A human society needs the active co-operation and productive energy of every person in it. A man who is present as a consumer, yet who does not contribute either by land, labor, or capital to the work of society, is a burden. On no sound political theory ought such a person to share in the political power of the State. He drops out of the ranks of workers and producers. Society must support him. It accepts the burden, but he must be cancelled from the ranks of the rulers likewise. So much for the pauper. About him no more need be said. But he is not the "poor man." The "poor man" is an elastic term, under which any number of social fallacies may be hidden.

Neither is there any possible definition of "the weak." Some are weak in one way, and some in another; and those who are weak in one sense are strong in another. In general, however, it may be said that those whom humanitarians and philanthropists call the weak are the ones through whom the productive and conservative forces of society are wasted. They constantly neutralize and destroy the finest efforts of the wise and industrious, and are a dead-weight on the society in all its struggles to realize any better things. Whether the people who mean no harm, but are weak in the essential powers necessary to the performance of one's duties in life, or those who are malicious and vicious, do the more mischief, is a question not easy to answer.

Under the names of the poor and the weak, the negligent, shiftless, inefficient, silly, and imprudent are fastened upon the industrious and prudent as a responsibility and a duty. On the one side, the terms are extended to cover the idle, intemperate, and vicious, who, by the combination, gain credit which they do not deserve, and which they could not get if they stood alone. On the other hand, the terms are extended to include wage-receivers of the humblest rank, who are degraded by the combination. The reader who desires to guard himself against fallacies should always scrutinize the terms "poor" and "weak" as used, so as to see which or how many of these classes they are made to cover.

The humanitarians, philanthropists, and reformers, looking at the facts of life as they present themselves, find enough which is sad and unpromising in the condition of many members of society. They see wealth and poverty side by side. They note great inequality of social position and social chances. They eagerly set about the attempt to account for what they see, and to devise schemes for remedying what they do not like. In their eagerness to recommend the less fortunate classes to pity and consideration they forget all about the right of other classes; they gloss over all the faults of the classes in question, and they exaggerate their misfortunes and their virtues. They invent new theories of property, distorting rights and perpetrating injustice, as any one is sure to do who sets about the re-adjustment of social relations with the interests of one group distinctly before his mind, and the interests of all other groups thrown into the background. When I have read certain of these discussions I have thought that it must be quite disreputable to be respectable, quite dishonest to own property, quite unjust to go one's own way and earn one's own living, and that the only really admirable person was the good-for-nothing. The man who by his own effort raises himself above poverty appears, in these discussions, to be of no account. The man who has done nothing to raise himself above poverty finds that the social doctors flock about him, bringing the capital which they have collected from the other class, and promising him the aid of the State to give him what the other had to work for. In all these schemes and projects the organized intervention of society through the State is either planned or hoped for, and the State is thus made to become the protector and guardian of certain classes. The agents who are to direct the State action are, of course, the reformers and philanthropists. Their schemes, therefore, may always be reduced to this type—that A and B decide what C shall do for D. It will be interesting to inquire, at a later period of our discussion, who C is, and what the effect is upon him of all these arrangements. In all the discussions attention is concentrated on A and B, the noble social reformers, and on D, the "poor man." I call C the Forgotten Man, because I have never seen that any notice was taken of him in any of the discussions. When we have disposed of A, B, and D we can better appreciate the case of C, and I think that we shall find that he deserves our attention, for the worth of his character and the magnitude of his unmerited burdens. Here it may suffice to observe that, on the theories of the social philosophers to whom I have referred, we should get a new maxim of judicious living: Poverty is the best policy. If you get wealth, you will have to support other people; if you do not get wealth, it will be the duty of other people to support you.

No doubt one chief reason for the unclear and contradictory theories of class relations lies in the fact that our society, largely controlled in all its organization by one set of doctrines, still contains survivals of old social theories which are totally inconsistent with the former. In the Middle

Ages men were united by custom and prescription into associations, ranks, guilds, and communities of various kinds. These ties endured as long as life lasted. Consequently society was dependent, throughout all its details, on status, and the tie, or bond, was sentimental. In our modern state, and in the United States more than anywhere else, the social structure is based on contract, and status is of the least importance. Contract, however, is rational—even rationalistic. It is also realistic, cold, and matter-of-fact. A contract relation is based on a sufficient reason, not on custom or prescription. It is not permanent. It endures only so long as the reason for it endures. In a state based on contract sentiment is out of place in any public or common affairs. It is relegated to the sphere of private and personal relations, where it depends not at all on class types, but on personal acquaintance and personal estimates. The sentimentalists among us always seize upon the survivals of the old order. They want to save them and restore them. Much of the loose thinking also which troubles us in our social discussions arises from the fact that men do not distinguish the elements of status and of contract which may be found in our society.

Whether social philosophers think it desirable or not, it is out of the question to go back to status or to the sentimental relations which once united baron and retainer, master and servant, teacher and pupil, comrade and comrade. That we have lost some grace and elegance is undeniable. That life once held more poetry and romance is true enough. But it seems impossible that any one who has studied the matter should doubt that we have gained immeasurably, and that our farther gains lie in going forward, not in going backward. The feudal ties can never be restored. If they could be restored they would bring back personal caprice, favoritism, sycophancy, and intrigue. A society based on contract is a society of free and independent men, who form ties without favor or obligation, and co-operate without cringing or intrigue. A society based on contract, therefore, gives the utmost room and chance for individual development, and for all the self-reliance and dignity of a free man. That a society of free men, co-operating under contract, is by far the strongest society which has ever yet developed the full measure of strength of which it is capable; and that the only social improvements which are now conceivable lie in the direction of more complete realization of a society of free men united by contract, are points which cannot be controverted. It follows, however, that one man, in a free state, cannot claim help from, and cannot be charged to give help to, another. . . .

On the Value, as a Sociological Principle, of the Rule to Mind One's Own Business

. . . Every man and woman in society has one big duty. That is, to take care of his or her own self. This is a social duty. For, fortunately, the matter stands so that the duty of making the best of one's self individually is not a separate thing from the duty of filling one's place in society, but the two are one, and the latter is accomplished when the former is done. The common notion, however, seems to be that one has a duty to society, as a special and separate thing, and that this duty consists in considering and deciding what other people ought to do. Now, the man who can do anything for or about anybody else than himself is fit to be head of a family; and when he becomes head of a family he has duties to his wife and his children, in addition to the former big duty. Then, again, any man who can take care of himself and his family is in a very exceptional position, if he does not find in his immediate surroundings people who need his care and have some sort of a personal claim upon him. If, now, he is able to fulfil all this, and to take care of anybody outside his family and his dependents, he must have a surplus of energy, wisdom, and moral virtue beyond what he needs for his own business. No man has this; for a family is a charge which is capable of infinite development, and no man could suffice to the full measure of duty for which a family may draw upon him. Neither can a man give to society so advantageous an employment of his services, whatever they are, in any other way as by spending them on his family. Upon this, however, I will not insist. I recur to the observation that a man who proposes to take care of other people must have himself and his family taken care of, after some sort of a fashion, and must have an as yet unexhausted store of energy.

The danger of minding other people's business is twofold. First, there is the danger that a man may leave his own business unattended to; and, second, there is the danger of an impertinent interference with another's affairs. The "friends of humanity" almost always run into both dangers. I am one of humanity, and I do not want any volunteer friends. I regard friendship as mutual, and I want to have my say about it. I suppose that other components of humanity feel in the same way about it. If so, they must regard any one who assumes the *rôle* of a friend of humanity as impertinent. The reference of the friend of humanity back to his own business is obviously the next step.

Yet we are constantly annoyed, and the legislatures are kept constantly busy, by the people who have made up their minds that it is wise and conducive to happiness to live in a certain way, and who want to compel everybody else to live in their way. Some people have decided to spend Sunday in a certain way, and they want laws passed to make other people

spend Sunday in the same way. Some people have resolved to be tee-
totalers, and they want a law passed to make everybody else a teetotaler.
Some people have resolved to eschew luxury, and they want taxes laid
to make others eschew luxury. The taxing power is especially something
after which the reformer's finger always itches. Sometimes there is an
element of self-interest in the proposed reformation, as when a publisher
wanted a duty imposed on books, to keep Americans from reading books
which would unsettle their Americanism; and when artists wanted a tax
laid on pictures, to save Americans from buying bad paintings. . . .

The social doctors enjoy the satisfaction of feeling themselves to be
more moral or more enlightened than their fellow-men. They are able to
see what other men ought to do when the other men do not see it. An
examination of the work of the social doctors, however, shows that they
are only more ignorant and more presumptuous than other people. We
have a great many social difficulties and hardships to contend with. Poverty, pain, disease, and misfortune surround our existence. We fight
against them all the time. The individual is a centre of hopes, affections,
desires, and sufferings. When he dies, life changes its form, but does not
cease. That means that the person—the centre of all the hopes, affections,
etc.—after struggling as long as he can, is sure to succumb at last. We
would, therefore, as far as the hardships of the human lot are concerned,
go on struggling to the best of our ability against them but for the social
doctors, and we would endure what we could not cure. But we have
inherited a vast number of social ills which never came from Nature.
They are the complicated products of all the tinkering, muddling, and
blundering of social doctors in the past. These products of social quackery
are now buttressed by habit, fashion, prejudice, platitudinarian thinking,
and new quackery in political economy and social science. It is a fact
worth noticing, just when there seems to be a revival of faith in legislative
agencies, that our States are generally providing against the experienced
evils of over-legislation by ordering that the Legislature shall sit only
every other year. During the hard times, when Congress had a real chance
to make or mar the public welfare, the final adjournment of that body
was hailed year after year with cries of relief from a great anxiety. The
greatest reforms which could now be accomplished would consist in un-
doing the work of statesmen in the past, and the greatest difficulty in the
way of reform is to find out how to undo their work without injury to
what is natural and sound. All this mischief has been done by men who
sat down to consider the problem (as I heard an apprentice of theirs once
express it), What kind of a society do we want to make? When they had
settled this question *a priori* to their satisfaction, they set to work to
make their ideal society, and to-day we suffer the consequences. Human
society tries hard to adapt itself to any conditions in which it finds itself,

and we have been warped and distorted until we have got used to it, as the foot adapts itself to an ill-made boot. Next, we have come to think that that is the right way for things to be; and it is true that a change to a sound and normal condition would for a time hurt us, as a man whose foot has been distorted would suffer if he tried to wear a well-shaped boot. Finally, we have produced a lot of economists and social philosophers who have invented sophisms for fitting our thinking to the distorted facts.

Society, therefore, does not need any care or supervision. If we can acquire a science of society, based on observation of phenomena and study of forces, we may hope to gain some ground slowly toward the elimination of old errors and the re-establishment of a sound and natural social order. Whatever we gain that way will be by growth, never in the world by any reconstruction of society on the plan of some enthusiastic social architect. The latter is only repeating the old error over again, and postponing all our chances of real improvement. Society needs first of all to be freed from these meddlers—that is, to be let alone. Here we are, then, once more back at the old doctrine—*Laissez faire*. Let us translate it into blunt English, and it will read, Mind your own business. It is nothing but the doctrine of liberty. Let every man be happy in his own way. If his sphere of action and interest impinges on that of any other man, there will have to be compromise and adjustment. Wait for the occasion. Do not attempt to generalize those interferences or to plan for them *a priori*. We have a body of laws and institutions which have grown up as occasion has occurred for adjusting rights. Let the same process go on. Practise the utmost reserve possible in your interferences even of this kind, and by no means seize occasion for interfering with natural adjustments. Try first long and patiently whether the natural adjustment will not come about through the play of interests and the voluntary concessions of the parties.

I have said that we have an empirical political economy and social science to fit the distortions of our society. The test of empiricism in this matter is the attitude which one takes up toward *laissez faire*. It no doubt wounds the vanity of a philosopher who is just ready with a new solution of the universe to be told to mind his own business. So he goes on to tell us that if we think that we shall, by being let alone, attain to perfect happiness on earth, we are mistaken. The half-way men—the professorial socialists—join him. They solemnly shake their heads, and tell us that he is right—that letting us alone will never secure us perfect happiness. Under all this lies the familiar logical fallacy, never expressed, but really the point of the whole, that we *shall* get perfect happiness if we put ourselves in the hands of the world-reformer. We never supposed that *laissez faire* would give us perfect happiness. We have left perfect happiness entirely out of our account. If the social doctors will mind their own business, we shall have no troubles but what belong to Nature. Those we will endure or combat as we can. What we desire is, that the friends of humanity should cease to add to them. Our disposition toward the ills which our fellow-man inflicts on us through malice or meddling is quite different from our disposition toward the ills which are inherent in the conditions of human life.

To mind one's own business is a purely negative and unproductive injunction, but, taking social matters as they are just now, it is a sociological principle of the first importance. There might be developed a grand philosophy on the basis of minding one's own business.

Andrew Carnegie
Wealth
(1889)

THE PROBLEM of our age is the proper administration of wealth, so that the ties of brotherhood may still bind together the rich and poor in harmonious relationship. The conditions of human life have not only been changed, but revolutionized, within the past few hundred years. In former days there was little difference between the dwelling, dress, food, and environment of the chief and those of his retainers. The Indians are to-day where civilized man then was. When visiting the Sioux, I was led to the wigwam of the chief. It was just like the others in external appearance, and even within the difference was trifling between it and those of the poorest of his braves. The contrast between the palace of the millionaire and the cottage of the laborer with us to-day measures the change which has come with civilization.

This change, however, is not to be deplored, but welcomed as highly beneficial. It is well, nay, essential for the progress of the race, that the houses of some should be homes for all that is highest and best in literature and the arts, and for all the refinements of civilization, rather than that none should be so. Much better this great irregularity than universal squalor. Without wealth there can be no Mæcenas. The "good old times" were not good old times. Neither master nor servant was as well situated then as to-day. A relapse to old conditions would be disastrous to both—not the least so to him who serves—and would sweep away civilization with it. But whether the change be for good or ill, it is upon us, beyond our power to alter, and therefore to be accepted and made the best of. It is a waste of time to criticise the inevitable.

It is easy to see how the change has come. One illustration will serve for almost every phase of the cause. In the manufacture of products we have the whole story. It applies to all combinations of human industry,

[From *The North American Review* (June 1889).]

as stimulated and enlarged by the inventions of this scientific age. Formerly articles were manufactured at the domestic hearth or in small shops which formed part of the household. The master and his apprentices worked side by side, the latter living with the master, and therefore subject to the same conditions. When these apprentices rose to be masters, there was little or no change in their mode of life, and they, in turn, educated in the same routine succeeding apprentices. There was, substantially, social equality, and even political equality, for those engaged in industrial pursuits had then little or no political voice in the State.

But the inevitable result of such a mode of manufacture was crude articles at high prices. To-day the world obtains commodities of excellent quality at prices which even the generation preceding this would have deemed incredible. In the commercial world similar causes have produced similar results, and the race is benefited thereby. The poor enjoy what the rich could not before afford. What were the luxuries have become the necessaries of life. The laborer has now more comforts than the farmer had a few generations ago. The farmer has more luxuries than the landlord had, and is more richly clad and better housed. The landlord has books and pictures rarer, and appointments more artistic, than the King could then obtain.

The price we pay for this salutary change is, no doubt, great. We assemble thousands of operatives in the factory, in the mine, and in the counting-house, of whom the employer can know little or nothing, and to whom the employer is little better than a myth. All intercourse between them is at an end. Rigid Castes are formed, and, as usual, mutual ignorance breeds mutual distrust. Each Caste is without sympathy for the other, and ready to credit anything disparaging in regard to it. Under the law of competition, the employer of thousands is forced into the strictest economies, among which the rates paid to labor figure prominently, and often there is friction between the employer and the employed, between capital and labor, between rich and poor. Human society loses homogeneity.

The price which society pays for the law of competition, like the price it pays for cheap comforts and luxuries, is also great; but the advantages of this law are also greater still, for it is to this law that we owe our wonderful material development, which brings improved conditions in its train. But, whether the law be benign or not, we must say of it, as we say of the change in the conditions of men to which we have referred: It is here; we cannot evade it; no substitutes for it have been found; and while the law may be sometimes hard for the individual, it is best for the race, because it insures the survival of the fittest in every department. We accept and welcome, therefore, as conditions to which we must accommodate ourselves, great inequality of environment, the concentration of business, industrial and commercial, in the hands of a few, and the law of competition between these, as being not only beneficial, but essential for the future progress of the race. Having accepted these, it follows that there must be great scope for the exercise of special ability in the merchant and in the manufacturer who has to conduct affairs upon a great scale. That this talent for organization and management is rare among men is proved by the fact that it invariably secures for its possessor enormous rewards, no matter where or under what laws or conditions. The experienced in affairs always rate the MAN whose services can be obtained as a partner as not only the first consideration, but such as to render the question of his capital scarcely worth considering, for such men soon create capital; while, without the special talent required, capital soon takes wings. Such men become interested in firms or corporations using millions; and estimating only simple interest to be made upon the capital invested, it is inevitable that their income must exceed their expenditures, and that they must accumulate wealth. Nor is there any middle ground which such men can occupy, because the great manufacturing or commercial concern which does not earn at least interest upon its capital soon becomes bankrupt. It must either go forward or fall behind: to stand still is impossible. It is a condition essential for its successful operation that it should be thus far profitable, and even that, in addition to interest on capital, it should make profit. It is a law, as certain as any of the others named, that men possessed of this peculiar talent for affairs, under the free play of economic forces, must, of necessity, soon be in receipt of more revenue than can be judiciously expended upon themselves; and this law is as beneficial for the race as the others.

Objections to the foundations upon which society is based are not in order, because the condition of the race is better with these than it has been with any others which have been tried. Of the effect of any new substitutes proposed we cannot be sure. The Socialist or Anarchist who seeks to overturn present conditions is to be regarded as attacking the foundation upon which civilization itself rests, for civilization took its start from the day that the capable, industrious workman said to his incompetent and lazy fellow, "If thou dost not sow, thou shalt not reap," and thus ended primitive Communism by separating the drones from the bees. One who studies this subject will soon be brought face to face with the conclusion that upon the sacredness of property civilization itself depends—the right of the laborer to his hundred dollars in the savings bank, and equally the legal right of the millionaire to his millions. To those who propose to substitute Communism for this intense Individualism the answer, therefore, is: The race has tried that. All progress from that barbarous day to the present time has resulted from its displacement. Not evil, but good, has come to the race from the accumulation of wealth by those who have the ability and energy that produce it. But even if we admit for a moment that it might be better for the race to discard its present foundation, Individualism,—that it is a nobler ideal that man should labor, not for himself alone, but in and for a brotherhood of his fellows, and share with them all in common, realizing Swedenborg's idea of Heaven, where, as he says, the angels derive their happiness, not from laboring for self, but for each other,—even admit all this, and a sufficient answer is, This is not evolution, but revolution. It necessitates the changing of human nature itself—a work of æons, even if it were good to change it, which we cannot know. It is not practicable in our day or in our age. Even if desirable theoretically, it belongs to another and long-succeeding sociological stratum. Our duty is with what is practicable now; with the next step possible in our day and generation. It is criminal to waste our energies in endeavoring to uproot, when all we can profitably or possibly accomplish is to bend the universal tree of humanity a little in the direction most favorable to the production of good fruit under existing circumstances. We might as well urge the destruction of the highest existing type of man because he failed to reach our ideal as to favor the destruction of Individualism, Private Property, the Law of Accumulation of Wealth, and the Law of Competition; for these are the highest results of human experience, the soil in which society so far has produced the best fruit. Unequally or unjustly, perhaps, as these laws sometimes operate, and imperfect as they appear to the Idealist, they are, nevertheless, like the highest type of man, the best and most valuable of all that humanity has yet accomplished.

We start, then, with a condition of affairs under which the best interests of the race are promoted, but which inevitably gives wealth to the few. Thus far, accepting conditions as they exist, the situation can be surveyed and pronounced good. The question then arises,—and, if the foregoing be correct, it is the only question with which we have to deal,—What is the proper mode of administering wealth after the laws upon which civilization is founded have thrown it into the hands of the few? And it is of this great question that I believe I offer the true solution. It will be understood that *fortunes* are here spoken of, not moderate sums saved by many years of effort, the returns from which are required for the comfortable maintenance and education of families. This is not *wealth*, but only *competence*, which it should be the aim of all to acquire.

There are but three modes in which surplus wealth can be disposed of. It can be left to the families of the decedents; or it can be bequeathed for public purposes; or, finally, it can be administered during their lives by its possessors. Under the first and second modes most of the wealth of the world that has reached the few has hitherto been applied. Let us in turn consider each of these modes. The first is the most injudicious.

In monarchical countries, the estates and the greatest portion of the wealth are left to the first son, that the vanity of the parent may be gratified by the thought that his name and title are to descend to succeeding generations unimpaired. The conditions of this class in Europe to-day teaches the futility of such hopes or ambitions. The successors have become impoverished through their follies or from the fall in the value of land. Even in Great Britain the strict law of entail has been found inadequate to maintain the status of an hereditary class. Its soil is rapidly passing into the hands of the stranger. Under republican institutions the division of property among the children is much fairer, but the question which forces itself upon thoughtful men in all lands is: Why should men leave great fortunes to their children? If this is done from affection, is it not misguided affection? Observation teaches that, generally speaking, it is not well for the children that they should be so burdened. Neither is it well for the state. Beyond providing for the wife and daughters moderate sources of income, and very moderate allowances indeed, if any, for the sons, men may well hesitate, for it is no longer questionable that great sums bequeathed oftener work more for the injury than for the good of the recipients. Wise men will soon conclude that, for the best interests of the members of their families and of the state, such bequests are an improper use of their means.

It is not suggested that men who have failed to educate their sons to earn a livelihood shall cast them adrift in poverty. If any man has seen fit to rear his sons with a view to their living idle lives, or, what is highly commendable, has instilled in them the sentiment that they are in a position to labor for public ends without reference to pecuniary considerations, then, of course, the duty of the parent is to see that such are provided for *in moderation*. There are instances of millionaires' sons unspoiled by wealth, who, being rich, still perform great services in the community. Such are the very salt of the earth, as valuable as, unfortunately, they are rare; still it is not the exception, but the rule, that men must regard, and, looking at the usual result of enormous sums conferred upon legatees, the thoughtful man must shortly say, "I would as soon leave to my son a curse as the almighty dollar," and admit to himself that it is not the welfare of the children, but family pride, which inspires these enormous legacies.

As to the second mode, that of leaving wealth at death for public uses, it may be said that this is only a means for the disposal of wealth, provided a man is content to wait until he is dead before it becomes of much good in the world. Knowledge of the results of legacies bequeathed is not calculated to inspire the brightest hopes of much posthumous good being accomplished. The cases are not few in which the real object sought by the testator is not attained, nor are they few in which his real wishes are thwarted. In many cases the bequests are so used as to become only monuments of his folly. It is well to remember that it requires the exercise of not less ability than that which acquired the wealth to use it so as to be really beneficial to the community. Besides this, it may fairly be said that no man is to be extolled for doing what he cannot help doing, nor is he to be thanked by the community to which he only leaves wealth at death. Men who leave vast sums in this way may fairly be thought men who would not have left it at all, had they been able to take it with them. The memories of such cannot be held in grateful remembrance, for there is no grace in their gifts. It is not to be wondered at that such bequests seem so generally to lack the blessing.

The growing disposition to tax more and more heavily large estates left at death is a cheering indication of the growth of a salutary change in public opinion. The State of Pennsylvania now takes—subject to some exceptions—one-tenth of the property left by its citizens. The budget presented in the British Parliament the other day proposes to increase the death-duties; and, most significant of all, the new tax is to be a graduated one. Of all forms of taxation, this seems the wisest. Men who continue hoarding great sums all their lives, the proper use of which for public ends would work good to the community, should be made to feel that the community, in the form of the state, cannot thus be deprived of its proper share. By taxing estates heavily at death the state marks its condemnation of the selfish millionaire's unworthy life.

It is desirable that nations should go much further in this direction. Indeed, it is difficult to set bounds to the share of a rich man's estate which should go at his death to the public through the agency of the state, and by all means such taxes should be graduated, beginning at nothing upon moderate sums to dependents, and increasing rapidly as the amounts swell, until of the millionaire's hoard, as of Shylock's, at least

> "——— The other half
> Comes to the privy coffer of the state."

This policy would work powerfully to induce the rich man to attend to the administration of wealth during his life, which is the end that society should always have in view, as being that by far most fruitful for the people. Nor need it be feared that this policy would sap the root of enterprise and render men less anxious to accumulate, for to the class whose ambition it is to leave great fortunes and be talked about after their death, it will attract even more attention, and, indeed, be a somewhat nobler ambition to have enormous sums paid over to the state from their fortunes.

There remains, then, only one mode of using great fortunes; but in this we have the true antidote for the temporary unequal distribution of wealth, the reconciliation of the rich and the poor—a reign of harmony—another ideal, differing, indeed, from that of the Communist in requiring only the further evolution of existing conditions, not the total overthrow of our civilization. It is founded upon the present most intense individualism, and the race is prepared to put it in practice by degrees whenever it pleases. Under its sway we shall have an ideal state, in which the surplus wealth of the few will become, in the best sense, the property of the many, because administered for the common good, and this wealth, passing through the hands of the few, can be made a much more potent force for the elevation of our race than if it had been distributed in small sums to the people themselves. Even the poorest can be made to see this, and to agree that great sums gathered by some of their fellow-citizens and spent for public purposes, from which the masses reap the principal benefit, are more valuable to them than if scattered among them through the course of many years in trifling amounts.

If we consider what results flow from the Cooper Institute, for instance, to the best portion of the race in New York not possessed of means, and compare these with those which would have arisen for the good of the masses from an equal sum distributed by Mr. Cooper in his lifetime in the form of wages, which is the highest form of distribution, being for work done and not for charity, we can form some estimate of the possibilities for the improvement of the race which lie embedded in the present law of the accumulation of wealth. Much of this sum, if distributed in small quantities among the people, would have been wasted in the indulgence of appetite, some of it in excess, and it may be doubted whether even the part put to the best use, that of adding to the comforts of the home, would have yielded results for the race, as a race, at all comparable to those which are flowing and are to flow from the Cooper Institute from generation to generation. Let the advocate of violent or radical change ponder well this thought.

We might even go so far as to take another instance, that of Mr. Tilden's bequest of five millions of dollars for a free library in the city of New York, but in referring to this one cannot help saying involuntarily, How much better if Mr. Tilden had devoted the last years of his own life to the proper administration of this immense sum; in which case neither legal contest nor any other cause of delay could have interfered with his aims. But let us assume that Mr. Tilden's millions finally become the means of giving to this city a noble public library, where the treasures of the world contained in books will be open to all forever, without money and without price. Considering the good of that part of the race which congregates in and around Manhattan Island, would its permanent benefit have been better promoted had these millions been allowed to circulate in small sums through the hands of the masses? Even the most strenuous advocate of Communism must entertain a doubt upon this subject. Most of those who think will probably entertain no doubt whatever.

Poor and restricted are our opportunities in this life; narrow our horizon; our best work most imperfect; but rich men should be thankful for one inestimable boon. They have it in their power during their lives to busy themselves in organizing benefactions from which the masses of their fellows will derive lasting advantage, and thus dignify their own lives. The highest life is probably to be reached, not by such imitation of the life of Christ as Count Tolstoï gives us, but, while animated by Christ's spirit, by recognizing the changed conditions of this age, and adopting modes of expressing this spirit suitable to the changed conditions under which we live; still laboring for the good of our fellows, which was the essence of his life and teaching, but laboring in a different manner.

This, then, is held to be the duty of the man of Wealth: First, to set an example of modest, unostentatious living, shunning display or extravagance; to provide moderately for the legitimate wants of those dependent upon him; and after doing so to consider all surplus revenues which come to him simply as trust funds, which he is called upon to administer, and strictly bound as a matter of duty to administer in the manner which, in his judgment, is best calculated to produce the most beneficial results for the community—the man of wealth thus becoming the mere agent and trustee for his poorer brethren, bringing to their service his superior wisdom, experience, and ability to administer, doing for them better than they would or could do for themselves.

We are met here with the difficulty of determining what are moderate sums to leave to members of the family; what is modest, unostentatious living; what is the test of extravagance. There must be different standards for different conditions. The answer is that it is as impossible to name exact amounts or actions as it is to define good manners, good taste, or the rules of propriety; but, nevertheless, these are verities, well known although undefinable. Public sentiment is quick to know and to feel what offends these. So in the case of wealth. The rule in regard to good taste in the dress of men or women applies here. Whatever makes one conspicuous offends the canon. If any family be chiefly known for display, for extravagance in home, table, equipage, for enormous sums ostentatiously spent in any form upon itself,—if these be its chief distinctions, we have no difficulty in estimating its nature or culture. So likewise in regard to the use or abuse of its surplus wealth, or to generous, free-handed cooperation in good public uses, or to unabated efforts to accumulate and hoard to the last, whether they administer or bequeath. The verdict rests with the best and most enlightened public sentiment. The community will surely judge, and its judgments will not often be wrong.

The best uses to which surplus wealth can be put have already been indicated. Those who would administer wisely must, indeed, be wise, for one of the serious obstacles to the improvement of our race is indiscriminate charity. It were better for mankind that the millions of the rich were thrown into the sea than so spent as to encourage the slothful, the drunken, the unworthy. Of every thousand dollars spent in so called charity to-day, it is probable that $950 is unwisely spent; so spent, indeed, as to produce the very evils which it proposes to mitigate or cure. A well-known writer of philosophic books admitted the other day that he had given a quarter of a dollar to a man who approached him as he was coming to visit the house of his friend. He knew nothing of the habits of this beggar; knew not the use that would be made of this money, although he had every reason to suspect that it would be spent improperly. This man professed to be a disciple of Herbert Spencer; yet the quarter-dollar given that night will probably work more injury than all the money which its thoughtless donor will ever be able to give in true charity will do good. He only gratified his own feelings, saved himself from annoyance,—and this was probably one of the most selfish and very worst actions of his life, for in all respects he is most worthy.

In bestowing charity, the main consideration should be to help those who will help themselves; to provide part of the means by which those who desire to improve may do so; to give those who desire to rise the aids by which they may rise; to assist, but rarely or never to do all. Neither the individual nor the race is improved by alms-giving. Those worthy of assistance, except in rare cases, seldom require assistance. The really valuable men of the race never do, except in cases of accident or sudden change. Every one has, of course, cases of individuals brought to his own knowledge where temporary assistance can do genuine good, and these he will not overlook. But the amount which can be wisely given by the individual for individuals is necessarily limited by his lack of knowledge of the circumstances connected with each. He is the only true reformer who is as careful and as anxious not to aid the unworthy as he is to aid the worthy, and, perhaps, even more so, for in alms-giving more injury is probably done by rewarding vice than by relieving virtue.

The rich man is thus almost restricted to following the examples of Peter Cooper, Enoch Pratt of Baltimore, Mr. Pratt of Brooklyn, Senator Stanford, and others, who know that the best means of benefiting the community is to place within its reach the ladders upon which the aspiring can rise—parks, and means of recreation, by which men are helped in body and mind; works of art, certain to give pleasure and improve the public taste, and public institutions of various kinds, which will improve the general condition of the people;—in this manner returning their surplus wealth to the mass of their fellows in the forms best calculated to do them lasting good.

Thus is the problem of Rich and Poor to be solved. The laws of accumulation will be left free; the laws of distribution free. Individualism will continue, but the millionaire will be but a trustee for the poor; intrusted for a season with a great part of the increased wealth of the community, but administering it for the community far better than it could or would have done for itself. The best minds will thus have reached a stage in the development of the race in which it is clearly seen that there is no mode of disposing of surplus wealth creditable to thoughtful and earnest men into whose hands it flows save by using it year by year for the general good. This day already dawns. But a little while, and although, without incurring the pity of their fellows, men may die sharers in great business enterprises from which their capital cannot be or has not been withdrawn, and is left chiefly at death for public uses, yet the man who dies leaving behind him millions of available wealth, which was his to administer during life, will pass away "unwept, unhonored, and unsung," no matter to what uses he leaves the dross which he cannot take with him. Of such as these the public verdict will then be: "The man who dies thus rich dies disgraced."

Such, in my opinion, is the true Gospel concerning Wealth, obedience to which is destined some day to solve the problem of the Rich and the Poor, and to bring "Peace on earth, among men Good-Will."

Thorstein Veblen
Industrial Exemption and Conservatism
(1899)

THE LIFE of man in society, just like the life of other species, is a struggle for existence, and therefore it is a process of selective adaptation. The evolution of social structure has been a process of natural selection of institutions. The progress which has been and is being made in human institutions and in human character may be set down, broadly, to a natural selection of the fittest habits of thought and to a process of enforced adaptation of individuals to an environment which has progressively changed with the growth of the community and with the changing institutions under which men have lived. Institutions are not only themselves the result of a selective and adaptive process which shapes the prevailing or dominant types of spiritual attitude and aptitudes; they are at the same time special methods of life and of human relations, and are therefore in their turn efficient factors of selection. So that the changing institutions in their turn make for a further selection of individuals endowed with the fittest temperament, and a further adaptation of individual temperament and habits to the changing environment through the formation of new institutions.

The forces which have shaped the development of human life and of social structure are no doubt ultimately reducible to terms of living tissue and material environment; but proximately for the purpose in hand, these forces may best be stated in terms of an environment, partly human, partly non-human, and a human subject with a more or less definite physical and intellectual constitution. Taken in the aggregate or average, this human subject is more or less variable; chiefly, no doubt, under a rule of selective conservation of favorable variations. The selection of favorable variations is perhaps in great measure a selective conservation of ethnic types. In the life history of any community whose population is

[From *The Theory of the Leisure Class* (1899).]

made up of a mixture of divers ethnic elements, one or another of several persistent and relatively stable types of body and of temperament rises into dominance at any given point. The situation, including the institutions in force at any given time, will favor the survival and dominance of one type of character in preference to another; and the type of man so selected to continue and to further elaborate the institutions handed down from the past will in some considerable measure shape these institutions in his own likeness. But apart from selection as between relatively stable types of character and habits of mind, there is no doubt simultaneously going on a process of selective adaptation of habits of thought within the general range of aptitudes which is characteristic of the dominant ethnic type or types. There may be a variation in the fundamental character of any population by selection between relatively stable types; but there is also a variation due to adaptation in detail within the range of the type, and to selection between specific habitual views regarding any given social relation or group of relations. . . .

. . . Institutions must change with changing circumstances, since they are of the nature of an habitual method of responding to the stimuli which these changing circumstances afford. The development of these institutions is the development of society. The institutions are, in substance, prevalent habits of thought with respect to particular relations and particular functions of the individual and of the community; and the scheme of life, which is made up of the aggregate of institutions in force at a given time or at a given point in the development of any society, may, on the psychological side, be broadly characterized as a prevalent spiritual attitude or a prevalent theory of life. . . .

The situation of today shapes the institutions of tomorrow through a selective, coercive process, by acting upon men's habitual view of things, and so altering or fortifying a point of view or a mental attitude handed down from the past. . . . Institutions are products of the past process, are adapted to past circumstances, and are therefore never in full accord with the requirements of the present. In the nature of the case, this process of selective adaptation can never catch up with the progressively changing situation in which the community finds itself at any given time; for the environment, the situation, the exigencies of life which enforce the adaptation and exercise the selection, change from day to day; and each successive situation of the community in its turn tends to obsolescence as soon as it has been established. . . .

It is to be noted then . . . that the institutions of today . . . do not entirely fit the situation of today. At the same time, men's present habits of thought tend to persist indefinitely, except as circumstances enforce a change. These institutions which have been handed down, these habits of thought, points of view, mental attitudes and aptitudes . . . are therefore themselves a conservative factor. . . .

Social structure changes, develops, adapts itself to an altered situation, only through a change in the habits of thought of the several classes of the community; or in the last analysis, through a change in the habits of thought of the individuals which make up the community. The evolution of society is substantially a process of mental adaptation on the part of individuals under the stress of circumstances which will no longer tolerate habits of thought formed under and conforming to a different set of circumstances in the past. . . .

Social advance, especially as seen from the point of view of economic theory, consists in a continued progressive approach to an approximately exact "adjustment of inner relations to outer relations"; but this adjustment is never definitively established, since the "outer relations" are subject to constant change as a consequence of the progressive change going on in the "inner relations." But the degree of approximation may be greater or less, depending on the facility with which an adjustment is made. A readjustment of men's habits of thought to conform with the exigencies of an altered situation is in any case made only tardily and reluctantly, and only under the coercion exercised by a stipulation which has made the accredited views untenable. The readjustment of institutions and habitual views to an altered environment is made in response to pressure from without; it is of the nature of a response to stimulus. Freedom and facility of readjustment, that is to say capacity for growth in social structure, therefore depends in great measure on the degree of freedom with which the situation at any given time acts on the individual members of the community. . . .

If any portion or class of society is sheltered from the action of the environment in any essential respect, that portion . . . or that class, will adapt its views and its scheme of life more tardily to the altered general situation; it will in so far tend to retard the process of social transformation. The wealthy leisure class is in such a sheltered position with respect to the economic forces that make for change and readjustment. And it may be said that the forces which make for a readjustment of institutions, especially in the case of a modern industrial community, are, in the last analysis, almost entirely of an economic nature. . . .

These institutions are habitual methods of carrying on the life process of the community in contact with the material environment in which it lives. When given methods of unfolding human activity in this given environment have been elaborated in this way, the life of the community will express itself with some facility in these habitual directions. The community will make use of the forces of the environment for the purposes of its life according to methods learned in the past and embodied in these institutions. But as population increases, and as men's knowledge and skill in directing the forces of nature widen, the habitual methods of relation between the members of the group, and the habitual method of carrying on the life process of the group as a whole, no longer give the same result as before; nor are the resulting conditions of life distributed and apportioned in the same manner or with the same effect among the various members as before. If the scheme according to which the life process of the group was carried on under the earlier conditions gave approximately the highest attainable result—under the circumstances—in the way of efficiency or facility of the life process of the group; then the same scheme of life unaltered will not yield the highest result attainable . . . under the altered conditions. Under the altered conditions of population, skill, and knowledge, the facility of life as carried on according to the traditional scheme may not be lower than under the earlier conditions; but the chances are always that it is less than might be if the scheme were altered to suit the altered conditions.

The group is made up of individuals, and the group's life is the life of individuals carried on in at least ostensible severalty. The group's accepted scheme of life is the consensus of views held by the body of these individuals as to what is right, good, expedient, and beautiful in the way of human life. In the redistribution of the conditions of life that comes of the altered method of dealing with the environment, the outcome is not an equable change in the facility of life throughout the group. The altered conditions may increase the facility of life for the group as a whole, but the redistribution will usually result in a decrease of facility or fullness of life for some members of the group. An advance in technical methods, in population, or in industrial organization will require at least some of the members of the community to change their habits of life, if they are to enter with facility and effect into the altered industrial methods; and in doing so they will be unable to live up to the received notions as to what are the right and beautiful habits of life.

Any one who is required to change his habits of life and his habitual relations to his fellow men will feel the discrepancy between the method of life required of him by the newly arisen exigencies, and the traditional scheme of life to which he is accustomed. It is the individuals placed in this position who have the liveliest incentive to reconstruct the received scheme of life and are most readily persuaded to accept new standards; and it is through the need of the means of livelihood that men are placed in such a position. The pressure exerted by the environment upon the group, and making for a readjustment of the group's scheme of life, impinges upon the members of the group in the form of pecuniary exigencies; and it is owing to this fact . . . that we can say that the forces which count toward a readjustment of institutions in any modern industrial community are chiefly economic forces. . . . Such a readjustment as is here contemplated is substantially a change in men's views as to what is good and right, and the means through which a change is wrought in men's apprehension of what is good and right is in large part the pressure of pecuniary exigencies.

Any change in men's views as to what is good and right in human life makes its way but tardily at the best. Especially is this true of any change in the direction of what is called progress. . . . Retrogression, reapproach to a standpoint to which the race has been long habituated in the past, is easier. . . .

The cultural stage which lies immediately back of the present in the life history of Western civilization is . . . the quasi-peaceable stage. At this quasi-peaceable stage the law of status is the dominant feature in the scheme of life. There is no need of pointing out how prone the men of today are to revert to the spiritual attitude of mastery and of personal subservience which characterizes that stage. It may rather be said to be held in an uncertain abeyance by the economic exigencies of today, than to have been definitely supplanted by a habit of mind that is in full accord with these later-developed exigencies. The predatory and quasi-peaceable stages of economic evolution seem to have been of long duration in the life history of all the chief ethnic elements which go to make up the populations of the Western culture. The temperament and the propensities proper to those cultural stages have, therefore, attained such a persistence as to make a speedy reversion to the broad features of the corresponding psychological constitution inevitable in the case of any class or community which is removed from the action of those forces that make for a maintenance of the later-developed habits of thought.

It is a matter of common notoriety that when individuals, or even considerable groups of men, are segregated from a higher industrial culture and exposed to a lower cultural environment, or to an economic situation of a more primitive character, they quickly show evidence of reversion toward the spiritual features which characterize the predatory type. . . . [T]he case of the American colonies might be cited as an example of such a reversion. . . .

The leisure class is the conservative class. The exigencies of the general economic situation of the community do not freely or directly impinge upon the members of this class. They are not required under penalty of forfeiture to change their habits of life and their theoretical views of the external world to suit the demands of an altered industrial technique, since they are not in the full sense an organic part of the industrial community. Therefore these exigencies do not readily produce, in the members of this class, that degree of uneasiness with the existing order which alone can lead any body of men to give up views and methods of life that have become habitual to them. The office of the leisure class in social evolution is to retard the movement and to conserve what is obsolescent. . . . The opposition of the class to changes in the cultural

scheme is instinctive, and does not rest primarily on an interested calculation of material advantages; it is an instinctive revulsion at any
departure from the accepted way of doing and of looking at things—a
revulsion common to all men and only to be overcome by stress of circumstances. All change in habits of life and of thought is irksome. The
difference in this respect between the wealthy and the common run of
mankind lies not so much in the motive which prompts to conservatism
as in the degree of exposure to the economic forces that urge a change.
The members of the wealthy class do not yield to the demand for innovation as readily as other men because they are not constrained to do
so. . . .

Since conservatism is a characteristic of the wealthier and therefore
more reputable portion of the community, it has acquired a certain hon-
orific or decorative value. It has become prescriptive to such an extent
that an adherence to conservative views is comprised as a matter of course
in our notions of respectability; and it is imperatively incumbent on all
who would lead a blameless life in point of social repute. Conservatism,
being an upper-class characteristic, is decorous; and conversely, innovation, being a lower-class phenomenon, is vulgar. . . . So that even in
cases where one recognizes the substantial merits of the case for which
the innovator is spokesman—as may easily happen if the evils which he
seeks to remedy are sufficiently remote in point of time or space or
personal contact—still one cannot but be sensible of the fact that the
innovator is a person with whom it is at least distasteful to be associated,
and from whose social contact one must shrink. Innovation is bad form.

The fact that the usages, actions, and views of the well-to-do leisure
class acquire the character of a prescriptive canon of conduct for the rest
of society, gives added weight and reach to the conservative influence of
that class. It makes it incumbent upon all reputable people to follow their
lead. So that, by virtue of its high position as the avatar of good form,
the wealthier class comes to exert a retarding influence upon social development far in excess of that which the simple numerical strength of
the class would assign it. Its prescriptive example acts to greatly stiffen
the resistance of all other classes against any innovation, and to fix men's
affections upon the good institutions handed down from an earlier generation.

There is a second way in which the influence of the leisure class acts
in the same direction, so far as concerns hindrance to the adoption of a
conventional scheme of life more in accord with the exigencies of the
time. . . . The code of proprieties, conventionalities, and usages in vogue
at any given time and among any given people has more or less of the
character of an organic whole; so that any appreciable change in one point
of the scheme involves something of a change or readjustment at other

points also, if not a reorganization all along the line. When a change is made which immediately touches only a minor point in the scheme, the consequent derangement of the structure of conventionalities may be inconspicuous; but even in such a case it is safe to say that some derangement of the general scheme, more or less far-reaching, will follow. On the other hand, when an attempted reform involves the suppression or thorough-going remodelling of an institution of first-rate importance in the conventional scheme, it is immediately felt that a serious derangement of the entire scheme would result; it is felt that a readjustment of the structure to the new form taken on by one of its chief elements would be a painful and tedious, if not a doubtful process. . . .

The revulsion felt by good people at any proposed departure from the accepted methods of life is a familiar fact of everyday experience. It is not unusual to hear those persons who dispense salutary advice and admonition to the community express themselves forcibly upon the far-reaching pernicious effects which the community would suffer from such relatively slight changes as the disestablishment of the Anglican Church, an increased facility of divorce, adoption of female suffrage, prohibition of the manufacture and sale of intoxicating beverages, abolition or restriction of inheritances, etc. Any one of these innovations would, we are told, "shake the social structure to its base," "reduce society to chaos," "subvert the foundations of morality," "make life intolerable," "confound the order of nature," etc. These various locutions are, no doubt, of the nature of hyperbole; but, at the same time, like all overstatement, they are evidence of a lively sense of the gravity of the consequences which they are intended to describe. The effect of these and like innovations in deranging the accepted scheme of life is felt to be of much graver consequence than the simple alteration of an isolated item in a series of contrivances for the convenience of men in society. What is true in so obvious a degree of innovations of first-rate importance is true in a less degree of changes of a smaller immediate importance. The aversion to change is in large part an aversion to the bother of making the readjustment which any given change will necessitate; and this solidarity of the system of institutions of any given culture or of any given people strengthens the instinctive resistance offered to any change in men's habits of thought, even in matters which, taken by themselves, are of minor importance.

A consequence of this increased reluctance . . . is that any innovation calls for a greater expenditure of nervous energy in making the necessary readjustment than would otherwise be the case. It is not only that a change in established habits of thought is distasteful. The process of readjustment of the accepted theory of life involves . . . a more or less protracted and laborious effort to find and to keep one's bearings under the altered circumstances. This process requires a certain expenditure of energy, and so presumes, for its successful accomplishment, some surplus of energy beyond that absorbed in the daily struggle for subsistence. Consequently it follows that progress is hindered by underfeeding and excessive physical hardship, no less effectually than by such a luxurious life as will shut out discontent by cutting off the occasion for it. The abjectly poor, and all those persons whose energies are entirely absorbed by the struggle for daily sustenance, are conservative because they cannot afford the effort of taking thought for the day after tomorrow; just as the highly prosperous are conservative because they have small occasion to be discontented with the situation as it stands today.

From this proposition it follows that the institution of a leisure class acts to make the lower classes conservative by withdrawing from them as much as it may of the means of sustenance, and so reducing their consumption, and consequently their available energy, to such a point as to make them incapable of the effort required for the learning and adoption of new habits of thought. The accumulation of wealth at the upper end of the pecuniary scale implies privation at the lower end of the scale. It is a commonplace that, wherever it occurs, a considerable degree of privation among the body of the people is a serious obstacle to any innovation.

This direct inhibitory effect of the unequal distribution of wealth is seconded by an indirect effect tending to the same result. . . . [T]he imperative example set by the upper class in fixing the canons of reputability fosters the practice of conspicuous consumption. The prevalence of conspicuous consumption as one of the main elements in the standard of decency among all classes is of course not traceable wholly to the example of the wealthy leisure class, but the practice and the insistence on it are no doubt strengthened by the example of the leisure class. The requirements of decency in this matter are very considerable and very imperative; so that even among classes whose pecuniary position is sufficiently strong to admit a consumption of goods considerably in excess of the subsistence minimum, the disposable surplus left over after the more imperative physical needs are satisfied is not infrequently diverted to the purpose of a conspicuous decency, rather than to added physical comfort and fullness of life. Moreover, such surplus energy as is available is also likely to be expended in the acquisition of goods for conspicuous consumption or conspicuous hoarding. The result is that the requirements of pecuniary reputability tend (1) to leave but a scanty subsistence minimum available for other than conspicuous consumption, and (2) to absorb any surplus energy which may be available after the bare physical necessities of life have been provided for. The outcome of the whole is a strengthening of the general conservative attitude of the community. . . .

To this is to be added that the leisure class has also a material interest in leaving things as they are. Under the circumstances prevailing at any given time this class is in a privileged position, and any departure from the existing order may be expected to work to the detriment of the class rather than the reverse. The attitude of the class, simply as influenced by its class interest, should therefore be to let well-enough alone. . . .

All this, of course, has nothing to say in the way of eulogy or deprecation of the office of the leisure class as an exponent and vehicle of conservatism or reversion in social structure. The inhibition which it exercises may be salutary or the reverse. Whether it is the one or the other in any given case is a question of casuistry rather than of general theory. There may be truth in the view . . . so often expressed by the spokesmen of the conservative element, that without some such substantial and consistent resistance to innovation as is offered by the conservative well-to-do classes, social innovation and experiment would hurry the community into untenable and intolerable situations; the only possible result of which would be discontent and disastrous reaction. . . .

But apart from all deprecation, and aside from all question as to the indispensability of some such check on headlong innovation, the leisure class, in the nature of things, consistently acts to retard that adjustment to the environment which is called social advance or development. The characteristic attitude of the class may be summed up in the maxim: "Whatever is, is right"; whereas the law of natural selection, as applied to human institutions, gives the axiom: "Whatever is, is wrong." Not that the institutions of today are wholly wrong for the purposes of the life of today, but they are, always and in the nature of things, wrong to some extent. They are the result of a more or less inadequate adjustment of the methods of living to a situation which prevailed at some point in the past development; and they are therefore wrong by something more than the interval which separates the present situation from that of the past. "Right" and "wrong" are of course here used without conveying any reflection as to what ought or ought not to be. They are applied simply from the (morally colorless) evolutionary standpoint, and are intended to designate compatibility or incompatibility with the effective evolutionary process. The institution of a leisure class, by force or class interest and instinct, and by precept and prescriptive example, makes for the perpetuation of the existing maladjustment of institutions, and even favors a reversion to a somewhat more archaic scheme of life; a scheme which would be still farther out of adjustment with the exigencies of life under the existing situation even than the accredited, obsolescent scheme that has come down from the immediate past.

But after all has been said on the head of conservation of the good old ways, it remains true that institutions change and develop. There is a cumulative growth of customs and habits of thought; a selective adaptation of conventions and methods of life. Something is to be said of the office of the leisure class in guiding this growth as well as in retarding it; but little can be said here of its relation to institutional growth except as it touches the institutions that are primarily and immediately of an economic character. These institutions . . . may be roughly distinguished into two classes or categories, according as they serve one or the other of two divergent purposes of economic life.

To adapt the classical terminology, they are institutions of acquisition or of production; . . . they are pecuniary or industrial institutions; they are institutions serving either the invidious or the non-invidious economic interest. The former category have to do with "business," the latter with industry, taking the latter word in the mechanical sense. The latter class are not often recognized as institutions, in great part because they do not immediately concern the ruling class, and are, therefore, seldom the subject of legislation or of deliberate convention. When they do receive attention they are commonly approached from the pecuniary or business side; that being the side or phase of economic life that chiefly occupies men's deliberations in our time, especially the deliberations of the upper classes. These classes have little else than a business interest in things economic, and on them at the same time it is chiefly incumbent to deliberate upon the community's affairs.

The relation of the leisure (that is, propertied non-industrial) class to the economic process is a pecuniary relation—a relation of acquisition, not of production; of exploitation, not of serviceability. Indirectly their economic office may, of course, be of the utmost importance to the economic life process; and it is by no means here intended to depreciate the economic function of the propertied class or of the captains of industry. The purpose is simply to point out what is the nature of the relation of these classes to the industrial process and to economic institutions. Their office is of a parasitic character, and their interest is to divert what substance they may to their own use, and to retain whatever is under their hand. The conventions of the business world have grown up under the selective surveillance of this principle of predation or parasitism. They are conventions of ownership; derivatives, more or less remote, of the ancient predatory culture. But these pecuniary institutions do not entirely fit the situation of today, for they have grown up under a past situation differing somewhat from the present. Even for effectiveness in the pecuniary way, therefore, they are not as apt as might be. The changed industrial life requires changed methods of acquisition; and the pecuniary classes have some interest in so adapting the pecuniary institutions as to give them the best effect for acquisition of private gain that is compatible with the continuance of the industrial process out of which this gain arises. Hence there is a more or less consistent trend in the leisure-class guidance of institutional growth, answering to the pecuniary ends which shape leisure-class economic life.

The effect of the pecuniary interest and the pecuniary habit of mind upon the growth of institutions is seen in those enactments and conventions that make for security of property, enforcement of contracts, facility of pecuniary transactions, vested interests. Of such bearing are changes affecting bankruptcy and receiverships, limited liability, banking and currency, coalitions of laborers or employers, trusts and pools. The community's institutional furniture of this kind is of immediate consequence only to the propertied classes, and in proportion as they are propertied; that is to say, in proportion as they are to be ranked with the leisure class. But indirectly these conventions of business life are of the gravest consequence for the industrial process and for the life of the community. And in guiding the institutional growth in this respect, the pecuniary classes, therefore, serve a purpose of the most serious importance to the community, not only in the conservation of the accepted social scheme, but also in shaping the industrial process proper.

The immediate end of this pecuniary institutional structure and of its amelioration is the greater facility of peaceable and orderly exploitation; but its remoter effects far outrun this immediate object. Not only does the more facile conduct of business permit industry and extra-industrial life to go on with less perturbation; but the resulting elimination of disturbances and complications calling for an exercise of astute discrimination in everyday affairs acts to make the pecuniary class itself superfluous. As fast as pecuniary transactions are reduced to routine, the captain of industry can be dispensed with. This consummation, it is needless to say, lies yet in the indefinite future. The ameliorations wrought in favor of the pecuniary interest in modern institutions tend, in another field, to substitute the "soulless" joint-stock corporation for the captain, and so they make also for the dispensability of the great leisure-class function of ownership. . . .

Woodrow Wilson
The Old Order Changeth
(1913)

THERE IS one great basic fact which underlies all the questions that are discussed on the political platform at the present moment. That singular fact is that nothing is done in this country as it was done twenty years ago.

We are in the presence of a new organization of society. Our life has broken away from the past. The life of America is not the life that it was twenty years ago; it is not the life that it was ten years ago. We have changed our economic conditions, absolutely, from top to bottom; and, with our economic society, the organization of our life. The old political formulas do not fit the present problems; they read now like documents taken out of a forgotten age. The older cries sound as if they belonged to a past age which men have almost forgotten. Things which used to be put into the party platforms of ten years ago would sound antiquated if put into a platform now. We are facing the necessity of fitting a new social organization, as we did once fit the old organization, to the happiness and prosperity of the great body of citizens; for we are conscious that the new order of society has not been made to fit and provide the convenience or prosperity of the average man. The life of the nation has grown infinitely varied. It does not centre now upon questions of governmental structure or of the distribution of governmental powers. It centres upon questions of the very structure and operation of society itself, of which government is only the instrument. Our development has run so fast and so far along the lines sketched in the earlier day of constitutional definition, has so crossed and interlaced those lines, has piled upon them such novel structures of trust and combination, has elaborated within them a life so manifold, so full of forces which transcend the boundaries of the country itself and fill the eyes of the world, that a new nation seems to have been created which the old formulas do not fit or afford a vital interpretation of.

We have come upon a very different age from any that preceded us. We have come upon an age when we do not do business in the way in which we used to do business,—when we do not carry on any of the operations of manufacture, sale, transportation, or communication as men used to carry them on. There is a sense in which in our day the individual has been submerged. In most parts of our country men work, not for themselves, not as partners in the old way in which they used to work, but generally as employees,—in a higher or lower grade,—of great corporations. There was a time when corporations played a very minor part in our business affairs, but now they play the chief part, and most men are the servants of corporations.

You know what happens when you are the servant of a corporation. You have in no instance access to the men who are really determining the policy of the corporation. If the corporation is doing the things that it ought not to do, you really have no voice in the matter and must obey the orders, and you have oftentimes with deep mortification to co-operate in the doing of things which you know are against the public interest. Your individuality is swallowed up in the individuality and purpose of a great organization.

It is true that, while most men are thus submerged in the corporation, a few, a very few, are exalted to a power which as individuals they could never have wielded. Through the great organizations of which they are the heads, a few are enabled to play a part unprecedented by anything in history in the control of the business operations of the country and in the determination of the happiness of great numbers of people.

Yesterday, and ever since history began, men were related to one another as individuals. To be sure there were the family, the Church, and the State, institutions which associated men in certain wide circles of relationship. But in the ordinary concerns of life, in the ordinary work, in the daily round, men dealt freely and directly with one another. To-day, the everyday relationships of men are largely with great impersonal concerns, with organizations, not with other individual men.

Now this is nothing short of a new social age, a new era of human relationships, a new stage-setting for the drama of life.

In this new age we find, for instance, that our laws with regard to the relations of employer and employee are in many respects wholly anti-quated and impossible. They were framed for another age, which nobody now living remembers, which is, indeed, so remote from our life that it would be difficult for many of us to understand it if it were described to us. The employer is now generally a corporation or a huge company of some kind; the employee is one of hundreds or of thousands brought together, not by individual masters whom they know and with whom they have personal relations, but by agents of one sort or another. Workingmen are marshaled in great numbers for the performance of a multitude of particular tasks under a common discipline. They generally use dangerous and powerful machinery, over whose repair and renewal they have no control. New rules must be devised with regard to their obligations and their rights, their obligations to their employers and their responsibilities to one another. Rules must be devised for their protection, for their compensation when injured, for their support when disabled.

There is something very new and very big and very complex about these new relations of capital and labor. A new economic society has sprung up, and we must effect a new set of adjustments. We must not pit power against weakness. The employer is generally, in our day, as I have said, not an individual, but a powerful group; and yet the workingman when dealing with his employer is still, under our existing law, an individual. . . .

So what we have to discuss is, not wrongs which individuals intentionally do,—I do not believe there are a great many of those,—but the wrongs of a system. I want to record my protest against any discussion of this matter which would seem to indicate that there are bodies of our fellow-citizens who are trying to grind us down and do us injustice. There are some men of that sort. I don't know how they sleep o' nights, but there are men of that kind. Thank God, they are not numerous. The truth is, we are all caught in a great economic system which is heartless. The modern corporation is not engaged in business as an individual. When we deal with it, we deal with an impersonal element, an immaterial piece of society. . . .

And do our laws take note of this curious state of things? Do they even attempt to distinguish between a man's act as a corporation director and as an individual? They do not. Our laws still deal with us on the basis of the old system. The law is still living in the dead past which we have left behind. . . .

Since I entered politics, I have chiefly had men's views confided to me privately. Some of the biggest men in the United States, in the field of commerce and manufacture, are afraid of somebody, are afraid of something. They know that there is a power somewhere so organized, so subtle, so watchful, so interlocked, so complete, so pervasive, that they had better not speak above their breath when they speak in condemnation of it.

They know that America is not a place of which it can be said, as it used to be, that a man may choose his own calling and pursue it just as far as his abilities enable him to pursue it; because to-day, if he enters certain fields, there are organizations which will use means against him that will prevent his building up a business which they do not want to have built up; organizations that will see to it that the ground is cut from under him and the markets shut against him. For if he begins to sell to certain retail dealers, to any retail dealers, the monopoly will refuse to sell to those dealers, and those dealers, afraid, will not buy the new man's wares.

And this is the country which has lifted to the admiration of the world its ideals of absolutely free opportunity, where no man is supposed to be under any limitation except the limitations of his character and of his mind; where there is supposed to be no distinction of class, no distinction of blood, no distinction of social status, but where men win or lose on their merits. . . .

American industry is not free, as once it was free; American enterprise is not free; the man with only a little capital is finding it harder to get into the field, more and more impossible to compete with the big fellow. Why? Because the laws of this country do not prevent the strong from crushing the weak. That is the reason, and because the strong have crushed the weak the strong dominate the industry and the economic life of this country. No man can deny that the lines of endeavor have more and more narrowed and stiffened; no man who knows anything about the development of industry in this country can have failed to observe that the larger kinds of credit are more and more difficult to obtain, unless you obtain them upon the terms of uniting your efforts with those who already control the industries of the country; and nobody can fail to observe that any man who tries to set himself up in competition with any process of manufacture which has been taken under the control of large combinations of capital will presently find himself either squeezed out or obliged to sell and allow himself to be absorbed.

There is a great deal that needs reconstruction in the United States. I should like to take a census of the business men,—I mean the rank and file of the business men,—as to whether they think that business conditions in this country, or rather whether the organization of business in this country, is satisfactory or not. I know what they would say if they dared. If they could vote secretly they would vote overwhelmingly that the present organization of business was meant for the big fellows and was not meant for the little fellows; that it was meant for those who are at the top and was meant to exclude those who are at the bottom; that it was meant to shut out beginners, to prevent new entries in the race, to prevent the building up of competitive enterprises that would interfere with the monopolies which the great trusts have built up.

What this country needs above everything else is a body of laws which will look after the men who are on the make rather than the men who are already made. Because the men who are already made are not going to live indefinitely, and they are not always kind enough to leave sons as able and as honest as they are.

The originative part of America, the part of America that makes new enterprises, the part into which the ambitious and gifted working-man makes his way up, the class that saves, that plans, that organizes, that presently spreads its enterprises until they have a national scope and character,—that middle class is being more and more squeezed out by the processes which we have been taught to call processes of prosperity. Its members are sharing prosperity, no doubt; but what alarms me is that they are not *originating* prosperity. No country can afford to have its prosperity originated by a small controlling class. The treasury of America does not lie in the brains of the small body of men now in control of the great enterprises that have been concentrated under the direction of a very small number of persons. The treasury of America lies in those ambitions, those energies, that cannot be restricted to a special favored class. It depends upon the inventions of unknown men, upon the originations of unknown men, upon the ambitions of unknown men. Every country is renewed out of the ranks of the unknown, not out of the ranks of those already famous and powerful and in control.

There has come over the land that un-American set of conditions which enables a small number of men who control the government to get favors from the government; by those favors to exclude their fellows from equal business opportunity; by those favors to extend a network of control that will presently dominate every industry in the country, and so make men forget the ancient time when America lay in every hamlet, when America was to be seen in every fair valley, when America displayed her great forces on the broad prairies, ran her fine fires of enterprise up over the mountainsides and down into the bowels of the earth, and eager men were everywhere captains of industry, not employees; not looking to a distant city to find out what they might do, but looking about among their neighbors, finding credit according to their character, not according to their connections, finding credit in proportion to what was known to be in them and behind them, not in proportion to the securities they held that were approved where they were not known. In order to start an enterprise now, you have to be authenticated, in a perfectly impersonal way, not according to yourself, but according to what you own that somebody else approves of your owning. You cannot begin such an enterprise as those that have made America until you are so authenticated, until you have succeeded in obtaining the good-will of large allied capitalists. Is that freedom? That is dependence, not freedom.

We used to think in the old-fashioned days when life was very simple that all that government had to do was to put on a policeman's uniform, and say, "Now don't anybody hurt anybody else." We used to say that the ideal of government was for every man to be left alone and not interfered with, except when he interfered with somebody else; and that the best government was the government that did as little governing as possible. That was the idea that obtained in Jefferson's time. But we are coming now to realize that life is so complicated that we are not dealing with the old conditions, and that the law has to step in and create new conditions under which we may live, the conditions which will make it tolerable for us to live. . . .

Why are we in the presence, why are we at the threshold, of a revolution? Because we are profoundly disturbed by the influences which we see reigning in the determination of our public life and our public policy. There was a time when America was blithe with self-confidence. She boasted that she, and she alone, knew the processes of popular government; but now she sees her sky overcast; she sees that there are at work forces which she did not dream of in her hopeful youth.

Don't you know that some man with eloquent tongue, without conscience, who did not care for the nation, could put this whole country into a flame? Don't you know that this country from one end to the other believes that something is wrong? What an opportunity it would be for some man without conscience to spring up and say: "This is the way. Follow me!"—and lead in paths of destruction!

The old order changeth—changeth under our very eyes, not quietly and equably, but swiftly and with the noise and heat and tumult of reconstruction.

I suppose that all struggle for law has been conscious, that very little of it has been blind or merely instinctive. It is the fashion to say, as if with superior knowledge of affairs and of human weakness, that every age has been an age of transition, and that no age is more full of change than another; yet in very few ages of the world can the struggle for change have been so widespread, so deliberate, or upon so great a scale as in this in which we are taking part.

The transition we are witnessing is no equable transition of growth and normal alteration; no silent, unconscious unfolding of one age into another, its natural heir and successor. Society is looking itself over, in our day, from top to bottom; is making fresh and critical analysis of its very elements; is questioning its oldest practices as freely as its newest, scrutinizing every arrangement and motive of its life; and it stands ready to attempt nothing less than a radical reconstruction, which only frank and honest counsels and the forces of generous co-operation can hold back from becoming a revolution. We are in a temper to reconstruct economic society, as we were once in a temper to reconstruct political society, and political society may itself undergo a radical modification in the process. I doubt if any age was ever more conscious of its task or more unanimously desirous of radical and extended changes in its economic and political practice.

We stand in the presence of a revolution,—not a bloody revolution;

America is not given to the spilling of blood,—but a silent revolution, whereby America will insist upon recovering in practice those ideals which she has always professed, upon securing a government devoted to the general interest and not to special interests.

We are upon the eve of a great reconstruction. It calls for creative statesmanship as no age has done since that great age in which we set up the government under which we live, that government which was the admiration of the world until it suffered wrongs to grow up under it which have made many of our own compatriots question the freedom of our institutions and preach revolution against them. I do not fear revolution. I have unshaken faith in the power of America to keep its self-possession. Revolution will come in peaceful guise, as it came when we put aside the crude government of the Confederation and created the great Federal Union which governs individuals, not States, and which has been these hundred and thirty years our vehicle of progress. Some radical changes we must make in our law and practice. Some reconstructions we must push forward, which a new age and new circumstances impose upon us. But we can do it all in calm and sober fashion, like statesmen and patriots.

I do not speak of these things in apprehension, because all is open and above-board. This is not a day in which great forces rally in secret. The whole stupendous program must be publicly planned and canvassed. Good temper, the wisdom that comes of sober counsel, the energy of thoughtful and unselfish men, the habit of co-operation and of compromise which has been bred in us by long years of free government, in which reason rather than passion has been made to prevail by the sheer virtue of candid and universal debate, will enable us to win through to still another great age without violence.

George Santayana
Materialism and Idealism
in American Life
(1920)

THE LANGUAGE and traditions common to England and America are like other family bonds: they draw kindred together at the greater crises in life, but they also occasion at times a little friction and fault-finding. The groundwork of the two societies is so similar, that each nation, feeling almost at home with the other, and almost able to understand its speech, may instinctively resent what hinders it from feeling at home altogether. Differences will tend to seem anomalies that have slipped in by mistake and through somebody's fault. Each will judge the other by his own standards, not feeling, as in the presence of complete foreigners, that he must make an effort of imagination and put himself in another man's shoes.

In matters of morals, manners, and art, the danger of comparisons is not merely that they may prove invidious, by ranging qualities in an order of merit which might wound somebody's vanity; the danger is rather that comparisons may distort comprehension, because in truth good qualities are all different in kind, and free lives are different in spirit. Comparison is the expedient of those who cannot reach the heart of the things compared; and no philosophy is more external and egotistical than that which places the essence of a thing in its relation to something else. In reality, at the centre of every natural being there is something individual and incommensurable, a seed with its native impulses and aspirations, shaping themselves as best they can in their given environment. Variation is a consequence of freedom, and the slight but radical diversity of souls in turn makes freedom requisite. Instead of instituting in his mind any

[From *Character and Opinion in the United States* (1920).]

comparisons between the United States and other nations, I would accordingly urge the reader to forget himself and, in so far as such a thing may be possible for him or for me, to transport himself ideally with me into the outer circumstances of American life, the better to feel its inner temper, and to see how inevitably the American shapes his feelings and judgments, honestly reporting all things as they appear from his new and unobstructed station.

I speak of the American in the singular, as if there were not millions of them, north and south, east and west, of both sexes, of all ages, and of various races, professions, and religions. Of course the one American I speak of is mythical; but to speak in parables is inevitable in such a subject, and it is perhaps as well to do so frankly. There is a sort of poetic ineptitude in all human discourse when it tries to deal with natural and existing things. Practical men may not notice it, but in fact human discourse is intrinsically addressed not to natural existing things but to ideal essences, poetic or logical terms which thought may define and play with. When fortune or necessity diverts our attention from this congenial ideal sport to crude facts and pressing issues, we turn our frail poetic ideas into symbols for those terrible irruptive things. In that paper money of our own stamping, the legal tender of the mind, we are obliged to reckon all the movements and values of the world. The universal American I speak of is one of these symbols; and I should be still speaking in symbols and creating moral units and a false simplicity, if I spoke of classes pedantically subdivided, or individuals ideally integrated and defined. As it happens, the symbolic American can be made largely adequate to the facts; because, if there are immense differences between individual Americans—for some Americans are black—yet there is a great uniformity in their environment, customs, temper, and thoughts. They have all been uprooted from their several soils and ancestries and plunged together into one vortex, whirling irresistibly in a space otherwise quite empty. To be an American is of itself almost a moral condition, an education, and a career. Hence a single ideal figment can cover a large part of what each American is in his character, and almost the whole of what most Americans are in their social outlook and political judgments.

The discovery of the new world exercised a sort of selection among the inhabitants of Europe. All the colonists, except the negroes, were voluntary exiles. The fortunate, the deeply rooted, and the lazy remained at home; the wilder instincts or dissatisfaction of others tempted them beyond the horizon. The American is accordingly the most adventurous, or the descendant of the most adventurous, of Europeans. It is in his blood to be socially a radical, though perhaps not intellectually. What has existed in the past, especially in the remote past, seems to him not only not authoritative, but irrelevant, inferior, and outworn. He finds it rather a sorry waste of time to think about the past at all. But his enthusiasm for the future is profound; he can conceive of no more decisive way of recommending an opinion or a practice than to say that it is what everybody is coming to adopt. This expectation of what he approves, or approval of what he expects, makes up his optimism. It is the necessary faith of the pioneer.

Such a temperament is, of course, not maintained in the nation merely by inheritance. Inheritance notoriously tends to restore the average of a race, and plays incidentally many a trick of atavism. What maintains this temperament and makes it national is social contagion or pressure—something immensely strong in democracies. The luckless American who is born a conservative, or who is drawn to poetic subtlety, pious retreats, or gay passions, nevertheless has the categorical excellence of work, growth, enterprise, reform, and prosperity dinned into his ears: every door is open in this direction and shut in the other; so that he either folds up his heart and withers in a corner—in remote places you sometimes find such a solitary gaunt idealist—or else he flies to Oxford or Florence or Montmartre to save his soul—or perhaps not to save it.

The optimism of the pioneer is not limited to his view of himself and his own future: it starts from that; but feeling assured, safe, and cheery within, he looks with smiling and most kindly eyes on everything and everybody about him. Individualism, roughness, and self-trust are supposed to go with selfishness and a cold heart; but I suspect that is a prejudice. It is rather dependence, insecurity, and mutual jostling that poison our placid gregarious brotherhood; and fanciful passionate demands upon people's affections, when they are disappointed, as they soon must be, breed ill will and a final meanness. The milk of human kindness is less apt to turn sour if the vessel that holds it stands steady, cool, and separate, and is not too often uncorked. In his affections the American is seldom passionate, often deep, and always kindly. If it were given me to look into the depths of a man's heart, and I did not find goodwill at the bottom, I should say without any hesitation, You are not an American. But as the American is an individualist his goodwill is not officious. His instinct is to think well of everybody, and to wish everybody well, but in a spirit of rough comradeship, expecting every man to stand on his own legs and to be helpful in his turn. When he has given his neighbour a chance he thinks he has done enough for him; but he feels it is an absolute duty to do that. It will take some hammering to drive a coddling socialism into America.

As self-trust may pass into self-sufficiency, so optimism, kindness, and goodwill may grow into a habit of doting on everything. To the good American many subjects are sacred: sex is sacred, women are sacred, children are sacred, business is sacred, America is sacred, Masonic lodges

and college clubs are sacred. This feeling grows out of the good opinion
he wishes to have of these things, and serves to maintain it. If he did not
regard all these things as sacred he might come to doubt sometimes if
they were wholly good. Of this kind, too, is the idealism of single ladies
in reduced circumstances who can see the soul of beauty in ugly things,
and are perfectly happy because their old dog has such pathetic eyes,
their minister is so eloquent, their garden with its three sunflowers is so
pleasant, their dead friends were so devoted, and their distant relations
are so rich.

Consider now the great emptiness of America: not merely the primitive
physical emptiness, surviving in some regions, and the continental spacing
of the chief natural features, but also the moral emptiness of a settlement
where men and even houses are easily moved about, and no one, almost,
lives where he was born or believes what he has been taught. Not that
the American has jettisoned these impedimenta in anger; they have simply
slipped from him as he moves. Great empty spaces bring a sort of freedom to both soul and body. You may pitch your tent where you will; or
if ever you decide to build anything, it can be in a style of your own
devising. You have room, fresh materials, few models, and no critics. You
trust your own experience, not only because you must, but because you
find you may do so safely and prosperously; the forces that determine
fortune are not yet too complicated for one man to explore. Your de-
tachable condition makes you lavish with money and cheerfully experi-
mental; you lose little if you lose all, since you remain completely yourself.
At the same time your absolute initiative gives you practice in coping
with novel situations, and in being original; it teaches you shrewd management. Your life and mind will become dry and direct, with few decorative flourishes. In your works everything will be stark and pragmatic;
you will not understand why anybody should make those little sacrifices
to instinct or custom which we call grace. The fine arts will seem to you
academic luxuries, fit to amuse the ladies, like Greek and Sanskrit; for
while you will perfectly appreciate generosity in men's purposes, you will
not admit that the execution of these purposes can be anything but business. Unfortunately the essence of the fine arts is that the execution should
be generous too, and delightful in itself; therefore the fine arts will suffer,
not so much in their express professional pursuit—for then they become
practical tasks and a kind of business—as in that diffused charm which
qualifies all human action when men are artists by nature. Elaboration,
which is something to accomplish, will be preferred to simplicity, which
is something to rest in; manners will suffer somewhat; speech will suffer
horribly. For the American the urgency of his novel attack upon matter,
his zeal in gathering its fruits, precludes meanderings in primrose paths;
devices must be short cuts, and symbols must be mere symbols. If his

wife wants luxuries, of course she may have them; if he has vices, that can be provided for too; but they must all be set down under those headings in his ledgers.

At the same time, the American is imaginative; for where life is intense, imagination is intense also. Were he not imaginative he would not live so much in the future. But his imagination is practical, and the future it forecasts is immediate; it works with the clearest and least ambiguous terms known to his experience, in terms of number, measure, contrivance, economy, and speed. He is an idealist working on matter. Understanding as he does the material potentialities of things, he is successful in invention, conservative in reform, and quick in emergencies. All his life he jumps into the train after it has started and jumps out before it has stopped; and he never once gets left behind, or breaks a leg. There is an enthusiasm in his sympathetic handling of material forces which goes far to cancel the illiberal character which it might otherwise assume. The good workman hardly distinguishes his artistic intention from the potency in himself and in things which is about to realise that intention. Accordingly his ideals fall into the form of premonitions and prophecies; and his studious prophecies often come true. So do the happy workmanlike ideals of the American. When a poor boy, perhaps, he dreams of an education, and presently he gets an education, or at least a degree; he dreams of growing rich, and he grows rich—only more slowly and modestly, perhaps, than he expected; he dreams of marrying his Rebecca and, even if he marries a Leah instead, he ultimately finds in Leah his Rebecca after all. He dreams of helping to carry on and to accelerate the movement of a vast, seething, progressive society, and he actually does so. Ideals clinging so close to nature are almost sure of fulfilment; the American beams with a certain self-confidence and sense of mastery; he feels that God and nature are working with him.

Idealism in the American accordingly goes hand in hand with present contentment and with foresight of what the future very likely will actually bring. He is not a revolutionist; he believes he is already on the right track and moving towards an excellent destiny. In revolutionists, on the contrary, idealism is founded on dissatisfaction and expresses it. What exists seems to them an absurd jumble of irrational accidents and bad habits, and they want the future to be based on reason and to be the pellucid embodiment of all their maxims. All their zeal is for something radically different from the actual and (if they only knew it) from the possible; it is ideally simple, and they love it and believe in it because their nature craves it. They think life would be set free by the destruction of all its organs. They are therefore extreme idealists in the region of hope, but not at all, as poets and artists are, in the region of perception and memory. In the atmosphere of civilised life they miss all the refraction and all the fragrance; so that in their conception of actual things they are apt to be crude realists; and their ignorance and inexperience of the moral world, unless it comes of ill-luck, indicates their incapacity for education. Now incapacity for education, when united with great inner vitality, is one root of idealism. It is what condemns us all, in the region of sense, to substitute perpetually what we are capable of imagining for what things may be in themselves; it is what condemns us, wherever it extends, to think *a priori;* it is what keeps us bravely and incorrigibly pursuing what we call the good—that is, what would fulfil the demands of our nature—however little provision the fates may have made for it. But the want of insight on the part of revolutionists touching the past and the present infects in an important particular their idealism about the future; it renders their dreams of the future unrealisable. For in human beings—this may not be true of other animals, more perfectly preformed—experience is necessary to pertinent and concrete thinking; even our primitive instincts are blind until they stumble upon some occasion that solicits them; and they can be much transformed or deranged by their first partial satisfactions. Therefore a man who does not idealise his experience, but idealises *a priori,* is incapable of true prophecy; when he dreams he raves, and the more he criticises the less he helps. American idealism, on the contrary, is nothing if not helpful, nothing if not pertinent to practicable transformations; and when the American frets, it is because whatever is useless and impertinent, be it idealism or inertia, irritates him; for it frustrates the good results which he sees might so easily have been obtained.

The American is wonderfully alive; and his vitality, not having often found a suitable outlet, makes him appear agitated on the surface; he is always letting off an unnecessarily loud blast of incidental steam. Yet his vitality is not superficial; it is inwardly prompted, and as sensitive and quick as a magnetic needle. He is inquisitive, and ready with an answer to any question that he may put to himself of his own accord; but if you try to pour instruction into him, on matters that do not touch his own spontaneous life, he shows the most extraordinary powers of resistance and oblivescence; so that he often is remarkably expert in some directions and surprisingly obtuse in others. He seems to bear lightly the sorrowful burden of human knowledge. In a word, he is young.

What sense is there in this feeling, which we all have, that the American is young? His country is blessed with as many elderly people as any other, and his descent from Adam, or from the Darwinian rival of Adam, cannot be shorter than that of his European cousins. Nor are his ideas always very fresh. Trite and rigid bits of morality and religion, with much seemly and antique political lore, remain axiomatic in him, as in the mind of a child; he may carry all this about with an unquestioning familiarity which does not comport understanding. To keep traditional sentiments in this way insulated and uncriticised is itself a sign of youth. A good young man is naturally conservative and loyal on all those subjects which his experience has not brought to a test; advanced opinions on politics, marriage, or literature are comparatively rare in America; they are left for the ladies to discuss, and usually to condemn, while the men get on with their work. In spite of what is old-fashioned in his more general ideas, the American is unmistakably young; and this, I should say, for two reasons: one, that he is chiefly occupied with his immediate environment, and the other, that his reactions upon it are inwardly prompted, spontaneous, and full of vivacity and self-trust. His views are not yet lengthened; his will is not yet broken or transformed. The present moment, however, in this, as in other things, may mark a great change in him; he is perhaps now reaching his majority, and all I say may hardly apply to-day, and may not apply at all to-morrow. I speak of him as I have known him; and whatever moral strength may accrue to him later, I am not sorry to have known him in his youth. The charm of youth, even when it is a little boisterous, lies in nearness to the impulses of nature, in a quicker and more obvious obedience to that pure, seminal principle which, having formed the body and its organs, always directs their movements, unless it is forced by vice or necessity to make them crooked, or to suspend them. Even under the inevitable crust of age the soul remains young, and, wherever it is able to break through, sprouts into something green and tender. We are all as young at heart as the most youthful American, but the seed in his case has fallen upon virgin soil, where it may spring up more bravely and with less respect for the giants of the wood. Peoples seem older when their perennial natural youth is encumbered with more possessions and prepossessions, and they are mindful of the many things they have lost or missed. The American is not mindful of them.

In America there is a tacit optimistic assumption about existence, to the effect that the more existence the better. The soulless critic might urge that quantity is only a physical category, implying no excellence, but at best an abundance of opportunities both for good and for evil. Yet the young soul, being curious and hungry, views existence *a priori* under the form of the good; its instinct to live implies a faith that most things it can become or see or do will be worth while. Respect for quantity is accordingly something more than the childish joy and wonder at bigness; it is the fisherman's joy in a big haul, the good uses of which he can take for granted. Such optimism is amiable. Nature cannot afford that we should begin by being too calculating or wise, and she encourages us by the pleasure she attaches to our functions in advance of their fruits, and often in excess of them; as the angler enjoys catching his fish more than eating it, and often, waiting patiently for the fish to bite, misses his own supper. The pioneer must devote himself to preparations; he must work for the future, and it is healthy and dutiful of him to love his work for its own sake. At the same time, unless reference to an ultimate purpose is at least virtual in all his activities, he runs the danger of becoming a living automaton, vain and ignominious in its mechanical constancy. Idealism about work can hide an intense materialism about life. Man, if he is a rational being, cannot live by bread alone nor be a labourer merely; he must eat and work in view of an ideal harmony which overarches all his days, and which is realised in the way they hang together, or in some ideal issue which they have in common. Otherwise, though his technical philosophy may call itself idealism, he is a materialist in morals; he esteems things, and esteems himself, for mechanical uses and energies. Even sensualists, artists, and pleasure-lovers are wiser than that, for though their idealism may be desultory or corrupt, they attain something ideal, and prize things only for their living effects, moral though perhaps fugitive. Sensation, when we do not take it as a signal for action, but arrest and peruse what it positively brings before us, reveals something ideal— a colour, shape, or sound; and to dwell on these presences, with no thought of their material significance, is an æsthetic or dreamful idealism. To pass from this idealism to the knowledge of matter is a great intellectual advance, and goes with dominion over the world; for in the practical arts the mind is adjusted to a larger object, with more depth and potentiality in it; which is what makes people feel that the material world is real, as they call it, and that the ideal world is not. Certainly the material world is real; for the philosophers who deny the existence of matter are like the critics who deny the existence of Homer. If there was never any Homer, there must have been a lot of other poets no less Homeric than he; and, if matter does not exist, a combination of other things exists which is just as material. But the intense reality of the material world would not prevent it from being a dreary waste in our eyes, or even an abyss of horror, if it brought forth no spiritual fruits. In fact, it does bring forth spiritual fruits, for otherwise we should not be here to find fault with it, and to set up our ideals over against it. Nature is material, but not materialistic; it issues in life, and breeds all sorts of warm passions and idle beauties. And just as sympathy with the mechanical travail and turmoil of nature, apart from its spiritual fruits, is moral materialism, so the continual perception and love of these fruits is moral idealism—happiness in the presence of immaterial objects and harmonies, such as we envisage in affection, speculation, religion, and all the forms of the beautiful.

The circumstances of his life hitherto have necessarily driven the American into moral materialism; for in his dealings with material things he can hardly stop to enjoy their sensible aspects, which are ideal, nor proceed at once to their ultimate uses, which are ideal, too. He is practical as against the poet, and worldly as against the clear philosopher or the saint. The most striking expression of this materialism is usually supposed to be his love of the almighty dollar; but that is a foreign and unintelligent view. The American talks about money, because that is the symbol and measure he has at hand for success, intelligence, and power; but as to money itself he makes, loses, spends, and gives it away with a very light heart. To my mind the most striking expression of his materialism is his singular preoccupation with quantity. If, for instance, you visit Niagara Falls, you may expect to hear how many cubic feet or metric tons of water are precipitated per second over the cataract; how many cities and towns (with the number of their inhabitants) derive light and motive power from it; and the annual value of the further industries that might very well be carried on by the same means, without visibly depleting the world's greatest wonder or injuring the tourist trade. That is what I confidently expected to hear on arriving at the adjoining town of Buffalo; but I was deceived. The first thing I heard instead was that there are more miles of asphalt pavement in Buffalo than in any city in the world. Nor is this insistence on quantity confined to men of business. The President of Harvard College, seeing me once by chance soon after the beginning of a term, inquired how my classes were getting on; and when I replied that I thought they were getting on well, that my men seemed to be keen and intelligent, he stopped me as if I was about to waste his time. "I meant," said he, "*what is the number* of students in your classes?"

Here I think we may perceive that this love of quantity often has a silent partner, which is diffidence as to quality. The democratic conscience recoils before anything that savours of privilege; and lest it should concede an unmerited privilege to any pursuit or person, it reduces all things as far as possible to the common denominator of quantity. Numbers cannot lie: but if it came to comparing the ideal beauties of philosophy with those of Anglo-Saxon, who should decide? All studies are good—why else have universities?—but those must be most encouraged which attract the greatest number of students. Hence the President's question. Democratic faith, in its diffidence about quality, throws the reins of education upon the pupil's neck, as Don Quixote threw the reins on the neck of Rocinante, and bids his divine instinct choose its own way.

The American has never yet had to face the trials of Job. Great crises, like the Civil War, he has known how to surmount victoriously; and now that he has surmounted a second great crisis victoriously, it is possible that he may relapse, as he did in the other case, into an apparently complete absorption in material enterprise and prosperity. But if serious and irremediable tribulation ever overtook him, what would his attitude be? It is then that we should be able to discover whether materialism or idealism lies at the base of his character. Meantime his working mind is not without its holiday. He spreads humour pretty thick and even over the surface of conversation, and humour is one form of moral emancipation. He loves landscape, he loves mankind, and he loves knowledge; and in music at least he finds an art which he unfeignedly enjoys. In music and landscape, in humour and kindness, he touches the ideal more truly, perhaps, than in his ponderous academic idealisms and busy religions; for it is astonishing how much even religion in America (can it possibly be so in England?) is a matter of meetings, building-funds, schools, charities, clubs, and picnics. To be poor in order to be simple, to produce less in order that the product may be more choice and beautiful, and may leave us less burdened with unnecessary duties and useless possessions—that is an ideal not articulate in the American mind; yet here and there I seem to have heard a sigh after it, a groan at the perpetual incubus of business and shrill society. Significant witness to such aspirations is borne by those new forms of popular religion, not mere variations on tradition, which have sprung up from the soil—revivalism, spiritualism, Christian Science, the New Thought. Whether or no we can tap, through these or other channels, some cosmic or inner energy not hitherto at the disposal of man (and there is nothing incredible in that), we certainly may try to remove friction and waste in the mere process of living; we may relax morbid strains, loosen suppressed instincts, iron out the creases of the soul, discipline ourselves into simplicity, sweetness, and peace. These religious movements are efforts toward such physiological economy and hygiene; and while they are thoroughly plebeian, with no great lights, and no idea of raising men from the most vulgar and humdrum worldly existence, yet they see the possibility of physical and moral health on that common plane, and pursue it. That is true morality. The dignities of various types of life or mind, like the gifts of various animals, are relative. The snob adores one type only, and the creatures supposed by him to illustrate it perfectly; or envies and hates them, which is just as snobbish. Veritable lovers of life, on the contrary, like Saint Francis or like Dickens, know that in every tenement of clay, with no matter what endowment or station, happiness and perfection are possible to the soul. There must be no brow-beating, with shouts of work or progress or revolution, any more than with threats of hell-fire. What does it profit a man to free the whole world if his soul is not free? Moral freedom is not an artificial condition, because the ideal is the mother tongue of both the heart and the senses. All that is requisite is that we should pause in living to enjoy life, and should lift up our hearts to things that are pure goods in themselves, so that once to have found and loved them, whatever else may betide, may remain a happiness that nothing can sully. This natural idealism does not imply that we are immaterial, but only that we are animate and truly alive. When the senses are sharp, as they are in the American, they are already half liberated, already a joy in themselves; and when the heart is warm, like his, and eager to be just, its ideal destiny can hardly be doubtful. It will not be always merely pumping and working; time and its own pulses will lend it wings.

DISENCHANTMENT AND DEPRESSION

John Dos Passos
The Body of an American
(1932)

Whereasthe Congressoftheunitedstates byaconcurrentresolutionadopted
on the4thdayofmarch lastauthorizedthe Secretaryofwar to cause to be
brought to theunitedstatesthe body of an Americanwhowasamemberofthe
americanexpeditionaryforce ineurope wholostthislifeduringtheworldwarand
whoseidentityhasnotbeenestablished for burial inthememorialamphitheaters
ofthenationalcemeteryatarlingtonvirginia

In the tarpaper morgue at Châlons-sur-Marne in the reek of chloride
of lime and the dead, they picked out the pine box that held all that was
left of
enie menie minie moe plenty other pine boxes stacked up there containing what they'd scraped up of Richard Roe
and other person or persons unknown. Only one can go. How did they
pick John Doe?
Make sure he ain't a dinge, boys.
make sure he ain't a guinea or a kike,
how can you tell a guy's a hundredpercent when all you've got's a
gunnysack full of bones, bronze buttons stamped with the screaming eagle
and a pair of roll puttees?
. . . and the gagging chloride and the puky dirtstench of the yearold
dead . . .

The day withal was too meaningful and tragic for applause. Silence,
tears, songs and prayer, muffled drums and soft music were the instrumentalities today of national approbation.

John Doe was born (thudding din of blood in love into the shuddering
soar of a man and a woman alone indeed together lurching into
and ninemonths sick drowse walking into scared agony and the pain
and blood and mess of birth). John Doe was born
and raised in Brooklyn, in Memphis, near the lakefront in Cleveland,

Ohio, in the stench of the stockyards in Chi, on Beacon Hill, in an old brick house in Alexandria, Virginia, on Telegraph Hill, in a halftimbered Tudor cottage in Portland, the city of roses

in the Lying-In Hospital old Morgan endowed on Stuyvesant Square,

across the railroad tracks, out near the country club, in a shack cabin tenement apartmenthouse exclusive residential suburb;

scion of one of the best families in the social register, won first prize in the baby parade at Coronado Beach, was marbles champion of the Little Rock grammarschools, crack basketballplayer at the Booneville High, quarterback at the State Reformatory, having saved the sheriff's kid from drowning in the Little Missouri River was invited to Washington to be photographed shaking hands with the President on the White House steps;—

> though this was a time of mourning, such an assemblage necessarily has about it a touch of color. In the boxes are seen the court uniforms of foreign diplomats, the gold braid of our own and foreign fleets and armies, the black of the conventional morning dress of American statesmen, the vari-colored furs and outdoor wrapping garments of mothers and sisters come to mourn the drab and blue of soldiers and sailors, the glitter of musical instruments and the white and black of a vested choir

—busboy harveststiff hogcaller boyscout champeen cornshucker of Western Kansas bellhop at the United States Hotel at Saratoga Springs officeboy callboy fruiter telephonelineman longshoreman lumberjack plumber's helper,

worked for an exterminating company in Union City, filled pipes in an opium joint in Trenton, New Jersey.

Y.M.C.A. secretary, express agent, truckdriver, ford-mechanic, sold books in Denver, Colorado: Madam would you be willing to help a young man work his way through college?

> President Harding, with a reverence seemingly more significant because of his high temporal station, concluded his speech:
> *We are met today to pay the impersonal tribute;*
> *the name of him whose body lies before us took flight with his imperishable soul . . .*
> *as a typical soldier of this representative democracy he fought and died believing in the indisputable justice of his country's cause . . .*

> by raising his right hand and asking the thousands within the sound of his voice to join in the prayer:
> *Our Father which art in heaven hallowed be thy name . . .*

Naked he went into the army;

they weighed you, measured you, looked for flat feet, squeezed your penis to see if you had clap, looked up your anus to see if you had piles, counted your teeth, made you cough, listened to your heart and lungs, made you read the letters on the card, charted your urine and your intelligence,

gave you a service record for a future (imperishable soul)

and an identification tag stamped with your serial number to hang around your neck, issued O.D. regulation equipment, a condiment can and a copy of the articles of war.

Atten'SHUN suck in your gut you c——r wipe that smile off your face eyes right wattja tink dis is a choirch-social? For-war-D'ARCH.

John Doe

and Richard Roe and other person or persons unknown

drilled, hiked, manual of arms, ate slum, learned to salute, to soldier, to loaf in the latrines, forbidden to smoke on deck, overseas guard duty, forty men and eight horses, shortarm inspection and the ping of shrapnel and the shrill bullets combing the air and the sorehead woodpeckers the machineguns mud cooties gasmasks and the itch.

Say feller tell me how I can get back to my outfit.

John Doe had a head

for twentyodd years intensely the nerves of the eyes the ears the palate the tongue the fingers the toes the armpits, the nerves warmfeeling under the skin charged the coiled brain with hurt sweet warm cold mine must don't sayings print headlines:

Thou shalt not the multiplication table long division, Now is the time for all good men knocks but once at a young man's door, It's a great life if Ish gebibbel, The first five years'll be the Safety First, Suppose a Hun tried to rape your my country right or wrong, Catch 'em young What he don't know won't treat 'em rough, Tell 'em nothin', He got what was coming to him he got his, This is a white man's country, Kick the bucket, Gone West, If you don't like it you can croaked him

Say buddy can't you tell me how I can get back to my outfit?

Can't help jumpin' when them things go off, give me the trots them things do. I lost my identification tag swimmin' in the Marne, roughhousin' with a guy while we was waitin' to be deloused, in bed with a girl named Jeanne (Love moving picture wet French postcard dream began with saltpeter in the coffee and ended at the propho station);—

Say soldier for chrissake can't you tell me how I can get back to my outfit?

John Doe's

heart pumped blood:

alive thudding silence of blood in your ears

down in the clearing in the Oregon forest where the pumpkins were punkincolor pouring into the blood through the eyes and the fallcolored trees and the bronze hoopers were hopping through the dry grass, where tiny striped snails hung on the underside of the blades and the flies hummed, wasps droned, bumblebees buzzed, and the woods smelt of wine and mushrooms and apples, homey smell of fall pouring into the blood,

and I dropped the tin hat and the sweaty pack and lay flat with the dogday sun licking my throat and adamsapple and the tight skin over the breastbone.

The shell had his number on it.

The blood ran into the ground.

The service record dropped out of the filing cabinet when the quartermaster sergeant got blotto that time they had to pack and leave the billets in a hurry.

The identification tag was in the bottom of the Marne.

The blood ran into the ground, the brains oozed out of the cracked skull and were licked up by the trenchrats, the belly swelled and raised a generation of bluebottle flies,

and the incorruptible skeleton,

and the scraps of dried viscera and skin bundled in khaki

they took to Châlons-sur-Marne

and laid it out neat in a pine coffin

and took it home to God's Country on a battleship

and buried it in a sarcophagus in the Memorial Amphitheater in the Arlington National Cemetery

and draped the Old Glory over it

and the bugler played taps

and Mr. Harding prayed to God and the diplomats and the generals and the admirals and the brasshats and the politicians and the handsomely dressed ladies out of the society column of the *Washington Post* stood up solemn

and thought how beautiful sad Old Glory God's Country it was to have the bugler play taps and the three volleys made their ears ring.

Where his chest ought to have been they pinned the Congressional Medal, the D.S.C., the Médaille Militaire, the Belgian Croix de Guerre, the Italian gold medal, the Vitutea Militara sent by Queen Marie of Rumania, the Czechoslovak War Cross, the Virtuti

Militari of the Poles, a wreath sent by Hamilton Fish, Jr., of New York, and a little wampum presented by a deputation of Arizona redskins in warpaint and feathers. All the Washingtonians brought flowers.

Woodrow Wilson brought a bouquet of poppies.

Ezra Pound
Hugh Selwyn Mauberley
(1920)

These fought in any case,
and some believing,

            pro domo, in any case . . .

Some quick to arm,
some for adventure,
some from fear of weakness,
some from fear of censure,
some for love of slaughter, in imagination,
learning later . . .
some in fear, learning love of slaughter;

Died some, pro patria,
            non "dulce" non "et decor" . . .
walked eye-deep in hell
believing in old men's lies, then unbelieving
came home, home to a lie,
home to many deceits,
home to old lies and new infamy;
usury age-old and age-thick
and liars in public places.

Daring as never before, wastage as never before.
Young blood and high blood,
fair cheeks, and fine bodies;

fortitude as never before

frankness as never before,
disillusions as never told in the old days,

hysterias, trench confessions,
laughter out of dead bellies.

There died a myriad,
And of the best, among them,
For an old bitch gone in the teeth,
For a botched civilization . . .

F. Scott Fitzgerald
Echoes of the Jazz Age
(1931)

IT IS too soon to write about the Jazz Age with perspective, and without being suspected of premature arteriosclerosis. Many people still succumb to violent retching when they happen upon any of its characteristic words— words which have since yielded in vividness to the coinages of the underworld. It is as dead as were the Yellow Nineties in 1902. Yet the present writer already looks back to it with nostalgia. It bore him up, flattered him and gave him more money than he had dreamed of, simply for telling people that he felt as they did, that something had to be done with all the nervous energy stored up and unexpended in the War.

The ten-year period that, as if reluctant to die outmoded in its bed, leaped to a spectacular death in October, 1929, began about the time of the May Day riots in 1919. When the police rode down the demobilized country boys gaping at the orators in Madison Square, it was the sort of measure bound to alienate the more intelligent young men from the prevailing order. We didn't remember anything about the Bill of Rights until Mencken began plugging it, but we did know that such tyranny belonged in the jittery little countries of South Europe. If goose-livered business men had this effect on the government, then maybe we had gone to war for J. P. Morgan's loans after all. But, because we were tired of Great Causes, there was no more than a short outbreak of moral indignation, typified by Dos Passos' "Three Soldiers." Presently we began to have slices of the national cake and our idealism only flared up when the newspapers made melodrama out of such stories as Harding and the Ohio Gang or Sacco and Vanzetti. The events of 1919 left us cynical rather than revolutionary, in spite of the fact that now we are all rummaging around in our trunks wondering where the hell we left the liberty cap— "I know I *had* it"—and the moujik blouse. It was characteristic of the Jazz Age that it had no interest in politics at all.

* * *

It was an age of miracles, it was an age of art, it was an age of excess, and it was an age of satire. A Stuffed Shirt, squirming to blackmail in a lifelike way, sat upon the throne of the United States; a stylish young man hurried over to represent to us the throne of England. A world of girls yearned for the young Englishman; the old American groaned in his sleep as he waited to be poisoned by his wife, upon the advice of the female Rasputin who then made the ultimate decision in our national affairs. But such matters apart, we had things our way at last. With Americans ordering suits by the gross in London, the Bond Street tailors perforce agreed to moderate their cut to the American long-waisted figure and loose-fitting taste, something subtle passed to America, the style of man. During the Renaissance, Francis the First looked to Florence to trim his leg. Seventeenth-century England aped the court of France, and fifty years ago the German Guards officer bought his civilian clothes in London. Gentleman's clothes—symbol of "the power that man must hold and that passes from race to race."

We were the most powerful nation. Who could tell us any longer what was fashionable and what was fun? Isolated during the European War, we had begun combing the unknown South and West for folkways and pastimes and there were more ready to hand.

The first social revelation created a sensation out of all proportion to its novelty. As far back as 1915 the unchaperoned young people of the smaller cities had discovered the mobile privacy of that automobile given to young Bill at sixteen to make him "self-reliant." At first petting was a desperate adventure even under such favorable conditions, but presently confidences were exchanged and the old commandment broke down. As early as 1917 there were references to such sweet and casual dalliance in any number of the *Yale Record* or the *Princeton Tiger*.

But petting in its more audacious manifestations was confined to the wealthier classes—among other young people the old standards prevailed until after the War, and a kiss meant that a proposal was expected, as young officers in strange cities sometimes discovered to their dismay. Only in 1920 did the veil finally fall—the Jazz Age was in flower.

Scarcely had the staider citizens of the republic caught their breaths when the wildest of all generations, the generation which had been adolescent during the confusion of the War, brusquely shouldered my contemporaries out of the way and danced into the limelight. This was the generation that corrupted its elders and eventually overreached itself less through lack of morals than through lack of taste. May one offer in exhibit the year 1922! That was the peak of the younger generation, for though the Jazz Age continued, it became less and less an affair of youth.

The sequel was like a children's party taken over by the elders, leaving the children puzzled and rather neglected and rather taken aback. By 1923 their elders, tired of watching the carnival with ill-concealed envy, had discovered that young liquor will take the place of young blood, and with a whoop the orgy began. The younger generation was starred no longer.

A whole race going hedonistic, deciding on pleasure. The precocious intimacies of the younger generation would have come about with or without prohibition—they were implicit in the attempt to adapt English customs to American conditions. (Our South, for example, is tropical and early maturing—it has never been part of the wisdom of France and Spain to let young girls go unchaperoned at sixteen and seventeen.) But the general decision to be amused that began with the cocktail parties of 1921 had more complicated origins.

The word jazz in its progress toward respectability has meant first sex, then dancing, then music. It is associated with a state of nervous stimulation, not unlike that of big cities behind the lines of a war. To many English the War still goes on because all the forces that menace them are still active—Wherefore eat, drink and be merry, for to-morrow we die. But different causes had now brought about a corresponding state in America—though there were entire classes (people over fifty, for example) who spent a whole decade denying its existence even when its puckish face peered into the family circle. Never did they dream that they had contributed to it. The honest citizens of every class, who believed in a strict public morality and were powerful enough to enforce the necessary legislation, did not know that they would necessarily be served by criminals and quacks, and do not really believe it to-day. Rich righteousness had always been able to buy honest and intelligent servants to free the slaves or the Cubans, so when this attempt collapsed our elders stood firm with all the stubbornness of people involved in a weak case, preserving their righteousness and losing their children. Silver-haired women and men with fine old faces, people who never did a consciously dishonest thing in their lives, still assure each other in the apartment hotels of New York and Boston and Washington that "there's a whole generation growing up that will never know the taste of liquor." Meanwhile their granddaughters pass the well-thumbed copy of "Lady Chatterley's Lover" around the boarding-school and, if they get about at all, know the taste of gin or corn at sixteen. But the generation who reached maturity between 1875 and 1895 continue to believe what they want to believe.

Even the intervening generations were incredulous. In 1920 Heywood Broun announced that all this hubbub was nonsense, that young men didn't kiss but told anyhow. But very shortly people over twenty-five came in for an intensive education. Let me trace some of the revelations vouchsafed them by reference to a dozen works written for various types of mentality during the decade. We begin with the suggestion that Don Juan leads an interesting life ("Jurgen," 1919); then we learn that there's a lot of sex around if we only knew it ("Winesburg, Ohio," 1920), that adolescents lead very amorous lives ("This Side of Paradise," 1920), that there are a lot of neglected Anglo-Saxon words ("Ulysses," 1921), that older people don't always resist sudden temptations ("Cytherea," 1922), that girls are sometimes seduced without being ruined ("Flaming Youth," 1922), that even rape often turns out well ("The Sheik," 1922), that glamorous English ladies are often promiscuous ("The Green Hat," 1924), that in fact they devote most of their time to it ("The Vortex," 1926), that it's a damn good thing too ("Lady Chatterley's Lover," 1928), and finally that there are abnormal variations ("The Well of Loneliness," 1928, and "Sodome and Gomorrhe," 1929).

In my opinion the erotic element in these works, even "The Sheik" written for children in the key of "Peter Rabbit," did not one particle of harm. Everything they described, and much more, was familiar in our contemporary life. The majority of the theses were honest and eluci-dating—their effect was to restore some dignity to the male as opposed to the he-man in American life. ("And what is a 'He-man'?" demanded Gertrude Stein one day. "Isn't it a large enough order to fill out to the dimensions of all that 'a man' has meant in the past? A 'He-man'!") The married woman can now discover whether she is being cheated, or whether sex is just something to be endured, and her compensation should be to establish a tyranny of the spirit, as her mother may have hinted. Perhaps many women found that love was meant to be fun. Anyhow the objectors lost their tawdry little case, which is one reason why our literature is now the most living in the world.

Contrary to popular opinion the movies of the Jazz Age had no effect upon its morals. The social attitude of the producers was timid, behind the times and banal—for example no picture mirrored even faintly the younger generation until 1923, when magazines had already been started to celebrate it and it had long ceased to be news. There were a few feeble splutters and then Clara Bow in "Flaming Youth"; promptly the Holly-wood hacks ran the theme into its cinematographic grave. Throughout the Jazz Age the movies got no farther than Mrs. Jiggs, keeping up with its most blatant superficialities. This was no doubt due to the censorship as well as to innate conditions in the industry. In any case the Jazz Age now raced along under its own power, served by great filling stations full of money.

The people over thirty, the people all the way up to fifty, had joined in the dance. We graybeards (to tread down F.P.A. [Franklin P. Adams]) remember the uproar when in 1912 grandmothers of forty tossed away their crutches and took lessons in the Tango and the Castle-Walk. A dozen years later a woman might pack the Green Hat with her other affairs as she set off for Europe or New York, but Savonarola was too busy flogging dead horses in Augean stables of his own creation to notice. Society, even in small cities, now dined in separate chambers, and the sober table learned about the gay table only from hearsay. There were very few people left at the sober table. One of its former glories, the less sought-after girls who had become resigned to sublimating a probable celibacy, came across Freud and Jung in seeking their intellectual recompense and came tearing back into the fray.

By 1926 the universal preoccupation with sex had become a nuisance. (I remember a perfectly mated, contented young mother asking my wife's advice about "having an affair right away," though she had no one especially in mind, "because don't you think it's sort of undignified when you get much over thirty?") For a while bootleg negro records with their phallic euphemisms made everything suggestive, and simultaneously came a wave of erotic plays—young girls from finishing schools packed the galleries to hear about the romance of being a Lesbian and George Jean Nathan protested. Then one young producer lost his head entirely, drank a beauty's alcoholic bath-water and went to the penitentiary. Somehow his pathetic attempt at romance belongs to the Jazz Age, while his contemporary in prison, Ruth Snyder, had to be hoisted into it by the tabloids—she was, as *The Daily News* hinted deliciously to gourmets, about "to cook, *and sizzle, AND FRY!*" in the electric chair.

The gay elements of society had divided into two main streams, one flowing toward Palm Beach and Deauville, and the other, much smaller, toward the summer Riviera. One could get away with more on the summer Riviera, and whatever happened seemed to have something to do with art. From 1926 to 1929, the great years of the Cap d'Antibes, this corner of France was dominated by a group quite distinct from that American society which is dominated by Europeans. Pretty much of anything went at Antibes—by 1929 at the most gorgeous paradise for swimmers on the Mediterranean no one swam any more, save for a short hang-over dip at noon. There was a picturesque graduation of steep rocks over the sea and somebody's valet and an occasional English girl used to dive from them but the Americans were content to discuss each other in the bar. This was indicative of something that was taking place in the homeland—Americans were getting soft. There were signs everywhere: we still won the Olympic games but with champions whose names had few vowels in them—teams composed, like the fighting Irish combination of Notre Dame, of fresh overseas blood. Once the French became really interested the Davis Cup gravitated automatically to their intensity in competition. The vacant lots of the Middle-Western cities were built up now—except for a short period in school we were not turning out to be an athletic people like the British after all. The hare and the tortoise. Of course if we wanted to we could be in a minute; we still had all those reserves of ancestral vitality, but one day in 1926 we looked down and found we had flabby arms and a fat pot and couldn't say boop-boop-a-doop to a Sicilian. Shades of Van Bibber!—no utopian ideal, God knows. Even golf, once considered an effeminate game, had seemed very strenuous of late—an emasculated form appeared and proved just right.

By 1927 a wide-spread neurosis began to be evident, faintly signalled, like a nervous beating of the feet, by the popularity of cross-word puzzles. I remember a fellow expatriate opening a letter from a mutual friend of ours, urging him to come home and be revitalized by the hardy, bracing qualities of the native soil. It was a strong letter and it affected us both deeply, until we noticed that it was headed from a nerve sanitarium in Pennsylvania.

By this time contemporaries of mine had begun to disappear into the dark maw of violence. A classmate killed his wife and himself on Long Island, another tumbled "accidentally" from a skyscraper in Philadelphia, another purposely from a skyscraper in New York. One was killed in a speak-easy in Chicago; another was beaten to death in a speak-easy in New York and crawled home to the Princeton Club to die; still another had his skull crushed by a maniac's axe in an insane asylum where he was confined. These are not catastrophes that I went out of my way to look for—these were my friends; moreover, these things happened not during the depression but during the boom.

In the spring of '27, something bright and alien flashed across the sky. A young Minnesotan who seemed to have had nothing to do with his generation did a heroic thing, and for a moment people set down their glasses in country clubs and speak-easies and thought of their old best dreams. Maybe there was a way out by flying, maybe our restless blood could find frontiers in the illimitable air. But by that time we were all pretty well committed; and the Jazz Age continued; we would all have one more.

Nevertheless, Americans were wandering ever more widely—friends seemed eternally bound for Russia, Persia, Abyssinia and Central Africa. And by 1928 Paris had grown suffocating. With each new shipment of Americans spewed up by the boom the quality fell off, until toward the end there was something sinister about the crazy boatloads. They were no longer the simple pa and ma and son and daughter, infinitely superior in their qualities of kindness and curiosity to the corresponding class in Europe, but fantastic neanderthals who believed something, something vague, that you remembered from a very cheap novel. I remember an

Italian on a steamer who promenaded the deck in an American Reserve Officer's uniform picking quarrels in broken English with Americans who criticised their own institutions in the bar. I remember a fat Jewess, inlaid with diamonds, who sat behind us at the Russian ballet and said as the curtain rose, "Thad's luffly, dey ought to baint a bicture of it." This was low comedy but it was evident that money and power were falling into the hands of people in comparison with whom the leader of a village Soviet would be a gold-mine of judgment and culture. There were citizens travelling in luxury in 1928 and 1929 who, in the distortion of their new condition, had the human value of Pekinese bivalves, cretins, goats. I remember the Judge from some New York district who had taken his daughter to see the Bayeux Tapestries and made a scene in the papers advocating their segregation because one scene was immoral. But in those days life was like the race in "Alice in Wonderland," there was a prize for every one.

The Jazz Age had had a wild youth and a heady middle age. There was the phase of the necking parties, the Leopold-Loeb murder (I remember the time my wife was arrested on Queensborough Bridge on the suspicion of being the "Bob-haired Bandit") and the John Held Clothes. In the second phase such phenomena as sex and murder became more mature, if much more conventional. Middle age must be served and pajamas came to the beach to save fat thighs and flabby calves from competition with the one-piece bathing-suit. Finally skirts came down and everything was concealed. Everybody was at scratch now. Let's go——

But it was not to be. Somebody had blundered and the most expensive orgy in history was over.

It ended two years ago, because the utter confidence which was its essential prop received an emormous jolt and it didn't take long for the flimsy structure to settle earthward. And after two years the Jazz Age seems as far away as the days before the War. It was borrowed time anyhow—the whole upper tenth of a nation living with the insouciance of grand ducs and the casualness of chorus girls. But moralizing is easy now and it was pleasant to be in one's twenties in such a certain and unworried time. Even when you were broke you didn't worry about money, because it was in such profusion around you. Toward the end one had a struggle to pay one's share; it was almost a favor to accept hospitality that required any travelling. Charm, notoriety, mere good manners, weighed more than money as a social asset. This was rather splendid but things were getting thinner and thinner as the eternal necessary human values tried to spread over all that expansion. Writers were geniuses on the strength of one respectable book or play; just as during the War officers of four months' experience commanded hundreds of men, so there were now many little fish lording it over great big bowls. In the theatrical world extravagant productions were carried by a few second-rate stars, and so on up the scale into politics where it was difficult to interest good men in positions of the highest importance and responsibility, importance and responsibility far exceeding that of business executives but which paid only five or six thousand a year.

Now once more the belt is tight and we summon the proper expression of horror as we look back at our wasted youth. Sometimes, though, there is a ghostly rumble among the drums, an asthmatic whisper in the trombones that swings me back into the early twenties when we drank wood alcohol and every day in every way grew better and better, and there was a first abortive shortening of the skirts, and girls all looked alike in sweater dresses, and people you didn't want to know said "Yes, we have no bananas," and it seemed only a question of a few years before the older people would step aside and let the world be run by those who saw things as they were—and it all seems rosy and romantic to us who were young then, because we will never feel quite so intensely about our surroundings any more.

Herbert Hoover
Principles and Ideals
of the United States Government
(1928)

THIS CAMPAIGN now draws near a close. The platforms of the two parties defining principles and offering solutions of various national problems have been presented and are being earnestly considered by our people.

After four months' debate it is not the Republican Party which finds reason for abandonment of any of the principles it has laid down or of the views it has expressed for solution of the problems before the country. The principles to which it adheres are rooted deeply in the foundations of our national life. The solutions which it proposes are based on experience with government and on a consciousness that it may have the responsibility for placing those solutions in action.

In my acceptance speech I endeavored to outline the spirit and ideals by which I would be guided in carrying that platform into administration. Tonight, I will not deal with the multitude of issues which have been already well canvassed. I intend rather to discuss some of those more fundamental principles and ideals upon which I believe the government of the United States should be conducted. . . .

Nor do I need to remind you that government today deals with an economic and social system vastly more intricate and delicately adjusted than ever before. That system now must be kept in perfect tune if we would maintain uninterrupted employment and the high standards of living of our people. The government has come to touch this delicate web at a thousand points. Yearly the relations of government to national prosperity become more and more intimate. Only through keen vision and

[Originally, this text was a campaign speech delivered in Madison Square Garden, New York City, on 22 October 1928.]

helpful co-operation by the government has stability in business and stability in employment been maintained during this past seven and one-half years. There always are some localities, some industries, and some individuals who do not share the prevailing prosperity. The task of government is to lessen these inequalities.

Never has there been a period when the Federal Government has given such aid and impulse to the progress of our people, not alone to economic progress but to the development of those agencies which make for moral and spiritual progress.

But in addition to this great record of contributions of the Republican Party to progress, there has been a further fundamental contribution—a contribution underlying and sustaining all the others—and that is the resistance of the Republican Party to every attempt to inject the government into business in competition with its citizens.

After the war, when the Republican Party assumed administration of the country, we were faced with the problem of determination of the very nature of our national life. During one hundred and fifty years we have builded up a form of self-government and a social system which is peculiarly our own. It differs essentially from all others in the world. It is the American system. It is just as definite and positive a political and social system as has ever been developed on earth. It is founded upon a particular conception of self-government in which decentralized local responsibility is the very base. Further than this, it is founded upon the conception that only through ordered liberty, freedom, and equal opportunity to the individual will his initiative and enterprise spur on the march of progress. And in our insistence upon equality of opportunity has our system advanced beyond all the world.

During the war we necessarily turned to the government to solve every difficult economic problem. The government having absorbed every energy of our people for war, there was no other solution. For the preservation of the state the Federal Government became a centralized despotism which undertook unprecedented responsibilities, assumed autocratic powers, and took over the business of citizens. To a large degree we regimented our whole people temporarily into a socialistic state. However justified in time of war, if continued in peace-time it would destroy not only our American system but with it our progress and freedom as well.

When the war closed, the most vital of all issues both in our own country and throughout the world was whether governments should continue their war-time ownership and operation of many instrumentalities of production and distribution. We were challenged with a peace-time choice between the American system of rugged individualism and a European philosophy of diametrically opposed doctrines—doctrines of paternalism and state socialism. The acceptance of these ideas would have meant the destruction of self-government through centralization of government. It would have meant the undermining of the individual initiative and enterprise through which our people have grown to unparalleled greatness.

The Republican Party from the beginning resolutely turned its face away from these ideas and these war practices. A Republican Congress co-operated with the Democratic administration to demobilize many of our war activities. At that time the two parties were in accord upon that point. When the Republican Party came into full power it went at once resolutely back to our fundamental conception of the state and the rights and responsibilities of the individual. Thereby it restored confidence and hope in the American people, it freed and stimulated enterprise, it restored the government to its position as an umpire instead of a player in the economic game. For these reasons the American people have gone forward in progress while the rest of the world has halted, and some countries have even gone backward. If anyone will study the causes of retarded recuperation in Europe, he will find much of it due to stifling of private initiative on one hand, and overloading of the government with business on the other.

There has been revived in this campaign, however, a series of proposals which, if adopted, would be a long step toward the abandonment of our American system and a surrender to the destructive operation of governmental conduct of commercial business. Because the country is faced with difficulty and doubt over certain national problems—that is, prohibition, farm relief, and electrical power—our opponents propose that we must thrust government a long way into the businesses which give rise to these problems. In effect, they abandon the tenets of their own party and turn to state socialism as a solution for the difficulties presented by all three. It is proposed that we shall change from prohibition to the state purchase and sale of liquor. If their agricultural relief program means anything, it means that the government shall directly or indirectly buy and sell and fix prices of agricultural products. And we are to go into the hydro-electric power business. In other words, we are confronted with a huge program of government in business.

There is, therefore, submitted to the American people a question of fundamental principle. That is: shall we depart from the principles of our American political and economic system, upon which we have advanced beyond all the rest of the world, in order to adopt methods based on principles destructive of its very foundations? And I wish to emphasize the seriousness of these proposals. I wish to make my position clear; for this goes to the very roots of American life and progress.

I should like to state to you the effect that this projection of government in business would have upon our system of self-government and our economic system. That effect would reach to the daily life of every man and woman. It would impair the very basis of liberty and freedom not only for those left outside the fold of expanded bureaucracy but for those embraced within it.

Let us first see the effect upon self-government. When the Federal Government undertakes to go into commercial business it must at once set up the organization and administration of that business, and it immediately finds itself in a labyrinth, every alley of which leads to the destruction of self-government.

Commercial business requires a concentration of responsibility. Self-government requires decentralization and many checks and balances to safeguard liberty. Our government to succeed in business would need become in effect a despotism. There at once begins the destruction of self-government.

The first problem of the government about to adventure in commercial business is to determine a method of administration. It must secure leadership and direction. Shall this leadership be chosen by political agencies or shall we make it elective? The hard practical fact is that leadership in business must come through the sheer rise in ability and character. That rise can only take place in the free atmosphere of competition. Competition is closed by bureaucracy. Political agencies are feeble channels through which to select able leaders to conduct commercial business.

Government, in order to avoid the possible incompetence, corruption, and tyranny of too great authority in individuals entrusted with commercial business, inevitably turns to boards and commissions. To make sure that there are checks and balances, each member of such boards and commissions must have equal authority. Each has his separate responsibility to the public, and at once we have the conflict of ideas and the lack of decision which would ruin any commercial business. It has contributed greatly to the demoralization of our shipping business. Moreover, these commissions must be representative of different sections and different political parties, so that at once we have an entire blight upon co-ordinated action within their ranks which destroys any possibility of effective administration.

Moreover, our legislative bodies cannot in fact delegate their full authority to commissions or to individuals for the conduct of matters vital to the American people; for if we would preserve government by the people we must preserve the authority of our legislators in the activities of our government.

Thus every time the Federal Government goes into a commercial business, five hundred and thirty-one Senators and Congressmen become the actual board of directors of that business. Every time a state government goes into business one or two hundred state senators and legislators become the actual directors of that business. Even if they were supermen and if there were no politics in the United States, no body of such numbers could competently direct commercial activities; for that requires initiative, instant decision, and action. It took Congress six years of constant discussion to even decide what the method of administration of Muscle Shoals should be.

When the Federal Government undertakes to go into business, the state governments are at once deprived of control and taxation of that business; when a state government undertakes to go into business, it at once deprives the municipalities of taxation and control of that business. Municipalities, being local and close to the people, can, at times, succeed in business where federal and state governments must fail. We have trouble enough with log-rolling in legislative bodies today. It originates naturally from desires of citizens to advance their particular section or to secure some necessary service. It would be multiplied a thousandfold were the federal and state governments in these businesses.

The effect upon our economic progress would be even worse. Business progressiveness is dependent on competition. New methods and new ideas are the outgrowth of the spirit of adventure, of individual initiative, and of individual enterprise. Without adventure there is no progress. No government administration can rightly take chances with taxpayers' money. . . .

The government in commercial business does not tolerate amongst its customers the freedom of competitive reprisals to which private business is subject. Bureaucracy does not tolerate the spirit of independence; it spreads the spirit of submission into our daily life and penetrates the temper of our people not with the habit of powerful resistance to wrong but with the habit of timid acceptance of irresistible might.

Bureaucracy is ever desirous of spreading its influence and its power. You cannot extend the mastery of the government over the daily working life of a people without at the same time making it the master of the people's souls and thoughts. Every expansion of government in business means that government in order to protect itself from the political consequences of its errors and wrongs is driven irresistibly without peace to greater and greater control of the nation's press and platform. Free speech does not live many hours after free industry and free commerce die.

It is a false liberalism that interprets itself into the government operation of commercial business. Every step of bureaucratizing of the business of our country poisons the very roots of liberalism—that is, political equality, free speech, free assembly, free press, and equality of opportunity. It is the road not to more liberty, but to less liberty. Liberalism should be found not striving to spread bureaucracy but striving to set bounds to it. True liberalism seeks all legitimate freedom first in the confident belief that without such freedom the pursuit of all other blessings and benefits is vain. That belief is the foundation of all American progress, political as well as economic.

Liberalism is a force truly of the spirit, a force proceeding from the deep realization that economic freedom cannot be sacrificed if political freedom is to be preserved. Even if governmental conduct of business could give us more efficiency instead of less efficiency, the fundamental objection to it would remain unaltered and unabated. It would destroy political equality. It would increase rather than decrease abuse and corruption. It would stifle initiative and invention. It would undermine the development of leadership. It would cramp and cripple the mental and spiritual energies of our people. It would extinguish equality and opportunity. It would dry up the spirit of liberty and progress. For these reasons primarily it must be resisted. For a hundred and fifty years liberalism has found its true spirit in the American system, not in the European systems.

I do not wish to be misunderstood in this statement. I am defining a general policy. It does not mean that our government is to part with one iota of its national resources without complete protection to the public interest. I have already stated that where the government is engaged in public works for purposes of flood control, of navigation, of irrigation, of scientific research or national defense, or in pioneering a new art, it will at times necessarily produce power or commodities as a by-product. But they must be a by-product of the major purpose, not the major purpose itself.

Nor do I wish to be misinterpreted as believing that the United States is free-for-all and devil-take-the-hindmost. The very essence of equality of opportunity and of American individualism is that there shall be no domination by any group or combination in this republic, whether it be business or political. On the contrary, it demands economic justice as well as political and social justice. It is no system of laissez faire.

I feel deeply on this subject because during the war I had some practical experience with governmental operation and control. I have witnessed not only at home but abroad the many failures of government in business. I have seen its tyrannies, its injustices, its destructions of self-government, its undermining of the very instincts which carry our people forward to progress. I have witnessed the lack of advance, the lowered standards of living, the depressed spirits of people working under such a system. My objection is based not upon theory or upon a failure to recognize wrong or abuse, but I know the adoption of such methods would strike at the very roots of American life and would destroy the very basis of American progress.

Our people have the right to know whether we can continue to solve our great problems without abandonment of our American system. I know we can. We have demonstrated that our system is responsive enough to meet any new and intricate development in our economic and business life. We have demonstrated that we can meet any economic problem and still maintain our democracy as master in its own house, and that we can at the same time preserve equality of opportunity and individual freedom.

In the last fifty years we have discovered that mass production will produce articles for us at half the cost they required previously. We have seen the resultant growth of large units of production and distribution. This is big business. Many businesses must be bigger, for our tools are bigger, our country is bigger. We now build a single dynamo of a hundred thousand horsepower. Even fifteen years ago that would have been a big business all by itself. Yet today advance in production requires that we set ten of these units together in a row.

The American people from bitter experience have a rightful fear that great business units might be used to dominate our industrial life and by illegal and unethical practices destroy quality of opportunity.

Years ago the Republican administration established the principle that such evils could be corrected by regulation. It developed methods by which abuses could be prevented while the full value of industrial progress could be retained for the public. It insisted upon the principle that when great public utilities were clothed with the security of partial monopoly, whether it be railways, power plants, telephones, or what not, then there must be the fullest and most complete control of rates, services, and finances by government or local agencies. It declared that these businesses must be conducted with glass pockets.

As to our great manufacturing and distributing industries, the Republican Party insisted upon the enactment of laws that not only would maintain competition but would destroy conspiracies to destroy the smaller units or dominate and limit the equality of opportunity amongst our people.

One of the great problems of government is to determine to what extent the government shall regulate and control commerce and industry and how much it shall leave it alone. No system is perfect. We have had many abuses in the private conduct of business. That every good citizen resents. It is just as important that business keep out of government as that government keep out of business.

Nor am I setting up the contention that our institutions are perfect. No human ideal is ever perfectly attained, since humanity itself is not perfect.

The wisdom of our forefathers in their conception that progress can only be attained as the sum of the accomplishment of free individuals has been reinforced by all of the great leaders of the country since that day. Jackson, Lincoln, Cleveland, McKinley, Roosevelt, Wilson, and Coolidge have stood unalterably for these principles.

And what have been the results of our American system? Our country has become the land of opportunity to those born without inheritance, not merely because of the wealth of its resources and industry but because of this freedom of initiative and enterprise. Russia has natural resources equal to ours. Her people are equally industrious, but she has not had the blessings of one hundred and fifty years of our form of government and of our social system.

By adherence to the principles of decentralized self-government, ordered liberty, equal opportunity, and freedom to the individual, our American experiment in human welfare has yielded a degree of well-being unparalleled in all the world. It has come nearer to the abolition of poverty, to the abolition of fear of want, than humanity has ever reached before. Progress of the past seven years is the proof of it. This alone furnishes the answer to our opponents, who ask us to introduce destructive elements into the system by which this has been accomplished.

Let us see what this sytem has done for us in our recent years of difficult and trying reconstruction and then solemnly ask ourselves if we now wish to abandon it.

As a nation we came out of the war with great losses. We made no profits from it. The apparent increases in wages were at that time fictitious. We were poorer as a nation when we emerged from the war. Yet during these last eight years we have recovered from these losses and increased our national income by over one-third, even if we discount the inflation of the dollar. That there has been a wide diffusion of our gain in wealth and income is marked by a hundred proofs. I know of no better test of the improved conditions of the average family than the combined increase in assets of life and industrial insurance, building and loan associations, and savings deposits. These are the savings banks of the average man. These agencies alone have in seven years increased by nearly one hundred per cent to the gigantic sum of over fifty billions of dollars, or nearly one-sixth of our whole national wealth. We have increased in home ownership, we have expanded the investments of the average man.

In addition to these evidences of larger savings, our people are steadily increasing their spending for higher standards of living. Today there are almost nine automobiles for each ten families, where seven and one-half years ago only enough automobiles were running to average less than four for each ten families. The slogan of progress is changing from the full dinner pail to the full garage. Our people have more to eat, better things to wear, and better homes. We have even gained in elbow room, for the increase of residential floor space is over twenty-five per cent, with less than ten per cent increase in our number of people. Wages have increased, the cost of living has decreased. The job of every man and woman has been made more secure. We have in this short period decreased the fear of poverty, the fear of unemployment, the fear of old age; and these are fears that are the greatest calamities of humankind.

All this progress means far more than increased creature comforts. It finds a thousand interpretations into a greater and fuller life. A score of new helps save the drudgery of the home. In seven years we have added seventy per cent to the electric power at the elbows of our workers and further promoted them from carriers of burdens to directors of machines. We have steadily reduced the sweat in human labor. Our hours of labor are lessened; our leisure has increased. We have expanded our parks and playgrounds. We have nearly doubled our attendance at games. We pour into outdoor recreation in every direction. The visitors at our national parks have trebled and we have so increased the number of sportsmen fishing in our streams and lakes that the longer time between bites is becoming a political issue. In these seven and one-half years the radio has brought music and laughter, education and political discussion to almost every fireside.

Springing from our prosperity with its greater freedom, its vast endowment of scientific research, and the greater resources with which to care for public health, we have according to our insurance actuaries during this short period since the war lengthened the average span of life by nearly eight years. We have reduced infant mortality, we have vastly decreased the days of illness and suffering in the life of every man and woman. We have improved the facilities for the care of the crippled and helpless and deranged.

From our increasing resources we have expanded our educational system in eight years from an outlay of twelve hundred millions to twenty-seven hundred millions of dollars. The education of our youth has become almost our largest and certainly our most important activity. From our greater income and thus our ability to free youth from toil we have increased the attendance in our grade schools by fourteen per cent, in our high schools by eighty per cent, and in our institutions of higher learning by ninety-five per cent. Today we have more youth in these institutions of higher learning twice over than all the rest of the world put together. We have made notable progress in literature, in art, and in public taste.

We have made progress in the leadership of every branch of American life. Never in our history was the leadership in our economic life more distinguished in its abilities than today, and it has grown greatly in its consciousness of public responsibility. Leadership in our professions and in moral and spiritual affairs of our country was never of a higher order.

And our magnificent educational system is bringing forward a host of recruits for the succession to this leadership.

I do not need to recite more figures and more evidence. I cannot believe that the American people wish to abandon or in any way to weaken the principles of economic freedom and self-government which have been maintained by the Republican Party and which have produced results so amazing and so stimulating to the spiritual as well as to the material advance of the nation.

Your city has been an outstanding beneficiary of this great progress and of these safeguarded principles. With its suburbs it has, during the last seven and one-half years, grown by over a million and a half of people until it has become the largest metropolitan district of all the world. Here you have made abundant opportunity not only for the youth of the land but for the immigrant from foreign shores. This city is the commercial center of the United States. It is the commercial agent of the American people. It is a great organism of specialized skill and leadership in finance, industry, and commerce which reaches every spot in our country. Its progress and its beauty are the pride of the whole American people. It leads our nation in its benevolences to charity, to education, and to scientific research. It is the center of art, music, literature, and drama. It has come to have a more potent voice than any other city in the United States.

But when all is said and done, the very life, progress, and prosperity of this city is wholly dependent on the prosperity of the 115,000,000 people who dwell in our mountains and valleys across the three thousand miles to the Pacific Ocean. Every activity of this city is sensitive to every evil and every favorable tide that sweeps this great nation of ours. Be there a slackening of industry in any place, it affects New York far more than any other part of the country. In a time of depression one-quarter of all the unemployed in the United States can be numbered in this city. In a time of prosperity the citizens of the great interior of our country pour into your city for business and entertainment at the rate of one hundred and fifty thousand a day. In fact, so much is this city the reflex of the varied interests of our country that the concern of every one of your citizens for national stability, for national prosperity, for national progress, for preservation of our American system is far greater than that of any other single part of our country.

We still have great problems if we would achieve the full economic advancement of our country. In these past few years some groups in our country have lagged behind others in the march of progress. I refer more particularly to those engaged in the textile, coal, and agricultural industries. We can assist in solving these problems by co-operation of our government. To the agricultural industry we shall need to advance initial capital to assist them to stabilize their industry. But this proposal implies that they shall conduct it themselves, and not the government. It is in the interest of our cities that we shall bring agriculture and all industries into full stability and prosperity. I know you will gladly co-operate in the faith that in the common prosperity of our country lies its future.

In bringing this address to a conclusion I should like to restate to you some of the fundamental things I have endeavored to bring out.

The foundations of progress and prosperity are dependent as never before upon the wise policies of government, for government now touches at a thousand points the intricate web of economic and social life.

Under administration by the Republican Party in the last seven and one-half years our country as a whole has made unparalleled progress and this has been in generous part reflected to this great city. Prosperity is no idle expression. It is a job for every worker; it is the safety and the safeguard of every business and every home. A continuation of the policies of the Republican Party is fundamentally necessary to the further advancement of this progress and to the further building up of this prosperity.

I have dwelt at some length on the principles of relationship between the government and business. I make no apologies for dealing with this subject. The first necessity of any nation is the smooth functioning of the vast business machinery for employment, feeding, clothing, housing, and providing luxuries and comforts to a people. Unless these basic elements are properly organized and function, there can be no progress in business, in education, literature, music, or art. There can be no advance in the fundamental ideals of a people. A people cannot make progress in poverty.

I have endeavored to present to you that the greatness of America has grown out of a political and social system and a method of control of economic forces distinctly its own—our American system—which has carried this great experiment in human welfare farther than ever before in all history. We are nearer today to the ideal of the abolition of poverty and fear from the lives of men and women than ever before in any land. And I again repeat that the departure from our American system by injecting principles destructive to it which our opponents propose will jeopardize the very liberty and freedom of our people, will destroy equality of opportunity not alone to ourselves but to our children.

To me the foundation of American life rests upon the home and the family. I read into these great economic forces, these intricate and delicate relations of the government with business and with our political and social life, but one supreme end—that we reinforce the ties that bind together the millions of our families, that we strengthen the security, the happiness, and the independence of every home.

My conception of America is a land where men and women may walk in ordered freedom in the independent conduct of their occupations; where they may enjoy the advantages of wealth, not concentrated in the hands of the few but spread through the lives of all; where they build and safeguard their homes, and give to their children the fullest advantages and opportunities of American life; where every man shall be respected in the faith that his conscience and his heart direct him to follow; where a contented and happy people, secure in their liberties, free from poverty and fear, shall have the leisure and impulse to seek a fuller life.

Some may ask where all this may lead beyond mere material progress. It leads to a release of the energies of men and women from the dull drudgery of life to a wider vision and a higher hope. It leads to the opportunity for greater and greater service, not alone from man to man in our own land, but from our country to the whole world. It leads to an America, healthy in body, healthy in spirit, unfettered, youthful, eager— with a vision searching beyond the farthest horizons, with an open mind, sympathetic and generous. It is to these higher ideals and for these purposes that I pledge myself and the Republican Party.

Edmund Wilson
A Man in the Street
(1932)

HE IS a tall man with square shoulders—looks able-bodied and self-dependent. A pure Nordic type, he has straight brows and a long straight nose. But his color is pale and he seems soiled, as if his quarters and food were poor; and though there is no demoralization in his face, he looks dazed as if he were not a part of the world in which he is walking, as if life had come suddenly under a shadow which he could see no way of getting out of and had no means of accounting for. His dark brown overcoat is old; his flat-topped straight-brimmed hat is too small for him. You can't tell whether he is a skilled mechanic or a former auto dealer or a bank cashier or a department store manager—he might even have been a provincial lawyer. But he wanders incongruously along West Fifty-eighth Street past the restaurants with smart French names and the half-empty apartment houses where liveried doormen guard the doors.

John Dewey
Individualism Old and New
(1930)

THE UNITED STATES, INCORPORATED

IT WAS not long ago that it was fashionable for both American and foreign observers of our national scene to sum up the phenomena of our social life under the title of "individualism." Some treated this alleged individualism as our distinctive achievement; some critics held that it was the source of our backwardness, the mark of a relatively uncivilized estate. To-day both interpretations seem equally inept and outmoded. Individualism is still carried on our banners and attempts are made to use it as a war cry, especially when it is desired to defeat governmental regulation of any form of industry previously exempt from legal control. Even in high quarters, rugged individualism is praised as the glory of American life. But such words have little relation to the moving facts of that life.

There is no word which adequately expresses what is taking place. "Socialism" has too specific political and economic associations to be appropriate. "Collectivism" is more neutral, but it, too, is a party-word rather than a descriptive term. Perhaps the constantly increasing rôle of corporations in our economic life gives a clue to a fitting name. The word may be used in a wider sense than is conveyed by its technical legal meaning. We may then say that the United States has steadily moved from an earlier pioneer individualism to a condition of dominant corporateness. The influence business corporations exercise in determining present industrial and economic activities is both a cause and a symbol of the tendency to combination in all phases of life. Associations tightly or loosely organized more and more define the opportunities, the choices and the actions of individuals.

I have said that the growth of legal corporations in manufacturing, transportation, distribution and finance is symbolic of the development of corporateness in all phases of life. The era of trust-busting is an almost forgotten age. Not only are big mergers the order of the day, but popular sentiment now looks upon them with pride rather than with fear. Size is our current measure of greatness in this as in other matters. It is not necessary to ask whether the opportunity for speculative manipulation for the sake of private gain, or increased public service at a lower cost, is the dominant motive. Personal motives hardly count as productive causes in comparison with impersonal forces. Mass production and mass distribution inevitably follow in the wake of an epoch of steam and electricity. These have created a common market, the parts of which are held together by intercommunication and interdependence; distance is eliminated and the tempo of action enormously accelerated. Aggregated capital and concentrated control are the contemporary responses.

Political control is needed, but the movement cannot be arrested by legislation. Witness the condition of nearly innocuous desuetude of the Sherman Anti-Trust Act. Newspapers, manufacturing plants, utilities supplying light, power and local transportation, banks, retail stores, theaters and the movies, have all joined in the movement toward integration. General Motors, the American Telegraph and Telephone Company, United States Steel, the rapid growth of chain-store systems, combinations of radio companies with companies controlling theaters all over the country, are familiar facts. Railway consolidations have been slowed up by politics and internal difficulties, but few persons doubt that they, too, are coming. The political control of the future to be effective must take a positive instead of negative form.

For the forces at work in this movement are too vast and complex to cease operation at the behest of legislation. Aside from direct evasions of laws, there are many legal methods of carrying the movement forward. Interlocking directorates, interpurchase of stocks by individuals and corporations, grouping into holding companies, investing companies with enough holdings to sway policies, effect the same end as do direct mergers. It was stated at a recent convention of bankers that eighty per cent of the capitalization of all the banks of the country is now in the hands of twelve financial concerns. It is evident that virtual control of the other twenty per cent, except for negligible institutions having only local importance, automatically ensues.

An economist could multiply instances and give them a more precise form. But I am not an economist, and the facts in any case are too well known to need detailed rehearsal. For my purpose is only to indicate the bearing of the development of these corporations upon the change of social life from an individual to a corporate affair. Reactions to the change are psychological, professional, political; they affect the working ideas, beliefs and conduct of all of us. . . .

Mass production causes a kind of mass education in which individual capacity and skill are submerged. While the artisan becomes more of a mechanic and less of an artist, those who are still called artists either put themselves, as writers and designers, at the disposal of organized business, or are pushed out to the edge as eccentric bohemians. The artist remains, one may say, as a surviving individual force, but the esteem in which the calling is socially held in this country measures the degree of his force. The status of the artist in any form of social life affords a fair measure of the state of its culture. The inorganic position of the artist in American life to-day is convincing evidence of what happens to the isolated individual who lives in a society growing corporate.

Attention has recently been called to a new phenomenon in human culture:—the business mind, having its own conversation and language, its own interests, its own intimate groupings in which men of this mind, in their collective capacity, determine the tone of society at large as well as the government of industrial society, and have more political influence than the government itself. I am not concerned here with their political power. The fact significant for present discussion is that we now have, although without formal or legal status, a mental and moral corporateness for which history affords no parallel. Our indigenous heroes are the Fords and Edisons who typify this mind to the public. Critics may find amusement in ridiculing Rotarians, Kiwanians and Lions, but the latter can well afford to disregard the ridicule because they are representatives of the dominant corporate mentality.

Nowhere is the decline of the old-fashioned individual and individualism more marked than in leisure life, in amusements and sports. Our colleges only follow the movement of the day when they make athletics an organized business, aroused and conducted under paid directors in the spirit of pure collectivism. The formation of theater chains is at once the cause and the effect of the destruction of the older independent life of leisure carried on in separate homes. The radio, the movies, the motor car, all make for a common and aggregate mental and emotional life. With technical exceptions, to be found in special publications and in some portion of all newspapers, the press is the organ of amusement for a hurried leisure time, and it reflects and carries further the formation of mental collectivism by massed methods. Crime, too, is assuming a new form; it is organized and corporate.

Our apartments and our subways are signs of the invasion and decline of privacy. Private "rights" have almost ceased to have a definable meaning. We live exposed to the greatest flood of mass suggestion that any people has ever experienced. The need for united action, and the supposed need of integrated opinion and sentiment, are met by organized propaganda and advertising. The publicity agent is perhaps the most significant symbol of our present social life. There are individuals who resist; but, for a time at least, sentiment can be manufactured by mass methods for almost any person or any cause.

* * *

These things are not said to be deplored, nor even in order to weigh their merits and demerits. They are merely reported as indications of the nature of our social scene, of the extent to which it is formed and directed by corporate and collective factors toward collective ends. Coincident with these changes in mentality and prestige are basic, if hardly acknowledged, changes in the ideas by which life is interpreted. Industry, again, provides the striking symbols.

What has become of the old-fashioned ideal of thrift? Societies for the promotion of savings among the young were much hurt in their feelings when Henry Ford urged a free scale of expenditures instead of a close scale of personal savings. But his recommendation was in line with all the economic tendencies of the day. Speeded-up mass production demands increased buying. It is promoted by advertising on a vast scale, by instalment selling, by agents skilled in breaking down sales resistance. Hence buying becomes an economic "duty" which is as consonant with the present epoch as thrift was with the period of individualism. For the industrial mechanism depends upon maintaining some kind of an equilibrium between production and consumption. If the equilibrium is disturbed, the whole social structure is affected and prosperity ceases to have a meaning. Replacement and extension of capital are indeed more required than they ever were. But the savings of individuals, as such, are petty and inadequate to the task. New capital is chiefly supplied by the surplus earnings of big corporate organizations, and it becomes meaningless to tell individual buyers that industry can be kept going only by their abstinence from the enjoyments of consumption. The old plea for "sacrifice" loses its force. In effect, the individual is told that by indulging in the enjoyment of free purchasing he performs his economic duty, transferring his surplus income to the corporate store where it can be most effectively used. Virtue departs from mere thrift. . . .

. . . But certain changes do not go backward. Those who have enjoyed high wages and a higher standard of consumption will not be content to return to a lower level. A new condition has been created with which we shall have to reckon constantly in the future. Depressions and slumps will come, but they can never be treated in the future in the casual and fatalistic way in which they have been accepted in the past. They will appear abnormal instead of normal, and society, including the industrial captains, will have to assume a responsibility from which it and they were previously exempt. The gospel of general prosperity in this life will have to meet tests to which that of salvation in the next world, as a compensation for the miseries of this one, was not subjected. "Prosperity" is not such an assured fact in 1930 as it seemed to many to be in the earlier part of 1929. The slump or the depression makes the problem caused by the growth of corporate industry and finance the more acute. An excess income of eight billions a year will only aggravate the economic situation unless it can find outlet in productive channels. It cannot do this unless consumption is sustained. This cannot happen unless organization and control extend from production and distribution to consumption. The alternatives seem to be either a definite expansion of social corporateness to include the average consumer or else economic suffering on a vast scale.

. . . [T]he instances cited of the reaction of the growing corporateness of society upon social mind and habit were not given in order to be either deplored or approved. They are set forth only to call out the picture of the decline of an individualistic philosophy of life, and the formation of a collectivistic scheme of interdependence, which finds its way into every cranny of life, personal, intellectual, emotional, affecting leisure as well as work, morals as well as economics. But because the purpose was to indicate the decay of the older conceptions, although they are still those that are most loudly and vocally professed, the illustrations given inevitably emphasize those features of growing standardization and mass uniformity which critics justly deplore. It would be unfair, accordingly, to leave the impression that these traits are the whole of the story of the "corporization" of American life.

The things which are criticized are the outward signs of an inner movement toward integration on a scale never known before. "Socialization" is not wholly a eulogistic term nor a desirable process. It involves danger to some precious values; it involves a threat of danger to some things which we should not readily lose. But in spite of much cant which is talked about "service" and "social responsibility," it marks the beginning of a new era of integration. What its ultimate possibilities are, and to what extent these possibilities will be realized, is for the future to tell. The need of the present is to apprehend the fact that, for better or worse, we are living in a corporate age.

It is of the nature of society as of life to contain a balance of opposed forces. Actions and reactions are ultimately equal and counterpart. At present the "socialization" is largely mechanical and quantitative. The system is kept in a kind of precarious balance by the movement toward lawless and reckless overstimulation among individuals. If the chaos and the mechanism are to generate a mind and soul, an integrated personality, it will have to be an intelligence, a sentiment and an individuality of a new type.

Meanwhile, the lawlessness and irregularity (and I have in mind not so much outward criminality as emotional instability and intellectual confusion) and the uniform standardization are two sides of the same emerging corporate society. Hence only in an external sense does society maintain a balance. When the corporateness becomes internal, when, that is, it is realized in thought and purpose, it will become qualitative. In this change, law will be realized not as a rule arbitrarily imposed from without but as the relations which hold individuals together. The balance of the individual and the social will be organic. The emotions will be aroused and satisfied in the course of normal living, not in abrupt deviations to secure the fulfillment which is denied them in a situation which is so incomplete that it cannot be admitted into the affections and yet is so pervasive that it cannot be escaped: a situation which defines an individual divided within himself.

Toward a New Individualism

Our material culture, as anthropologists would call it, is verging upon the collective and corporate. Our moral culture, along with our ideology is, on the other hand, still saturated with ideals and values of an individualism derived from the prescientific, pretechnological age. Its spiritual roots are found in medieval religion, which asserted the ultimate nature of the individual soul and centered the drama of life about the destiny of that soul. Its institutional and legal concepts were framed in the feudal period.

This moral and philosophical individualism anteceded the rise of modern industry and the era of the machine. It was the context in which the latter operated. The apparent subordination of the individual to established institutions often conceals from recognition the vital existence of a deep-seated individualism. But the fact that the controlling institution was the Church should remind us that in ultimate intent it existed to secure the salvation of the individual. That this individual was conceived as a soul, and that the end served by the institution was deferred to another and everlasting life conceal from contemporary realization the underlying individualism. In its own time, its substance consisted in just this eternal spiritual character of the personal soul; the power of the established institutions proceeded from their being the necessary means of accomplishing the supreme end of the individual.

The early phase of the industrial revolution wrought a great transformation. It gave a secular and worldly turn to the career of the individual, and it liquefied the static property concepts of feudalism by the shift of emphasis from agriculture to manufacturing. Still, the idea persisted that property and reward were intrinsically individual. There were, it is true, incompatible elements in the earlier and later versions of individualism. But a fusion of individual capitalism, of natural rights, and of morals founded in strictly individual traits and values remained, under the influence of Protestantism, the dominant intellectual synthesis.

The basis of this synthesis was destroyed, however, by the later development of the industrial system, which brought about the merging of personal capacity, effort and work into collective wholes. Meanwhile, the control of natural energies eliminated time and distance, so that action once adapted to local conditions was swallowed up in complex undertakings of indefinite extent. Yet the older mental equipment remained after its causes and foundations had disappeared. This, fundamentally, is the inner division out of which spring our present confusion and insincerities.

The earlier economic individualism had a definite creed and function. It sought to release from legal restrictions man's wants and his efforts to satisfy those wants. It believed that such emancipation would stimulate latent energy into action, would automatically assign individual ability to the work for which it was suited, would cause it to perform that work under stimulus of the advantage to be gained, and would secure for capacity and enterprise the reward and position to which they were entitled. At the same time, individual energy and savings would be serving the needs of others, and thus promoting the general welfare and effecting a general harmony of interests.

We have gone a long way since this philosophy was formulated. Today, the most stalwart defenders of this type of individualism do not venture to repeat its optimistic assertions. At most, they are content to proclaim its consistency with unchanging human nature—which is said to be moved to effort only by the hope of personal gain—and to paint dire pictures of the inevitable consequences of change to any other régime. They ascribe all the material benefits of our present civilization to this individualism—as if machines were made by the desire for money profit, not by impersonal science; and as if they were driven by money alone, and not by electricity and steam under the direction of a collective technology.

In America, the older individualism assumed a romantic form. It was hardly necessary to elaborate a theory which equated personal gain with social advance. The demands of the practical situation called for the initiative, enterprise and vigor of individuals in all immediate work that urgently asked for doing, and their operation furthered the national life. . . .

Where is the wilderness which now beckons creative energy and affords untold opportunity to initiative and vigor? Where is the pioneer who goes forth rejoicing, even in the midst of privation, to its conquest? The wilderness exists in the movie and the novel; and the children of the pioneers, who live in the midst of surroundings artificially made over by the machine, enjoy pioneer life idly in the vicarious film. I see little social unrest which is the straining of energy for outlet in action; I find rather the protest against a weakening of vigor and a sapping of energy that emanate from the absence of constructive opportunity; and I see a confusion that is an expression of the inability to find a secure and morally rewarding place in a troubled and tangled economic scene.

Because of the bankruptcy of the older individualism, those who are aware of the breakdown often speak and argue as if individualism were itself done and over with. I do not suppose that those who regard socialism and individualism as antithetical really mean that individuality is going to die out or that it is not something intrinsically precious. But in speaking as if the only individualism were the local episode of the last two centuries, they play into the hands of those who would keep it alive in order to serve their own ends, and they slur over the chief problem—that of remaking society to serve the growth of a new type of individual. There are many who believe that socialism of some form is needed to realize individual initiative and security on a wide scale. They are concerned about the restriction of power and freedom to a few in the present régime, and they think that collective social control is necessary, at least for a time, in order to achieve its advantages for all. But they too often seem to assume that the result will be merely an extension of the earlier individualism to the many.

Such thinking treats individualism as if it were something static, having a uniform content. It ignores the fact that the mental and moral structure of individuals, the pattern of their desires and purposes, changes with every great change in social constitution. Individuals who are not bound together in associations, whether domestic, economic, religious, political, artistic or educational, are monstrosities. It is absurd to suppose that the ties which hold them together are merely external and do not react into mentality and character, producing the framework of personal disposition.

The tragedy of the "lost individual" is due to the fact that while individuals are now caught up into a vast complex of associations, there is no harmonious and coherent reflection of the import of these conditions into the imaginative and emotional outlook on life. This fact is of course due in turn to the absence of harmony within the state of society. There is an undoubted circle. But it is a vicious circle only as far as men decline to accept—in the intellectual, observing and inquiring spirit defined in the previous chapter—the realities of the social estate, and because of this refusal either surrender to the division or seek to save their individuality by escape or sheer emotional revolt. The habit of opposing the corporate and collective to the individual tends to the persistent continuation of the confusion and uncertainty. It distracts attention from the crucial issue: How shall the individual refind himself in an unprecedentedly new social situation, and what qualities will the new individualism exhibit?

* * *

That the problem is not merely one of extending to all individuals the traits of economic initiative, opportunity and enterprise; that it is one of forming a new psychological and moral type, is suggested by the great pressure now brought to bear to effect conformity and standardization of American opinion. Why should regimentation, the erection of an average struck from the opinions of large masses into regulative norms, and in general the domination of quantity over quality, be so characteristic of present American life? I see but one fundamental explanation. The individual cannot remain intellectually a vacuum. If his ideas and beliefs are not the spontaneous function of a communal life in which he shares, a seeming consensus will be secured as a substitute by artificial and mechanical means. In the absence of mentality that is congruous with the new social corporateness that is coming into being, there is a desperate effort to fill the void by external agencies which obtain a factitious agreement.

In consequence, our uniformity of thought is much more superficial than it seems to be. The standardization is deplorable, but one might almost say that one of the reasons it is deplorable is because it does not go deep. It goes far enough to effect suppression of original quality of thought, but not far enough to achieve enduring unity. Its superficial character is evident in its instability. All agreement of thought obtained by external means, by repression and intimidation, however subtle, and by calculated propaganda and publicity, is of necessity superficial; and whatever is superficial is in continual flux. The methods employed produce mass credulity, and this jumps from one thing to another according to the dominant suggestions of the day. We think and feel alike—but only for a month or a season. Then comes some other sensational event or personage to exercise a hypnotizing uniformity of response. At a given time, taken in cross-section, conformity is the rule. In a time span, taken longitudinally, instability and flux dominate. . . . I suppose there are others who have a feeling of irritation at such terms as "radio-conscious" and "air-minded," now so frequently forced upon us. I do not think the irritation is wholly due to linguistic causes. It testifies to a half-conscious sense of the external ways in which our minds are formed and swayed and of the superficiality and inconsistency of the result. . . .

Just as the new individualism cannot be achieved by extending the benefits of the older economic individualism to more persons, so it cannot be obtained by a further development of generosity, good will and altruism. Such traits are desirable, but they are also more or less constant expressions of human nature. There is much in the present situation that stimulates them to active operation. They are probably more marked features of American life than of that of any other civilization at any time. Our charity and philanthropy are partly the manifestation of an uneasy conscience. As such a manifestation, they testify to a realization that a régime of industry carried on for private gain does not satisfy the full human nature of even those who profit by it. The impulse and need which the existing economic régime chokes, through preventing its articulated expression, find outlet in actions that acknowledge a social responsibility which the system as a system denies. Hence the development of philanthropic measures is not only compensatory to a stifling of human nature undergone in business, but it is in a way prophetic. Construction is better than relief; prevention than cure. Activities by way of relief of poverty and its attendant mental strains and physical ills—and our philanthropic activities including even the endowment of educational institutions have their ultimate causes in the existence of economic insecurity and distress— suggest, in dim forecast, a society in which daily occupations and relationships will give independence and substantial living to all normal individuals who share in its ongoings, reserving relief for extraordinary emergencies. One does not need to reflect upon the personal motives of great philanthropists to see in what they do an emphatic record of the breakdown of our existing economic organization.

For the chief obstacle to the creation of a type of individual whose pattern of thought and desire is enduringly marked by consensus with others, and in whom sociability is one with coöperation in all regular human associations, is the persistence of that feature of the earlier individualism which defines industry and commerce by ideas of private pecuniary profit. Why, once more, is there such zeal for standardized likeness? It is not, I imagine, because conformity for its own sake appears to be a great boon. It is rather because a certain kind of conformity gives defense and protection to the pecuniary features of our present régime. The foreground may be filled with depiction of the horror of change, and with clamor for law and order and the support of the Constitution. But behind there is desire for perpetuation of that régime which defines individual initiative and ability by success in conducting business so as to make money.

It is not too much to say that the whole significance of the older individualism has now shrunk to a pecuniary scale and measure. The virtues that are supposed to attend rugged individualism may be vocally proclaimed, but it takes no great insight to see that what is cherished is measured by its connection with those activities that make for success in business conducted for personal gain. Hence, the irony of the gospel of "individualism" in business conjoined with suppression of individuality in thought and speech. One cannot imagine a bitterer comment on any professed individualism than that it subordinates the only creative individuality—that of mind—to the maintenance of a régime which gives the few an opportunity for being shrewd in the management of monetary business.

It is claimed, of course, that the individualism of economic self-seeking, even if it has not produced the adjustment of ability and reward and the harmony of interests earlier predicted, has given us the advantage of material prosperity. It is not needful to raise here the question of how far that material prosperity extends. For it is not true that its moving cause is pecuniary individualism. That has been the cause of some great fortunes, but not of national wealth; it counts in the process of distribution, but not in ultimate creation. Scientific insight taking effect in machine technology has been the great productive force. For the most part, economic individualism interpreted as energy and enterprise devoted to private profit has been an adjunct, often a parasitical one, to the movement of technical and scientific forces.

The scene in which individuality is created has been transformed. The pioneer . . . had no great need for any ideas beyond those that sprang up in the immediate tasks in which he was engaged. His intellectual problems grew out of struggle with the forces of physical nature. The wilderness was a reality and it had to be subdued. The type of character that evolved was strong and hardy, often picturesque, and sometimes heroic. Individuality was a reality because it corresponded to conditions. Irrelevant traditional ideas in religion and morals were carried along, but they were reduced to a size where they did no harm; indeed, they could easily be interpreted in such a way as to be a reinforcement to the sturdy and a consolation to the weak and failing.

But it is no longer a physical wilderness that has to be wrestled with. Our problems grow out of social conditions: they concern human relations rather than man's direct relationship to physical nature. The adventure of the individual, if there is to be any venturing of individuality and not a relapse into the deadness of complacency or of despairing discontent, is an unsubdued social frontier. The issues cannot be met with ideas improvised for the occasion. The problems to be solved are general, not local. They concern complex forces that are at work throughout the whole country, not those limited to an immediate and almost face-to-face environment. Traditional ideas are more than irrelevant. They are an encumbrance; they are the chief obstacle to the formation of a new individuality integrated within itself and with a liberated function in the society wherein it exists. A new individualism can be achieved only through the controlled use of all the resources of the science and technology that have mastered the physical forces of nature.

They are not controlled now in any fundamental sense. Rather do they control us. They are indeed physically controlled. Every factory, powerhouse and railway system testifies to the fact that we have attained this measure of control. But control of power through the machine is not control of the machine itself. Control of the energies of nature by science is not controlled use of science. We are not even approaching a climax of control; we are hardly at its feeble beginnings. For control is relative to consequences, ends, values; and we do not manage, we hardly have commenced to dream of managing, physical power for the sake of projected purposes and prospective goods. The machine took us unawares and unprepared. Instead of forming new purposes commensurate with its potentialities, we accordingly tried to make it the servant of aims that were the expression of an age when mastery of natural energies on any large scale was the fantasy of magic. . . .

There is no greater sign of the paralysis of the imagination which custom and involvement in immediate detail can induce than the belief, sedulously propagated by some who pride themselves on superior taste, that the machine is itself the source of our troubles. Of course immense potential resources impose responsibility, and it has yet to be demonstrated whether human capacity can rise to utilization of the opportunities which the machine and technology have opened to us. But it is hard to think of anything more childish than the animism that puts the blame on machinery. For machinery means an undreamed-of reservoir of power. If we have harnessed this power to the dollar rather than to the liberation and enrichment of human life, it is because we have been content to stay within the bounds of traditional aims and values although we are in possession of a revolutionary transforming instrument. Repetition of the older credo of individualism is but the evidence of contentment within these bonds. I for one think it is incredible that this particular form of confession of inferiority will endure very much longer. When we begin to ask what can be done with the machine for the creation and fulfillment of values corresponding to its potency and begin organized planning to effect these goods, a new individual correlative to the realities of the age in which we live will also begin to take form.

Revolt against the machine as the author of social evils usually has an esthetic origin. A more intellectual and quasi-philosophic reaction finds natural science to be their source; or if not science itself (which is allowed to be all very well if it keeps its appropriate humble place) then the attitude of those who depend upon science as an organ of vision and light. Contempt for nature is understandable, at least historically; even though it seems both intellectually petty and morally ungracious to feel contempt for the matrix of our being and the inescapable condition of our lives. But that men should fear and dislike the method of approach to nature I do not find understandable. The eye sees many foul things and the arm and hand do many cruel things. Yet the fanatic who would pluck out the eye and cut off the arm is recognized for what he is. Science, one may say, is but the extension of our natural organs of approach to nature. And I do not mean merely an extension in quantitative range and penetration, as a microscope multiplies the capacity of the unaided eye, but an extension of insight and understanding through bringing relationships and interactions into view. Since we must in any case approach nature in some fashion and by some path—if only that of death—I confess my total inability to understand those who object to an intelligently controlled approach—for that is what science is.

The only way in which I can obtain any sympathetic realization of their attitude is by recalling that there have been those who have professed adoration of science—writing it with a capital S—; those who have thought of it not as a method of approach but as a kind of self-enclosed entity and end in itself, a new theology of self-sufficient authoritatively revealed inherent and absolute Truth. It would, however, seem simpler to correct their misapprehension than first to share it and then to reverse their worship into condemnation. The opposite of intelligent method is no method at all or blind and stupid method. It is a curious state of mind which finds pleasure in setting forth the "limits of science." For the intrinsic limit of knowledge is simply ignorance; and the point in extolling ignorance is not clear except when expressed by those who profit by keeping others in ignorance. There is of course an extrinsic limit of science. But that limitation lies in the ineptitude of those who put it to use; its removal lies in rectification of its use, not in abuse of the thing used.

This reference to science and technology is relevant because they are the forces of present life which are finally significant. It is through employing them with understanding of their possible import that a new individualism, consonant with the realities of the present age, may be brought into operative being. There are many levels and many elements in both the individual and his relations. Neither can be comprehended nor dealt with in mass. Discriminative sensitivity, selection, is imperative. Art is the fruit of such selection when it is given objective effect. The art which our times needs in order to create a new type of individuality is the art which, being sensitive to the technology and science that are the moving forces of our time, will envisage the expansive, the social, culture which they may be made to serve. I am not anxious to depict the form which this emergent individualism will assume. Indeed, I do not see how it can be described until more progress has been made in its production. But such progress will not be initiated until we cease opposing the socially corporate to the individual, and until we develop a constructively imaginative observation of the rôle of science and technology in actual society. The greatest obstacle to that vision is, I repeat, the perpetuation of the older individualism now reduced, as I have said, to the utilization of science and technology for ends of private pecuniary gain. I sometimes wonder if those who are conscious of present ills but who direct their blows of criticism at everything except this obstacle are not stirred by motives which they unconsciously prefer to keep below consciousness.

Mary Heaton Vorse
School for Bums
(1931)

THEY TOOK a census of the floating unemployed on the East Side, which covered the homeless men. In the Municipal Lodging House, in the missions and shelters, in flop-houses and speakeasies where a man can stay all night, sleeping on sawdust, if he buys a drink, they took a census.

The regular salaried census takers had a force of between two and three hundred volunteers, divided up into teams. Each captain had working under him a team of six or more people, flung across the Bowery, down Doyers Street, through Chrystie Street, on to the waterfront.

They are rounding up the misery of the East Side. Doing it "intensively" as one census taker puts it. This is a queer census. It is a census of misery. It is the count of despair. In New York City for future reference they will tabulate the hopeless and put between covers of books how many men are wandering around shelterless, no prospect of jobs, no place to stay in the daytime, no place to sleep at night. How many are there—the wanderers from Municipal Lodging House to Salvation Army shelter, to flop-house, to speakeasy? How many are there sleeping in the subway or under the bridge at One Hundred and Eighty-fourth Street?

Well, at this writing the figures are being compiled. They are not yet accurate, but it looks as if there are about fifteen thousand homeless men in New York—which would include a couple of hundred homeless women.

The unemployed homeless do not take so kindly to the count. Social workers reported that in the flop-houses and twenty-five-cent-a-bed hotels they were hard to talk to—different from what they had been two years before when a similar count had been taken. Some men did not answer at all. Nor did the social workers wonder at this.

Everyone said the missions were the easiest places in which to take the unemployed census. Take the mission in Doyers Street. It is where the Chinese Theatre used to be. You come into a large irregular room.

They hold the mission service where the Chinese actors used to play their interminable plays. Go down a flight of stairs. Here is an underground place. Toward one end, a counter, men in aprons behind it. This is where the men get their food. After that, after they have praised God with hymns, after the prayers, the beds stacked up high against bricked-in arches will be spread down in this space, which holds perhaps three hundred.

The line, before the men are fed, shuffles patiently in front of the census takers. One is a young girl in a raccoon coat, with a clear-cut profile. Her eyes are open with surprise. She has never seen anything like this before. She is embarrassed asking questions—name, age, where born, what trade? They file along, the men in the mission, a long shuffling line. A patient line. Weary feet, broken shoes, worn clothes, unshaven faces.

Very few young men in the missions now. The young men don't go in so much for religion. Many of them over forty, comparatively few under thirty. They crawl along, glad enough to answer the questions and get on. They shuffle along like men already accustomed to waiting, easing themselves on one foot, then on the other. After a couple of hours they get their handout.

A queer census. What happened to John Bentley, 29, house painter, born in Kansas of American parents, union member? Well, there was this depression in the building trades, and he heard of a job farther east. He had a job for a short time. Now here he is in the line. His face is clear-cut, English, with a long upper lip. The type of man who should be upstanding and brisk. His shoulders sag, his shoes are broken. Defeat and bitterness are in his expression. The slight defiance in his answers is of the man who dares you to ask him how he happened to come on a breadline. There are hundreds more with his story.

The beds are being spread out. The girl in the raccoon coat cries out, "My God, they're lying on the floor!" There are not beds enough for everyone. Enough handouts, enough free food of a kind "that don't stand by you," all the drifters will tell you. But not enough flops.

A group of some twenty well dressed people suddenly appears on the stairs. "Ladies and gentlemen," chants a guide, "this was one of the underground resorts of old Chinatown. This used to be the place where Chinatown came to hit the pipe. You would find white people and Chinese together sodden in opium dreams. Behind those bricked-in arches was where the plutocrats and the society people used to come to smoke their pipes in privacy. . . ."

"My Lord!" says the girl in the raccoon coat. *"Tourists!"*

The people from the sightseeing bus peer at the men rolling themselves in blankets. They peer at the bricked-in archways behind which in the old days "plutocrats and society women" supposedly came for an opium debauch. Then they go on.

The census is over. No one else will be allowed in tonight. They are taking care of all they can.

The groups of census takers go on from the mission to the speakeasies. In some of these there is a free lunch. Here, if you buy a drink, they let you stay and sleep on the sawdust or on a chair. In some of them there is a drink of free whiskey all around at midnight.

It is not hard to understand why a man would rather sleep in the filthy sawdust than at a mission or in that place of massed misery, the Municipal Lodging House—where there is a somewhat ghastly moment after a man has given up his clothes to be sterilized. After his shower, he stands naked, with all his other naked and miserable comrades, waiting for a nightshirt. The speakeasy, after all, has a touch of home about it, a place where a man can keep his personality, what there is of it.

A group of volunteer census takers meet, men and women. They have together accumulated a series of nightmare pictures of our civilization. They have seen where the men sleep and how inadequate the beds of New York are for the homeless. One social worker sums it up as he exclaims:

"It's a school for bums."

It is a school for bums—crawling breadlines—81,000 free meals daily. No certain place to sleep, no organized shelter.

If you want to know how to make a bum out of a workingman who has had trade, home, security and ambition taken from him, talk to any of the young fellows on the breadline who have been in town long enough to have become experienced in misery. Say a man in this town goes to the Municipal Lodging House for his first night. Until lately, he would have been routed out at five in the morning. Now he can stay until six. He is given breakfast, then he must leave, blizzard or rain. He can go next to a Salvation Army shelter for a handout, and get down to the City Free Employment Bureau before it opens. Or he can find shelter in subways and mark the Want Ads in a morning paper.

If he decides on the Employment Bureau, he is wise to arrive there before the doors open. He will find himself in the midst of a huge company which augments all the time until the opening of the doors. He may have spent two hours there—from nine to eleven. After that, he will not have eaten since his handout at seven at the Salvation Army, and he will have walked quite a lot. The next thing to do will be to put himself on some other breadline. It will take him one and a half or two hours to get his noonday meal.

In the afternoon there isn't very much use hunting jobs; yet there may be a chance at something; at some of the agencies, or perhaps by looking through the scanty Want Ads in the afternoon papers. There is a question then as to how and where to spend the rest of the time. If he has good enough clothes he can kill some time in the library. With discretion, hours can be spent in the terminals of stations. He can go to a museum. If he has a nickel, he can "ride the subways." But if he can panhandle some money, he can at least stay indoors in a speakeasy or Bowery hotel.

It will take him an hour and a half or two hours for his evening meal, and if he is going to the Municipal Lodging House again, he had best be early on the line.

Until recently the Municipal Lodging House was open only one night a month to non-residents and five nights to residents of New York. This restriction has now been removed. There are 3,300 people sleeping at the Municipal Lodging House, of which one hundred are women. The beds are full, and they are sleeping on benches, on the floor.

In the life of this drifting worker there is never any security. He is never sure where he is going to sleep. It is easy to learn to panhandle twenty-five or fifty cents for a night's flop. Between the agencies who help homeless men—the Salvation Army, Municipal lodging houses, the Y.M.C.A. and missions—there are not enough beds. Make a count of all the agencies, even including the new pier, which furnishes shelter for seven hundred more, and the Salvation Army boat that gives lodging to six hundred seamen, besides its other shelters. There is still a slack of thousands for whom there is no free accommodation at present in the city.

The present situation is indeed a school for bums. A thing to sap moral and physical strength. A situation which in a few weeks would make most employable men unemployable, and which puts a premium upon panhandling. It is the deadly frustration of each unsuccessful day of job hunting when, tired and footsore, a man again stands in the long gray queue of the breadline only to seek an uncertain shelter. It is astonishing how soon a newcomer learns the ropes, how quickly it spreads from mouth to mouth where food is better, where flops are to be had.

Usually when times are hard and people are out of work, Fifth Avenue and Broadway know nothing about it. This is the first time these streets have lost their glittering shine. The shabby, shifting, ebbing men out of work have taken it from them.

On a street corner near Fiftieth Street was a store which had been turned into a free restaurant for the unemployed. Well dressed young ladies were cutting sandwiches for all who wanted to come in and get one. In the middle of each table stood a pot of mustard. There were men with well brushed clothes, men who looked like old bums, young white-collar men, all engulfing enormous sandwiches, cheese spread with mustard—three sandwiches to a person and coffee.

There were men whose faces made a spot of yellow, famine color. They had been starving. The men eating behind the plate-glass windows of the corner store were being gaped at by a crowd. Outside two men discussed them.

"That's to keep 'em from riotin'; it's to keep 'em quiet that they're feedin' 'em," said a man who talked like a play by Upton Sinclair.

"Har! Ye talk like a radical," said a man with an English accent. "That's fir hadvertising that they're feedin' 'em, them's society girls in there."

"It's to keep 'em quiet, I say. If they didn't feed 'em, they'd come marchin' down to the markets. They'd break the windows and loot 'em and help 'emselves. An' what's to prevent 'em from takin' what they want? They's a million of 'em in the city; if they was to march they'd make a procession!"

What if they should march, one wonders—all of them. What if having had their census taken and their misery compiled, they should give an exhibition of their numbers? What then? Tear gas and clubs and arrests, no doubt.

There are other sides to the avalanche of despair. As a part of the widespread slump, the people who thought themselves secure have been thrown into it. The people who have been able to have a college education suddenly find themselves out of a job. No one can take the census of this misery. It doesn't walk the street. It sits and shivers in cold houses. It hides itself.

They hunt in vain for jobs. Or, if they have homes to go to, they return, defeated, to be dependent. Or perhaps, having no home to go to, these people, too, may slip gradually downhill where they must apply for charity.

And what about such people as a friend of mine told me of recently? She was working in one of the emergency employment bureaus on the East Side where daily men came to get the Prosser jobs which are now nonexistent. Daily the little crowd of people gathers outside and waits in vain.

I watched this flood of people who had been once well-to-do, judging by their clothing. People used to steady work, coming in vain with their stories of five children, no work, savings gone.

"It's not nearly as hard as the employment agency I used to work with in Queens," my friend told me. The first day she worked there, she went to nine houses, which had in each case been lost by the young people who were in the process of buying them. Here was a little suburban community where young people, many of them with college educations, had come to found homes, to live where their children could be brought up healthfully.

"There was something more desperate in Queens," my friend told me, "than there is on the East Side, where people are used to the idea of insecurity. The car goes first: the furniture goes; then the house goes; confidence in life goes."

Of the number of people losing their all, because they cannot raise a few dollars, there is no record as yet. Maybe there will never be. One can only generalize and say that the white-collar class is suffering today with the mechanic. The man who has spent thousands upon his education is no more secure than a laborer. The misery, doubt and defeat piles up, an incalculable mountain. There is no census yet of these.

Walter Lippmann
The New Imperative
(1935)

HERE IN this university there is performed the miracle which distinguishes civilized man from all the other animals. He can transmit from one generation to another the knowledge which he discovers, the skill which he acquires, the wisdom which he perceives. But though man has the faculty of tradition, it is an uncertain one. Oftener than not he has been unable to absorb and to transmit the vital essence of his tradition. Then he has fallen into dark ages when he has lost his inheritance, into dull ages when he is uninterested in it, and into ages of bewilderment when he cries out for it and cannot find it.

So the history of man is heavy with the tragedy of his unrealized possibilities. For had he been able to transmit the human heritage unimpaired in its full vitality from ancient times to the present day, so that no skill was lost and none of the lessons of experience forgotten, the compounded wisdom of mankind would have produced a civilization so splendid as to surpass our ability to imagine it.

But again and again the tradition of the good life has become dim and has been interrupted, and then it has had laboriously to be rediscovered and realized and learned once more.

I

We live in an age when men are dismayed because they feel that they have lost the tradition of the good life. They are acutely aware of the unrealized possibilities of human societies. The intellectual life of the western world is distracted, its spirit is impaired, by the paradoxes of poverty when there is plenty, of science triumphant in political disorder,

[The text is from Lippmann's Phi Beta Kappa speech at Sanders Theater, Harvard University, on 21 June 1935.]

of conscience become sensitive to human dignity in the midst of a re-version to the primitive. To these paradoxes men cannot become resigned. They can accept a fate which it is beyond their power to avert. They can endure pain and hardship and natural calamity. But they will not resign themselves to a failure which originates—so they must believe—in their own behavior and could be remedied by intelligence and courage and good will.

A civilization tormented by these paradoxes is sick, like the Roman world of which Lucretius said that it had a malady of which its masters did not know the cause. For us the point at which the malady is most ominous is when young men come asking us what tradition we possess by which they can confront this contradictory world. The older generation who sit in the seats of authority, and in the nature of things determine the answer, do not have an answer. They do not know what to say when they are asked what ideas they possess which offer the new generation valid purposes and noble duties. They are embarrassed at the question. Though they love their country and believe in it, they cannot put into words, because they do not have it in their minds, a conception of the American commonwealth in which the young men can find direction and meaning for their lives.

Thus we are unable to transmit from our generation to the next a credible and coherent tradition. This is our danger. The nation is secure against conquest. Its resources are ample. Its people are energetic and cheerful and brave. But those who determine what schools and colleges and the press shall transmit as the American tradition do not know what to tell the young men. There is a breach, which is threatening and sinister, between the energy of youth and the experience of age.

This new generation, to whom we can offer skill rather than wisdom and specialized knowledge without philosophy, is cheated and feels it is cheated if we do not know how to offer it a part in some great enterprise. For these men are young and they are not yet tired and they do not yet prefer comfort and security above all other things. They have courage unspoiled by the commitments of maturity and they have not lived until they have known a duty that transcends personal ambition. They must believe that they are needed. They must enter into an idea that will inform and transfigure their private worlds.

But they cannot find this idea in the teachings and the warnings of those who sit in the seats of authority. Some, therefore, have sought it, and believe they have found it, in the revolutionary fervors and alien faiths of central and eastern Europe. Others (and they are the great majority) go out into the world without political convictions. The consequences are ominous. For they mean that those who will rule the American commonwealth tomorrow are spiritually isolated from those

who rule it today. The fathers do not know what their sons will do with
the estate and so they cannot act in the present with the conviction of
permanence. The sons cannot prepare for the future with the enthusiasm
of loyalty. The circuits of tradition, by which purposes are transmitted
from one generation to another, are seriously interrupted.

This is the condition, which has preceded so many of the tragedies of
history, when the successful and the dominant live for the moment,
defensively, dreading the future and not daring to engage it, irresolute
because they have lost purpose and intention and the conviction of a great
destiny. When this happens, wisdom acquired through many ages is blown
about by all the winds of doctrine; then the government of the commonwealth is not in the hands of confident men.

II

The articulate belief of the industrial and financial leaders of America
is the doctrine of *laissez faire*. Though they recognize that government
has certain duties to perform, that it must defend the frontiers against
aggression, and domestic peace against violence, that it must provide
social services, such as education, that it must regulate many abuses, they
hold that it has no function to perform in governing the national economy
as a whole, either to maintain it in a working equilibrium or to see to it
that its products are well distributed. They insist that the vital balance
is automatically self-regulating and that deliberate policy in regard to it
is meddlesome, expensive, and subversive.

On the major issues of the modern world they believe in an ideal of
masterly inactivity. This is the ideal they would have the schools and
colleges profess. To the young men asking how they can serve their
country—how they can mitigate booms and depressions, maintain a healthy
relation between agriculture and industry, conserve and develop the natural resources, prevent the congestion of population and the concentration
of wealth and power, the orthodox answer must be that these matters are
not the concern of the state and that the only sound policy is to have no
policy.

It is perfectly true that this tradition has an honorable history. It has
served the country well for more than a hundred years. How is it, then,
that this conception of the commonwealth has lost its authority? It has
lost it, I believe, because those who preached this gospel do not practice
it. It is no longer the rule of their own conduct. They argue zealously
that the economy is automatically self-regulating—that the free play of
supply and demand will regulate the production and distribution of wealth
more efficiently than conscious and concerted management and administration. But they do not in fact apply this principle. Those who are most

insistent upon the ideal of *laissez faire* are the very men who by means of tariffs and combinations have organized the industrial life of the country into corporate systems subject to highly centralized control. In their articulate thinking they are free traders. In their actual practice they suspend the free play of supply and demand and substitute for it, whenever it is practicable to do so, the conscious management of production and the administrative determination of prices and wages. Not only that, but put to the acid test in the crisis which began in 1929, the party with which they are most in sympathy abandoned the whole ideal of *laissez faire* and organized what President Hoover described as "the most gigantic program of economic defense and counter attack ever evolved in the history of the Republic."

Is it astonishing that a doctrine which is not practiced should lack vitality and authority? Sermons on the danger of interfering with economic laws are somehow unimpressive when they are preached by men who in their own markets have suspended those laws. It is intellectually confusing to live in an age when the dominant tradition is so deeply at variance with the dominant practice. Yet if the inconsistency were merely theoretical, it might not greatly matter: nations get along very well in spite of many logical contradictions in their thinking. But this inconsistency has great practical consequences. For when the automatism of competition is suspended by big business, the automatism of the rest of the economy is radically impaired.

III

A social order flexibly competitive in all its parts, as the free traders of the nineteenth century imagined it, is theoretically conceivable and might be very attractive. It is an ideal which a modern state might consciously pursue, using all its powers against monopoly of any kind. But an economy which is automatic and inflexible in some of its parts, managed and inflexible in others, can be self-regulating only by subjecting its unorganized parts to an intolerable strain.

The doctrine of *laissez faire* is open to the devastating criticism that it is preached by men who wish other men to practice it. From such logical, moral, and practical confusion it is impossible to derive a whole tradition which will engage the enthusiasm of young men. They have perceived the humiliating paradoxes of our time. They have seen the glut of food while there is hunger in the land, homeless men and untenanted houses, idle men and unused machinery, stagnant money and desperate debtors, and when they ask those who speak with authority, What shall we do? they are told in substance that there is nothing to do. These things are beyond human control and the only wisdom is resignation. They are not even told to go West and start a new life. They are told to sit and wait, like Chinese coolies in a famine, until, for some mysterious reason, the warm blood of confidence rises once more in the veins of bank directors and corporation executives.

This is not a doctrine to inspire young men, especially American young men, the sons of pioneers and of immigrants and of those who dared to undertake great enterprises and to settle a continent. If you wish to know why the young men are tempted by communism, by fascism, by almost anything which is emphatic and bold and positive, this is the reason: those who sit in the seats of authority are preaching a gospel of frustration. If you wish to know why, in spite of all our schools and colleges, the level of competence in public life is low, this is the reason: we are not training men to govern; we are teaching them to believe that in great matters it is unnecessary to govern. If you wish to know why the political sciences are not a true discipline for the future guardians of our civilization, but are a haphazard collection of disconnected specialties, this is the reason: it is disreputable to hold and to declare a positive and coherent conception of the function of the state in a modern economy.

The basic question is not whether we ought to have state socialism, regimentation, inflation or a flexible and competitive economy. It is whether we can have any coherent and working economy by having no conscious policy, allowing those who are strong to escape automatism in their own efforts and to subject others to its intensified consequences. The truth is that in the modern state even a policy of *laissez faire* would have to be deliberately administered, the free play of supply and demand would have to be deliberately maintained. This would be my own deepest preference. I should rather have economic liberty than centralized direction and command. But if we are to have economic liberty we must accept the ancient truth that liberty is not the natural state of man, but the achievement of an organized society. Liberty is a right which only vigilant and wise government can provide. It is the artificial product of civilized effort and is lost almost instantly when the primitive passions of men are unleashed.

The association between liberty and the absence of purpose in government is merely a temporary coincidence due to the fact that in the nineteenth century the English-speaking peoples had an open frontier in America and a head start in the export of manufactures from England. The coincidence will not be repeated in this century. We have to govern the great interests of the commonwealth or we perish. We have to govern them or we lose our liberties. We have to teach young men to govern them or we shall not teach the young men their inescapable duty. But we cannot begin until we have said farewell to the assumption that Utopia is in the old American frontier and in the Lancashire of Cobden.

We cannot begin until we have renounced the illusion that in a world of highly organized national states, with gigantic corporate organizations within those states, the vital interests of the whole economy will be automatically self-regulating. We shall be utterly confused, we shall mumble and fumble when the young men examine us, we shall be defensive and impotent and without moral authority until we reconcile our philosophy with our practice.

The issue of automatism as against governing is obsolete. The real issue is not whether the major interests of the commonwealth shall be matters of conscious policy. It is what the policy shall be and by what means it shall be applied. I am not pleading that we indoctrinate young men with a belief that all social arrangements should be planned and directed by highly centralized government. Far from it. On that question I shall be in the ranks with those who think no government is wise enough or good enough to be trusted with so much power, with those who will fight as best they can for the utmost that is possible in decentralization and in voluntary agreement. But it is precisely because this great issue of the omnivorous state confronts us that it is so urgent to rid ourselves of the fictitious and distracting issues raised by the automatists with their program of know-nothing and do-nothing.

IV

For I hold that the transition from automatism to the deliberate government of the main elements of the modern economy is already so far advanced that it is impossible to retrace our steps. But I hold also that a historic transition of this kind can be effected safely only if those who have the experience to appreciate its difficulties participate sincerely in guiding the people. Does not the history of America and of Britain since the revolutionary period of the eighteenth century teach us that radical transitions in a nation's life are best carried through by conservative men?

If we are not to be swallowed by an imperious state socialism in some one of its many possible forms, then we have to govern successfully this capitalist democracy. Ungoverned, it will not drift through stormy seas into safe harbors. Those who say that it cannot be governed without sacrificing personal liberties to the authority of the state are in effect saying that our civilization is doomed. I do not believe them. They have never given the problem their undivided attention. They cannot see the way because they have not the will. They are like the men who once thought it sacrilegious to examine the constitution of the universe. Like those men they are able to learn little about the constitution of the universe. For the progress of scientific knowledge is the work of men who have believed that it was noble to seek for truth and possible to find it.

So it is with those who believe in the fatalism of human affairs and the impossibility of human intervention. It is imperative that we find a true balance between liberty and authority in the modern state. The fatalists do not find it today because they are not looking for it. They are afraid to look. They think it disreputable to look. They would like nobody to look. The only result of this obscurantism is to inhibit the minds of men from seizing and working upon a problem which historic necessity compels them to face.

We must answer the question that young men put to us. We must tell them that they will have to manage the social order. We must call them to the study, not warn them away from it, of how to achieve the healthy balance of a well ordered commonwealth. We must call them to the task of preserving the integrity of our civilization as against proletarianism and plutocracy and the fatal diseases of concentrated power and concentrated wealth. We must call them to the defense of freedom, now imperiled throughout the world, by showing them not only its value but the method of its defense. We must dedicate them by rededicating ourselves to the promise of American life which is that men can govern a state in order to enlarge and to preserve the rights of men.

Let us not rebuff them and thwart them and deny them by telling them please to be good enough to do nothing. Let us rather tell them the truth, that our civilization is in peril and that they have a great duty, a duty comparable in its grandeur with that of any generation that ever entered the arena of events. For theirs is the duty in an age when darkness is again setting in elsewhere, and the barbarians are again at the gates, to make invincible on this continent a commonwealth that invites the souls of men.

PART FOUR

IRONY IN AMERICAN LIFE

"next to of course god america i
love you land of the pilgrims' and so forth oh
say can you see by the dawn's early my
country 'tis of centuries come and go
and are no more what of it we should worry
in every language even deafanddumb
thy sons acclaim your glorious name by gorry
by jingo by gee by gosh by gum
why talk of beauty what could be more beautiful than these heroic happy dead
who rushed like lions to the roaring slaughter
they did not stop to think they died instead
then shall the voice of liberty be mute?"

He spoke. And drank rapidly a glass of water

next to of course god america i
E. E. Cummings (1926)

Two of the nation's Founders, Thomas Jefferson and John Adams, died only hours apart on 4 July 1826. In his 1975 poem "Great American Fourth of July Parade," Archibald MacLeish portrays them visiting a contemporary celebration of the signing of the Declaration of Independence. Jefferson and Adams listen to the poem's Orator, who delivers a patriotic pep talk. They also exchange views with his audience. Observing that Americans now seem to find Jefferson's philosophy too optimistic, Adams nonetheless concludes with the final words he uttered on his deathbed a century and a half before: "Jefferson still lives." On that day in 1826, Adams's proposition was literally false; it was and still is figuratively true, however. But if Americans retain hopeful outlooks, their current mood may contrast with the bombast of MacLeish's Orator, which at one point becomes an hysterical yell: "The U.S.A. is Number One!"

The reasons for that contrast have much to do with an increased awareness that America's ebullient sense of possibility promised more than it ever could deliver. Within the consequent disillusionment, moreover, there is a double sense of irony. On the one hand, Americans were doomed to disappointment precisely because so many found that this was indeed a land of opportunity; on the other, those same successes conspired with the natural limitations of human finitude to restrict equal access to opportunity. Acting on the premise that there are unalienable rights to life, liberty, and the pursuit of happiness, Americans have undercut their own dreams by honoring self-interest at the expense of the commonwealth. The land reflects that heritage.

Once, the West was fabled but yet unexplored; America was a young country, with such a vast expanse of fertile open space and time before it that an infinite number of new starts was conceivable. America is no longer young and never will be again; its open space is mostly taken, its vaunted natural plenitude clearly finite, its reputation as the land of opportunity suspect both at home and abroad. Once, America prided itself on the freedom of its individuals and on the nation's freedom from foreign entanglements; after all, Europe was an ocean away and Americans had done with it. Now things are different: the individual's freedom to be "a simple, separate person" seems increasingly hamstrung by a bureaucratically regulated order, the nation as a whole entangled with every other nation in the world. Once America was innocent enough to dream that it could not only control its own destiny but that the rest of the world would emulate its brand of democracy. Today that destiny is far from manifest, and yet the truth remains: Jefferson still lives. He does so in particular because he wrote and believed a proposition destined to be as inspiring as it was ambiguous, as troublesome as American practices rendered it ironic: "All men are created equal."

SOME DREAMS DEFERRED: COLOR AND GENDER

The black sociologist W. E. B. Du Bois (1868–1963) believed that "the problem of the Twentieth Century is the problem of the color line." He stated that conviction in *The Souls of Black Folk*, which utilizes an image of "the Veil" to designate the racial barrier that has separated whites and blacks on American ground. The Veil is no stone wall. Contact occurs among those it hangs between. But it also effects separation, thus leading Du Bois to remind Frederick Jackson Turner that "America is not another word for Opportunity to *all* her sons." Yet, like the brothers and sisters for whom he spoke, Du Bois claimed equality of opportunity as his American birthright. Indeed because his reading of Thomas Jefferson would not let him settle for less, Du Bois found himself at odds with the most formidable black leader of the day, Booker T. Washington.

Washington's philosophy concerning relations between blacks and whites was that "in all things that are purely social we can be as separate as the fingers, yet one as the hand in all things essential to mutual progress." Du Bois found that dictum unacceptable, for where did the category "purely social" begin and end? Separate and equal, as the Supreme Court would concur a half century later, were not justly compatible terms. Refusing to settle for the strategies of accommodation, Du Bois discovered how impenetrable the American Veil of race could be. Thus, he concluded his early book with a chapter on the Sorrow Songs, referring to many of the spirituals that still influence American music, religion, and politics. They sing about exile, poverty, flight and freedom, strife, and death. But those themes are the beginning, not the end. For "through all the sorrow of the Sorrow Songs," Du Bois writes, "there breathes a hope—a faith in the ultimate justice of things." Du Bois's meditation proceeds to ask whether that hope is justified, whether the Sorrow Songs sing true. His answer, however, had been given before the asking. It is found in Du Bois's protesting grief over his son's untimely death. His little boy might have seen the Veil lifted, although Du Bois understood the chance was slim. Refusal to settle for that outcome, however, ultimately shines through: "Surely," he protests, "surely this is not the end. Surely there shall yet dawn some mighty morning to lift the Veil and set the prisoned free . . . a morning when men ask of the workman, not 'Is he white?' but 'Can he work?' When men ask artists, not 'Are they black?' but 'Do they know?' " If Du Bois's "surely" has not been disproven, neither has it been fully confirmed.

Experiencing the ironic gap between what America offered and what its black citizens received, Du Bois contended with "a dream deferred." That phrase was deftly coined by the black poet Langston Hughes (1902–1967). "America," he wrote in 1938, "never was America to me, / And yet I swear this oath— / America will be!" Like Du Bois, Hughes knew the Sorrow Songs—he heard them Harlem-style in the black jazz riffs and blues that inspired his verse. Du Bois had told his white readers how discouraging it was for blacks to live "haunted by the ghost of an untrue dream." Hughes did not forsake his vow—"America will be!"—but by 1951 he had to ask, "What happens to a dream deferred?" Hughes's response, steeped in an anger frustrated, impatient, and yet hopeful all at once, supplied the unsettling correction. A dream deferred, Hughes warned, well might explode.

Hughes's premonition hit the target. By mid-century the struggle for racial equality heated up, erupting violently across the land—in Newark, Detroit, Watts, and elsewhere—during the 1960s. Early on Hughes had identified some of the reasons. Then and now, an American dream deferred will keep the have-nots tantalized with hope. Still seeking what they do not possess, "a certain amount of nothing" makes their self-determination impotent because the powers insist on asking not "Can he work?" or "Does she know?" but "Are they white?" If all men, however, are created equal and granted certain unalienable rights by God, including those to life, liberty, and the pursuit of happiness, such results are bound to cause confusion. The confusion they breed, moreover, teeters between despair and rage. Either is more than sufficient to unleash violence.

"There comes a time when the cup of endurance runs over, and men are no longer willing to be plunged into the abyss of despair." Those words were written in a Birmingham jail cell by Martin Luther King, Jr. (1929–1968). King was not opposed to letting "a dream deferred" explode. But that explosion, he counseled, must be governed neither by despair nor by rage. It had to clear a path of resistance that would heal, not deepen, the wounds of inequality. The time was ripe to take self-conscious, self-controlled action to make America live the meaning of its creed. So King rejected the view that he was pressing too hard and fast for fundamental changes in American life. "Wait," the code word for "never," meant "a dream deferred." That painful realization, King went on to say, contained an unforgettable lesson: "Freedom is never voluntarily given by the oppressor; it must be demanded by the oppressed."

King's campaigns of nonviolent resistance succeeded in rending part of the Veil of race in the United States, but his hopes, too, remained in part "a dream deferred." As King himself predicted, he never got to the promised land. An assassin's bullet in Memphis saw to that. In the longer run, however, everything depends on whether King, despite his realistic views of what happens when human nature is infested with racism, was still too optimistic. For in spite of his tough appraisal that those holding privileges established by the color line never give up their prerogatives easily, King proclaimed that "I still have a dream." America's "hard-won heritage of freedom," he believed, "is ultimately more powerful than our traditions of cruelty and injustice." Hence justice shall prevail here. Thus far events have not proved King completely correct, but will King's confidence yet be justified? Will American ground, "from every mountainside, let freedom ring"? Final answers to those questions are ironically deferred because they cannot be written in black and white alone.

The Veil of race is woven of many multicolored strands. Nor does the complexity end with skin color and race alone. American ground is peopled by Asians and Latinos of diverse traditions, Middle Eastern Arabs and Jews of varied persuasions, as well as by the multiple Native American cultures that were here long before the hordes of ethnically different European whites and African blacks arrived. The variety of heritage and life style in America has often been celebrated in the United States, but ironically it makes living together harder for Americans, not easier. One reason is that these domestic relationships, which are never very far removed from the color line, have international implications. Americans see each other, not to mention their country as a whole, in foreign affairs. American foreign policy is influenced by ethnic coalitions and rivalries within the nation's borders. Such factors would be more than enough to guarantee that the tranquility promised by the American Constitution is much more to be wished for than to be taken for granted. Yet no current appraisal of the state of the Union could begin to be complete if it ignored the fact that Americans are divided not only by color, race, and ethnicity but also by that most fundamental, natural difference of all, the one between male and female. Here, too, there are various rivalries and coalitions, all of them affected by the cultural particularity of their constituents. The resulting stew is bubbling not in a melting pot but in a pressure cooker, suggesting that Thomas Wolfe saw the situation clearly in his 1940 novel *You Can't Go Home Again*. The "true discovery of America," wrote Wolfe, "is before us." The problem is that his predictive judgment may turn out to be more ironic than inspiring.

A century and a half after Tocqueville took the pulse of democracy in the United States, Studs Terkel (1912–   ) made his own survey of American ground. Earlier, in *Working* he had appraised American attitudes toward work; this time his project broadened to assay *American Dreams: Lost and Found*. Reporting Terkel's interviews with men and women—young and old, from diverse geographical regions, economic classes, and ethnic backgrounds, but each thoroughly American—the book displays what some contemporaries think about their homeland and its future. Three samples further illustrate the irony in American experience.

Seattle residents Aki and Jun Kurose, both American citizens, are *Nisei*, second-generation Japanese immigrants. Their civil rights were violated by internment in an American concentration camp during World War II; that experience is not the only one that has taught them how far the Veil of race extends. Presently a schoolteacher, Aki Kurose once asked whether her school's library could get some books about Japanese-American history. The librarian's not-so-innocent response was a question: "Why do you have to bring up the past?"

Ramona Bennett, a Puyallup Indian, helps Mrs. Kurose supply the answer. For they concur that the history officially packaged for American schools is still white-male dominated. It obscures what most needs honest illumination, and, ironically, too few are the wiser. Take, for example, violated treaties. Trusting Puyallups accepted reservation status from the United States government. In Bennett's experience, however, reservation never meant preservation. The government persuaded people that its encroachments were at least virtuous necessities, if not obviously warranted rights. Stripped of its irony, "What happened," dissents Ramona Bennett simply, "is we had land the whites wanted."

Land, Stephen Cruz might add, is not all they wanted. His grandparents entered the United States when, as he puts it, "controls at the border didn't exist as they do now." Their grandson did well—graduated college with a degree in engineering ("where the bucks were" in the early sixties), then did graduate work in business. He got fourteen job offers, took the one from Procter & Gamble and was on his way. Irony and, with his recognition of it, ambivalence began to intrude. How much did his advancement have to do with his abilities and how much did it have to do with his being "a minority"? No hypocrite, Cruz did not deplore the Civil Rights Acts that were raising his chances. He just was not sure whether his own success reflected a real change of spirit in America or whether it was an indication that the letter of the law was being fulfilled so that white domination could be maintained. "Every time I turned around," he told Terkel, "America seemed to be treating me very well." Admitting that he felt a real internal conflict between the temptations of financial gain and the lure of integrity, Cruz eventually decided that America was treating him a little too well for his or the nation's good. Finding that established power conferred so much on him but so little on others who were on the wrong side of the color line, the young man concluded that his success, unfortunately, was symptomatic that America is ruled by the fear of losing. Convinced that "a counterpower is needed," Cruz set aside his corporate image and became a teacher.

Adrienne Rich (1929–   ), ardent feminist poet, scans similar terrain "From an Old House in America" but views it differently. She likens the body of a pioneer American woman to "a hollow ship bearing sons to the wilderness . . . daughters whose juices drain like mine into the *arroyo* of stillbirths, massacres." The nation has not treated its women too well, at least not enough of them. If Du Bois was correct to dissent from Turner—America has not been "another word for Opportunity to *all* her sons"—his indictment rings even truer for their sisters, mothers, and daughters. The domestic "separation of powers," Rich contends, left American women in a lonely, "savagely fathered" land where they got more than their fair share of suffering, less than their equitable portion of satisfaction. Rich's poem, however, is no man-hating recital of complaint and resentment. It celebrates the resourceful endurance of American women, the know-how and determination embodied in and borne through "the frontier woman leveling her rifle along the homestead fence." Urging the American woman, and by implication all Americans, to "come to terms with the women in the mirror," Rich hopes they will activate untapped power to soften, if not to erase, the lines that divide so much, so needlessly and destructively. To the extent that they do, "we are in the open, on our way." Like that of many others represented in these pages, Rich's faith in the future shows that her "Old House" has foundations deep in American ground. Whether they stand on solid rock or on shifting sand, however, remains undetermined. The land is still in the making.

WHERE HAVE WE BEEN? WHERE ARE WE GOING?

Late at night on Saturday, 21 May 1927, Charles A. Lindbergh and "The Spirit of St. Louis" touched down at Le Bourget, bringing his solo New York-to-Paris flight to a successful conclusion. Transatlantic radio broadcast his landing and excited reception. The trip's significance, moreover, was not missed by American ministers who preached the next day. A typical expression of the sermonic rhetoric that Sunday belonged to Dr. Russell Bowie of Grace Episcopal Church in New York City, who testified that Lindbergh "manifested the indomitable heroism which, whether . . . in victory or defeat, has made possible the progress of the human race toward the mastery of its world."

On that same Sunday morning, far to the west of Paris and New York, another Christian pastor, Reinhold Niebuhr (1892–1971) preached to his congregation. Undoubtedly that predominantly blue-collar church in Detroit got a message different from Russell Bowie's, for Niebuhr's outlook was sterner. For example, about the time of Lindbergh's flight, Niebuhr entered these words in his diary, which is now a book entitled *Leaves from the Notebook of a Tamed Cynic*: "I wish that some of our romanticists and sentimentalists could sit through a series of meetings where the real social problems of the city are discussed. They would be cured of their optimism. A city which is built around a productive process and which gives only casual thought and incidental attention to human problems is really a kind of hell. Thousands in this town are living in torment while the rest of us eat, drink, and make merry. What a civilization!"

Soon Niebuhr left Detroit behind, though never his heartfelt concern for its people and their problems, to begin forty years in New York as a writer and teacher. His career would mark him as one of the greatest Protestant theologians of the twentieth century and as one of the most perceptive and influential social theorists the United States has yet produced. Believing that "the powers of human self-deception are seemingly endless," especially insofar as people think they can make history conform to their hearts' desires, it cannot be surprising that one of Niebuhr's best books is *The Irony of American History*. It focuses on the Soviet-American "Cold War" that loomed so large at midcentury, but Niebuhr's historical awareness lent the book a wide-ranging scope that gives even the temporal particulars of his account a lasting relevance.

Undergirding his interpretation of American experience were at least two premises especially important for grasping his philosophy of irony. First, he believed, human beings are infected by *original sin*. Niebuhr's understanding of that admittedly old-fashioned notion, however, was very much down to earth, even commonsensical, for he located its significance in "the obvious fact that all men are persistently inclined to regard themselves more highly and are more assiduously concerned with their own interests than any 'objective' view of their importance would warrant." Second, he found the American version of this original sin to be located in the nation's presumption that its ways not only represent a clean break from a corrupted past but also that they remain so fundamentally innocent and virtuous that they could rightly be identified with God's will for the world. As Niebuhr saw them, the facts suggested an alternative view. "The irony of our situation," he argued, "lies in the fact that we could not be virtuous (in the sense of practicing the virtues which are implicit in meeting our vast world responsibilities) if we were really as innocent as we pretend to be."

American ground spawns power. Such might, Niebuhr affirmed, is never won, used, or even lost innocently. American ground, however, is riddled with irony when people persuade themselves differently. To make this case, Niebuhr distinguished irony from *pathos* and *tragedy*. Pathos resides in unmerited suffering that results from events in which none of the agents involved can rightly be held responsible or guilty. Its clearest examples are found in the pain and grief brought on by nature's fury in earthquakes or tornados. Tragedy arises from conflict of another kind. The many claims life makes are not always harmonious. One good must sometimes be sacrificed for another, but even more unfortunate is the fact that life so often involves what Niebuhr called "conscious choices of evil for the sake of good." Such choices are the essence of tragedy. By contrast with both pathos and tragedy, irony dwells in gaps between intention and consequence that yawn neither by accident nor by conscious design alone.

Niebuhr's point was not that American life lacks pathos or tragedy, or even, for that matter, an abundance of blatant wrongdoing. But neither did Niebuhr think that the United States is the most corrupt nation on earth. Just the opposite is closer to the truth, and therefore he anguished over the peculiar degree to which Americans wreak havoc in the world and upon each other because they know themselves insufficiently. Niebuhr tried to show Americans that their virtues contain hidden defects, that their nation's strength is weak just to the extent that the nation is vain, that its yearnings for security will breed insecurity if they go too far, that America's considerable wisdom may be reduced to folly unless limits are better recognized. Grandiose pretension, excessive pride, and unwarranted self-righteousness—these perennial idols were the objects of Niebuhr's criticism. He wanted Americans, not to their sorrow but before it became too late, to learn that their reach may exceed their grasp. Yet he recognized one irony more, namely, that such disillusionment has no foregone conclusion. It "either must lead," he warned, "to an abatement of the pretension, which means contrition; or it leads to a desperate accentuation of the vanities to the point where irony turns into pure evil." In a nuclear age, Niebuhr's ultimate "either/or" is especially harsh, for it portends apocalypse if Americans fail to mend their ways. But even if they do, Niebuhr would be the first to admit, such action may not be enough. For the United States is not the only responsible party or even the one most likely to bring about the end. The United States cannot save the world or even itself singlehandedly. That was one of Niebuhr's fundamental points. Yet his critique was offered with a hopeful expectation that looked for Americans to do their best.

Stylistically, Niebuhr's *Irony in American History* is a far cry from the "beat generation" poetry of Lawrence Ferlinghetti's "I Am Waiting." Their ways of life contrasted, too. Unlike Niebuhr, Ferlinghetti (1919–   ) could find no home in the traditional religions of his native land, hence turned to Buddhism. Niebuhr worked in the East, primarily the Boston-New York-Washington corridor where he hobnobbed with the political leaders who sought his advice and consent. Meanwhile Ferlinghetti explored the West, leading a rebellious literary movement from his haunts in San Francisco. He wanted to free people from the conventions of business-as-usual, replete with their suburban trappings and political power plays. Indeed, Ferlinghetti might have seen Reinhold Niebuhr as part of the problem, not of the solution, for in the 1950s Niebuhr was engaged in helping to construct some of the political strategies that became central targets of the so-called "Beatniks." Niebuhr, on the other hand, would not have approved of Ferlinghetti altogether, more than likely finding him politically naive, too much the innocent. Their writings, though, identify them much more as brothers than either might have realized. At the very least, they are kindred spirits in wanting America to wake up. They both love the land and its people.

Niebuhr wrote about irony. In "I Am Waiting," Ferlinghetti uses it— wistfully, humorously, sardonically. He wants to cross "the Great Divide" of incongruity between what America is and what it ought to be. Anticipating the arrival of "a reconstructed Mayflower," he also watches "for the day / that maketh all things clear." Ferlinghetti's expectation, however, is anything but passive nonactivity. Restless and insistent, "I Am Waiting" is paradoxically a pilgrimage, an odyssey of self-discovery in verses beating with hope that the atomic tests shall end, willing for things to get worse if eventually they do get better. Some would say those desires are futile, like expecting "the fleeing lovers on the Grecian Urn / to catch each other up at last / and embrace." Ferlinghetti rejects such realism. He concludes by "awaiting / perpetually and forever / a renaissance of wonder." Such wonder can help Americans arrive where his poem begins: looking within "for someone / to really discover America / and wail. . . ."

To wail Ferlinghetti-style is not to yell hysterically "The U.S.A. is Number One." Nor is it to intone the gaggle of vacuous clichés and pious platitudes that rush so thoughtlessly from the mouth of E. E. Cummings's 1926 counterpart to MacLeish's Orator. Cummings (1894–1962) does not make explicit the occasion for the banalities uttered by his speaker in "next to of course god america i." Memorial Day or Veterans' Day, however, seems more likely than the Fourth of July, for this poem is an ironic tribute to those "who rushed like lions to the roaring slaughter." Himself a veteran of World War I, Cummings sets forth the incoherence of a patriotism that sends a nation's youth to die and then compounds the waste by claiming that nothing "could be more beautiful than these heroic happy dead." Such blindness is a reason to lament and grieve, and Ferlinghetti joins Cummings in doing both. But that wailing is not the end. Unmasking the pretense, hurting through the pathos, tragedy, and irony, they pair to wail a jazz duet that soars beyond the blues and the Sorrow Songs, yearning "for the American Eagle / to really spread its wings / and straighten up and fly right." If that is where we are going, then where we have been has its virtues, too.

SOME DREAMS DEFERRED: COLOR AND GENDER

William Edward Burghardt Du Bois
The Souls of Black Folk
(1903)

THE FORETHOUGHT

HEREIN LIE buried many things which if read with patience may show the strange meaning of being black here at the dawning of the Twentieth Century. This meaning is not without interest to you, Gentle Reader; for the problem of the Twentieth Century is the problem of the color line. . . .

I have sought here to sketch, in vague, uncertain outline, the spiritual world in which ten thousand thousand Americans live and strive. . . . I have stepped within the Veil, raising it that you may view faintly its deeper recesses,—the meaning of its religion, the passion of its human sorrow, and the struggle of its greater souls. . . . I have ended with a chapter of song. . . .

Before each chapter . . . stands a bar of the Sorrow Songs,—some echo of haunting melody from the only American music which welled up from black souls in the dark past. And, finally, need I add that I who speak here am bone of the bone and flesh of the flesh of them that live within the Veil?

OF OUR SPIRITUAL STRIVINGS

Between me and the other world there is ever an unasked question: unasked by some through feelings of delicacy; by others through the difficulty of rightly framing it. All, nevertheless, flutter round it. They approach me in a half-hesitant sort of way, eye me curiously or compassionately, and then, instead of saying directly, How does it feel to be a problem? they say, I know an excellent colored man in my town; or, I fought at Mechanicsville; or, Do not these Southern outrages make your blood boil? At these I smile, or am interested, or reduce the boiling to a simmer, as the occasion may require. To the real question, How does it feel to be a problem? I answer seldom a word.

And yet, being a problem is a strange experience,—peculiar even for one who has never been anything else, save perhaps in babyhood and in Europe. It is in the early days of rollicking boyhood that the revelation first bursts upon one, all in a day, as it were. I remember well when the shadow swept across me. I was a little thing, away up in the hills of New England, where the dark Housatonic winds between Hoosac and Taghkanic to the sea. In a wee wooden schoolhouse, something put it into the boys' and girls' heads to buy gorgeous visiting-cards—ten cents a package—and exchange. The exchange was merry, till one girl, a tall newcomer, refused my card,—refused it peremptorily, with a glance. Then it dawned upon me with a certain suddenness that I was different from the others; or like, mayhap, in heart and life and longing, but shut out from their world by a vast veil. I had thereafter no desire to tear down that veil, to creep through; I held all beyond it in common contempt, and lived above it in a region of blue sky and great wandering shadows. That sky was bluest when I could beat my mates at examination-time, or beat them at a foot-race, or even beat their stringy heads. Alas, with the years all this fine contempt began to fade; for the worlds I longed for, and all their dazzling opportunities, were theirs, not mine. But they should not keep these prizes, I said; some, all, I would wrest from them. Just how I would do it I could never decide: by reading law, by healing the sick, by telling the wonderful tales that swam in my head,—some way. With other black boys the strife was not so fiercely sunny: their youth shrunk into tasteless sycophancy, or into silent hatred of the pale world about them and mocking distrust of everything white; or wasted itself in a bitter cry, Why did God make me an outcast and a stranger in mine own house? The shades of the prison-house closed round about us all: walls strait and stubborn to the whitest, but relentlessly narrow, tall, and unscalable to sons of night who must plod darkly on in resignation, or beat unavailing palms against the stone, or steadily, half hopelessly, watch the streak of blue above.

After the Egyptian and Indian, the Greek and Roman, the Teuton and Mongolian, the Negro is a sort of seventh son, born with a veil, and gifted with second-sight in this American world,—a world which yields him no

true self-consciousness, but only lets him see himself through the revelation of the other world. It is a peculiar sensation, this double-consciousness, this sense of always looking at one's self through the eyes of others,
of measuring one's soul by the tape of a world that looks on in amused
contempt and pity. One ever feels his twoness,—an American, a Negro;
two souls, two thoughts, two unreconciled strivings; two warring ideals
in one dark body, whose dogged strength alone keeps it from being torn
asunder.

The history of the American Negro is the history of this strife,—this
longing to attain self-conscious manhood, to merge his double self into a
better and truer self. In this merging he wishes neither of the older selves
to be lost. He would not Africanize America, for America has too much
to teach the world and Africa. He would not bleach his Negro soul in a
flood of white Americanism, for he knows that Negro blood has a message
for the world. He simply wishes to make it possible for a man to be both
a Negro and an American, without being cursed and spit upon by his
fellows, without having the doors of Opportunity closed roughly in his
face. . . .

OF THE PASSING OF THE FIRST-BORN

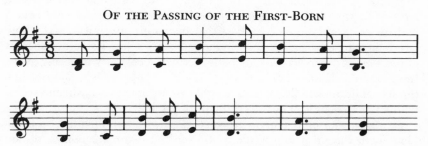

"Unto you a child is born," sang the bit of yellow paper that fluttered
into my room one brown October morning. Then the fear of fatherhood
mingled wildly with the joy of creation; I wondered how it looked and
how it felt,—what were its eyes, and how its hair curled and crumpled
itself. And I thought in awe of her,—she who had slept with Death to
tear a man-child from underneath her heart, while I was unconsciously
wandering. I fled to my wife and child, repeating the while to myself half
wonderingly, "Wife and child? Wife and child?"—fled fast and faster than
boat and steam-car, and yet must ever impatiently await them; away from
the hard-voiced city, away from the flickering sea into my own Berkshire
Hills that sit all sadly guarding the gates of Massachusetts.

Up the stairs I ran to the wan mother and whimpering babe, to the
sanctuary on whose altar a life at my bidding had offered itself to win a
life, and won. What is this tiny formless thing, this newborn wail from

an unknown world,—all head and voice? I handle it curiously, and watch perplexed its winking, breathing, and sneezing. I did not love it then; it seemed a ludicrous thing to love; but her I loved, my girl-mother, she whom now I saw unfolding like the glory of the morning—the transfigured woman. Through her I came to love the wee thing, as it grew strong; as its little soul unfolded itself in twitter and cry and half-formed word, and as its eyes caught the gleam and flash of life. How beautiful he was, with his olive-tinted flesh and dark gold ringlets, his eyes of mingled blue and brown, his perfect little limbs, and the soft voluptuous roll which the blood of Africa had moulded into his features! I held him in my arms, after we had sped far away to our Southern home,—held him, and glanced at the hot red soil of Georgia and the breathless city of a hundred hills, and felt a vague unrest. Why was his hair tinted with gold? An evil omen was golden hair in my life. Why had not the brown of his eyes crushed out and killed the blue?—for brown were his father's eyes, and his father's father's. And thus in the Land of the Color-line I saw, as it fell across my baby, the shadow of the Veil.

Within the Veil was he born, said I; and there within shall he live,— a Negro and a Negro's son. Holding in that little head—ah, bitterly!— the unbowed pride of a hunted race, clinging with that tiny dimpled hand—ah, wearily!—to a hope not hopeless but unhopeful, and seeing with those bright wondering eyes that peer into my soul a land whose freedom is to us a mockery and whose liberty a lie. I saw the shadow of the Veil as it passed over my baby, I saw the cold city towering above the blood-red land. I held my face beside his little cheek, showed him the star-children and the twinkling lights as they began to flash, and stilled with an even-song the unvoiced terror of my life.

So sturdy and masterful he grew, so filled with bubbling life, so tremulous with the unspoken wisdom of a life but eighteen months distant from the All-life,—we were not far from worshipping this revelation of the divine, my wife and I. Her own life builded and moulded itself upon the child; he tinged her every dream and idealized her every effort. No hands but hers must touch and garnish those little limbs; no dress or frill must touch them that had not wearied her fingers; no voice but hers could coax him off to Dreamland, and she and he together spoke some soft and unknown tongue and in it held communion. I too mused above his little white bed; saw the strength of my own arm stretched onward through the ages through the newer strength of his; saw the dream of my black fathers stagger a step onward in the wild phantasm of the world; heard in his baby voice the voice of the Prophet that was to rise within the Veil.

And so we dreamed and loved and planned by fall and winter, and the full flush of the long Southern spring, till the hot winds rolled from the fetid Gulf, till the roses shivered and the still stern sun quivered its awful light over the hills of Atlanta. And then one night the little feet pattered wearily to the wee white bed, and the tiny hands trembled; and a warm flushed face tossed on the pillow, and we knew baby was sick. Ten days he lay there,—a swift week and three endless days, wasting, wasting away. Cheerily the mother nursed him the first days, and laughed into the little eyes that smiled again. Tenderly then she hovered round him, till the smile fled away and Fear crouched beside the little bed.

Then the day ended not, and night was a dreamless terror, and joy and sleep slipped away. I hear now that Voice at midnight calling me from dull and dreamless trance,—crying, "The Shadow of Death! The Shadow of Death!" Out into the starlight I crept, to rouse the gray physician,—the Shadow of Death, the Shadow of Death. The hours trembled on; the night listened; the ghastly dawn glided like a tired thing across the lamplight. Then we two alone looked upon the child as he turned toward us with great eyes, and stretched his stringlike hands,—the Shadow of Death! And we spoke no word, and turned away.

He died at eventide, when the sun lay like a brooding sorrow above the western hills, veiling its face; when the winds spoke not, and the trees, the great green trees he loved, stood motionless. I saw his breath beat quicker and quicker, pause, and then his little soul leapt like a star that travels in the night and left a world of darkness in its train. The day changed not; the same tall trees peeped in at the windows, the same green grass glinted in the setting sun. Only in the chamber of death writhed the world's most piteous thing—a childless mother.

I shirk not. I long for work. I pant for a life full of striving. I am no coward, to shrink before the rugged rush of the storm, nor even quail before the awful shadow of the Veil. But hearken, O Death! Is not this my life hard enough,—is not that dull land that stretches its sneering web about me cold enough,—is not all the world beyond these four little walls pitiless enough, but that thou must needs enter here,—thou, O Death? About my head the thundering storm beat like a heartless voice, and the crazy forest pulsed with the curses of the weak; but what cared I, within my home beside my wife and baby boy? Wast thou so jealous of one little coign of happiness that thou must needs enter there,—thou, O Death?

A perfect life was his, all joy and love, with tears to make it brighter,— sweet as a summer's day beside the Housatonic. The world loved him; the women kissed his curls, the men looked gravely into his wonderful eyes, and the children hovered and fluttered about him. I can see him now, changing like the sky from sparkling laughter to darkening frowns, and then to wondering thoughtfulness as he watched the world. He knew no color-line, poor dear,—and the Veil, though it shadowed him, had not yet darkened half his sun. He loved the white matron, he loved his black nurse; and in his little world walked souls alone, uncolored and unclothed. I—yea, all men—are larger and purer by the infinite breadth of that one little life. She who in simple clearness of vision sees beyond the stars said when he had flown, "He will be happy There; he ever loved beautiful things." And I, far more ignorant, and blind by the web of mine own weaving, sit alone winding words and muttering, "If still he be, and he be There, and there be a There, let him be happy, O Fate!"

Blithe was the morning of his burial, with bird and song and sweet-smelling flowers. The trees whispered to the grass, but the children sat with hushed faces. And yet it seemed a ghostly unreal day,—the wraith of Life. We seemed to rumble down an unknown street behind a little white bundle of posies, with the shadow of a song in our ears. The busy city dinned about us; they did not say much, those pale-faced hurrying men and women; they did not say much,—they only glanced and said, "Niggers!"

We could not lay him in the ground there in Georgia, for the earth there is strangely red; so we bore him away to the northward, with his flowers and his little folded hands. In vain, in vain!—for where, O God! beneath thy broad blue sky shall my dark baby rest in peace,—where Reverence dwells, and Goodness, and a Freedom that is free?

All that day and all that night there sat an awful gladness in my heart,— nay, blame me not if I see the world thus darkly through the Veil,—and my soul whispers ever to me, saying, "Not dead, not dead, but escaped; not bond, but free." No bitter meanness now shall sicken his baby heart till it die a living death, no taunt shall madden his happy boyhood. Fool that I was to think or wish that this little soul should grow choked and deformed within the Veil! I might have known that yonder deep unworldly look that ever and anon floated past his eyes was peering far beyond this narrow Now. In the poise of his little curl-crowned head did there not sit all that wild pride of being which his father had hardly crushed in his own heart? For what, forsooth, shall a Negro want with pride amid the studied humiliations of fifty million fellows? Well sped, my boy, before the world had dubbed your ambition insolence, had held your ideals unattainable, and taught you to cringe and bow. Better far this nameless void that stops my life than a sea of sorrow for you.

Idle words; he might have borne his burden more bravely than we,— aye, and found it lighter too, some day; for surely, surely this is not the end. Surely there shall yet dawn some mighty morning to lift the Veil and set the prisoned free. Not for me,—I shall die in my bonds,—but for fresh young souls who have not known the night and waken to the morning; a morning when men ask of the workman, not "Is he white?" but "Can he work?" When men ask artists, not "Are they black?" but

"Do they know?" Some morning this may be, long, long years to come. But now there wails, on that dark shore within the Veil, the same deep voice, *Thou shalt forgo!* And all have I forgone at that command, and with small complaint,—all save that fair young form that lies so coldly wed with death in the nest I had builded.

If one must have gone, why not I? Why may I not rest me from this restlessness and sleep from this wide waking? Was not the world's alembic, Time, in his young hands, and is not my time waning? Are there so many workers in the vineyard that the fair promise of this little body could lightly be tossed away? The wretched of my race that line the alleys of the nation sit fatherless and unmothered; but Love sat beside his cradle, and in his ear Wisdom waited to speak. Perhaps now he knows the All-love, and needs not to be wise. Sleep, then, child,—sleep till I sleep and waken to a baby voice and the ceaseless patter of little feet—above the Veil.

OF THE SORROW SONGS

> I walk through the churchyard
>   To lay this body down;
> I know moon-rise, I know star-rise;
> I walk in the moonlight, I walk in the starlight;
> I'll lie in the grave and stretch out my arms,
> I'll go to judgment in the evening of the day,
> And my soul and thy soul shall meet that day,
>   When I lay this body down.
>   —*Negro Song.*

They that walked in darkness sang songs in the olden days—Sorrow Songs—for they were weary at heart. And so before each thought that I have written in this book I have set a phrase, a haunting echo of these weird old songs in which the soul of the black slave spoke to men. Ever since I was a child these songs have stirred me strangely. They came out of the South unknown to me, one by one, and yet at once I knew them as of me and of mine. Then in after years when I came to Nashville I saw the great temple builded of these songs towering over the pale city. To

me Jubilee Hall seemed ever made of the songs themselves, and its bricks
were red with the blood and dust of toil. Out of them rose for me morning,
noon, and night, bursts of wonderful melody, full of the voices of my
brothers and sisters, full of the voices of the past.

Little of beauty has America given the world save the rude grandeur
God himself stamped on her bosom; the human spirit in this new world
has expressed itself in vigor and ingenuity rather than in beauty. And so
by fateful chance the Negro folk-song—the rhythmic cry of the slave—
stands to-day not simply as the sole American music, but as the most
beautiful expression of human experience born this side the seas. It has
been neglected, it has been, and is, half despised, and above all it has
been persistently mistaken and misunderstood; but notwithstanding, it
still remains as the singular spiritual heritage of the nation and the greatest
gift of the Negro people.

Away back in the thirties the melody of these slave songs stirred the
nation, but the songs were soon half forgotten. Some, like "Near the lake
where drooped the willow," passed into current airs and their source was
forgotten; others were caricatured on the "minstrel" stage and their memory died away. Then in war-time came the singular Port Royal experiment
after the capture of Hilton Head, and perhaps for the first time the North
met the Southern slave face to face and heart to heart with no third
witness. The Sea Islands of the Carolinas, where they met, were filled
with a black folk of primitive type, touched and moulded less by the world
about them than any others outside the Black Belt. Their appearance was
uncouth, their language funny, but their hearts were human and their
singing stirred men with a mighty power. . . . But the world listened
only half credulously until the Fisk Jubilee Singers sang the slave songs
so deeply into the world's heart that it can never wholly forget them again.

. . . [I]n 1871 the pilgrimage of the Fisk Jubilee Singers began. North
to Cincinnati they rode,—four half-clothed black boys and five girl-women,—
led by a man with a cause and a purpose. They stopped at Wilberforce,
the oldest of Negro schools, where a black bishop blessed them. Then
they went, fighting cold and starvation, shut out of hotels, and cheerfully
sneered at, ever northward; and ever the magic of their song kept thrilling
hearts, until a burst of applause in the Congregational Council at Oberlin
revealed them to the world. They came to New York and Henry Ward
Beecher dared to welcome them, even though the metropolitan dailies
sneered at his "Nigger Minstrels." So their songs conquered till they sang
across the land and across the sea, before Queen and Kaiser, in Scotland
and Ireland, Holland and Switzerland. Seven years they sang, and brought
back a hundred and fifty thousand dollars to found Fisk University. . . .

What are these songs, and what do they mean? I know little of music
and can say nothing in technical phrase, but I know something of men,

and knowing them, I know that these songs are the articulate message of the slave to the world. They tell us in these eager days that life was joyous to the black slave, careless and happy. I can easily believe this of some, of many. But not all the past South, though it rose from the dead, can gainsay the heart-touching witness of these songs. They are the music of an unhappy people, of the children of disappointment; they tell of death and suffering and unvoiced longing toward a truer world, of misty wanderings and hidden ways.

The songs are indeed the siftings of centuries; the music is far more ancient than the words, and in it we can trace here and there signs of development. My grandfather's grandmother was seized by an evil Dutch trader two centuries ago; and coming to the valleys of the Hudson and Housatonic, black, little, and lithe, she shivered and shrank in the harsh north winds, looked longingly at the hills, and often crooned a heathen melody to the child between her knees, thus:

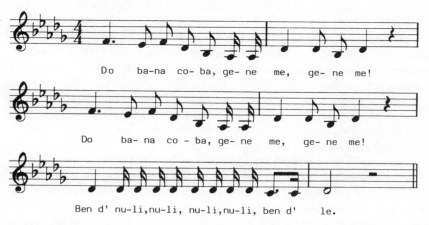

The child sang it to his children and they to their children's children, and so two hundred years it has travelled down to us and we sing it to our children, knowing as little as our fathers what its words may mean, but knowing well the meaning of its music.

This was primitive African music; it may be seen in larger form in the strange chant which heralds "The Coming of John":

> "You may bury me in the East,
> You may bury me in the West,
> But I'll hear the trumpet sound in that morning,"

—the voice of exile.

Ten master songs, more or less, one may pluck from this forest of melody—songs of undoubted Negro origin and wide popular currency,

and songs peculiarly characteristic of the slave. One of these I have just
mentioned. Another whose strains begin this book is "Nobody knows the
trouble I've seen." When, struck with a sudden poverty, the United States
refused to fulfill its promises of land to the freedmen, a brigadier-general
went down to the Sea Islands to carry the news. An old woman on the
outskirts of the throng began singing this song; all the mass joined with
her, swaying. And the soldier wept.

The third song is the cradle-song of death which all men know,—
"Swing low, sweet chariot." . . . Then there is the song of many waters,
"Roll, Jordan, roll," a mighty chorus with minor cadences. There were
many songs of the fugitive like that which opens "The Wings of Atalanta,"
and the more familiar "Been a-listening." The seventh is the song of the
End and the Beginning—"My Lord, what a morning! when the stars
begin to fall". . . . The ninth is the song of this chapter—"Wrestlin' Jacob,
the day is a-breaking,"—a pæan of hopeful strife. The last master song is
the song of songs—"Steal away,"—sprung from "The Faith of the Fathers."

There are many others of the Negro folk-songs as striking and characteristic as these . . . and others I am sure could easily make a selection
on more scientific principles. There are, too, songs that seem to be a step
removed from the more primitive types: there is the maze-like medley,
"Bright sparkles." . . . ; the Easter carol, "Dust, dust and ashes"; the
dirge, "My mother's took her flight and gone home"; and that burst of
melody hovering over "The Passing of the First-Born"—"I hope my mother
will be there in that beautiful world on high."

These represent a third step in the development of the slave song, of
which "You may bury me in the East" is the first, and songs like "March
on" . . . and "Steal away" are the second. The first is African music, the
second Afro-American, while the third is a blending of Negro music with
the music heard in the foster land. The result is still distinctively Negro
and the method of blending original, but the elements are both Negro
and Caucasian. One might go further and find a fourth step in this development, where the songs of white America have been distinctively
influenced by the slave songs or have incorporated whole phrases of Negro
melody, as "Swanee River" and "Old Black Joe." Side by side, too, with
the growth have gone the debasements and imitations—the Negro "minstrel" songs, many of the "gospel" hymns, and some of the contemporary
"coon" songs,—a mass of music in which the novice may easily lose himself
and never find the real Negro melodies.

In these songs, I have said, the slave spoke to the world. Such a message
is naturally veiled and half articulate. Words and music have lost each
other and new and cant phrases of a dimly understood theology have
displaced the older sentiment. Once in a while we catch a strange word
of an unknown tongue, as the "Mighty Myo," which figures as a river of

death; more often slight words or mere doggerel are joined to music of singular sweetness. Purely secular songs are few in number, partly because many of them were turned into hymns by a change of words, partly because the frolics were seldom heard by the stranger, and the music less often caught. Of nearly all the songs, however, the music is distinctly sorrowful. The ten master songs I have mentioned tell in word and music of trouble and exile, of strife and hiding; they grope toward some unseen power and sigh for rest in the End.

The words that are left to us are not without interest, and, cleared of evident dross, they conceal much of real poetry and meaning beneath conventional theology and unmeaning rhapsody. Like all primitive folk, the slave stood near to Nature's heart. Life was a "rough and rolling sea" like the brown Atlantic of the Sea Islands; the "Wilderness" was the home of God, and the "lonesome valley" led to the way of life. "Winter'll soon be over," was the picture of life and death to a tropical imagination. The sudden wild thunder-storms of the South awed and impressed the Negroes,—at times the rumbling seemed to them "mournful," at times imperious:

> "My Lord calls me,
> He calls me by the thunder,
> The trumpet sounds it in my soul."

The monotonous toil and exposure are painted in many words. One sees the ploughmen in the hot, moist furrow, singing:

> "Dere's no rain to wet you,
> Dere's no sun to burn you,
> Oh, push along, believer,
> I want to go home."

The bowed and bent old man cries, with thrice-repeated wail:

> "O Lord, keep me from sinking down,"

and he rebukes the devil of doubt who can whisper:

> "Jesus is dead and God's gone away."

Yet the soul-hunger is there, the restlessness of the savage, the wail of the wanderer, and the plaint is put in one little phrase:

My soul wants some thing that's new, that's new

Over the inner thoughts of the slaves and their relations one with another the shadow of fear ever hung, so that we get but glimpses here and there, and also with them, eloquent omissions and silences. Mother and child are sung, but seldom father; fugitive and weary wanderer call for pity and affection, but there is little of wooing and wedding; the rocks and the mountains are well known, but home is unknown. Strange blending of love and helplessness sighs through the refrain:

> "Yonder 's my ole mudder,
>   Been waggin' at de hill so long;
>   'Bout time she cross over,
>   Git home bime-by."

Elsewhere comes the cry of the "motherless" and the "Farewell, farewell, my only child."

Love-songs are scarce and fall into two categories—the frivolous and light, and the sad. Of deep successful love there is ominous silence, and in one of the oldest of these songs there is a depth of history and meaning:

Poor Ro-sy, poor gal; Poor Ro-sy, poor gal; Ro-sy break my poor heart, Heav'n shall-a-be my home.

A black woman said of the song, "It can't be sung without a full heart and a troubled sperrit." . . .

Of death the Negro showed little fear, but talked of it familiarly and even fondly as simply a crossing of the waters, perhaps—who knows?—back to his ancient forests again. Later days transfigured his fatalism, and amid the dust and dirt the toiler sang:

> "Dust, dust and ashes, fly over my grave,
>   But the Lord shall bear my spirit home."

The things evidently borrowed from the surrounding world undergo characteristic change when they enter the mouth of the slave. Especially is this true of Bible phrases. "Weep, O captive daughter of Zion," is quaintly turned into "Zion, weep-a-low," and the wheels of Ezekiel are turned every way in the mystic dreaming of the slave, till he says:

"There's a little wheel a-turnin' in-a-my heart."

As in olden time, the words of these hymns were improvised by some leading minstrel of the religious band. The circumstances of the gathering, however, the rhythm of the songs, and the limitations of allowable thought, confined the poetry for the most part to single or double lines, and they seldom were expanded to quatrains or longer tales, although there are some few examples of sustained efforts, chiefly paraphrases of the Bible. Three short series of verses have always attracted me,—the one that heads this chapter, of one line of which Thomas Wentworth Higginson has fittingly said, "Never, it seems to me, since man first lived and suffered was his infinite longing for peace uttered more plaintively." The second and third are descriptions of the Last Judgment,—the one a late improvisation, with some traces of outside influence:

"Oh, the stars in the elements are falling,
And the moon drips away into blood,
And the ransomed of the Lord are returning unto God,
Blessed be the name of the Lord."

And the other earlier and homelier picture from the low coast lands:

"Michael, haul the boat ashore,
Then you'll hear the horn they blow,
Then you'll hear the trumpet sound,
Trumpet sound the world around,
Trumpet sound for rich and poor,
Trumpet sound the Jubilee,
Trumpet sound for you and me."

Throughout all the sorrow of the Sorrow Songs there breathes a hope—a faith in the ultimate justice of things. The minor cadences of despair change often to triumph and calm confidence. Sometimes it is faith in life, sometimes a faith in death, sometimes assurance of boundless justice in some fair world beyond. But whichever it is, the meaning is always clear: that sometime, somewhere, men will judge men by their souls and not by their skins. Is such a hope justified? Do the Sorrow Songs sing true?

The silently growing assumption of this age is that the probation of races is past, and that the backward races of to-day are of proven inefficiency and not worth the saving. Such an assumption is the arrogance of peoples irreverent toward Time and ignorant of the deeds of men. A thousand years ago such an assumption, easily possible, would have made it difficult for the Teuton to prove his right to life. Two thousand years ago such dogmatism, readily welcome, would have scouted the idea of blond races ever leading civilization. So woefully unorganized is sociological knowledge that the meaning of progress, the meaning of "swift" and "slow" in human doing, and the limits of human perfectability, are veiled, unanswered sphinxes on the shores of science. Why should Æschylus have sung two thousand years before Shakespeare was born? Why has civilization flourished in Europe, and flickered, flamed, and died in Africa? So long as the world stands meekly dumb before such questions, shall this nation proclaim its ignorance and unhallowed prejudices by denying freedom of opportunity to those who brought the Sorrow Songs to the Seats of the Mighty?

Your country? How came it yours? Before the Pilgrims landed we were here. Here we have brought our three gifts and mingled them with yours: a gift of story and song—soft, stirring melody in an ill-harmonized and unmelodious land; the gift of sweat and brawn to beat back the wilderness, conquer the soil, and lay the foundations of this vast economic empire two hundred years earlier than your weak hands could have done it; the third, a gift of the Spirit. Around us the history of the land has centred for thrice a hundred years; out of the nation's heart we have called all that was best to throttle and subdue all that was worst; fire and blood, prayer and sacrifice, have billowed over this people, and they have found peace only in the altars of the God of Right. Nor has our gift of the Spirit been merely passive. Actively we have woven ourselves with the very warp and woof of this nation,—we fought their battles, shared their sorrow, mingled our blood with theirs, and generation after generation have pleaded with a headstrong, careless people to despise not Justice, Mercy, and Truth, lest the nation be smitten with a curse. Our song, our toil, our cheer, and warning have been given to this nation in blood-brotherhood. Are not these gifts worth the giving? Is not this work and striving? Would America have been America without her Negro people?

Even so is the hope that sang in the songs of my fathers well sung. If somewhere in this whirl and chaos of things there dwells Eternal Good, pitiful yet masterful, then anon in His good time America shall rend the Veil and the prisoned shall go free. . . .

FIFTY YEARS AFTER (1953)

. . . [F]ifty years ago, *The Souls of Black Folk* appeared. It was well received and for the next generation it ran into a number of editions.

Several times I planned to revise the book and bring it abreast of my own thought and to answer criticism. But I hesitated and finally decided to leave the book as first printed, as a monument to what I thought and felt in 1903. I hoped in other books to set down changes of fact and reaction.

In the present edition I have clung to this decision, and my thoughts appear again as then written. I have made less than a half-dozen alterations in word or phrase and then not to change my thought as previously set down but to avoid any possible misunderstanding today of what I meant to say yesterday.

As I re-read these messages of more than half a century ago, I sense two matters which are not so much omission on my part as indications of what I then did not know or did not realize: one is the influence of Freud and his co-workers in their study of psychology; the other is the tremendous impact on the modern world of Karl Marx.

As a student of James, Santayana and Royce, I was not unprepared for the revolution in psychology which the Twentieth Century has brought; but *The Souls of Black Folk* does not adequately allow for unconscious thought and the cake of custom in the growth and influence of race prejudice.

My college training did not altogether omit Karl Marx. He was mentioned at Harvard and taken into account in Berlin. It was not omission but lack of proper emphasis or comprehension among my teachers of the revolution in thought and action which Marx meant. So perhaps I might end this retrospect simply by saying: I still think today as yesterday that the color line is a great problem of this century. But today I see more clearly than yesterday that back of the problem of race and color, lies a greater problem which both obscures and implements it: and that is the fact that so many civilized persons are willing to live in comfort even if the price of this is poverty, ignorance and disease of the majority of their fellowmen; that to maintain this privilege men have waged war until today war tends to become universal and continuous, and the excuse for this war continues largely to be color and race.

Langston Hughes
Let America Be America Again
(1938)

Let America be American again.
Let it be the dream it used to be.
Let it be the pioneer on the plain
Seeking a home where he himself is free.

(America never was America to me.)

Let America be the dream the dreamers dreamed—
Let it be that great strong land of love
Where never kings connive nor tyrants scheme
That any man be crushed by one above.

(It never was America to me.)

O, let my land be a land where Liberty
Is crowned with no false patriotic wreath,
But opportunity is real, and life is free,
Equality is in the air we breathe.

(There's never been equality for me,
Nor freedom in this "homeland of the free.")

Say who are you that mumbles in the dark?
And who are you that draws your veil across the stars?

I am the poor white, fooled and pushed apart,
I am the Negro bearing slavery's scars.
I am the red man driven from the land,
I am the immigrant clutching the hope I seek—
And finding only the same old stupid plan
Of dog eat dog, of mighty crush the weak.

I am the young man, full of strength and hope,
Tangled in that ancient endless chain
Of profit, power, gain, of grab the land!
Of grab the gold! Of grab the ways of satisfying need!
Of work the men! Of take the pay!
Of owning everything for one's own greed!

I am the farmer, bondsman to the soil.
I am the worker sold to the machine.
I am the Negro, servant to you all.
I am the people, worried, hungry, mean—
Hungry yet today despite the dream.
Beaten yet today—O, Pioneers!
I am the man who never got ahead,
The poorest worker bartered through the years.

Yet I'm the one who dreamt our basic dream
In that Old World while still a serf of kings,
Who dreamt a dream so strong, so brave, so true,
That even yet its mighty daring sings
In every brick and stone, in every furrow turned
That's made America the land it has become.
O, I'm the man who sailed those early seas
In search of what I meant to be my home—
For I'm the one who left dark Ireland's shore,
And Poland's plain, and England's grassy lea,
And torn from Black Africa's strand I came
To build a "homeland of the free."

The free?

A dream—
Still beckoning to me!

O, let America be America again—
The land that never has been yet—
And yet must be—
The land where *every* man is free.
The land that's mine—
The poor man's, Indian's, Negro's, ME—
Who made America,
Whose sweat and blood, whose faith and pain,
Whose hand at the foundry, whose plow in the rain,
Must bring back our mighty dream again.

Sure, call me any ugly name you choose—
The steel of freedom does not stain.
From those who live like leeches on the people's lives,
We must take back our land again,
America!

Oh, yes,
I say it plain,
America never was America to me,
And yet I swear this oath—
America will be!
An ever-living seed,
Its dream
Lies deep in the heart of me.

We, the people, must redeem
Our land, the mines, the plants, the rivers,
The mountains and the endless plain—
All, all the stretch of these great green states—
And make America again!

Langston Hughes
Lenox Avenue Mural
(1951)

HARLEM

What happens to a dream deferred?

Does it dry up
like a raisin in the sun?
Or fester like a sore——
And then run?
Does it stink like rotten meat?
Or crust and sugar over——
like a syrupy sweet?

Maybe it just sags
like a heavy load.

Or does it explode?

GOOD MORNING

Good morning, daddy!
I was born here, he said,
watched Harlem grow
until colored folks spread
from river to river
across the middle of Manhattan
out of Penn Station
dark tenth of a nation,
planes from Puerto Rico,
and holds of boats, chico,
up from Cuba Haiti Jamaica,
in busses marked NEW YORK

from Georgia Florida Louisiana
to Harlem Brooklyn the Bronx
but most of all to Harlem
dusky sash across Manhattan
I've seen them come dark
　　　wondering
　　　wide-eyed
　　　dreaming
out of Penn Station——
but the trains are late.
The gates open——
but there're bars
at each gate.

　　　What happens
　　　to a dream deferred?

Daddy, ain't you heard?

Same In Blues

I said to my baby,
Baby, take it slow.
I can't, she said, I can't!
I got to go!

　　　There's a certain
　　　amount of traveling
　　　in a dream deferred.

Lulu said to Leonard,
I want a diamond ring.
Leonard said to Lulu,
You won't get a goddamn thing!

　　　A certain
　　　amount of nothing
　　　in a dream deferred.

Daddy, daddy, daddy,
All I want is you.
You can have me, baby——
but my lovin' days is through.

A certain
amount of impotence
in a dream deferred.

Three parties
On my party line——
But that third party,
Lord, ain't mine!

There's liable
to be confusion
in a dream deferred.

From river to river,
Uptown and down,
There's liable to be confusion
when a dream gets kicked around.

COMMENT ON CURB

You talk like
they don't kick
dreams around
Downtown.

I expect they do——
But I'm talking about
Harlem to you!

LETTER

Dear Mama,
      Time I pay rent and get my food
and laundry I don't have much left
but here is five dollars for you
to show you I still appreciates you.
My girl-friend send her love and say
she hopes to lay eyes on you sometime in life.
Mama, it has been raining cats and dogs up
here. Well, that is all so I will close.

      Your son baby

            Respectably as ever,

                  Joe

ISLAND

Between two rivers,
North of the park,
Like darker rivers
The streets are dark.

Black and white,
Gold and brown——
Chocolate-custard
Pie of a town.

Dream within a dream,
Our dream deferred.

Good morning, daddy!

Ain't you heard?

Martin Luther King, Jr.
Letter from Birmingham Jail*
(1963)

April 16, 1963

My Dear Fellow Clergymen:

While confined here in the Birmingham city jail, I came across your recent statement calling my present activities "unwise and untimely." Seldom do I pause to answer criticism of my work and ideas. If I sought to answer all the criticisms that cross my desk, my secretaries would have little time for anything other than such correspondence in the course of the day, and I would have no time for constructive work. But since I feel that you are men of genuine good will and that your criticisms are sincerely set forth, I want to try to answer your statement in what I hope will be patient and reasonable terms.

I think I should indicate why I am here in Birmingham, since you have been influenced by the view which argues against "outsiders coming in." I have the honor of serving as president of the Southern Christian Leadership Conference, an organization operating in every southern state, with headquarters in Atlanta, Georgia. . . . Several months ago the affiliate here in Birmingham asked us to be on call to engage in a nonviolent direct-action program if such were deemed necessary. We readily consented, and when the hour came we lived up to our promise. So I, along with several members of my staff, am here because I was invited here. I am here because I have organizational ties here.

---

* Author's Note: This response to a published statement by eight fellow clergymen from Alabama (Bishop C. C. J. Carpenter, Bishop Joseph A. Durick, Rabbi Hilton L. Grafman, Bishop Paul Hardin, Bishop Holan B. Harmon, the Reverend George M. Murray, the Reverend Edward V. Ramage and the Reverend Earl Stallings) was composed under somewhat constricting circumstances. Begun on the margins of the newspaper in which the statement appeared while I was in jail, the letter was continued on scraps of writing paper supplied by a friendly Negro trusty, and concluded on a pad my attorneys were eventually permitted to leave me. Although the text remains in substance unaltered, I have indulged in the author's prerogative of polishing it for publication.

But more basically, I am in Birmingham because injustice is here. Just as the prophets of the eighth century B.C. left their villages and carried their "thus saith the Lord" far beyond the boundaries of their home towns, and just as the Apostle Paul left his village of Tarsus and carried the gospel of Jesus Christ to the far corners of the Greco-Roman world, so am I compelled to carry the gospel of freedom beyond my own home town. Like Paul, I must constantly respond to the Macedonian call for aid.

Moreover, I am cognizant of the interrelatedness of all communities and states. I cannot sit idly by in Atlanta and not be concerned about what happens in Birmingham. Injustice anywhere is a threat to justice everywhere. We are caught in an inescapable network of mutuality, tied in a single garment of destiny. Whatever affects one directly, affects all indirectly. Never again can we afford to live with the narrow, provincial "outside agitator" idea. Anyone who lives inside the United States can never be considered an outsider anywhere within its bounds.

You deplore the demonstrations taking place in Birmingham. But your statement, I am sorry to say, fails to express a similar concern for the conditions that brought about the demonstrations. I am sure that none of you would want to rest content with the superficial kind of social analysis that deals merely with effects and does not grapple with underlying causes. It is unfortunate that demonstrations are taking place in Birmingham, but it is even more unfortunate that the city's white power structure left the Negro community with no alternative.

In any nonviolent campaign there are four basic steps: collection of the facts to determine whether injustices exist; negotiation; self-purification; and direct action. We have gone through all these steps in Birmingham. There can be no gainsaying the fact that racial injustice engulfs this community. Birmingham is probably the most thoroughly segregated city in the United States. Its ugly record of brutality is widely known. Negros have experienced grossly unjust treatment in the courts. There have been more unsolved bombings of Negro homes and churches in Birmingham than in any other city in the nation. These are the hard, brutal facts of the case. On the basis of these conditions, Negro leaders sought to negotiate with the city fathers. But the latter consistently refused to engage in good-faith negotiation. . . .

As in so many past experiences, our hopes had been blasted, and the shadow of deep disappointment settled upon us. We had no alternative except to prepare for direct action, whereby we would present our very bodies as a means of laying our case before the conscience of the local and the national community. . . .

You may well ask: "Why direct action? Why sit-ins, marches and so forth? Isn't negotiation a better path?" You are quite right in calling for negotiation. Indeed, this is the very purpose of direct action. Nonviolent direct action seeks to create such a crisis and foster such a tension that a community which has constantly refused to negotiate is forced to confront the issue. It seeks so to dramatize the issue that it can no longer be ignored. My citing the creation of tension as part of the work of the nonviolent-resister may sound rather shocking. But I must confess that I am not afraid of the word "tension." I have earnestly opposed violent tension, but there is a type of constructive, nonviolent tension which is necessary for growth. Just as Socrates felt that it was necessary to create a tension in the mind so that individuals could rise from the bondage of myths and half-truths to the unfettered realm of creative analysis and objective appraisal, so must we see the need for nonviolent gadflies to create the kind of tension in society that will help men rise from the dark depths of prejudice and racism to the majestic heights of understanding and brotherhood.

The purpose of our direct-action program is to create a situation so crisis-packed that it will inevitably open the door to negotiation. I therefore concur with you in your call for negotiation. Too long has our beloved Southland been bogged down in tragic effort to live in monologue rather than dialogue.

One of the basic points in your statement is that the action that I and my associates have taken in Birmingham is untimely. . . . My friends, I must say to you that we have not made a single gain in civil rights without determined legal and nonviolent pressure. Lamentably, it is an historical fact that privileged groups seldom give up their privileges voluntarily. Individuals may see the moral light and voluntarily give up their unjust posture; but, as Reinhold Niebuhr has reminded us, groups tend to be more immoral than individuals.

We know through painful experience that freedom is never voluntarily given by the oppressor; it must be demanded by the oppressed. Frankly, I have yet to engage in a direct-action campaign that was "well timed" in the view of those who have not suffered unduly from the disease of segregation. For years now I have heard the word "Wait!" It rings in the ear of every Negro with piercing familiarity. This "Wait" has almost always meant "Never." We must come to see, with one of our distinguished jurists, that "justice too long delayed is justice denied."

We have waited for more than 340 years for our constitutional and God-given rights. The nations of Asia and Africa are moving with jetlike speed toward gaining political independence, but we still creep at horse-and-buggy pace toward gaining a cup of coffee at a lunch counter. Perhaps it is easy for those who have never felt the stinging darts of segregation to say, "Wait." But when you have seen vicious mobs lynch your mothers and fathers at will and drown your sisters and brothers at whim; when you have seen hate-filled policemen curse, kick and even kill your black brothers and sisters; when you see the vast majority of your twenty million Negro brothers smothering in an airtight cage of poverty in the midst of an affluent society; when you suddenly find your tongue twisted and your speech stammering as you seek to explain to your six-year-old daughter why she can't go to the public amusement park that has just been advertised on television, and see tears welling up in her eyes when she is told that Funtown is closed to colored children, and see ominous clouds of inferiority beginning to form in her little mental sky, and see her beginning to distort her personality by developing an unconscious bitterness toward white people; when you have to concoct an answer for a five-year-old son who is asking: "Daddy, why do white people treat colored people so mean?"; when you take a cross-country drive and find it necessary to sleep night after night in the uncomfortable corners of your automobile because no motel will accept you; when you are humiliated day in and day out by nagging signs reading "white" and "colored"; when your first name becomes "nigger," your middle name becomes "boy" (however old you are) and your last name becomes "John," and your wife and mother are never given the respected title "Mrs."; when you are harried by day and haunted by night by the fact that you are a Negro, living constantly at tiptoe stance, never quite knowing what to expect next, and are plagued with inner fears and outer resentments; when you are forever fighting a degenerating sense of "nobodiness"—then you will understand why we find it difficult to wait. There comes a time when the cup of endurance runs over, and men are no longer willing to be plunged into the abyss of despair. I hope, sirs, you can understand our legitimate and unavoidable impatience.

You express a great deal of anxiety over our willingness to break laws. This is certainly a legitimate concern. Since we so diligently urge people to obey the Supreme Court's decision of 1954 outlawing segregation in the public schools, at first glance it may seem rather paradoxical for us consciously to break laws. One may well ask: "How can you advocate breaking some laws and obeying others?" The answer lies in the fact that there are two types of laws: just and unjust. I would be the first to advocate obeying just laws. One has not only a legal but a moral responsibility to obey just laws. Conversely, one has a moral responsibility to disobey unjust laws. I would agree with St. Augustine that "an unjust law is no law at all."

Now, what is the difference between the two? How does one determine whether a law is just or unjust? A just law is a man-made code that squares with the moral law or the law of God. An unjust law is a code that is out of harmony with the moral law. To put it in the terms of St. Thomas Aquinas: An unjust law is a human law that is not rooted in eternal law and natural law. Any law that uplifts human personality is just. Any law that degrades human personality is unjust. All segregation statutes are unjust because segregation distorts the soul and damages the personality. It gives the segregator a false sense of superiority and the segregated a false sense of inferiority. Segregation, to use the terminology of the Jewish philosopher Martin Buber, substitutes an "I—it" relationship for an "I—thou" relationship and ends up relegating persons to the status of things. Hence segregation is not only politically, economically and sociologically unsound, it is morally wrong and sinful. Paul Tillich has said that sin is separation. Is not segregation an existential expression of man's tragic separation, his awful estrangement, his terrible sinfulness? Thus it is that I can urge men to obey the 1954 decision of the Supreme Court, for it is morally right; and I can urge them to disobey segregation ordinances, for they are morally wrong.

Let us consider a more concrete example of just and unjust laws. An unjust law is a code that a numerical or power majority group compels a minority group to obey but does not make binding on itself. This is *difference* made legal. By the same token, a just law is a code that a majority compels a minority to follow and that it is willing to follow itself. This is *sameness* made legal.

Let me give another explanation. A law is unjust if it is inflicted on a minority that, as a result of being denied the right to vote, had no part in enacting or devising the law. Who can say that the legislature of Alabama which set up that state's segregation laws was democratically elected? Throughout Alabama all sorts of devious methods are used to prevent Negroes from becoming registered voters, and there are some counties in which, even though Negroes constitute a majority of the population, not a single Negro is registered. Can any law enacted under such circumstances be considered democratically structured?

Sometimes a law is just on its face and unjust in its application. For instance, I have been arrested on a charge of parading without a permit. Now, there is nothing wrong in having an ordinance which requires a permit for a parade. But such an ordinance becomes unjust when it is used to maintain segregation and to deny citizens the First-Amendment privilege of peaceful assembly and protest.

I hope you are able to see the distinction I am trying to point out. In no sense do I advocate evading or defying the law, as would the rabid segregationist. That would lead to anarchy. One who breaks an unjust law that conscience tells him is unjust, and who willingly accepts the penalty of imprisonment in order to arouse the conscience of the community over its injustice, is in reality expressing the highest respect for law.

Of course, there is nothing new about this kind of civil disobedience. It was evidenced sublimely in the refusal of Shadrach, Meshach and

Abednego to obey the laws of Nebuchadnezzar, on the ground that a higher moral law was at stake. It was practiced superbly by the early Christians, who were willing to face hungry lions and the excruciating pain of chopping blocks rather than submit to certain unjust laws of the Roman Empire. To a degree, academic freedom is a reality today because Socrates practiced civil disobedience. In our own nation, the Boston Tea Party represented a massive act of civil disobedience.

We should never forget that everything Adolf Hitler did in Germany was "legal" and everything the Hungarian freedom fighters did in Hungary was "illegal." It was "illegal" to aid and comfort a Jew in Hitler's Germany. Even so, I am sure that, had I lived in Germany at the time, I would have aided and comforted my Jewish brothers. If today I lived in a Communist country where certain principles dear to the Christian faith are suppressed, I would openly advocate disobeying that country's antireligious laws.

I must make two honest confessions to you, my Christian and Jewish brothers. First, I must confess that over the past few years I have been gravely disappointed with the white moderate. I have almost reached the regrettable conclusion that the Negro's great stumbling block in his stride toward freedom is not the White Citizen's Counciler or the Ku Klux Klanner, but the white moderate, who is more devoted to "order" than to justice; who prefers a negative peace which is the absence of tension to a positive peace which is the presence of justice; who constantly says: "I agree with you in the goal you seek, but I cannot agree with your methods of direct action"; who paternalistically believes he can set the timetable for another man's freedom; who lives by a mythical concept of time and who constantly advises the Negro to wait for a "more convenient season." Shallow understanding from people of good will is more frustrating than absolute misunderstanding from people of ill will. Lukewarm acceptance is much more bewildering than outright rejection.

I had hoped that the white moderate would understand that law and order exist for the purpose of establishing justice and that when they fail in this purpose they become the dangerously structured dams that block the flow of social progress. I had hoped that the white moderate would understand that the present tension in the South is a necessary phase of the transition from an obnoxious negative peace, in which the Negro passively accepted his unjust plight, to a substantive and positive peace, in which all men will respect the dignity and worth of human personality. Actually, we who engage in nonviolent direct action are not the creators of tension. We merely bring to the surface the hidden tension that is already alive. We bring it out in the open, where it can be seen and dealt with. Like a boil that can never be cured so long as it is covered up but must be opened with all its ugliness to the natural medicines of air and light, injustice must be exposed, with all the tension its exposure creates, to the light of human conscience and the air of national opinion before it can be cured.

In your statement you assert that our actions, even though peaceful, must be condemned because they precipitate violence. But is this a logical assertion? Isn't this like condemning a robbed man because his possession of money precipitated the evil act of robbery? Isn't this like condemning Socrates because his unswerving commitment to truth and his philosophical inquiries precipitated the act by the misguided populace in which they made him drink hemlock? Isn't this like condemning Jesus because his unique God-consciousness and never-ceasing devotion to God's will precipitated the evil act of crucifixion? We must come to see that, as the federal courts have consistently affirmed, it is wrong to urge an individual to cease his efforts to gain his basic constitutional rights because the quest may precipitate violence. Society must protect the robbed and punish the robber.

I had also hoped that the white moderate would reject the myth concerning time in relation to the struggle for freedom. I have just received a letter from a white brother in Texas. He writes: "All Christians know that the colored people will receive equal rights eventually, but it is possible that you are in too great a religious hurry. It has taken Christianity almost two thousand years to accomplish what it has. The teachings of Christ take time to come to earth." Such an attitude stems from a tragic misconception of time, from the strangely irrational notion that there is something in the very flow of time that will inevitably cure all ills. Actually, time itself is neutral; it can be used either destructively or constructively. More and more I feel that the people of ill will have used time much more effectively than have the people of good will. We will have to repent in this generation not merely for the hateful words and actions of the bad people but for the appalling silence of the good people. Human progress never rolls in on wheels of inevitability; it comes through the tireless efforts of men willing to be co-workers with God, and without this hard work, time itself becomes an ally of the forces of social stagnation. We must use time creatively, in the knowledge that the time is always ripe to do right. Now is the time to make real the promise of democracy and transform our pending national elegy into a creative psalm of brotherhood. Now is the time to lift our national policy from the quicksand of racial injustice to the solid rock of human dignity. . . . I stand in the middle of two opposing forces in the Negro Community. One is a force of complacency, made up in part of Negroes who, as a result of long years of oppression, are so drained of self-respect and a sense of "somebodiness" that they have adjusted to segregation; and in part of a few middle-class Negroes who, because of a degree of academic and economic security and because in some ways they profit by segregation, have become insensitive to the problems of the masses. The other force is one of bitterness and hatred, and it comes perilously close to advocating violence. It is expressed in the various black nationalist groups that are springing up across the nation, the largest and best-known being Elijah Muhammad's Muslim movement. Nourished by the Negro's frustration over the continued existence of racial discrimination, this movement is made up of people who have lost faith in America, who have absolutely repudiated Christianity, and who have concluded that the white man is an incorrigible "devil."

I have tried to stand between these two forces, saying that we need emulate neither the "do-nothingism" of the complacent nor the hatred and despair of the black nationalist. For there is the more excellent way of love and nonviolent protest. I am grateful to God that, through the influence of the Negro church, the way of nonviolence became an integral part of our struggle.

If this philosophy had not emerged, by now many streets of the South would, I am convinced, be flowing with blood. And I am further convinced that if our white brothers dismiss as "rabble-rousers" and "outside agitators" those of us who employ nonviolent direct action, and if they refuse to support our nonviolent efforts, millions of Negroes will, out of frustration and despair, seek solace and security in black-nationalist ideologies—a development that would inevitably lead to a frightening racial nightmare.

Oppressed people cannot remain oppressed forever. The yearning for freedom eventually manifests iself, and that is what has happened to the American Negro. Something within has reminded him of his birthright of freedom, and something without has reminded him that it can be gained. Consciously or unconsciously, he has been caught up by the *Zeitgeist*, and with his black brothers of Africa and his brown and yellow brothers of Asia, South America and the Caribbean, the United States Negro is moving with a sense of great urgency toward the promised land of racial justice. If one recognizes this vital urge that has engulfed the Negro community, one should readily understand why public demonstrations are taking place. The Negro has many pent-up resentments and latent frustrations, and he must release them. So let him march; let him make prayer pilgrimages to the city hall; let him go on freedom rides—and try to understand why he must do so. If his repressed emotions are not released in nonviolent ways, they will seek expression through violence; this is not a threat but a fact of history. So I have not said to my people: "Get rid of your discontent." Rather, I have tried to say that this normal and healthy discontent can be channeled into the creative outlet of nonviolent direct action. And now this approach is being termed extremist.

But though I was initially disappointed at being categorized as an extremist, as I continued to think about the matter I gradually gained a measure of satisfaction from the label. Was not Jesus an extremist for love: "Love your enemies, bless them that curse you, do good to them that hate you, and pray for them which despitefully use you, and persecute you." Was not Amos an extremist for justice: "Let justice roll down like waters and righteousness like an ever-flowing stream." Was not Paul an extremist for the Christian gospel: "I bear in my body the marks of the Lord Jesus." Was not Martin Luther an extremist: "Here I stand; I cannot do otherwise, so help me God." And John Bunyan:"I will stay in jail to the end of my days before I make a butchery of my conscience." And Abraham Lincoln: "This nation cannot survive half slave and half free." And Thomas Jefferson: "We hold these truths to be self-evident, that all men are created equal . . ." So the question is not whether we will be extremists, but what kind of extremists we will be. Will we be extremists for hate or for love? Will we be extremists for the preservation of injustice or for the extension of justice? In that dramatic scene on Calvary's hill three men were crucified. We must never forget that all three were crucified for the same crime—the crime of extremism. Two were extremists for immorality, and thus fell below their environment. The other, Jesus Christ, was an extremist for love, truth and goodness, and thereby rose above his environment. Perhaps the South, the nation and the world are in dire need of creative extremists. . . .

I hope the church as a whole will meet the challenge of this decisive hour. But even if the church does not come to the aid of justice, I have no despair about the future. I have no fear about the outcome of our struggle in Birmingham, even if our motives are at present misunderstood. We will reach the goal of freedom in Birmingham and all over the nation, because the goal of America is freedom. Abused and scorned though we may be, our destiny is tied up with America's destiny. Before the pilgrims landed at Plymouth, we were here. Before the pen of Jefferson etched the majestic words of the Declaration of Independence across the pages of history, we were here. For more than two centuries our forebears labored in this country without wages; they made cotton king; they built the homes of their masters while suffering gross injustice and shameful humiliation—and yet out of a bottomless vitality they continued to thrive and develop. If the inexpressible cruelties of slavery could not stop us, the opposition we now face will surely fail. We will win our freedom because the sacred heritage of our nation and the eternal will of God are embodied in our echoing demands. . . .

One day the South will recognize its real heroes. They will be the James Merediths, with the noble sense of purpose that enables them to face jeering and hostile mobs, and with the agonizing loneliness that characterizes the life of the pioneer. They will be old, oppressed, battered Negro women, symbolized in a seventy-two-year-old woman in Montgomery, Alabama, who rose up with a sense of dignity and with her people decided not to ride segregated buses, and who responded with ungrammatical profundity to one who inquired about her weariness: "My feets is tired, but my soul is at rest." They will be the young high school and college students, the young ministers of the gospel and a host of their elders, courageously and nonviolently sitting in at lunch counters and willingly going to jail for conscience' sake. One day the South will know that when these disinherited children of God sat down at lunch counters, they were in reality standing up for what is best in the American dream and for the most sacred values in our Judaeo-Christian heritage, thereby bringing our nation back to those great wells of democracy which were dug deep by the founding fathers in their formulation of the Constitution and the Declaration of Independence.

Yours for the cause of Peace and Brotherhood,

MARTIN LUTHER KING, JR.

Martin Luther King, Jr.
I Have a Dream
(1963)

I SAY to you today, my friends, that in spite of the difficulties and frustrations of the moment, I still have a dream. It is a dream deeply rooted in the American dream.

I have a dream that one day this nation will rise up and live out the true meaning of its creed: "We hold these truths to be self-evident: that all men are created equal."

I have a dream that one day on the red hills of Georgia the sons of former slaves and the sons of former slaveowners will be able to sit down together at the table of brotherhood.

I have a dream that one day even the state of Mississippi, a desert state sweltering with the heat of injustice and oppression, will be transformed into an oasis of freedom and justice.

I have a dream that my four little children will one day live in a nation where they will not be judged by the color of their skin but the content of their character.

I have a dream today.

I have a dream that one day the state of Alabama, whose governor's lips are presently dripping with the words of interposition and nullification, will be transformed into a situation where little black boys and girls will be able to join hands with little white boys and white girls and walk together as sisters and brothers.

I have a dream today.

I have a dream that one day every valley shall be exalted, every hill and mountain shall be made low, the rough places will be made plains, and the crooked places will be made straight, and the glory of the Lord shall be revealed, and all flesh shall see it together.

[This text is from a speech that King delivered in Washington, D.C., on 28 August 1963.]

This is our hope. This is the faith with which I return to the South. With this faith we will be able to hew out of the mountains of despair a stone of hope. With this faith we will be able to transform the jangling discords of our nation into a beautiful symphony of brotherhood. With this faith we will be able to work together, to pray together, to struggle together, to go to jail together, to stand up for freedom together, knowing that we will be free one day.

This will be the day when all of God's children will be able to sing with new meaning "My country 'tis of thee, sweet land of liberty, of thee I sing. Land where my fathers died, land of the Pilgrim's pride, from every mountainside, let freedom ring."

And if America is to be a great nation this must become true. So let freedom ring from the prodigious hilltops of New Hampshire. Let freedom ring from the mighty mountains of New York. Let freedom ring from the heightening Alleghenies of Pennsylvania.

Let freedom ring from the snow-capped Rockies of Colorado.

Let freedom ring from the curvacious peaks of California!

But not only that; let freedom ring from Stone Mountain of Georgia!

Let freedom ring from every hill and mole hill of Mississippi. From every mountainside, let freedom ring.

When we let freedom ring, when we let it ring from every village and every hamlet, from every state and every city, we will be able to speed up that day when all of God's children, black men and white men, Jews and Gentiles, Protestants and Catholics, will be able to join hands and sing in the words of that old Negro spiritual, "Free at last! Free at last! Thank God almighty, we are free at last!"

Studs Terkel
American Dreams: Lost and Found
(1980)

THEM—AKI AND JUN KUROSE

Seattle. They are a middle-aged Nisei couple. Both were born and raised in Seattle. They have four grown children.

They live in a middle-class neighborhood. The house is comfortable, rambling; the street is tree-lined.

JUN: *Caucasians always ask me: Did you always live in an integrated area? My answer is: Yes, I did. Half Japanese ghetto and half white prostitutes. We lived in the only area in Seattle that did not have paved roads. When the government project went up, the Japanese and the prostitutes were moved out.*

We bought this house sixteen years ago from a very liberal man, and it was a hassle. Even though restrictive covenants were illegal, they had a verbal agreement among homeowners not to let Japanese or blacks over this side of the hill.

AKI: *There was an actual paper. I saw it. It said: no blacks, no Jews, no Asians. They had to be white Anglo-Saxon.*

AKI: The American Dream? I think: for whites only. I didn't feel that way before World War Two. The school I went to was ninety-nine percent Asian. We were already segregated, but we didn't realize it because this was the accepted norm. When the war broke out, we found out what it was to be a minority. When Japan bombed Pearl Harbor, we were not part of American society any more. It was a shock.

The principal was always pounding away about Americanism, being loyal to your country, waving the red, white, and blue. Every morning we stood out in the hallway, gave the pledge of allegiance, and saluted the flag. At that time, I really had the feeling that America was my country. I was very proud to be an American.

JUN: I wasn't as naïve as she was. I played sports at high school, and when the team would have a party, usually us Asian boys were excluded. The only time they wanted us around was if they got in a scrap with somebody. Being raised in a ghetto, you had to learn to fight pretty darn good. We lived south of the Mason-Dixon line, the Caucasians lived north. (Laughs.)

AKI: My mother was an educator. She was one of the very few women that migrated to America who had a college education. She told me from the time I was small: "This is your country. Work hard. To get places, you'll have to do twice as much as the whites." *Shikataganai*—that's the way it is. It can't be helped.

JUN: I always wanted to be a physical ed instructor. I was doing fairly well in school, scholastically, until my junior year. That's when I talked to my coach, and he told me to forget it. So I forgot it, books and all. I just sat through.

I used to work in the salmon canneries. We're sent up there to Alaska in the steerage of boats, in the hole. We're packed just like sardines. The machine klunks out, and it's *us* that are fixin' it because the machinist doesn't know how to do it. They're makin' three, four times the money we are. They're eating steak, we're eating fish.

AKI: My dad was a porter at the railroad station, and my mother used to work in the restaurant, waiting on tables. When they got married in 1913, they came to America. My mother taught Japanese language until World War Two. Then we were thrown into the concentration camp. After stayin' there three or four years, she went to live in Chicago. She ended up her life working as a chambermaid in a hotel.

I was about fifteen the day Pearl Harbor was bombed. On the next day, Monday, when I went to school, the teacher immediately treated me as an enemy. She said: "You people bombed Pearl Harbor." Everything changed completely. Our friends looked upon us with suspicion. The idea that we were Americans was shattered.

JUN: On *that* Sunday, I was workin' at this gas station. An hour or two after I got there, the extra started comin' out. I says: "Goddamn Hirohito." As bad as things were, I still loved my country. I figured: Dammit, one of these days I'm gonna make it. I was as mad as the next guy.

Within a week, I changed completely. I found out I'm not an American any more. We were being blamed for Pearl Harbor. I didn't even know where the hell Pearl Harbor was. (Laughs.)

AKI: You suddenly become someone without a country. We couldn't feel a closeness to Japan, a feeling of belonging. We were very much involved in our own community. Seattle was my world.

JUN: My dad served in the Coast Guard around 1910. Even at that, he wasn't accepted as a citizen. He was peddling fruits and vegetables in all-white areas. Quite a few name people were his customers. He was scared. He wouldn't go. I was workin' for this produce man, delivering at the University of Washington: lunchrooms, fraternities, dorms. My boss was scared. I said: "Aw, let's go." By then, I figured even if they kill me, by God, they're gonna have a fight on their hands. I wasn't gonna take it layin' down, because I didn't do anything wrong.

Even though we didn't have our constitutional rights, I thought the law would uphold us. As the months went by, I found out otherwise. Some of the students I ran into were pretty fair, but the cooks who worked at the university gave us a rough time. I figured they were just uneducated people. As time wore on, I saw everybody was that way.

They say we can't be trusted. I spent a little over a year in the concentration camp. Then I was in the army. Within another year, I had the highest security clearance in the United States. (Laughs.) I was put into the counterintelligence corps. From an untrusted guy, they sent me to the land of my ancestors to interrogate Japanese nationals. Still they say I can't be trusted. You face those kind of things, you wonder: Oh, what the hell.

My brother was an honor student at the University of Washington, with a master's in electrical engineering. He couldn't get a job at a time when the U.S. really needed engineers. 1940. We didn't even know there was gonna be a Pearl Harbor. He was offered a job by a company in Japan. The president of the university said: "Take it. You don't have a chance in this country." If he stayed here, he'd probably be down there selling vegetables, yelling: "Lettuce, five cents a head!" He went to Japan, to a good job. A couple of years later, someplace in the Philippines, he got killed by a bomb dropped by the U.S. Air Force.

At last they were gonna do us a favor and let us go into the army. I wanted to volunteer because all my friends did. My folks having lost one son already over there, I promised my mother I won't volunteer, but if I'm called I will go. Nine months later, I was called.

There were over ten thousand Japanese-American soldiers in Europe. There were six thousand in the Pacific. These guys had to really sneak to the front of the front. They'd go into caves, flush soldiers out. We were trusted enough to be sent into the Pacific to fight a lot of our ancestors.

AKI: Having served didn't make you a first-class citizen. These people came back in 1945 and weren't acceptable to the American Legion. My girlfriend lost her husband in the European theater. She was told: "Don't come down to the Legion hall. We don't accept Orientals." They were still in their uniforms, my brother one of them, and weren't served in many establishments. The drugstore on our corner would not serve "Japs," even in uniform. Finally, when they were told they must, they put ashes in the Coke. When we were given our release, there were signs: *No Japs allowed.*

Dave Beck* refused produce from Japanese-American farmers. My brother-in-law was a prisoner of war in Germany and was all shot up. He came back to produce row to see Teamster signs: *Japs not wanted.*

JUN: Before we joined the army, they gave us all a loyalty test. Question number one: Will you drop all allegiance to the emperor and be loyal to the United States? Answer yes or no. If you said yes, it means you had allegiance to the emperor. I answered: No. I would not drop allegiance to the emperor because I never had any. I wrote a sentence. That master sergeant gave me hell. The other was: Will you volunteer? I wrote no. I will go if I'm drafted. He called me disloyal. I said: "Did you volunteer or were you drafted?" He said: "I was drafted." I said: "You and I are in the same boat." That stopped him right there. Most of the guys wrote yes, yes, yes, because they were scared. Some of the fellows who answered no were known as the no-no boys. They were ostracized by the Japanese community as disloyal. There's a group in Seattle called Nisei Veterans Committee, they are so gung ho, they made it tough for anyone who didn't serve.

When I came back from overseas in the United States uniform, I was walking downtown, with ribbons and all, by God. A guy walks by, looks at me, and says: "You lousy Jap." This was after the war. I said: "Man, this is it." I'm pretty violent in my ways. I didn't fight because I had a girl with me. Doggone, if I was by myself, I woulda ended up in jail. By God, giving so much of your life to your country, you're not gonna take it. Being young, being hard-headed, being a man, there's certain things like honor.

AKI: That was the most impressive thing to me: all of a sudden to see so much fear in adults, it was constant. My parents were trying to hide it from us as much as possible. As soon as Eseis** would get together, it was always: What's going to happen to us? The leaders of the community were immediately taken into camps, sent to Missoula, Montana.

The FBI was surveilling the house across the street. They come into our house and suddenly it wasn't our home any more. Here were these strangers taking it over. I remember one FBI that came, looking around for contrabands of war. Even the Japanese kimono became contraband. And Japanese children's books, readers. We went to Japanese school on Saturday to learn the language. This became an indication that we were disloyal.

Many people in my peer group would deny that they could even

---

* Lived in Seattle and was, at the time, president of the International Brotherhood of Teamsters. He was subsequently sent to prison for racketeering and thereafter received a presidential pardon in 1975.

** Japanese-born.

understand Japanese and were showing a hatred to Japan because they didn't want to be considered disloyal. Many people, to this day, deny they can understand Japanese. I'm sure I must have had those feelings, too, though I try to deny it myself now.

JUN: We didn't think citizens had to go to these camps until about two weeks before it happened. We were born and raised here. We had nothin' goin' for us in Japan. To them, we were foreigners. The only thing we had was a Japanese vase. (Laughs.)

AKI: First, they imposed a curfew on us. That really made us angry. We were afraid to discuss it openly among white people. We became very careful not to say anything. I was afraid as to how anything might be interpreted. It was almost paranoia. I was always feeling that I was suspect.

I thought the war was coming right into Seattle. The hysteria was so great. I saw the Eseis taken away. Rumors started that we also were going to be herded off. All of a sudden, the orders came. We were gone six months after the war started.

JUN: I was one of the first to go, in April 1942. They took it by districts. (To Aki) You came sometime in May.

It was the whole family. We were told to meet at a certain location at a certain time in the morning, with no more than we could carry in our hands.

AKI: Two pieces of luggage.

JUN: No contraband. No radios, scissors, razors. You couldn't even take a kitchen knife. Some people did, and it was confiscated. My dad used a straightedge to shave, and he got that confiscated.

AKI: The whole family was given one room. We were six.

JUN: My father just sold everything, the whole business. He got about twenty-five dollars for his truck. It musta been worth about three, four thousand dollars. Everything that was accumulated from 1913, '14, when he and my mother came to America, just went down the drain. We didn't even have to put an ad in the paper. People just came to the house. "You selling anything? How much do you want for this?" I said: "I should get at least a hundred dollars." "I'll give you fifteen dollars." They were lookin' down our throats. I wouldn't sell my piano, so I loaned it to the church.

Just at the point it was gettin' better for the immigrant family, because the children were bringin' in a little income, pooling our hard-earned pennies, buying furniture and this and that, we had to go. My dad had all his customers owin' him money. Some paid back, some didn't.

AKI: People were offering twenty-five cents for a table. A very nice deacon of one of the main churches downtown came over and said he was so sorry this was happening to us. He'd like to help us. If we gave him power of attorney, he'd take over everything. My father and mother were so grateful. All of a sudden we heard, in camp, that all our furniture, all our savings from the bank, were gone. He took everything. We had believed he was an honest man. We were so naïve.

JUN: We were first sent to the state fairgrounds.

Ramona Bennett, a Puyallup Indian who is present, interjects: "It was the place where we used to have pony races and games and weddings. It was our traditional, tribal campground. We invited white people to come visit and share our food. Now we can't even get a booth out there."

JUN: We were fenced in behind barbed wire. We were put in sheds made of tar paper. The rain came through the walls, and it was all mud.

AKI: My father became very ill. He had appendicitis, and because of the red tape you have to go through, his appendix was ruptured. But he survived.

They gave us burlap bags. We were told to stuff straw in them and they would be our mattresses. My sister who was very asthmatic became very ill because she was allergic to straw. She was finally allotted a GI mattress. But you had to prove you were ill.

JUN: Machine-gun towers were in the main parking lot. If you jump through the fence, man, you're dead. This is what gets me today. They say: "We did it for your protection." When you protect somebody, you don't aim a gun at the guy you're protecting.

AKI: The guns were not aimed outside but inside, at us.

JUN: People would drive around in their cars, calling us names. You'd feel just like an animal in the zoo.

AKI: Animal shelters were converted to shelters for some of us.

JUN: Pretty near half of us lived in horse stalls and former pigpens.

You'd read in the papers where Dave Beck said kill 'em. And Walter Lippmann, he was a bad one.* Westbrook Pegler, Walter Winchell, they were out for blood.

Franklin Roosevelt, to all white Americans, he was a great president. New Deal. As far as I'm concerned, he was a crud. Concentration camps. My spine is not gonna quiver at the thought of him.

AKI: Our guards were very young soldiers with machine guns. They were frightened themselves when they heard a noise outside our barbed wire. One night, there was a gunshot and we heard a moo. They had killed a cow. It was terrifying.

Some of the soldiers had never seen a Japanese person before. I re-

---

** "On February 12 and 14, 1942, two extremely influential columns by Walter Lippmann, based on talks with Earl Warren, then attorney general of California, tipped the scales of national opinion in favor of mass evacuation." Carey McWilliams, *The Education of Carey McWilliams* (New York: Simon & Schuster, 1979).

member a young boy from the South. He was very lonely and started talking. He was surprised that we talked English. He was frightened and upset by the whole thing. A decent kid,

JUN: Then we were sent to Idaho. We were in altogether a little over a year.

AKI: The barracks and mess halls were converted into classrooms. I graduated in camp. I don't know if this is something I dreamed up, but I really think it was true. Everything was so surreal. The assignment one teacher gave us was: "Write why you are proud to be an American." (Laughs softly.) We had to salute the flag every day and sing the national anthem.

JUN: Some of us were released earlier. That's when they started accepting Japanese-Americans into service. Anyway, it was costing the damn government too much money, so it was better to have us out workin'. I left first chance I got to grab any old job. They gave us railroad fare plus twenty-five dollars. I went to Chicago.

AKI: The American Friends Service Committee had a student relocation program. We had to find housing before we could be relocated. There were many calls for domestic jobs. Many people wanted maids. I went to Salt Lake City, where I was supposed to work for my room and board and attend school. But this lady's idea was for me to work all day and go to night school. I would say to her: "I came to attend school." She says: "Go at night. If you complain, I can always send you back to camp." My brother, who came home from his furlough in the army, said: "You don't have to take that." Another lady took me in.

Do you know that many who were in with us tried to justify the camps? When we were told to evacuate, the American Friends Service Committee said: "Don't go, we will help you." They almost became our enemies. Some of the Japanese were saying: "Stay out of this, you're making it rougher for us." If we'd listened to the Friends, we might have been able to avert much suffering. We went willingly, we really did.

JUN: Us Nisei* were still too young and too naïve. Remember, all our community leaders were packed up within hours and sent far away to Montana. Most of us were still dependent on our parents for everything.

AKI: Many of the Nisei wanted to forget about all this. Why bring up the past? For a long time, they were blocking it out as unpleasant memories; also, they were afraid of being disloyal. They were real gung-ho Americans, waving the flag, never questioning the government.

JUN: I got into quite a few squabbles at Boeing, where I work as a machinist. During the fifties, before the civil rights movement, I'd kind of have to shut up for a while or I'd be out of a job. With my kids and all, if I'm not workin', I'm sunk. Since the sixties, now that my kids are

* First-generation American-born Japanese.

all grown, the job doesn't mean that much to me any more. I go gung
ho on tellin' 'em what it is.

They still say: "We did it for your protection." I said: "Protection, my
eye. The machine gun wasn't facing your way, it was facing ours." I don't
know why they want to justify the wrong so much. Thirty years later,
they still justify it. Especially with all this redress stuff.* Hayakawa, look
at him.** (Laughs.)

The younger kids who work in the shop are more educated than their
parents were. When I first went to Boeing, the journeymen machinists
had fourth- or fifth-grade educations. Everything they heard from the
rabble-rousers, they believed. But the kids have had some college, and
they have a better understanding.

AKI: He equates education with understanding. I don't. I'm a school-
teacher, and I'm still concerned about the attitude of my colleagues.
There's a desegregation program going on right now in Seattle to make
the schools more racially balanced. I was teaching in a school of black
and Asian children. Being of a minority myself, I was sent out to one of
the ritzier schools in the north end of town. I put up a fight. I didn't
want to go. I enjoyed my job and was more comfortable where I was. I
said: "I was educated to teach children, not certain kinds of children." It
was kindergarten.

The principal said: "We don't have Asians out here." Before, the term
was "Oriental." (Laughs.) She said: "The parents want to meet you." This
was summertime 1976. They set up a date in the middle of August. I cut
my vacation short. The principal was quite nervous about it. She drove
me there.

It was a beautiful home on the lake. Two guards were flashing their
lights so we'd find the house. I came on the scene at eight. Thirty parents
had been there since seven. They had a meeting. They were out to test
me. Where did you get your education? What degree do you have? What
was your major? Where did you learn English? I played the game very
well. I brought out Bruner and Piaget.

They didn't know what the hell you were talkin' about.

Neither did I. (Laughs.) But they didn't know it. These are all upper-
middle-class white parents. They were very impressed. (Laughs.) I happen not to like coffee. I prefer tea. They said: "Would you like coffee?"

---

* A movement for redress of grievances has come into being on behalf of Japanese-
Americans who were interned during the war years.

** Senator S. I. Hayakawa of California, who is opposed to redress, has described the
internment camp experience as beneficial and educational to the inmates.

I said: "I don't drink coffee." One of the parents said: "Of course!" (Laughs.)

When these women saw some black children coming into the classroom with a Nisei teacher, they really freaked out. Phones were ringing like crazy in the school district, parents were walking in and out of my classroom, constantly questioning me about the curriculum. My first year was really hell on earth.

The faculty, I thought, would make me feel welcome. First, one teacher said to me: "Kurose. What kind of name is that?" I said: "It's my husband's name." "What is he?" "He's my husband." "Where are you from?" "Seattle." "No, where *were* you from:" "I was born in Seattle." Finally, I said: "Are you trying to find out my ethnic background?" She said: "You really ought to be more careful." I asked why. She said: "The community still remembers this Japanese family that lived here. We were very nice to the family, but they stayed private. Their son joined the Japanese army and became an officer." I said: "I didn't know Japan sent a carrier over to pick up one person and put him in the Japanese army. I think you're referring to the Ishtane family that lived here. Their son was in the Japanese-American army. The U.S. Army did not allow Japanese boys to be in with regular white boys." She replied: "You really should be more careful."

I asked the librarian if they could put in some books about Japanese-American history. She said: "Why do you have to bring up the past?" I said: "It's part of history." She said: "You must remember, you people started the war." These are educated people.

JUN: At work, when I might disagree with a guy about politics, he'll tell me: "Why don't you go back where you came from?" I say: "I was born and raised here. If you don't like what I say, why don't *you* go back where you came from, Europe?" They're surprised. It's the first time they ever heard this.

(Mumbles) August 6, 1945 . . .

AKI: (Softly) The bombing of Hiroshima and Nagasaki. It was a shocking thing to the Japanese community. The Eseis were especially affected. Some of them tried to hide their grief because everybody was afraid to show any kind of feeling for the people of Japan. But you couldn't help feeling. It was just complete annihilation.

JUN: There's more immigrants from Hiroshima in America, percentage-wise, than any other part of Japan. Most of the people that came here were from agricultural families. Whether your brother's an enemy or not, you're gonna grieve. I think it was a racial thing. They had the bomb before Germany was defeated but didn't drop it there.

AKI: It was so unnecessary. And the bombing of Nagasaki, why? Why?

I feel we have to remind the people over and over again what that kind of bomb can do. Now we're talking about something many times more powerful!

I think things are changing. The new generation, the Sanseis,* are saying: "How could you have kept so quiet? Why haven't you told us?" There are so many families that never discussed it. Their kids are saying: "We're hearing about this from other people. How come?"

The civil rights movement did a lot to bring this out for us. They took the lead, and it's easier for others to follow. Many Niseis and Sanseis got involved in the black movement, yet they were reluctant to discuss their own situation. It took a long time for them to come out.

JUN: For a long time, we lived with *shikataganai*—it can't be helped. Until many of us said: "What the hell do you mean, it can't be helped?" No more of this silence, hell, no.

GIRL OF THE GOLDEN WEST—RAMONA BENNETT

We're on the highway, heading from the Seattle airport to Tacoma.

"Do you know we're on a reservation at this moment? It was reserved forever for the members of my tribe. 'Forever' meant until some white people wanted it. I'm a member of the Puyallup tribe. It's called that by the whites because they couldn't pronounce our foreign name: Spalalla-pubsh. (Laughs.)

"We were a fishing people. We had camps all the way from McNeill's Island to Salmon Bay and clear up to the Rodando. In 1854, agents of the United States government met with our people and did a treaty. They promised us they only needed land to farm. They assured us that our rights as commercial fishing people would not be disturbed. Because Indian people have always been generous, we agreed to share.

"Our tribes were consolidated onto this reservation, twenty-nine thou-sand acres. We lost eleven thousand in the survey, so we came down to eighteen thousand. We should have known, but we're a trusting people."

We were long-house people, matriarchal, where the whole extended family lived together. We didn't have real estate problems. There was lots of space for everybody, so we didn't have to stand our long houses on end and call them skyscrapers.

The white people decided we'd make good farmers, so they separated our long-house families into forty-, eighty-, and 160-acre tracts. If we didn't improve our land, we'd lose it. They really knew it wouldn't work, but it was a way of breaking up our society. Phil Lucas, who's a beautiful

* Second-generation American-born Japanese.

Indian folk singer, says the marriage between the non-Indians and the Indians was a perfect one. The Indian measures his success by his ability to share. The white man measures his importance by how much he can take. There couldn't have been two more perfect cultures to meet, with the white people taking everything and the Indians giving everything.

They then decided that because we couldn't read or write or speak English, we should all be assigned guardians. So the lawyers and judges and police and businessmen who came out with Milwaukee Railroad and Weyerhaeuser Lumber, all these good citizens were assigned their fair share of Indians to be guardians for. They sold the land to each other, kept the money for probate fees, and had the sheriffs come out and remove any Indians still living on this land. Those Indians unwilling to be removed were put on the railroad tracks and murdered. We became landless on our own reservations.

The kids were denied access to anything traditionally theirs. They had programs called Domestic Science, where little Indian girls were taught how to wash dishes for white people, cook meals for white people, mop floors for white people. If they were very, very smart, they were taught how to be beauticians and cut white people's hair, or to be waitresses and serve white people in restaurants, to be clerk typists, maybe, and type white people's ideas. All the boys went through a program called Agricultural Science, where they were taught how to plow white people's fields and take care of white people's cows and chickens and to care for the produce that was being raised on their own land, stolen by non-Indians. If these boys were very, very smart, they were taught to be unemployed welders or unemployed sheet-metal workers. People that do the hiring are whites, and they tend to be more comfortable with people who resemble them.

We are entering a complex of buildings. One stands out from among the others; it has the appearance of a stone fortress.

This is a jail for young Indian boys. It used to be a little Indian hospital. It was the only hospital for us in the whole region. That's Alaska, Montana, Idaho, Washington, and Oregon. The good white folks saw this new modern hospital going up and right away got mad. They started lobbying to get it away from us. About eighteen years ago, the government snatched it away.

I spent eight years as chairwoman of Puyallup Tribal Council, nonstop, working to reacquire the building. Right now, it's used by Washington State as a jail for children. It's called a juvenile diagnostic center. (She nods toward a young boy on the grounds.) You just saw an Indian child. Who the hell do you think gets locked up in this country? Children, minority and white. It's a system that is so goddamn sick that it abandons and locks up its children. Didn't you see the barbed wire? (Impatient with me) I mean, didn't you see the cyclone fence? See the bars on the windows over there?

We enter one of the smaller buildings across the road. It is noninstitutional in appearance and feeling. Small, delighted children are busy at their tasks or listening quietly to one of the young women teachers. A teacher says: "Most of our students and teachers are Indian. We concentrate on traditional crafts and arts and history. We teach respect for the visions of others. We honor elders for their wisdom. We prize good humor, especially when directed at oneself. All natural things are our brothers and sisters, and will teach us if we are aware and listen. We honor persons for what they've done for their people, not what they've done for themselves."

We demanded a school building to get our kids out of the public school system, where they were being failed. It was a struggle getting this school. I've learned from the whites how to grab and how to push. When the state would not return our hospital to us, we just pushed our way on this property and occupied it.

When you read about Indians or when you see them in movies, you see John Wayne theater. You see an Indian sneaking through the bushes to kill some innocent white. (She indicates people walking by, all of whom know her. On occasion, she chats with one or two.) You'd never think those two guys are fishermen and the guy that just walked by is an accountant. You think of the stereotype that everyone needs to be afraid of.

In school, I learned the same lies you learned: that Columbus discovered America, that there were no survivors at Little Big Horn, that the first baby born west of the Mississippi was born to Narcissa Whitman. All the same crap that you learned. Through those movies, I learned that an Irishman who stands up for his rights is a patriot, and an Indian who stands up for his rights is a savage. I learned that the pioneers made the West a fit place for decent folks to live. I learned that white people had to take land away from the Indian people because we didn't know how to use it. It wasn't plowed, logged, and paved. It wasn't strip-mined. It had to be taken from us because we had no environmental knowledge or concerns. We were just not destructive enough to be considered *really* civilized.

What happened is we had land the whites wanted. The government ordered the Indians to move. They were moved so many times, they might as well have had handles. There were always a few patriots who'd say: "For God's sake, we were born here, we buried our dead here. Leave us alone. My God, it's a federal promise. We got a contract. I'm not makin' my grandmother move, I'm not makin' my children move. Bullshit, I'm sick of this." They pick up arms and that would be an uprising. The cavalry rides in. Since we all look alike, they'd kill the first bunch of Indians they saw. This was just tradition. Every single one of those cavalry officers had one of those damn little flags and damn little Bibles. Oh, they were very, very religious. (Laughs.) They opened fire and did a genocide.

They always teach that the only survivor at Little Big Horn was that cavalry horse. Since then, I've realized there were many survivors of Little Big Horn. (Laughs.) They were Sioux and Cheyennes and therefore didn't count, apparently. You never see a roster with all of *their* names.

When I went to school, we learned history so we won't make the same mistakes. This is what I was told. I know damn good and well that if American children in school had learned that the beautiful Cheyenne women at Sand Creek put their shawls over their babies' faces so they wouldn't see the long knives, if the American schoolchildren learned that Indian mothers held their babies close to their bodies when the Gatling guns shot and killed three hundred, there would never have been a My Lai massacre. If the history teacher had really been truthful with American children, Calley would have given an order to totally noncooperating troops. There would have been no one to fight. There would have been a national conscience. The lie has made for an American nightmare, not dream.

When I was in first grade, really tiny, I played a small child in a school play. This was during World War Two. I was born in 1938. My mother was a little dark lady. Caucasians cannot tell people of color apart. To the average white, Chinese, Filipinos, Japanese, all look the same. When my mom came to the school grounds, a little boy named Charles made slanty eyes at her and called her ugly names. I didn't understand what he was saying, but I just jumped on him and started hitting him. He was a friend of mine, and he didn't know why I was doing it. Neither did I. When the play started, my clothes were all disheveled. I was confused, hurt, and really feeling bad. When I went on that stage and looked at all those faces, I realized for the first time my mother was a different color from the others and attracted attention. Her skin had always been rich and warm, while mine looked pale and cold. My father was white. It was such a shock that someone could hate my mother for being such a warm, beautiful woman. Much later I found out that Charles's father died in the Pacific and that his whole family was very uptight about the Japanese.

I think of Indian people who, at treaty time, offered to share with a few men from Boston. They never knew there'd be a Boeing Airplane

Company or a Weyerhaeuser. They never knew there would be a statue in the harbor inviting wretched masses and that those masses would come like waves of the sea, thousands and thousands of people seeking freedom. Freedoms that those Indian people would never be afforded. With all those waves coming at us, we were just drowning in the American Dream.

The median lifespan for Indians is somewhere in the forties. That's deceptive because our infant mortality rate is four times higher than the national average. We have the magic age of nineteen, the age of drinking, violent deaths, and suicides. Our teenage suicide rate is thirty-four times higher than the national average.

Forty-five is another magic age for the Indian. That's the age of deaths from alcoholism. Our people have gone from the highest protein diet on the face of the earth—buffalo and salmon—to macaroni. If we're not alcoholics, we're popoholics. Ninety percent of us, eighteen and older, are alcoholics. It's a daily suicide: "I can't face my life, lack of future. I can't face the ugly attitudes toward me. I can't face the poverty. So I'll just drink this bottle of Ripple, and I'll kill myself for a few hours. I'll kill some brain cells. Tomorrow, when I get sober, maybe things will be different. When I get sober and things are no different, I'll drink again. I'm not so hopeless that I'll kill myself." It's an optimistic form of suicide.

I once drank very heavily. A little seventeen-year-old girl, who I considered just a child, would just get in my face and give me hell. She would say: "Don't you care about yourself? Don't you realize you're killing an Indian? Why do you want to hurt yourself?" At that point I stopped, and I can't be around people who drink. Oh, I don't mind if you drink. I don't care what non-Indian people do to themselves. But I hate to see an Indian killing himself or herself. That Indian is waiting, marking time and wasting, decade after decade. The family is broken up.

They rush through our communities and gather our children. Thirty-five percent of our children have been removed from their families to boarding schools, foster homes, and institutions. A Shoshone or Sioux or Navajo woman lives in a house like mine. Substandard, no sanitation. No employment on the reservation. Inadequate education. The Mormons have a relocation—child-removal—program. Here's the routine:

A woman from the LDS* knocks on my door. I'm gracious and I invite her in because that's our way. She says: "Oh, look at all your pretty children. Oh, what a nice family. I see that your roof leaks and your house is a little cold and you don't have sanitation. By the looks of your kitchen, you don't have much food, and I notice you have very little furniture. You don't have running water and you have an outdoor toilet. And the nearest school is sixty miles away. Wouldn't you like your children to go and live in this nice house, where they'll have their own bedrooms,

---

* Latter Day Saints.

wonderful people who care about them, lots of money to buy food, indoor plumbing, posturepedic mattresses and Cannon sheets, and wonderful television sets, and well-landscaped yards? And a neighborhood school, so your children won't have to spend three hours a day on a bus?" And then she says: "If you reeeeeeeally, reeeeeeeally love your children, you wouldn't want them to live like this. You would want them to have all the good things they need." And that mother thinks: My God, I love my children and what a monster I am! How can I possibly keep them from this paradise?

"My mother grew up poor, like many Indians. She was taken away to boarding school, where they forbade the use of her language, her religion. But she kept her wits about her. She learned to look at things with a raised eyebrow. When she hears something that's funny, she laughs out loud. She provided me with pride, humor, and strength: you don't snivel, you don't quit, you don't back off.

"She talks to graves, talks to plants, talks to rivers. Aside from knowing the traditional things, she was busy growing things, digging clams, smoking fish, sewing. She's an excellent seamstress. At the same time, she's politically and socially sharp.

"When I was a little girl, a couple of FBI agents came to the house. I was maybe four years old. World War Two had just broken out. In a secretive way, they said: 'We'd like to talk to you about security risks. Next-door is this German family, and on the other side these Italians. We want to know if you think they're loyal.' My maiden name was Church, a very British, acceptable name. She said that the Germans were third-generation and are Americans to the core, and the Italian family had already lost a son in the Pacific. Then she said: 'If you're looking for a security risk, I suggest you investigate me, because I don't see any reason for an Indian to be fighting for a government that has stolen lands from the Indian people.' She just shouted at them to get the hell off her porch. Gee, they just back-pedaled off and went." (Laughs.)

I met a bunch of Eskimos from Alaska that the Methodists got hold of. They call it the Methodist ethic. If you work, you're good, if you don't, you're bad. I don't impose that ethic on other people. These Eskimos are now so task-oriented, they're very, very hyper. They don't know how to relax. The Methodists got hold of their heads, and they lost what they had. They're in a mad dash all the time and don't know how to sit and cogitate.

My little six-year-old will go out, just sit and talk to one of those trees or observe the birds. He can be calm and comfortable doing that. He hasn't been through the same brainwash that the rest of us have.

There's a knowledge born in these little ones that ties back to the spirit

world, to the Creator. Those little kids in school can tell you that the
nations of fish are their brothers and sisters. They'll tell you that their
life is no more important than the life of that animal or that tree or that
flower. They're born knowing that. It's that our school doesn't beat it out
of them.

History's important, what happened in the past is important. But I'm
not satisfied with just talking about what happened in 1855 or what happened in 1903, during the murders, or 1961, when they seized our hospital. I want my children to have something good to say in 1990 about
what happened in 1979. They're not gonna look in the mirror and see
themselves as Indians with no future.

My little son shares the continent with 199,999,999 other folks. (Laughs.)
If your government screws up and creates one more damned war, his
little brown ass will get blown away, right along with all your people. All
those colors (laughs) and all those attitudes. The bombs that come don't
give a damn if he's got cute little braids, is a little brown boy, talks to
cedar trees, and is a sweet little person.

I see the United States government as a little baby brat. If you say
no, it throws something at you. If it sees something, it just grabs. Just
drools all over and soils itself, and has to have others come in and clean
it up. It's a 200-year-old kid. They gave us dual citizenship in 1924. How
can a little teeny stupid 150-year-old government grant citizenship to a
Yakima Indian who has been here for eight million years? To a Puyallup?
What an insult! (Laughs.) How can a lying little trespasser that doesn't
know how to act right grant anything to anybody? Why doesn't somebody
get that kid in line? Eventually, some stranger will go over and grab that
little kid and shake 'im up. I think the United States is just rapidly heading
to be shaken around. Unfortunately, I'm living right here and I'm gonna
get shaken around right along with the rest of us. (Laughs.) We're all in
the same canoe.

GATHERING AND LETTING GO—STEPHEN CRUZ

He is thirty-nine.
   *"The family came in stages from Mexico. Your grandparents usually
came first, did a little work, found little roots, put together a few bucks,
and brought the family in, one at a time. Those were the days when
controls at the border didn't exist as they do now."*

You just tried very hard to be whatever it is the system wanted of you.
I was a good student and, as small as I was, a pretty good athlete. I was
well liked, I thought. We were fairly affluent, but we lived down where
all the trashy whites were. It was the only housing we could get. As kids,
we never understood why. We did everything right. We didn't have those

Mexican accents, we were never on welfare. Dad wouldn't be on welfare to save his soul. He woulda died first. He worked during the depression. He carries that pride with him, even today.

Of the five children, I'm the only one who really got into the business world. We learned quickly that you have to look for opportunities and add things up very quickly. I was in liberal arts, but as soon as Sputnik went up, well, golly, hell, we knew where the bucks were. I went right over to the registrar's office and signed up for engineering. I got my degree in '62. If you had a master's in business as well, they were just paying all kinds of bucks. So that's what I did. Sure enough, the market was super. I had fourteen job offers. I could have had a hundred if I wanted to look around.

I never once associated these offers with my being a minority. I was aware of the Civil Rights Act of 1964, but I was still self-confident enough to feel they wanted me because of my abilities. Looking back, the reason I got more offers than the other guys was because of the government edict. And I thought it was because I was so goddamned brilliant. (Laughs.) In 1962, I didn't get as many offers as those who were less qualified. You have a tendency to blame the job market. You just don't want to face the issue of discrimination.

I went to work with Procter & Gamble. After about two years, they told me I was one of the best supervisors they ever had and they were gonna promote me. Okay, I went into personnel. Again, I thought it was because I was such a brilliant guy. Now I started getting wise to the ways of the American Dream. My office was glass-enclosed, while all the other offices were enclosed so you couldn't see into them. I was the visible man.

They made sure I interviewed most of the people that came in. I just didn't really think there was anything wrong until we got a new plant manager, a southerner. I received instructions from him on how I should interview blacks. Just check and see if they smell, okay? That was the beginning of my training program. I started asking: Why weren't we hiring more minorities? I realized I was the only one in a management position.

I guess as a Mexican I was more acceptable because I wasn't really black. I was a good compromise. I was visibly good. I hired a black secretary, which was *verboten*. When I came back from my vacation, she was gone. My boss fired her while I was away. I asked why and never got a good reason.

Until then, I never questioned the American Dream. I was convinced if you worked hard, you could make it. I never considered myself different. That was the trouble. We had been discriminated against a lot, but I never associated it with society. I considered it an individual matter. Bad people, my mother used to say. In '68 I began to question.

I was doing fine. My very first year out of college, I was making twelve thousand dollars. I left Procter & Gamble because I really saw no opportunity. They were content to leave me visible, but my thoughts were not really solicited. I may have overreacted a bit, with the plant manager's attitude, but I felt there's no way a Mexican could get ahead here.

I went to work for Blue Cross. It's 1969. The Great Society is in full swing. Those who never thought of being minorities before are being turned on. Consciousness raising is going on. Black programs are popping up in universities. Cultural identity and all that. But what about the one issue in this country: economics? There are very few management jobs for minorities, especially blacks.

The stereotypes popped up again. If you're Oriental, you're real good in mathematics. If you're Mexican, you're a happy guy to have around, pleasant but emotional, Mexicans are either sleeping or laughing all the time. Life is just one big happy kind of event. *Mañana*. Good to have as part of the management team, as long as you weren't allowed to make decisions.

I was thinking there were two possibilities why minorities were not making it in business. One was deep, ingrained racism. But there was still the possibility that they were simply a bunch of bad managers who just couldn't cut it. You see, until now I believed everything I was taught about the dream: the American businessman is omnipotent and fair. If we could show these turkeys there's money to be made in hiring minorities, these businessmen—good managers, good decision makers—would respond. I naïvely thought American businessmen gave a damn about society, that given a choice they would do the right thing. I had that faith.

I was hungry for learning about decision-making criteria. I was still too far away from top management to see exactly how they were working. I needed to learn more. Hey, just learn more and you'll make it. That part of the dream hadn't left me yet. I was still clinging to the notion of work your ass off, learn more than anybody else, and you'll get in that sphere.

During my fifth year at Blue Cross, I discovered another flaw in the American Dream. Minorities are as bad to other minorities as whites are to minorities. The strongest weapon the white manager had is the old divide and conquer routine. My mistake was thinking we were all at the same level of consciousness.

I had attempted to bring together some blacks with the other minorities. There weren't too many of them anyway. The Orientals never really got involved. The blacks misunderstood what I was presenting, perhaps I said it badly. They were on the cultural kick: a manager should be crucified for saying "Negro" instead of "black." I said as long as the Negro or the black gets the job, it doesn't mean a damn what he's called. We got into a huge hassle. Management, of course, merely smiled. The whole struggle fell flat on its face. It crumpled from divisiveness. So I learned another lesson. People have their own agenda. It doesn't matter what group you're with, there is a tendency to put the other guy down regardless.

The American Dream began to look so damn complicated, I began to think: Hell, if I wanted, I could just back away and reap the harvest myself. By this time, I'm up to twenty-five thousand dollars a year. It's beginning to look good, and a lot of people are beginning to look good. And they're saying: "Hey, the American Dream, you got it. Why don't you lay off?" I wasn't falling in line.

My bosses were telling me I had all the "ingredients" for top management. All that was required was to "get to know our business." This term comes up all the time. If I could just warn all minorities and women whenever you hear "get to know our business," they're really saying "fall in line." Stay within that fence, and glory can be yours. I left Blue Cross disillusioned. They offered me a director's job at thirty thousand dollars before I quit.

All I had to do was behave myself. I had the "ingredients" of being the good Chicano, the equivalent of the good nigger. I was smart. I could articulate well. People didn't know by my speech patterns that I was of Mexican heritage. Some tell me I don't look Mexican, that I have a certain amount of Italian, Lebanese, or who knows. (Laughs.)

One could easily say: "Hey, what's your bitch? The American Dream has treated you beautifully. So just knock it off and quit this crap you're spreading around." It was a real problem. Every time I turned around, America seemed to be treating me very well.

Hell, I even thought of dropping out, the hell with it. Maybe get a job in a factory. But what happened? Offers kept coming in. I just said to myself: God, isn't this silly? You might as well take the bucks and continue looking for the answer. So I did that. But each time I took the money, the conflict in me got more intense, not less.

Wow, I'm up to thirty-five thousand a year. This is a savings and loan business. I have faith in the executive director. He was the kind of guy I was looking for in top management: understanding, humane, also looking for the formula. Until he was up for consideration as executive v.p. of the entire organization. All of a sudden everything changed. It wasn't until I saw this guy flip-flop that I realized how powerful vested interests are. Suddenly he's saying: "Don't rock the boat. Keep a low profile. Get in line." Another disappointment.

Subsequently, I went to work for a consulting firm. I said to myself: Okay, I've got to get close to the executive mind. I need to know how they work. Wow, a consulting firm.

Consulting firms are saving a lot of American businessmen. They're doing it in ways that defy the whole notion of capitalism. They're not allowing these businesses to fail. Lockheed was successful in getting U.S. funding guarantees because of the efforts of consulting firms working on their behalf, helping them look better. In this kind of work, you don't find minorities. You've got to be a proven success in business before you get there.

The American Dream, I see now, is governed not by education, opportunity, and hard work, but by power and fear. The higher up in the organization you go, the more you have to lose. The dream is *not losing*. This is the notion pervading America today: Don't lose.

When I left the consulting business, I was making fifty-five thousand dollars a year. My last performance appraisal was: You can go a long way in business, you can be a partner, but you gotta know our business. It came up again. At this point, I was incapable of being disillusioned any more. How easy it is to be swallowed up by the same set of values that governs the top guy. I was becoming that way. I was becoming concerned about losing that fifty grand or so a year. So I asked other minorities who had it made. I'd go up and ask 'em: "Look, do you owe anything to others?" The answer was: "We owe nothing to anybody." They drew from the civil rights movement but felt no debt. They've quickly forgotten how it happened. It's like I was when I first got out of college. Hey, it's really me, I'm great. I'm as angry with these guys as I am with the top guys.

Right now, it's confused. I've had fifteen years in the business world as "a success." Many Anglos would be envious of my progress. Fifty thousand dollars a year puts you in the one or two top percent of all Americans. Plus my wife making another thirty thousand. We had lots of money. When I gave it up, my cohorts looked at me not just as strange, but as something of a traitor. "You're screwing it up for all of us. You're part of our union, we're the elite, we should govern. What the hell are you doing?" So now I'm looked at suspiciously by my peer group as well.

I'm teaching at the University of Wisconsin at Platteville. It's nice. My colleagues tell me what's on their minds. I got a farm next door to Platteville. With farm prices being what they are (laughs), it's a losing proposition. But with university work and what money we've saved, we're gonna be all right.

The American Dream is getting more elusive. The dream is being governed by a few people's notion of what the dream is. Sometimes I feel it's a small group of financiers that gets together once a year and decides all the world's issues.

It's getting so big. The small-business venture is not there any more. Business has become too big to influence. It can't be changed internally. A counterpower is needed.

Adrienne Rich
From an Old House in America
(1975)

1.

Deliberately, long ago
the carcasses

of old bugs crumbled
into the rut of the window

and we started sleeping here
Fresh June bugs batter this June's

screens, June-lightning batters
the spiderweb

I sweep the wood-dust
from the wood-box

the snout of the vacuum cleaner
sucks the past away

2.

Other lives were lived here:
mostly un-articulate

yet someone left her creamy signature
in the trail of rusticated

narcissus straggling up
through meadowgrass and vetch

Families breathed close
boxed-in from the cold

hard times, short growing season
the old rainwater cistern

hulks in the cellar

3.

Like turning through the contents of a drawer:
these rusted screws, this empty vial

useless, this box of watercolor paints
dried to insolubility—

but this—
this pack of cards with no card missing

still playable
and three good fuses

and this toy: a little truck
scarred red, yet all its wheels still turn

The humble tenacity of things
waiting for people, waiting for months, for years

4.

Often rebuked, yet always back returning[1]
I place my hand on the hand

of the dead, invisible palm-print
on the doorframe

spiked with daylillies, green leaves
catching in the screen door

or I read the backs of old postcards
curling from thumbtacks, winter and summer

fading through cobweb-tinted panes—
white church in Norway

Dutch hyacinths bleeding azure
red beach on Corsica

set-pieces of the world
stuck to this house of plank

[1] Borrowed from a poem, "Stanzas," by Emily Brontë [*Rich's note*].

I flash on wife and husband
embattled, in the years

that dried, dim ink was wet
those signatures

5.

If they call me man-hater, you
would have known it for a lie

but the *you* I want to speak to
has become your death

If I dream of you these days
I know my dreams are mine and not of you

yet something hangs between us
older and stranger than ourselves

like a translucent curtain, a sheet of water
a dusty window

the irreducible, incomplete connection
between the dead and living

or between man and woman in this
savagely fathered and unmothered world

6.

The other side of a translucent
curtain, a sheet of water

a dusty window, Non-being
utters its flat tones

the speech of an actor learning his lines
phonetically

the final autistic statement
of the self-destroyer

All my energy reaches out tonight
to comprehend a miracle beyond

raising the dead: the undead to watch
back on the road of birth

7.

I am an American woman:
I turn that over

like a leaf pressed in a book
I stop and look up from

into the coals of the stove
or the black square of the window

Foot-slogging through the Bering Strait
jumping from the *Arbella* to my death

chained to the corpse beside me[2]
I feel my pains begin

I am washed up on this continent
shipped here to be fruitful

my body a hollow ship
bearing sons to the wilderness

sons who ride away
on horseback, daughters

whose juices drain like mine
into the *arroyo* of stillbirths, massacres

Hanged as witches, sold as breeding-wenches
my sisters leave me

I am not the wheatfield
nor the virgin forest

I never chose this place
yet I am of it now

In my decent collar, in the daguerrotype
I pierce its legend with my look

my hands wring the necks of prairie chickens
I am used to blood

When the men hit the hobo track
I stay on with the children

---

[2] Many African women went into labor and gave birth on the slave-ships of the Middle
Passage, chained for the duration of the voyage to the dying or the dead [*Rich's note*].

my power is brief and local
but I know my power

I have lived in isolation
from other women, so much

in the mining camps, the first cities
the Great Plains winters

Most of the time, in my sex, I was alone

8.

Tonight in this northeast kingdom
striated iris stand in a jar with daisies

the porcupine gnaws in the shed
fireflies beat and simmer

caterpillars begin again
their long, innocent climb

the length of leaves of burdock
or webbing of a garden chair

plain and ordinary things
speak softly

the light square on old wallpaper
where a poster has fallen down

Robert Indiana's LOVE
leftover of a decade

9.

I do not want to simplify
Or: I would simplify

by naming the complexity
It was made over-simple all along

the separation of powers
the allotment of sufferings

her spine cracking in labor
his plow driving across the Indian graves

her hand unconscious on the cradle, her mind
with the wild geese

his mother-hatred driving him
into exile from the earth

the refugee couple with their cardboard luggage
standing on the ramshackle landing-stage

he with fingers frozen around his Law
she with her down quilt sewn through iron nights

—the weight of the old world, plucked
drags after them, a random feather-bed

10.

Her children dead of diphtheria, she
set herself on fire with kerosene

(O Lord I was unworthy
Thou didst find me out)

she left the kitchen scrubbed
down to the marrow of its boards

"The penalty for barrenness
is emptiness

my punishment is my crime
what I have failed to do, is me . . ."

—Another month without a show
and this the seventh year

O Father let this thing pass out of me
I swear to You

I will live for the others, asking nothing
I will ask nothing, ever, for myself

11.

Out back of this old house
*datura*³ tangles with a gentler weed

its spiked pods smelling
of bad dreams and death

³ A poisonous hallucinogenic weed. It has a spiky green pod and a white flower, and is
also known as jimson-weed, or deadly nightshade [*Rich's note*].

I reach through the dark, groping
past spines of nightmare

to brush the leaves of sensuality
A dream of tenderness

wrestles with all I know of history
I cannot now lie down

with a man who fears my power
or reaches for me as for death

or with a lover who imagines
we are not in danger

12.

If it was lust that had defined us—
their lust and fear of our deep places

we have done our time
as faceless torsos licked by fire

we are in the open, on our way—
our counterparts

the pinyon jay, the small
gilt-winged insect

the Cessna throbbing level
the raven floating in the gorge

the rose and violet vulva of the earth
filling with darkness

yet deep within a single sparkle
of red, a human fire

and near and yet above the western planet
calmly biding her time

13.

They were the distractions, lust and fear
but are

themselves a key
Everything that can be used, will be:

the fathers in their ceremonies
the genital contests

the cleansing of blood from pubic hair
the placenta buried and guarded

their terror of blinding
by the look of her who bore them

If you do not believe
that fear and hatred

read the lesson again
in the old dialect

14.

But can't you see me as a human being
he said

What is a human being
she said

I try to undertand
he said

what will you undertake
she said

will you punish me for history
he said

what will you undertake
she said

do you believe in collective guilt
he said

let me look in your eyes
she said

15.

Who is here? The Erinyes.
One to sit in judgment.

One to speak tenderness.
One to inscribe the verdict on the canyon wall.

If you have not confessed
the damage

if you have not recognized
the Mother of reparations

if you have not come to terms
with the women in the mirror

if you have not come to terms
with the inscription

the terms of the ordeal
the discipline   the verdict

if still you are on your way
still She awaits your coming

16.

"Such women are dangerous
to the order of things"

and yes, we will be dangerous
to ourselves

groping through spines of nightmare
(*datura* tangling with a simpler herb)

because the line dividing
lucidity from darkness

is yet to be marked out

Isolation, the dream
of the frontier woman

leveling her rifle along
the homestead fence

still snares our pride
—a suicidal leaf

laid under the burning-glass
in the sun's eye

Any woman's death diminishes me

WHERE HAVE WE BEEN? WHERE ARE WE GOING?

Reinhold Niebuhr
The Irony of American History
(1952)

PREFACE

. . . WE FREQUENTLY speak of "tragic" aspects of contemporary history;
and also call attention to a "pathetic" element in our present historical
situation. My effort to distinguish "ironic" elements in our history from
tragic and pathetic ones does not imply the denial of tragic and pathetic
aspects in our contemporary experience. It does rest upon the conviction
that the ironic elements are more revealing. The three elements might
be distinguished as follows: (a) Pathos is that element in an historic situation which elicits pity, but neither deserves admiration nor warrants
contrition. Pathos arises from fortuitous cross-purposes and confusions in
life for which no reason can be given, or guilt ascribed. Suffering caused
by purely natural evil is the clearest instance of the purely pathetic.
(b) The tragic element in a human situation is constituted of conscious
choices of evil for the sake of good. If men or nations do evil in a good
cause; if they cover themselves with guilt in order to fulfill some high
responsibility; or if they sacrifice some high value for the sake of a higher
or equal one they make a tragic choice. Thus the necessity of using the
threat of atomic destruction as an instrument for the preservation of peace
is a tragic element in our contemporary situation. Tragedy elicits admiration as well as pity because it combines nobility with guilt. (c) Irony
consists of apparently fortuitous incongruities in life which are discovered,
upon closer examination, to be not merely fortuitous. Incongruity as such
is merely comic. It elicits laughter. This element of comedy is never
completely eliminated from irony. But irony is something more than
comedy. A comic situation is proved to be an ironic one if a hidden relation
is discovered in the incongruity. If virtue becomes vice through some

hidden defect in the virtue; if strength becomes weakness because of the vanity to which strength may prompt the mighty man or nation; if security is transmuted into insecurity because too much reliance is placed upon it; if wisdom becomes folly because it does not know its own limits—in all such cases the situation is ironic. The ironic situation is distinguished from a pathetic one by the fact that the person involved in it bears some responsibility for it. It is differentiated from tragedy by the fact that the responsibility is related to an unconscious weakness rather than to a conscious resolution. While a pathetic or a tragic situation is not dissolved when a person becomes conscious of his involvement in it, an ironic situation must dissolve, if men or nations are made aware of their complicity in it. Such awareness involves some realization of the hidden vanity or pretension by which comedy is turned into irony. This realization either must lead to an abatement of the pretension, which means contrition; or it leads to a desperate accentuation of the vanities to the point where irony turns into pure evil.

Our modern liberal cultural, of which American civilization is such an unalloyed exemplar, is involved in many ironic refutations of its original pretensions of virtue, wisdom, and power. . . .

THE IRONIC ELEMENT IN THE AMERICAN SITUATION

Everybody understands the obvious meaning of the world struggle in which we are engaged. We are defending freedom against tyranny and are trying to preserve justice against a system which has, demonically, distilled injustice and cruelty out of its original promise of a higher justice. The obvious meaning is analyzed for us in every daily journal; and the various facets of this meaning are illumined for us in every banquet and commencement-day speech. The obvious meaning is not less true for having become trite. Nevertheless it is not the whole meaning.

We also have some awareness of an element of tragedy in this struggle, which does not fit into the obvious pattern. Could there be a clearer tragic dilemma than that which faces our civilization? Though confident of its virtue, it must yet hold atomic bombs ready for use so as to prevent a possible world conflagration. It may actually make the conflict the more inevitable by this threat; and yet it cannot abandon the threat. Furthermore, if the conflict should break out, the non-communist world would be in danger of destroying itself as a moral culture in the process of defending itself physically. For no one can be sure that a war won by the use of the modern means of mass destruction would leave enough physical and social substance to rebuild a civilization among either victors or vanquished. The victors would also face the "imperial" problem of using power in global terms but from one particular center of authority, so preponderant and unchallenged that its world rule would almost certainly violate basic standards of justice.

Such a tragic dilemma is an impressive aspect of our contemporary situation. But tragic elements in present history are not as significant as the ironic ones. Pure tragedy elicits tears of admiration and pity for the hero who is willing to brave death or incur guilt for the sake of some great good. Irony however prompts some laughter and a nod of comprehension beyond the laughter; for irony involves comic absurdities which cease to be altogether absurd when fully understood. Our age is involved in irony because so many dreams of our nation have been so cruelly refuted by history. Our dreams of a pure virtue are dissolved in a situation in which it is possible to exercise the virtue of responsibility toward a community of nations only by courting the prospective guilt of the atomic bomb. And the irony is increased by the frantic efforts of some of our idealists to escape this hard reality by dreaming up schemes of an ideal world order which have no relevance to either our present dangers or our urgent duties.

Our dreams of bringing the whole of human history under the control of the human will are ironically refuted by the fact that no group of idealists can easily move the pattern of history toward the desired goal of peace and justice. The recalcitrant forces in the historical drama have a power and persistence beyond our reckoning. Our own nation, always a vivid symbol of the most characteristic attitudes of a bourgeois culture, is less potent to do what it wants in the hour of its greatest strength than it was in the days of its infancy. The infant is more secure in his world than the mature man is in his wider world. The pattern of the historical drama grows more quickly than the strength of even the most powerful man or nation.

Our situation of historic frustration becomes doubly ironic through the fact that the power of recalcitrance against our fondest hopes is furnished by a demonic religio-political creed which had even simpler notions than we of finding an escape from the ambiguity of man's strength and weakness. For communism believes that it is possible for man, at a particular moment in history, to take "the leap from the realm of necessity to the realm of freedom." The cruelty of communism is partly derived from the absurd pretension that the communist movement stands on the other side of this leap and has the whole of history in its grasp. Its cruelty is partly due to the frustration of the communist overlords of history when they discover that the "logic" of history does not conform to their delineation of it. One has an uneasy feeling that some of our dreams of managing history might have resulted in similar cruelties if they had flowered into action. But there was fortunately no program to endow our elite of prospective philosopher-scientist-kings with actual political power.

Modern man's confidence in his power over historical destiny prompted the rejection of every older conception of an overruling providence in history. Modern man's confidence in his virtue caused an equally un-equivocal rejection of the Christian idea of the ambiguity of human virtue. In the liberal world the evils in human nature and history were ascribed to social institutions or to ignorance or to some other manageable defect in human nature or environment. Again the communist doctrine is more explicit and therefore more dangerous. It ascribes the origin of evil to the institution of property. The abolition of this institution by communism therefore prompts the ridiculous claim of innocency for one of the vastest concentrations of power in human history. This distillation of evil from the claims of innocency is ironic enough. But the irony is increased by the fact that the so-called free world must cover itself with guilt in order to ward off the peril of communism. The final height of irony is reached by the fact that the most powerful nation in the alliance of free peoples is the United States. For every illusion of a liberal culture has achieved a special emphasis in the United States, even while its power grew to phenomenal proportions.

We were not only innocent a half century ago with the innocency of irresponsibility; but we had a religious version of our national destiny which interpreted the meaning of our nationhood as God's effort to make a new beginning in the history of mankind. Now we are immersed in world-wide responsibilities; and our weakness has grown into strength. Our culture knows little of the use and the abuse of power; but we have to use power in global terms. Our idealists are divided between those who would renounce the responsibilities of power for the sake of pre-serving the purity of our soul and those who are ready to cover every ambiguity of good and evil in our actions by the frantic insistence that any measure taken in a good cause must be unequivocally virtuous. We take, and must continue to take, morally hazardous actions to preserve our civilization. We must exercise our power. But we ought neither to believe that a nation is capable of perfect disinterestedness in its exercise, nor become complacent about particular degrees of interest and passion which corrupt the justice by which the exercise of power is legitimatized. Communism is a vivid object lesson in the monstrous consequences of moral complacency about the relation of dubious means to supposedly good ends.

The ironic nature of our conflict with communism sometimes centers in the relation of power to justice and virtue. The communists use power without scruple because they are under the illusion that their conception of an unambiguously ideal end justifies such use. Our own culture is schizophrenic upon the subject of power. Sometimes it pretends that a liberal society is a purely rational harmony of interests. Sometimes it achieves a tolerable form of justice by a careful equilibration of the powers and vitalities of society, though it is without a conscious philosophy to justify these policies of statesmanship. Sometimes it verges on that curious combination of cynicism and idealism which characterizes communism, and is prepared to use any means without scruple to achieve its desired end.

The question of "materialism" leads to equally ironic consequences in our debate and contest with communism. The communists are consistent philosophical materialists who believe that mind is the fruit of matter; and that culture is the product of economic forces. Perhaps the communists are not as consistently materialistic in the philosophical sense as they pretend to be. For they are too Hegelian to be mechanistic materialists. They have the idea of a "dialectic" or "logic" running through both nature and history which means that a rational structure of meaning runs through the whole of reality. Despite the constant emphasis upon the "dignity of man" in our own liberal culture, its predominant naturalistic bias frequently results in views of human nature in which the dignity of man is not very clear.

It is frequently assumed that human nature can be manipulated by methods analogous to those used in physical nature. Furthermore it is generally taken for granted that the highest ends of life can be fulfilled in man's historic existence. This confidence makes for utopian visions of historical possibilities on the one hand and for rather materialistic conceptions of human ends on the other. All concepts of immortality are dismissed as the fruit of wishful thinking. This dismissal usually involves indifference toward the tension in human existence, created by the fact that "our reach is beyond our grasp," and that every sensitive individual has a relation to a structure of meaning which is never fulfilled in the vicissitudes of actual history.

The crowning irony in this debate about materialism lies in the tremendous preoccupation of our own technical culture with the problem of gaining physical security against the hazards of nature. Since our nation has carried this preoccupation to a higher degree of consistency than any other we are naturally more deeply involved in the irony. Our orators profess abhorrence of the communist creed of "materialism" but we are rather more successful practitioners of materialism as a working creed than the communists, who have failed so dismally in raising the general standards of well-being.

Meanwhile we are drawn into an historic situation in which the paradise of our domestic security is suspended in a hell of global insecurity; and the conviction of the perfect compatibility of virtue and prosperity which we have inherited from both our Calvinist and our Jeffersonian ancestors is challenged by the cruel facts of history. For our sense of responsibility to a world community beyond our own borders is a virtue, even though it is partly derived from the prudent understanding of our own interests. But this virtue does not guarantee our ease, comfort, or prosperity. We are the poorer for the global responsibilities which we bear. And the fulfillments of our desires are mixed with frustrations and vexations.

Sometimes the irony in our historic situation is derived from the extravagant emphasis in our culture upon the value and dignity of the individual and upon individual liberty as the final value of life. Our cherished values of individualism are real enough; and we are right in preferring death to their annulment. But our exaltation of the individual involves us in some very ironic contradictions. On the one hand, our culture does not really value the individual as much as it pretends; on the other hand, if justice is to be maintained and our survival assured, we cannot make individual liberty as unqualifiedly the end of life as our ideology asserts. . . .

THE INNOCENT NATION IN AN INNOCENT WORLD

Practically all schools of modern culture, whatever their differences, are united in their rejection of the Christian doctrine of original sin. This doctrine asserts the obvious fact that all men are persistently inclined to regard themselves more highly and are more assiduously concerned with their own interests than any "objective" view of their importance would warrant. Modern culture in its various forms feels certain that, if men could be sufficiently objective or disinterested to recognize the injustice of excessive self-interest, they could also in time transfer the objectivity of their judgments as observers of the human scene to their judgments as actors and agents in human history. This is an absurd notion which every practical statesman or man of affairs knows how to discount because he encounters ambitions and passions in his daily experience, which refute the regnant modern theory of potentially innocent men and nations. There is consequently a remarkable hiatus between the shrewdness of practical men of affairs and the speculations of our wise men. The latter are frequently convinced that the predicament of our possible involvement in an atomic and global conflict is due primarily to failure of the statesmen to heed the advice of our psychological and social scientists. The statesmen on the other hand have fortunately been able to disregard the admonition of our wise men because they could still draw upon the native shrewdness of the common people who in smaller realms have had something of the same experience with human nature as the statesmen. The statesmen have not been particularly brilliant in finding solutions for our problems, all of which have reached global dimensions. But they have, at least, steered a course which still offers us minimal hope of avoiding a global conflict.

But whether or not we avoid another war, we are covered with pro-spective guilt. We have dreamed of a purely rational adjustment of in-terests in human society; and we are involved in "total" wars. We have dreamed of a "scientific" approach to all human problems; and we find that the tensions of a world-wide conflict release individual and collective emotions not easily brought under rational control. We had hoped to make neat and sharp distinctions between justice and injustice; and we discover that even the best human actions involve some guilt.

This vast involvement in guilt in a supposedly innocent world achieves a specially ironic dimension through the fact that the two leading powers engaged in the struggle are particularly innocent according to their own official myth and collective memory. The Russian-Communist pretensions of innocency and the monstrous evils which are generated from them, are the fruit of a variant of the liberal dogma. According to the liberal dogma men are excessively selfish because they lack the intelligence to consider interests other than their own. But this higher intelligence can be supplied, of course, by education. Or they are betrayed into selfishness by an unfavorable social and political environment. This can be remedied by the growth of scientifically perfected social institutions.

The communist dogma is more specific. Men are corrupted by a par-ticular social institution: the institution of property. The abolition of this institution guarantees the return of mankind to the state of original in-nocency which existed before the institution of property arose, a state which Engels describes as one of idyllic harmony with "no soldiers, no gendarmes, no policemen, prefects or judges, no prisons, laws or law-suits."

The initiators of this return to innocency are the proletarian class. This class is innocent because it has no interests to defend; and it cannot become "master of the productive forces of society except by abolishing their mode of appropriation." The proletarians cannot free themselves from slavery without emancipating the whole of mankind from injustice. Once this act of emancipation has been accomplished every action and event on the other side of the revolution participates in this new freedom from guilt. A revolutionary nation is guiltless because the guilt of "im-perialism" has been confined to "capitalistic" nations "by definition." Thus the lust for power which enters into most individual and collective human actions is obscured. The priest-kings of this new revolutionary state, though they wield inordinate power because they have gathered both economic and political control in the hands of a single oligarchy, are also, in theory, innocent of any evil. Their interests and those of the masses whom they control are, by definition, identical since neither owns property. . . .

It is difficult to conceive of a more implausible theory of human nature and conduct. Yet it is one which achieves a considerable degree of plausibility, once the basic assumptions are accepted. It has been plausible enough, at any rate, to beguile millions of people, many of whom are not under the direct control of the tyranny and are therefore free to consider critical challenges of its adequacy. So powerful has been this illusory restoration of human innocency that, for all we know, the present communist oligarchs, who pursue their ends with such cruelty, may still be believers. The powers of human self-deception are seemingly endless. The communist tyrants may well legitimatize their cruelties not only to the conscience of their devotees but to their own by recourse to an official theory which proves their innocence "by definition."

John Adams in his warnings to Thomas Jefferson would seem to have had a premonition of this kind of politics. At any rate, he understood the human situation well enough to have stated a theory which comprehended what we now see in communism. "Power," he wrote, "always thinks it has a great soul and vast views beyond the comprehension of the weak; and that it is doing God's service when it is violating all His laws. Our passions, ambitions, avarice, love and resentment, etc., possess so much metaphysical subtlety and so much overpowering eloquence that they insinuate themselves into the understanding and the conscience and convert both to their party." Adams's understanding of the power of the self's passions and ambitions to corrupt the self's reason is a simple recognition of the facts of life which refute all theories, whether liberal or Marxist, about the possibility of a completely disinterested self. Adams, as every Christian understanding of man has done, nicely anticipated the Marxist theory of an "ideological taint" in reason when men reason about each other's affairs and arrive at conclusions about each other's virtues, interests and motives. The crowning irony of the Marxist theory of ideology is that it foolishly and self-righteously confined the source of this taint to economic interest and to a particular class. It was, therefore, incapable of recognizing all the corruptions of ambition and power which would creep inevitably into its paradise of innocence.

In any event we have to deal with a vast religious-political movement which generates more extravagant forms of political injustice and cruelty out of the pretensions of innocency than we have ever known in human history.

The liberal world which opposes this monstrous evil is filled ironically with milder forms of the same pretension. Fortunately they have not resulted in the same evils, partly because they are not as consistently held; and partly because we have not invested our ostensible "innocents" with inordinate power. Though a tremendous amount of illusion about human nature expresses itself in American culture, our political institutions contain many of the safeguards against the selfish abuse of power which our Calvinist fathers insisted upon. According to the accepted theory, our democracy owes everything to the believers in the innocency and perfectibility of man and little to the reservations about human nature which emanated from the Christianity of New England. But fortunately there are quite a few accents in our constitution which spell out the warning of John Cotton: "Let all the world give mortall man no greater power than they are content they shall use, for use it they will. . . . And they that have the liberty to speak great things you will find that they will speak great blasphemies."

But these reservations of Christian realism in our culture cannot obscure the fact that, next to the Russian pretensions, we are (according to our traditional theory) the most innocent nation on earth. The irony of our situation lies in the fact that we could not be virtuous (in the sense of practicing the virtues which are implicit in meeting our vast world responsibilities) if we were really as innocent as we pretend to be. It is particularly remarkable that the two great religious-moral traditions which informed our early life—New England Calvinism and Virginian Deism and Jeffersonianism—arrive at remarkably similar conclusions about the meaning of our national character and destiny. Calvinism may have held too pessimistic views of human nature, and too mechanical views of the providential ordering of human life. But when it assessed the significance of the American experiment both its conceptions of American destiny and its appreciation of American virtue finally arrived at conclusions strikingly similar to those of Deism. Whether our nation interprets its spiritual heritage through Massachusetts or Virginia, we came into existence with the sense of being a "separated" nation, which God was using to make a new beginning for mankind. We had renounced the evils of European feudalism. We had escaped from the evils of European religious bigotry. We had found broad spaces for the satisfaction of human desires in place of the crowded Europe. Whether, as in the case of the New England theocrats, our forefathers thought of our "experiment" as primarily the creation of a new and purer church, or, as in the case of Jefferson and his coterie, they thought primarily of a new political community, they believed in either case that we had been called out by God to create a new humanity. We were God's "American Israel." Our pretensions of innocency therefore heightened the whole concept of a virtuous humanity which characterizes the culture of our era; and involve us in the ironic incongruity between our illusions and the realities which we experience. We find it almost as difficult as the communists to believe that anyone could think ill of us, since we are as persuaded as they that our society is so essentially virtuous that only malice could prompt criticism of any of our actions. . . .

One interesting aspect of these illusions of "new beginnings" in history is that they are never quite as new as is assumed, and never remain quite as pure as when they are new. . . .

Every nation has its own form of spiritual pride. . . . Our version is that our nation turned its back upon the vices of Europe and made a new beginning.

The Jeffersonian conception of virtue, had it not overstated the innocency of American social life, would have been a tolerable prophecy of some aspects of our social history which have distinguished us from Europe. For it can hardly be denied that the fluidity of our class structure, derived from the opulence of economic opportunities, saved us from the acrimony of the class struggle in Europe, and avoided the class rebellion, which Marx could prompt in Europe but not in America. When the frontier ceased to provide for the expansion of opportunities, our superior technology created ever new frontiers for the ambitious and adventurous. In one sense the opulence of American life has served to perpetuate Jeffersonian illusions about human nature. For we have thus far sought to solve all our problems by the expansion of our economy. This expansion cannot go on forever and ultimately we must face some vexatious issues of social justice in terms which will not differ too greatly from those which the wisest nations of Europe have been forced to use.

The idea that men would not come in conflict with one another, if the opportunities were wide enough, was partly based upon the assumption that all human desires are determinate and all human ambitions ordinate. This assumption was shared by our Jeffersonians with the French Enlightenment. "Every man," declared Tom Paine, "wishes to pursue his occupation and enjoy the fruits of his labors and the produce of his property in peace and safety and with the least possible expense. When these things are accomplished all objects for which governments ought to be established are accomplished." The same idea underlies the Marxist conception of the difference between an "economy of scarcity" and an "economy of abundance." In an economy of abundance there is presumably no cause for rivalry. Neither Jeffersonians nor Marxists had any understanding for the perennial conflicts of power and pride which may arise on every level of "abundance" since human desires grow with the means of their gratification. . . .

Since America developed as a bourgeois society, with only remnants of the older feudal culture to inform its ethos, it naturally inclined toward the bourgeois ideology which neglects the factor of power in the human community and equates interest with rationality.

Such a society regards all social relations as essentially innocent because it believes self-interest to be inherently harmless. It is, in common with Marxism, blind to the lust for power in the motives of men; but also to the injustices which flow from the disbalances of power in the community.

Both the bourgeois ideology and Marxism equate self-interest with the economic motive. The bourgeois world either regards economic desire as inherently ordinate or it hopes to hold it in check either by prudence (as in the thought of the utilitarians) or by the pressure of the self-interest of others (as in classical liberalism). Marxism, on the other hand, believes that the disbalance of power in industrial society, plus the inordinate character of the economic motive, must drive a bourgeois society to greater and greater injustice and more and more overt social conflict.

Thus the conflict between communism and the bourgeois world achieves a special virulence between the two great hegemonous nations of the respective alliances, because America is, in the eyes of communism, an exemplar of the worst form of capitalistic injustice, while it is, in its own eyes, a symbol of pure innocence and justice. This ironic situation is heightened by the fact that every free nation in alliance with us is more disposed to bring economic life under political control than our traditional theory allows. There is therefore considerable moral misunderstanding between ourselves and our allies. This represents a milder version of the contradiction between ourselves and our foes. The classes in our society, who pretend that only political power is dangerous, frequently suggest that our allies are tainted with the same corruption as that of our foes. European nations, on the other hand, frequently judge us according to our traditional theory. They fail to recognize that our actual achievements in social justice have been won by a pragmatic approach to the problems of power, which has not been less efficacious for its lack of consistent speculation upon the problems of power and justice. Our achievements in this field represent the triumph of common sense over the theories of both our business oligarchy and the speculations of those social scientists who are still striving for a "scientific" and disinterested justice. We are, in short, more virtuous than our detractors, whether foes or allies, admit, because we know ourselves to be less innocent than our theories assume. The force and danger of self-interest in human affairs are too obvious to remain long obscure to those who are not too blinded by either theory or interest to see the obvious. The relation of power to interest on the one hand, and to justice on the other, is equally obvious. In our domestic affairs we have thus builded better than we knew because we have not taken the early dreams of our peculiar innocency too seriously.

Our foreign policy reveals even more marked contradictions between our early illusions of innocency and the hard realities of the present day than do our domestic policies. We lived for a century not only in the illusion but in the reality of innocency in our foreign relations. We lacked the power in the first instance to become involved in the guilt of its use. As we gradually achieved power, through the economic consequences of our richly stored continent, the continental unity of our economy and the technical efficiency of our business and industrial enterprise, we sought for a time to preserve innocency by disavowing the responsibilities of power. We were, of course, never as innocent as we pretended to be, even as a child is not as innocent as is implied in the use of the child as the symbol of innocency. The surge of our infant strength over a continent, which claimed Oregon, California, Florida and Texas against any sovereignty which may have stood in our way, was not innocent. It was the expression of a will-to-power of a new community in which the land-hunger of hardy pioneers and settlers furnished the force of imperial expansion. The organs of government, whether political or military, played only a secondary role. From those early days to the present moment we have frequently been honestly deceived because our power availed itself of covert rather than overt instruments. One of the most prolific causes of delusion about power in a commercial society is that economic power is more covert than political or military power.

We believed, until the outbreak of the First World War, that there was a generic difference between us and the other nations of the world. This was proved by the difference between their power rivalries and our alleged contentment with our lot. The same President of the United States who ultimately interpreted the First World War as a crusade to "make the world safe for democracy" reacted to its first alarms with the reassuring judgment that the conflict represented trade rivalries with which we need not be concerned. We were drawn into the war by considerations of national interest, which we hardly dared to confess to ourselves. Our European critics may, however, overshoot the mark if they insist that the slogan of making "the world safe for democracy" was merely an expression of that moral cant which we seemed to have inherited from the British, only to express it with less subtlety than they. For the fact is that every nation is caught in the moral paradox of refusing to go to war unless it can be proved that the national interest is imperiled, and of continuing in the war only by proving that something much more than national interest is at stake. Our nation is not the only community of mankind which is tempted to hypocrisy. Every nation must come to terms with the fact that, though the force of collective self-interest is so great, national policy must be based upon it; yet also the sensitive conscience recognizes that the moral obligation of the individual transcends his particular community. Loyalty to the community is therefore morally tolerable only if it includes values wider than those of the community.

More significant than our actions and interpretations in the First World War was our mood after its conclusion. Our "realists" feared that our sense of responsibility toward a nascent world community had exceeded the canons of a prudent self-interest. Our idealists, of the thirties, sought to preserve our innocence by neutrality. The main force of isolationism came from the "realists," as the slogan "America First" signifies. But the abortive effort to defy the forces of history which were both creating a potential world community and increasing the power of America beyond that of any other nation, was supported by pacifist idealists, Christian and secular, and by other visionaries who desired to preserve our innocency. They had a dim and dark understanding of the fact that power cannot be wielded without guilt, since it is never transcendent over interest, even when it tries to subject itself to universal standards and places itself under the control of a nascent world-wide community. They did not understand that the disavowal of the responsibilities of power can involve an individual or nation in even more grievous guilt.

There are two ways of denying our responsibilities to our fellowmen. The one is the way of imperialism, expressed in seeking to dominate them by our power. The other is the way of isolationism, expressed in seeking to withdraw from our responsibilities to them. Geographic circumstances and the myths of our youth rendered us more susceptible to the latter than the former temptation. This has given our national life a unique color, which is not without some moral advantages. No powerful nation in history has ever been more reluctant to acknowledge the position it has achieved in the world than we. The moral advantage lies in the fact that we do not have a strong lust of power, though we are quickly acquiring the pride of power which always accompanies its possession. Our lack of the lust of power makes the fulminations of our foes against us singularly inept. On the other hand, we have been so deluded by the concept of our innocency that we are ill prepared to deal with the temptations of power which now assail us.

The Second World War quickly dispelled the illusions of both our realists and idealists; and also proved the vanity of the hopes of the legalists who thought that rigorous neutrality laws could abort the historical tendencies which were pushing our nation into the center of the world community. We emerged from that war the most powerful nation on earth. To the surprise of our friends and critics we seemed also to have sloughed off the tendencies toward irresponsibility which had characterized us in the long armistice between the world wars. We were determined to exercise the responsibilities of our power.

The exercise of this power required us to hold back the threat of Europe's inundation by communism through the development of all kinds of instruments of mass destruction, including atomic weapons. Thus an "innocent" nation finally arrives at the ironic climax of its history. It finds itself the custodian of the ultimate weapon which perfectly embodies and symbolizes the moral ambiguity of physical warfare. We could not disavow the possible use of the weapon, partly because no imperiled nation is morally able to dispense with weapons which might insure its survival. All nations, unlike some individuals, lack the capacity to prefer a noble death to a morally ambiguous survival. But we also could not renounce the weapon because the freedom or survival of our allies depended upon the threat of its use. Of this at least Mr. Winston Churchill and other Europeans have assured us. Yet if we should use it, we shall cover ourselves with a terrible guilt. We might insure our survival in a world in which it might be better not to be alive. Thus the moral predicament in which all human striving is involved has been raised to a final pitch for a culture and for a nation which thought it an easy matter to distinguish between justice and injustice and believed itself to be peculiarly innocent. In this way the perennial moral predicaments of human history have caught up with a culture which knew nothing of sin or guilt, and with a nation which seemed to be the most perfect fruit of that culture.

In this as in every other ironic situation of American history there is a footnote which accentuates the incongruity. This footnote is added by the fact that the greatness of our power is derived on the one hand from the technical efficiency of our industrial establishment and on the other from the success of our natural scientists. Yet it was assumed that science and business enterprise would insure the triumph of reason over power and passion in human history.

Naturally, a culture so confident of the possibility of resolving all incongruities in life and history was bound to make strenuous efforts to escape the tragic dilemma in which we find ourselves. These efforts fall into two categories, idealistic and realistic. The idealists naturally believe that we could escape the dilemma if we made sufficiently strenuous rational and moral efforts; if for instance we tried to establish a world government. Unfortunately the obvious necessity of integrating the global community politically does not guarantee its possibility. And all the arguments of the idealists finally rest upon a logic which derives the possibility of an achievement from its necessity. Other idealists believe that a renunciation of the use of atomic weapons would free us from the dilemma. But this is merely the old pacifist escape from the dilemma of war itself.

The realists on the other hand are inclined to argue that a good cause will hallow any weapon. They are convinced that the evils of communism are so great that we are justified in using any weapon against them. Thereby they closely approach the communist ruthlessness. The inadequacy of both types of escape from our moral dilemma proves that there is no purely moral solution for the ultimate moral issues of life; but neither is there a viable solution which disregards the moral factors. Men and nations must use their power with the purpose of making it an instrument of justice and a servant of interests broader than their own. Yet they must be ready to use it though they become aware that the power of a particular nation or individual, even when under strong religious and social sanctions, is never so used that there is a perfect coincidence between the value which justifies it and the interest of the wielder of it.

One difficulty of a nation, such as ours, which manifests itself long before we reach the ultimate dilemma of warfare with weapons of mass destruction, is that we have reached our position in the world community through forms of power which are essentially covert rather than overt. Or rather the overt military power which we wield has been directly drawn from the economic power, derived from the wealth of our natural resources and our technical efficiency. We have had little experience in the claims and counter-claims of man's social existence, either domestically or internationally. We therefore do not know social existence as an encounter between life and life, or interest with interest in which moral and non-moral factors are curiously compounded. It is therefore a weakness of our foreign policy, particularly as our business community conceives it, that we move inconsistently from policies which would overcome animosities toward us by the offer of economic assistance to policies which would destroy resistance by the use of pure military might. We can understand the neat logic of either economic reciprocity or the show of pure power. But we are mystified by the endless complexities of human motives and the varied compounds of ethnic loyalties, cultural traditions, social hopes, envies and fears which enter into the policies of nations, and which lie at the foundation of their political cohesion.

In our relations with Asia these inconsistencies are particularly baffling. We expect Asians to be grateful to us for such assistance as we have given them; and are hurt when we discover that Asians envy, rather than admire, our prosperity and regard us as imperialistic when we are "by definition" a non-imperialistic nation.

Nations are hardly capable of the spirit of forgiveness which is the final oil of harmony in all human relations and which rests upon the contrite recognition that our actions and attitudes are inevitably interpreted in a different light by our friends as well as foes than we interpret them. Yet it is necessary to acquire a measure of this spirit in the collective relations of mankind. Nations, as individuals, who are completely innocent in their own esteem, are insufferable in their human contacts. The whole world suffers from the pretensions of the communist oligarchs. Our pretensions are of a different order because they are not as consistently held. In any event, we have preserved a system of freedom in which they may be challenged. Yet our American nation, involved in its vast responsibilities, must slough off many illusions which were derived both from the experiences and the ideologies of its childhood. Otherwise either we will seek escape from responsibilities which involve unavoidable guilt, or we will be plunged into avoidable guilt by too great confidence in our virtue.

Lawrence Ferlinghetti
I Am Waiting
(1955)

I am waiting for my case to come up
and I am waiting
for a rebirth of wonder
and I am waiting for someone
to really discover America
and wail
and I am waiting
for the discovery
of a new symbolic western frontier
and I am waiting
for the American Eagle
to really spread its wings
and straighten up and fly right
and I am waiting
for the Age of Anxiety
to drop dead
and I am waiting
for the war to be fought
which will make the world safe
for anarchy
and I am waiting
for the final withering away
of all governments
and I am perpetually awaiting
a rebirth of wonder

I am waiting for the Second Coming
and I am waiting
for a religious revival

to sweep thru the state of Arizona
and I am waiting
for the Grapes of Wrath to be stored
and I am waiting
for them to prove
that God is really American
and I am seriously waiting
for Billy Graham and Elvis Presley
to exchange roles seriously
and I am waiting
to see God on television
piped onto church altars
if only they can find
the right channel
to tune in on
and I am waiting
for the Last Supper to be served again
with a strange new appetizer
and I am perpetually awaiting
a rebirth of wonder

I am waiting for my number to be called
and I am waiting
for the living end
and I am waiting
for dad to come home
his pockets full
of irradiated silver dollars
and I am waiting
for the atomic tests to end
and I am waiting happily
for things to get much worse
before they improve
and I am waiting
for the Salvation Army to take over
and I am waiting
for the human crowd
to wander off a cliff somewhere
clutching its atomic umbrella
and I am waiting
for Ike to act
and I am waiting
for the meek to be blessed

and inherit the earth
without taxes
and I am waiting
for forests and animals
to reclaim the earth as theirs
and I am waiting
for a way to be devised
to destroy all nationalisms
without killing anybody
and I am waiting
for linnets and planets to fall like rain
and I am waiting for lovers and weepers
to lie down together again
in a new rebirth of wonder

I am waiting for the Great Divide to be crossed
and I am anxiously waiting
for the secret of eternal life to be discovered
by an obscure general practitioner
and save me forever from certain death
and I am waiting
for life to begin
and I am waiting
for the storms of life
to be over
and I am waiting
to set sail for happiness
and I am waiting
for a reconstructed Mayflower
to reach America
with its picture story and tv rights
sold in advance to the natives
and I am waiting
for the lost music to sound again
in the Lost Continent
in a new rebirth of wonder

I am waiting for the day
that maketh all things clear
and I am waiting
for Ole Man River
to just stop rolling along
past the country club
and I am waiting

for the deepest South
to just stop Reconstructing itself
in its own image
and I am waiting
for a sweet desegregated chariot
to swing low
and carry me back to Ole Virginie
and I am waiting
for Ole Virginie to discover
just why Darkies are born
and I am waiting
for God to lookout
from Lookout Mountain
and see the *Ode to the Confederate Dead*
as a real farce
and I am awaiting retribution
for what America did
to Tom Sawyer
and I am perpetually awaiting
a rebirth of wonder

I am waiting for Tom Swift to grow up
and I am waiting
for the American Boy
to take off Beauty's clothes
and get on top of her
and I am waiting
for Alice in Wonderland
to retransmit to me
her total dream of innocence
and I am waiting
for Childe Roland to come
to the final darkest tower
and I am waiting
for Aphrodite
to grow live arms
at a final disarmament conference
in a new rebirth of wonder

I am waiting
to get some intimations
of immortality
by recollecting my early childhood
and I am waiting

for the green mornings to come again
youth's dumb green fields come back again
and I am waiting
for some strains of unpremeditated art
to shake my typewriter
and I am waiting to write
the great indelible poem
and I am waiting
for the last long careless rapture
and I am perpetually waiting
for the fleeing lovers on the Grecian Urn
to catch each other up at last
and embrace
and I am awaiting
perpetually and forever
a renaissance of wonder

THE SURVEY— FINISHED?

We wonder whether the dream of American liberty
Was two hundred years of pine and hardwood
And three generations of the grass

And the generations are up: the years over

We don't know

It was two hundred years from the smell of the tidewater
Up through the Piedmont: on through the piney woods:
Till we came out
With our led calves and our lean women
In the oak openings of Illinois

It was three generations from the oak trees—
From the islands of elm and the islands of oak in the prairie—

Till we heeled out with our plows and our steel harrows
On the grass-drowned reef bones of the Plains

"Four score and seven years" said the Orator

We remember it differently: we remember it
Kansas: Illinois: Ohio: Connecticut.
We remember it Council Bluffs: St. Louis:
Wills Creek: the Cumberland: Shenandoah—

The long harangues of the grass in the wind are our histories

We tell our freedom backward by the land
We tell our past by the gravestones and the apple trees

We wonder whether the great American dream
Was the singing of locusts out of the grass to the west and the
West is behind us now:
The west wind's away from us:

We wonder if the liberty is done:
The dreaming is finished

We can't say

We aren't sure

Or if there's something different men can dream
Or if there's something different men can mean by
Liberty

Or if there's liberty a man can mean that's
Men: not land

We wonder

We don't know

We're asking

LAND OF THE FREE: CONCLUSION OF THE SOUND TRACK
Archibald MacLeish   (1938)

LIONEL TRILLING, the literary and cultural critic, once said that
America "is the only nation that prides itself upon a dream and gives its
name to one, 'the American dream.' " In those words Trilling defined a
notable distinction between the United States and other countries. True,
as Reinhold Niebuhr points out in *The Irony of American History*, some
nations live by a blueprint for the future—notably those subscribing to a
communist ideology. But a blueprint is not a dream. A blueprint is a
model, which must be followed to the line and letter if the building or
machine for which it is modeled is to come out as planned. Was John
Winthrop's "A Model of Christian Charity" a blueprint? No. Was "The
Mayflower Compact" a blueprint? No. Was "The Declaration of Independence"? No: it was a *declaration*, a *manifesto*, a dream if you will,
but it lacks the details necessary to a blueprint. "We hold these truths
to be self-evident, that all men are created equal, that they are endowed
by their Creator with certain unalienable Rights, that among these are
Life, Liberty, and the pursuit of Happiness"—such a statement is hardly
a blueprint. It is, instead, the expression of a dream almost in the classic
Freudian sense, for it assumes the fulfillment of wishes that can probably
never be fully realized in actuality. Even the Constitution, the nearest
thing to a blueprint the United States has ever formulated, allows too

much room for interpretation to be anything other than a rough outline for implementation of certain ideals.

Americans have in fact historically resisted blueprints. That is to say, they have always been suspicious of formal ideologies, of closed systems. Practical though they are alleged to be, Americans are basically dreamers, not social engineers. And, as the selections in this anthology have illustrated, there are probably as many American dreams as there are American dreamers. "Our fate is to become one, and yet many—this is not prophecy, but description." So Ralph Ellison says of America in his novel *Invisible Man* (1952), and his assertion is equally true of American dreams. For what we call the American Dream is actually composed of a congeries of diverse dreams unified only by a commonly professed belief in a set of ideals: liberty, equality of opportunity, justice, the rights of the individual, the will of the majority. Everyone agrees that these ideals (and others) constitute the Dream—hence Ellison's "one." But the interpretations of the ideals and the preferred ways of turning them into concrete realities differ, as we have seen, from one person to another and from one era to another—hence the "many." This has been true from the beginning: Winthrop's dream was not precisely the same as Roger Williams's or William Penn's, Jefferson's not the same as Hamilton's. It continued to be true throughout the nineteenth century, and it continues so in our own time. One could even argue that the tensions among the various interpretations are necessary to maintain America's vitality. For perhaps, as Ellison also declares, "only in division is there true health."

Admittedly, these tensions are sometimes so painful and frustrating as to call the entire complex Dream into doubt. American history has, after all, been periodically dotted by events that have threatened to turn harmonious dreams into cacophonous nightmares: the Civil War, economic depressions, the rise of urban squalor, the oppression of minorities, the rape of nature, crime, violence, drug abuse, revelations of political corruption, even such military and diplomatic failures as Vietnam. *Land of the Free*, written by Archibald MacLeish (1892–1982) in the wake of the Great Depression, captures the pain, confusion, and doubt not only of that tumultuous era but of other critical times as well. For the questions MacLeish raises have been raised both before and after 1930. Have Americans taken their freedom too much for granted? Are the "truths" noted in the Declaration of Independence "self-evident," if in fact they are truths at all? Are there any such things as "unalienable rights"? MacLeish wonders. Most particularly, he wonders whether the American dream of liberty was principally a matter of open land, the "singing of locusts out of the grass to the west." And since the "West is behind us now," perhaps the "liberty is done: / The dreaming is finished." Yet MacLeish, who was not only a poet and playwright but also for a time filled important government positions, will not give up the Dream altogether. Perhaps, he says, "there's something different men can dream . . . / something different men can mean by / Liberty," a meaning that is based on people, not land. MacLeish knows that American ground is more than land, that the frontier is not just a geographical place but a state of mind, and that Americans are capable of re-defining both abstractions and landscapes to fit changing conditions.

The Western frontier promised Americans a new beginning, a place where their dreams could be realized. MacLeish implies that by revising the interpretation of liberty a new kind of frontier is still possible. Several recent presidents have expressed similar ideas, thereby reaffirming one of the central components of the Dream. John F. Kennedy punctuated his 1961 inaugural address with the phrase "Let us begin" and, like Henry Wallace before him, adopted as a slogan "The New Frontier." Lyndon B. Johnson, in turn, ended his "Great Society" speech (1964) with these words: "Those who came to this land sought to build more than just a new country. They sought a new world. . . . You can make their vision our reality." Richard M. Nixon's first inaugural address (1969) predicted the "beginning of the third millennium"; his second (1973), with unintended irony, urged America to "begin anew." And, not to be outdone, Ronald Reagan, whose path from smalltown Midwestern radio announcer to Hollywood movie star to president embodies an American dream in itself, repeated Thomas Paine's assertion that we can begin the world over again and centered his 1980 campaign on the promise to "make America great again."

However cynical Americans have become about such political rhetoric, there is considerable evidence that they have not entirely abandoned their faith in the possibility of a new beginning, or, for that matter, in the American Dream as a whole. The latter phrase itself pops up repeatedly—in advertisements, in newspaper headlines, in the titles of books, even in the names of a television show, a Las Vegas revue, and a table game. As for Americans' belief in a new beginning, the periodic popularity of such books as Charles A. Reich's *The Greening of America* or William Least Heat Moon's *Blue Highways: A Journey into America* remains significant.

A 1970s version of the myth of America as a New Eden, Reich's vision predicted that the American consciousness would transform itself into a new openness, a new honesty, a new awareness of individual worth that is less competitive than cooperative. Some current trends indicate that many Americans still share Reich's hopes for a rebirth of their personal lives if not for the life of society at large. The body failing? Take up aerobics, adopt a vegetarian diet, run a marathon. The psyche disintegrating? See a therapist who will put Humpty Dumpty back together again—or, if you cannot afford therapy, buy a self-help book and do the job yourself. Experiencing dark nights of the soul when, as F. Scott Fitzgerald said, it is always three o'clock in the morning? Become a born-again Christian, or a transcendental meditator, or go out of the now-all-too-much-for-us complexity back to the land on a communal farm.

Less sanguine than Reich, and persuaded that there was no quick or inevitable fix for his "nearly desperate sense of isolation and a growing suspicion that I lived in an alien land," Heat Moon chucked his Missouri routine on "the last night of winter," took to the back roads in a van named "Ghost Dancing," and looped America "from the heartland out and around." Searching for clarity and renewal in the 1980s, this half-Anglo half-Indian American concluded by wondering: "In a season on the blue roads, what had I accomplished?" The log of Heat Moon's journey answers, "In my own country, I had gone out, had met, had shared. I had stood as witness." The blend of change and permanence he found was far from perfect. Yet its hope was enough to keep him going because, as Heat Moon stresses, "I sometimes heard *human* voices that showed the power not of visions but of revision, the power to see again and revise."

America obviously differs in many ways from what it was two hundred, one hundred, fifty, or even ten years ago. Visions of some parts of its Dream have indeed been revised. In at least one respect, however, the country has not changed at all. Its vistas still empower a Dream, which perhaps no differences of interpretation and no ironic disparity between ideals and actuality can thoroughly destroy. At Willy Loman's funeral, near the end of Arthur Miller's play *Death of a Salesman*, Willy's friend Charley says: "A salesman is got to dream, boy. It comes with the territory." The same might be said of those who live on American ground.

SOME NOVELS ABOUT
AMERICAN GROUND

ANY READER who chooses, as we have done, to supplement the selections in this book will find a rich field of novels from which to pick. After all, American novelists have understandably dealt with many of the same issues that have concerned the poets and essayists.

This was certainly true of the classic nineteenth-century American novelists—James Fenimore Cooper, Herman Melville, Nathaniel Hawthorne, Mark Twain, and Henry James—as well as of less artistically gifted writers. Although great works of fiction resist all efforts to reduce them to a single theme, such novels as Cooper's *The Prairie* (1827), a romance of the frontier; Melville's *The Confidence-Man* (1857), a satirical look at American faith and optimism; Hawthorne's *The Scarlet Letter* (1850), set in Puritan times, and *The Blithedale Romance* (1852), a critical account of a nineteenth-century experiment in social reform and communal living; Twain's *A Connecticut Yankee in King Arthur's Court* (1889), with its ambivalent attitude toward modern technology; James's *The American* (1877), the story of a successful American businessman coming face to face with the powerful conventions of a class-conscious European society; Harriet Beecher Stowe's *Uncle Tom's Cabin* (1852), that melodramatic narrative about slavery; Henry Adams's *Democracy* (1880), a tale of political power and corruption—these are but a few examples of nineteenth-century works of fiction concerned with issues raised by our anthology selections.

So many twentieth-century novels treat the issues that selecting among them is a problem in itself. Among the most successful, however, are two that are set in earlier periods: Willa Cather's *My Ántonia* (1918) and William Styron's *The Confessions of Nat Turner* (1967). Cather's novel offers a striking image of both the beauty and hardships of provincial life on the Nebraska frontier in the 1880s, thereby implicitly providing a dramatic perspective on the essays by Frederick Jackson Turner (and, to a lesser extent, of Josiah Royce), while also depicting various responses of European immigrants, especially women, to the New World. Styron's novel, a fictional account of a slave uprising in Virginia in 1831, not only speculates on the psychology of a literate black slave and the conditions prompting the revolt but also suggests parallels to the militant black movements of the 1960s.

Styron calls his novel a "meditation on history." The same might be said of Ralph Ellison's *Invisible Man* (1952). Centrally concerned with the plight of a black man in twentieth-century America, Ellison's novel repeatedly alludes to the history that has helped to make his protagonist what he is. Moreover, it wrestles with problems faced by Americans in general, black or white, past or present: problems of an American identity, of individuality vs. conformity, of the one and the many.

All truly first-rate novels have the power to transcend their immediate time and place, of course. Some of the novels we have found to be effective supplements to the anthology pieces, though on the surface closely tied to particular periods, prove on closer reading to achieve that transcendence.

F. Scott Fitzgerald's *The Great Gatsby* (1925) is an expanded fictional counterpart of his "Echoes of the Jazz Age." But it is more than a picture of a decade. It is about the recurrent American dream of wealth as the means to success. Its protagonist, a self-made man governed, like the nation itself, by a "Platonic conception of himself," exemplifies Santayana's definition of the American as an "idealist working on matter." For Jay Gatsby believes—as, according to Fitzgerald, so many Americans do— that he can realize an ideal future by reclaiming and arresting a golden moment of the past.

Sinclair Lewis's *Babbitt* (1922) is a more heavy-handed and satirical picture of the twenties, emphasizing the period's materialism, its narrow provincialism and chauvinism, its glorification of "business," its pressures toward conformity, its shallow optimism. Like Jay Gatsby, George Babbitt has his romantic longings; but he lacks the former's "sense of wonder" and willingness to sacrifice everything to his dreams. He is, in essence, the American as Philistine.

In many respects, John Steinbeck's *The Grapes of Wrath* (1939) represents the 1930s as *The Great Gatsby* and *Babbitt* do the 1920s. Portraying the economic exploitation of the agrarian victims of the Dust Bowl when they migrated to California, Steinbeck captures much of the deprivation, disenchantment, and bewilderment that marked the Depression years. In addition, he shows the continuing power of the frontier dream, the ambivalent attitudes toward nature, the tensions between idealism and pragmatism and between individualism and collectivism that have persistently characterized the American experience. And he demonstrates that the old dream of a more perfect union still lives.

Joyce Carol Oates's *them* (1969) begins during the 1930s but ends with the social upheavals of the 1960s. Despite the novel's time scope, however, Oates's characters are in effect children of the Depression. Members of a lower-class urban family, the Wendalls are as much thwarted as Steinbeck's farmers by forces beyond their control. Nevertheless, they too cling to typical American dreams of freedom, self-determination, and an open future.

Curiously enough, the Wendalls seem relatively unaffected by World War II. Not so the characters in Willam Styron's *Sophie's Choice* (1979). Sophie Zawistowska, a Polish survivor of Auschwitz, has come to America hoping to start life anew, to put the past behind her as Americans have so often tried to do. She finds that hope impossible. Having been forced at Auschwitz to choose which of her children would be sent to the gas chamber, Sophie cannot rid herself of guilt. For her, the freedom of choice so prized by Americans leads to despair and then to suicide. Through Sophie, Stingo, the young American Southerner who narrates the novel, is forced to confront his own past and by extension his country's, including its racial guilt. In short, Stingo loses the innocence that America has prided itself on embodying, as Reinhold Niebuhr's *The Irony of American History* points out. Like Sophie, Stingo is forced to choose between hope and despair and, indeed, to decide whether freedom of choice makes life more worth living or less.

Finally, John Updike's trilogy about Harry "Rabbit" Angstrom—*Rabbit, Run* (1960), *Rabbit Redux* (1971), and *Rabbit Is Rich* (1981)—surveys three recent decades of American life. In the earliest novel, Harry suffers from a "closed-in feeling." A former high-school basketball star, the Rabbit has since experienced only mediocrity. And Harry cannot abide mediocrity. Consequently, like earlier Americans, he runs. The trouble is, he does not know where to run. Harry has a son, Nelson, and he fathers a daughter, Becky, who drowns while still an infant. Harry also takes up with a prostitute named Ruth and gets her pregnant. Nearly twenty years later—in *Rabbit Is Rich*—he thinks he meets his other daughter, but Harry never knows for sure. Meanwhile, the institutions—domestic, social, religious—that the younger Harry has been brought up to believe in fail to satisfy him; yet he can find no adequate replacements, no new frontiers where he can fan the "little flame" inside him.

Rabbit Redux is set at the time when America's involvement in Vietnam was being most strenuously criticized. Harry is not one of the critics. Desperate to find something to believe in, he has in fact substituted the idea of America for the "face of God." The America that Harry truly believes in, however, is an older America which, as he nostalgically remembers it, was epitomized by family solidarity, Sunday-morning church and Sunday-afternoon baseball games. It is not the nation he inhabits, In those late 1960s, America has penetrated outer space but, to Harry, has failed to fill its spiritual void. In the course of the novel, Harry struggles to come to terms with his feelings not only about Vietnam but also about the sexual revolution, the black civil-rights movement, the new technology, the drug culture, and, above all, with the question of how much responsibility he must assume for himself, for others, and for the country as a whole.

A decade later, Updike affirms that "Rabbit is rich." Now in his mid-forties, Harry manages Springer Motors and prospers by selling Japanese Toyotas to buyers in his hometown, Brewer, Pennsylvania. Harry has a country-club membership and a new house. His frequently rocky marriage seems to have stabilized. Harry, who thought God "never wanted him to have a daughter," has a new granddaughter, too. But Harry's contentment is not complete. Rabbit cares and so he still has reasons to wonder whether "the great American ride is ending." As in all the novels above, plus many others that could be mentioned, there is in Harry's asking a determination and a hope to renew American ground.